LIAM
LYNCH

TO DECLARE A REPUBLIC

Gerard Shannon

MERRION
PRESS

First published in 2023 by

Merrion Press

10 George's Street

Newbridge

Co. Kildare

Ireland

www.iap.ie

© Gerard Shannon, 2023

978 1 78855 821 1 (Paper)

978 1 78855 170 0 (Ebook)

978 1 78855 172 4 (PDF)

A CIP catalogue record for this book is
available from the British Library.

Typeset in Minion Pro 11/16 pt

Cover design: edit+ www.stuartcoughlan.com

Cover images courtesy of Cork Public Museum, Cork.

Merrion Press is a member of Publishing Ireland.

LIAM
LYNCH

Dedicated to my father, Gerard senior,
who inspired my interest in Irish history,

and

to the memory of his grandfather, Séamus Hennessy
(1894–1969), who served in the Mid-Clare Brigade,
Irish Republican Army from 1917 to 1924.

Gerard Shannon is a historian from Skerries in north County Dublin. In 2019 he completed a thesis on Liam Lynch during the Civil War as part of an MA in History with the Dublin City University School of History and Geography, which formed the basis for this book. Gerard has also written numerous articles and given talks on key figures of the Irish revolutionary period. He works as a civil servant in Dublin city.

Contents

'But through every disaster I preserved unbroken faith in the purpose and courage of my country. I believed, and still believe that her true heart is faithful to liberty and hopeful for the future …'

Michael Doheny in *The Felon's Track*, his account of the 1848 Young Ireland rebellion, one of Liam Lynch's favourite books

'Strange, is it not? That battles, martyrs, agonies, blood, even assassination, should so condense – perhaps only really condense – *a nationality*.'

Walt Whitman, speaking during a public lecture on the American Civil War (1861–65) in New York, 1879

PROLOGUE

ON HIS PASSING AT THE age of thirty, General Liam Lynch, chief of staff of the Irish Republican Army (IRA), was the undisputed leader of Irish republicanism.[1] The circumstances of his death for many since have been a demonstration of his devotion to the cause of the establishment of an independent Irish Republic, a cause in which many of his contemporaries had already given their lives. With his death in the closing weeks of the Irish Civil War, the already dwindling military resistance of the IRA to the new Irish state lost what little momentum it had left. IRA Volunteer Todd Andrews, who travelled with Lynch as an adjutant in his final weeks, summed it up best when he wrote that with 'Lynch's death I knew the end of the Civil War had come. Only his iron will had kept it going in the last few months.'[2]

In the decades since his death, Lynch has been mythologised, both by those who knew him during his short life as well as by latter-day admirers. This can be observed in the vast array of recorded recollections and memoirs of his contemporaries, and in tributes given in articles, at commemorations and in other forms of remembrance. As a result, Lynch has endured as a towering figure among several different political traditions who claim the mantle of Irish republicanism and trace a direct line to Irish republicans who resisted the forces of the Irish Free State during the Civil War. Various memorials to his brief life can be found across the south-west of Ireland, erected across the last century by former comrades, friends and family. Several commemorations by different groups and political parties continue to this day, with Lynch uniquely being remembered at different times of the year.

What emerges through all this is a particular image of Liam Lynch: that of a genuinely courageous, gifted military leader who gave it all for the overthrow of British rule in Ireland; a man devoted to the object of Irish freedom. This image of Lynch was maintained through the two previous biographies of his life, both of which provide great insights into Lynch yet are firmly embedded in the sub-genre of Irish republican hagiography in their celebration of their subject.[3] Both rarely acknowledge nuances in Lynch's personal character, motivations and actions, or his inherent contradictions.

However, an abundance of new scholarship and newly available sources on the extraordinary and eventful period of the Irish Revolution, has extended our knowledge and understanding of the time and the personalities involved, and this new biography of Liam Lynch is intended to contribute to this – particularly in consideration of his role in the Civil War. It was his leadership of the military republican resistance to the new Irish state during the eleven-month Civil War that made him a public figure beyond his familiar environs of north Cork, and it is striking that, given the mixed legacy of the conflict, Lynch's role and decision-making during those pivotal months has been little understood or contextualised in the century since. This will form an important part of this work.

In the introduction of the still impressive first biography of Lynch, *No Other Law*, its author, Florence O'Donoghue, remarked that it was his hope that future historians, 'having more ample leisure and access to a wider range of historical material, will ensure that men like Liam Lynch do not die a second death'.[4] As we approach the centenary of Lynch's passing, as O'Donoghue hoped, the availability of a wide array of archival material has created a major opportunity for new perspectives on an important historical figure and his place in that revolutionary generation. This is particularly pertinent in relation to discussion and debates on the continued contested historical legacies of the revolutionary decade, which have come to the fore during its centenary over matters such as the utilisation of political violence, the nature of commemoration and remembrance, and the endurance of Irish partition and the place of Northern Ireland in the make-up of the United Kingdom, alongside the lingering legacy of the recent 'Troubles'. Discussion and analysis on all these have re-emerged dramatically in the last decade, often in fraught public and political debates within both jurisdictions in Ireland and beyond. Underpinning these are the enormous political, economic and social upheavals caused by both Brexit and the recent global pandemic, which have greatly tested, in various ways, the Irish state's relationship with both Northern Ireland and Great Britain. Against the backdrop of all this is the rise in electoral and popular support of the modern-day iteration of the Sinn Féin political party both north and south – a party which makes no secret to voters in both jurisdictions of its unashamed ideological Irish republicanism and its main aspiration being that of Irish unification.

In consideration of the place of General Liam Lynch in history, it is the author's hope that the reader will find this a timely and revealing biography of a man whose life and death played an important part in the epochal events of the early twentieth-century Irish Revolution.

Chapter 1

'Quiet and gentle and you didn't notice him much' (1892–1916)

ABOUT FIVE MILES FROM THE town of Mitchelstown in north Cork, across the county's south-eastern border, lies the village of Anglesboro in rural Limerick. Near this village is the townland of Barnagurraha, whose residents live in view of the extraordinary sight of the western slopes of the Galtee mountains. It is in this townland that an 8-foot-tall monument can be found, just across from the birthplace of Liam Lynch. The monument, a large Celtic cross, was erected in his memory in a well-attended unveiling ceremony on 17 April 1978. The total cost of the cross was estimated at £3,000 and was financed through subscriptions from the United States and throughout Ireland.[1] On the monument is a side-profile relief of Lynch, and a plaque at the base proclaims: 'Your epitaph is your glorious service Liam'. This is a reference to the famous phrase from the Irish republican martyr Robert Emmet's courtroom speech before his execution in 1803: 'When my country takes her place among the nations of the Earth, then and not till then, let my epitaph be written.'

Liam was one of seven children, the second youngest of Jeremiah Lynch and his wife, Mary (née Kelly), and he was christened William Fanaghan Lynch.[2] His middle name was after St Fanahan, the patron saint of nearby Mitchelstown, who is said to have built an abbey near a well west of the town some 1,500 years ago.[3] Previously, the date provided for Liam's birth has often been incorrect. Both of his previous biographers gave it as 9 November 1893 (which also appears on the monument in Barnagurraha), and hence, most secondary sources list his age at death as twenty-nine.[4] While it is unclear why (or when) the confusion arose, the date listed, along with his parents' names and address, on the birth registration of the William Lynch of interest here is 20 November 1892.[5] This would match the later age given for him at the time of both the 1901 and 1911 censuses, thereby making him over thirty on his death in 1923.

Liam's siblings, in order of birth, were John (later known as Seán), Jeremiah, Margaret, Martin, James, then Liam himself, and finally Tom.[6] In an early family tragedy, the second-oldest, Jeremiah junior, died in 1904. He had been working as a civil servant in London and died of a heart attack while bathing. He was buried in St Pancras and Islington cemetery, in East Finchley, north London, and members of the Irish community there marked his grave with a cross. He was just nineteen years old.[7] Though Liam was only in his early teens at the time, he never forgot his late brother, even referring to him in one letter written during the Civil War.[8]

Typically for an Irish rural family of the time, the Lynches were firm devotees of the Catholic faith, and both Martin and Tom would later follow religious vocations. On joining the Christian Brothers, Martin became known as Brother Placidus, while Tom later emigrated, becoming a parish priest in the community of Bega, in New South Wales, Australia.[9] Liam was especially close to these two brothers, particularly Tom – his youngest sibling influenced him greatly and the two later shared an uncompromising militant republicanism. In addition, given Liam's deep religious faith and Tom being a priest, the latter provided important spiritual and moral counsel to his older brother in difficult times during Liam's revolutionary activities. Tom remarked in one account he wrote of Liam's life that being 'next to [Liam] in age (2 years 9 months younger) we were more attached to one another than to any other member of the family'.[10]

Both brothers also shared a great interest in Irish history. Tom, at Liam's suggestion, wrote a detailed history of the Lynch family. In his research, he indicated that the Lynches had strong farming roots going back hundreds of years in Anglesboro, originally referred to by its Gaelic name Gleann na gCreabhar. Their own family lands in Barnagurraha had been bought in the 1840s by their great-grandfather James Lynch, who had come into an inheritance from his own father. James then made an arrangement with the landlord in the area, Maxwell Lowe, to pay a fixed sum for 'all Barnagurraha for his lifetime'. As part of this arrangement, James became the landlord for the townland and accepted the rents from six to eight farmers nearby. The townland amounted to around 300 acres of land, and James kept around 100 acres for himself while letting out plots of 20 acres. James had a son, also James, who married Johanna Mary O'Donnell; they were Liam's grandparents, and they resided on the same land.

The Great Famine or Gorta Mór ('Great Hunger') also impacted on the Lynch family. The Famine, which spanned the years 1845 to 1852, was, in summary, the result of the failure of the potato crop due to blight and the subsequent failure of the British administration to help much of the starving and poor rural populace in Ireland who depended on the crop to survive. An estimated one million people died, with another million emigrating. By 1846, with such poverty and social upheaval dominating Ireland, a degree of lawlessness prevailed in the countryside, to which James Lynch senior fell victim. On 12 January 1846, James met a sudden, violent end when he was shot while walking to his son's family home in Barnagurraha. The culprits were apparently a group of local bandits called the 'Black Boys', who had been paid £2 by an unknown party to carry out the deed.

A contemporary news report suggested the incident was rooted in James having borrowed a sum of money several years prior and given a portion of his land as security. As part of this agreement, the land was not to be let or tilled, a stipulation which was then violated. When the loan was paid off, James had demanded the land be freed of tenants and began legal proceedings. For this, he received a violent warning, which he ignored. The report then described how he was attacked by three 'ruffians' who fired three shots, the first two passing through his spine and the third through his lungs. In Tom Lynch's narrative, James junior heard the shots and ran to the gate of the family home in time to see the bandits running off. On his death, James senior was seventy years old. There is no evidence to suggest the culprits were apprehended or faced justice. Tom commented that James' descendants still 'pray for him', demonstrating how vividly this story of agrarian violence was recalled within the family decades later; it must have been heard often by Liam.[11]

✳✳✳

The Ireland of the late nineteenth century into which Liam Lynch was born had seen a considerable degree of political upheaval in the years since the Famine.

In 1858, the Irish Republican Brotherhood (IRB) was founded. The stated aim of this secret oath-bound group was the overthrow of British rule in Ireland by physical force and the establishment of an independent Irish republic, in keeping with the enlightenment ideology espoused by the United Irishmen in the 1790s. An equivalent and closely associated body, the American-based Fenian Brotherhood, was founded by John O'Mahony in New York in the same year, and its members were largely Irish immigrants and exiles. Born in 1815, O'Mahony had grown up in Kilbehenny, east of Mitchelstown and not far from Anglesboro village.[12] A keen student of Irish history, O'Mahony named the organisation after the mythical Celtic warriors of the Fianna – the members of his group, and the IRB, thus became known as 'Fenians'.

The IRB's best-known action prior to the year of Liam's birth was the 1867 Fenian Rising, a poorly planned and resourced insurrection. After initial incidents on 14 February near Cork, further skirmishes between Fenians and the Irish Constabulary and British soldiers took place on 5 March at Cork city and within counties Dublin, Limerick and Tipperary. On that day, Peter O'Neill Crowley led a group of Fenians in the destruction of a coastguard station at Knockadoon, near Youghal, and also seized rifles from the police garrisoned there. When O'Neill Crowley learned that Fenians throughout Ireland had failed to rise and there were no reinforcements coming to his aid, he led his forces to Kilcooney wood, west of Mitchelstown. It was there that over 300 police and British military forces located them, and a dramatic shoot-out followed. As the insurrectionists faced defeat, O'Neill Crowley was mortally wounded. His massive funeral procession became embedded in popular folk memory.[13]

Lynch's father, Jeremiah, along with the latter's older brother, John, were both members of the local Fenians. Having stolen horses from a nearby wedding party, they had ridden to Kilmallock for the 1867 Rising, only to find the Fenian force there had withdrawn from the town and Kilmallock itself surrounded by British forces.[14] The Lynch brothers had been joined by their neighbour, fellow Fenian and distant cousin William Condon.[15]

Following the wholesale defeat of the Fenian movement in 1867, support for constitutional nationalism within Ireland began to increase. Since the Act of Union in 1800, all Irish political representatives had to sit in the British parliament at Westminster and in this political context, by 1882, the charismatic yet enigmatic Charles Stewart Parnell, a Protestant landowner, had ascended to the position of leader of the Irish Parliamentary Party (IPP). With the IPP, Parnell challenged the British parliament to bring about land reform for landowners throughout Ireland and at key junctures he aligned with the British Liberal Party under William Gladstone to try to achieve his aims. Parnell had also been elected president of the Irish National Land League in 1879, founded by a key ally, the radical nationalist Michael Davitt. The League's chief aim was to change the nature of land ownership in Ireland and abolish the landlord system. Though the organisational character of the League was radical, it did not advocate the use of violence. However, agrarian violence against landlords, their agents and their property became commonplace, often in response to the violent evictions of tenants on rural estates carried out by the Royal Irish Constabulary (RIC).

The League had an equivalent female organisation, the Ladies' Land League. Lynch's mother, Mary, was joint secretary of the Ballylanders

Branch during the Land War.[16] According to her son Seán, her involve-
ment in land agitation had its roots in a rental dispute that her father,
James Kelly, had had with a landlord over the family holding in
Ballylanders, County Limerick.[17]

From 1885, following the suppression of the Land League, Parnell
was determined to use the replacement organisation, the Irish National
League, to help promote his chief political goal: Home Rule. This would
see Ireland regain domestic self-government, while remaining part of
the British Empire. Unfortunately for Parnell, before he could achieve
this, his political career ended in disgrace when it was revealed he had
been having a long-time affair with the wife of one his party's MPs. This
immediately raised the ire of the Catholic Church hierarchy and other
forces opposed to Parnell within Irish society, not least his own opponents
within the IPP. The consequent party split and the stress of the situation
may well have been the reason Parnell died young, at the age of forty-
five. It was not until 1900, that both wings of the IPP reunited under the
leadership of one of Parnell's key lieutenants, John Redmond, who was
determined to pursue the goal of Home Rule anew.

It seems likely that Lynch's father, Jeremiah, was a supporter of Parnell,
the IPP and their efforts at constitutional agitation within Westminster,
and he probably remained so until his death.[18] Liam would have been
reared on stories of the Fenians and the land struggles, along with
anecdotes of his family's involvement in both.[19] This almost certainly
cemented his love for Irish history, particularly Irish revolutionary
history, along with a keen interest in politics and current affairs. Liam's
knowledge of his parents' militant political activism during such a pivotal
time in history prior to his birth was almost certainly one inspiration for
his own militancy some years later.

★★★

Liam Lynch was four years old when he first attended nearby Anglesboro
School in 1897.[20] His teacher, Patrick Kiely, who taught him from 1899,
recalled that the young boy 'had a mild, quiet disposition. I didn't notice

any aptitude in him.'[21] Kiely taught Lynch Irish as an extra subject but did not feel he picked up any great grasp of the language. For Kiely, one particular incident in his memory stood out when Lynch was in sixth class: 'the lads were reading aloud and when it came to his turn he burst out crying.'[22] Lynch complained to his teacher that his eyes were hurting him. On Kiely's advice, Liam's family took him to the local doctor, who advised that he needed glasses, which he wore regularly for the rest of his life. Whatever Lynch's initial difficulties, on leaving school in October 1909, Kiely wrote that his pupil was 'attentive to his studies … above average in intelligence', and also, 'possessed of a good, sound education, in so far as that provided by the primary school of his time.'[23]

In his childhood, Liam was close to Hanna Condon (later Cleary), a distant cousin of his several years his senior, who was also his godmother. The Condon family resided quite close to the Lynch farm and the young Liam was a regular visitor to their home.[24] Hanna has been described as a formative influence on Liam, and in her locality she was remembered as a 'Maud Gonne MacBride' type – in reference to the famous radical activist – and an enthusiastic balladeer.[25] In a later interview with Ernie O'Malley, she recalled some of the most detailed impressions of Liam in his youth. She regularly showed the young Liam the arrest warrant for her father from the hated Under-Secretary of Ireland, William 'Buckshot' Forster. (Forster's name was synonymous with violent suppression of agitation during the Land War.) In Cleary's opinion, Lynch was 'quiet and gentle and you didn't notice him much' among the other pupils of the school. She recalled, too, that her godson was 'unassuming, and more like a priest … He was more like the religious type than anything else, but he was always very much in earnest whatever he would do or wherever he would go.'[26] 'This frequent description of Lynch possessing a similar demeanour to a priest, endured well into his adulthood. George Lennon, a Waterford IRA leader, expressed great respect for Lynch but nonetheless felt, 'how can he be like a military man but have the appearance of a responsible superior of a great religious order? He was by nature most abstemious and he never raised his voice, which was gentle.'[27]

Cleary would also recall how in school Liam was 'very attentive to study' and 'a very good scholar'.[28] This intensely studious nature was noted by many during the revolutionary phase of his life. She remembered Liam as a voracious reader, especially of Irish history – William Condon owned many books on the subject, and Liam borrowed them from his collection. His favourite books from childhood were all notably sympathetic to the republican cause: *The Forge of Cloghogue* (a novel set against the backdrop of the 1798 rebellion against British rule), John Mitchel's *Jail Journal* (a first-hand account of the Young Ireland revolutionary's prison experiences in the 1850s), and *Speeches from the Dock* (a collection of courtroom speeches by Irish revolutionary figures when sentenced to execution or imprisonment). Cleary noted with amusement that if she and Liam were reading the same book at the same time, he tended to finish it before her.[29] Although not good at sports, Liam was a skilled draughts player. Tom Lynch speculated in one account that this may have contributed to Liam's later success as a guerrilla commander, in that 'it may have given him an idea of how to watch an opponent, attack him where least expected, watch your own weak defence and forestall the opponent's move at every turn'.[30]

One of Liam's childhood heroes was Patrick Sarsfield, the famed military commander and nationalist icon who aided the defeated King James II after the Battle of the Boyne in 1690. The main source of Sarsfield's fame among modern-day Irish nationalists is an episode that took place during the co-ordination of his army's retreat to Limerick, when he oversaw a successful and daring attack near Limerick on a siege train belonging to the forces of King William of Orange, resulting in the destruction of siege guns and other armaments and supplies. However, the real Sarsfield remains somewhat elusive and, as noted in one biographical sketch, his 'military reputation rests as much on the adulation of some of his followers and the myth-making of later nationalist writers as on his actual achievements'.[31] Nonetheless, the young Liam was naturally drawn to such stories of heroic deeds. A fellow pupil, who was part of a group that climbed Galtymore Mountain on the border of Limerick and Tipperary, recalled how, on reaching the peak, Liam pointed north to the site of the famed episode and told the story of Sarsfield masterminding the destruction of the Williamite siege train.[32]

* * *

A census was taken on 31 March 1901, when Liam was eight years old. It shows that the Lynch farm was one of eleven dwelling houses in Barnagurraha, with the household of Jeremiah and Mary consisting of nine residents. As well as the dwelling, the Lynch farm then consisted of one stable, one cow house and one piggery.[33]

The 1911 census, taken on 2 April that year, listed Liam as still residing at the Lynch family farm. His father, Jeremiah, had expanded the farm in the decade prior and it now consisted of one stable, two cow houses, two piggeries, one barn and one shed. Nineteen-year-old James now assisted both his father and brother Seán with farm duties. Of note is the fact that Liam's older brother Martin had by then departed the household, with a farmhand joining the family at home.[34] Hanna Cleary recalled that Jeremiah owned about ten cows and regularly brought milk to the creamery in Anglesboro.[35]

In 1910, then aged seventeen, Liam had begun a three-year apprenticeship in the hardware trade with Patrick O'Neill, whose store was based on Baldwin Street in Mitchelstown. He also joined a technical class to learn new skills, as well as continuing to read regularly. Though standing out at nearly six feet in height, he was recalled as a quiet, shy individual in this period.[36] According to Cleary, Patrick O'Neill's wife was a cousin of Jeremiah Lynch, which helped Liam secure the position at O'Neill's store.[37]

At some point not long into his apprenticeship, Liam left the family homestead for digs in Mitchelstown, though he returned home every Sunday.[38] Having now embarked on a profession quite different from the farming duties of his older brothers, Lynch later admitted to having had mixed feelings about it. Todd Andrews, Lynch's adjutant in his final weeks, remembered how in conversation, 'Liam sometimes talked of his home life on the family farm, regretting that family circumstances compelled him to leave the land. He seemed to regard farming as the ideal mode of life for an Irishman.'[39] In his youth, Liam assisted on the farm when he could, his teacher Patrick Kiely remembering that the young Liam regularly helped to bring his family's milk to the nearby village of Galbally.[40]

By the early twentieth century Mitchelstown had seen great social and economic progress. The town had been a major hub of activity for the Irish National League, which won out in its campaign against the Kingstown estate for reduced rents and the return of property to evicted tenants. From 1888 on, the town became the focal point for new industries and business. In 1896, a new British Army camp opened at Kilworth, providing important business opportunities as the nearby garrison required supplies for both soldiers and their cavalry horses. Along with this massive influx of commercial activity, between 1900 and 1915, social housing was built for labourers in the town in addition to cottages for agricultural labourers in rural areas outside.[41]

Like many major towns in Ireland, by the second decade of the twentieth century Mitchelstown was a major centre of cultural and political activity, and it was there, in the environs of north Cork, that Liam Lynch would first become active in Irish cultural nationalist and political circles.

✳✳✳

Combined with the political assertiveness that emerged among Irish nationalists during the period of land agitation and heightened efforts for Home Rule, cultural nationalism was on the rise among a large proportion of the Irish populace from the late nineteenth century. Cultural nationalism reinforced the idea of Ireland as a distinct political and cultural unit, a popular notion among a growing Catholic middle class increasingly expectant of Irish self-government. One major cultural organisation which came to the fore was the Gaelic Athletic Association (GAA), which was founded in 1884 and promoted distinctly Irish sports, such as hurling and Gaelic football – though there is no evidence the bookish Lynch ever took part in such sporting activities as he grew into adulthood. Indeed, his comrade Moss Twomey could not recall Lynch taking an interest in any sports.[42]

One organisation Lynch did join in Mitchelstown was the local branch of the Gaelic League, where he attended weekly classes.[43] The League was founded in 1893 and became a major movement devoted to the preservation of the Irish language. The organisation had two goals: the preservation of Irish as the national language, and the study and publication of Irish-themed literature. By 1908, the League had managed to achieve one of its key objectives, the teaching of Irish in primary schools. By the same year, it could boast over 600 branches across Ireland. At the direction of its founder, Douglas Hyde, the League avoided association with politics, but this created tensions – particularly with those deemed 'advanced nationalists' outside the political mainstream.[44]

It is not clear when Lynch adopted the Irish version of his name, but by 1917 the earliest letters we have from him show him signing his name Liam, though there is at least one example of a letter in the same year to his brother Tom which is signed 'William'.[44] It is possible his Gaelicised first name was used within the family and by friends long before his move to Mitchelstown and his enthusiastic involvement in the burgeoning Irish language movement. In one account, it is said that Lynch often encouraged fellow boarders in his digs to become interested in speaking Irish.[46] Ironically, Lynch, by his own admission, never had a great grasp of the language himself, with his subsequent revolutionary activities derailing his study of it, but the Gaelic League remained an important social outlet for him even after he joined the Volunteers in 1917.

At some point in these initial years in Mitchelstown, Lynch joined the local chapter of the Irish Catholic fraternal organisation known as the Ancient Order of Hibernians (AOH).[47] One noted historian has referred to the AOH as 'a confessedly sectarian institution, deriving from the eighteenth century … it represented the Catholic reaction to the [Protestant] Orange Order'. By 1909, the AOH had 60,000 members in Ireland and its charismatic leader – or 'Grand Master of the Board

of Erin' – was the Belfast-born nationalist MP Joe Devlin. The AOH
became a major supporter of the IPP and John Redmond's party
leadership, as well as mobilising people to vote for nationalists during
elections.[48] The Order also participated in parades and its members
wore green-coloured sashes, mirroring their Protestant rivals in the
Orange Order.

Like the Gaelic League, the AOH seemed, for a time, to function as
an important social outlet for Lynch in Mitchelstown. George Power, who
was to become a particularly close comrade in the later revolutionary
years, first met Lynch at a meeting of the Mitchelstown AOH.[49] Patrick
Luddy, later active in the IRA's Cork No. 2 Brigade, recalled meeting
Lynch as a fellow member in 1912.[50] It is difficult to determine how closely
Lynch was involved in the AOH's regular activities, but his membership
reflected a period in his life when he was a strong vocal supporter of the
IPP and the Home Rule cause. In an account he wrote on Liam's life, his
brother Tom recalled that by the time he was based in Fermoy, Liam had
dismissed the AOH as 'gas bags'.[51] Lynch, as a supporter of Home Rule,
was within the mainstream of Irish nationalist opinion for the time, and
it was an important phase of his political development.

Between 1912 and 1914, events in Ireland gathered pace by way
of major political developments at Westminster. Through a complex
arrangement with the ruling British Liberal Party, the IPP led by John
Redmond introduced the third Home Rule Bill to Parliament in 1912.
Irish unionists, mainly based in the north-east of Ireland, had long
been furiously opposed to Home Rule and deeply suspicious of any
attempt to break their strong cultural and economic ties with the rest
of Britain. Central to their opposition was the considerable latent
fear of the unionist minority being forced to reside in a self-governed
Ireland ruled by a Catholic majority. The most dramatic response to this
fear was the founding of the Ulster Volunteer Force (UVF) in January
1913, a volunteer militia dedicated to resisting the implementation of
Home Rule by whatever means deemed necessary, including force. The
unionists, led by the Dublin-born lawyer Edward Carson, were aided
in their efforts by the more Conservative-aligned elements within the

British political establishment. One effect of this alliance was the decision by leading members of the British military based at the Curragh camp in County Kildare not to oppose their actions. In April 1914, the UVF oversaw the successful importation of almost 25,000 rifles and between three and five million rounds of ammunition in different locations across Counties Down and Antrim. That there was no attempt by the British military authorities to prevent this would not have gone unnoticed by Irish nationalists.

Inevitably, within the more advanced elements of Irish nationalism, a major response to these developments was planned. Elements of a re-formed IRB had long been anticipating the founding of an exclusively Irish nationalist militia. With an eye to a pending European war, which would see the British military engaged on the continent and forced to defend the British mainland, the IRB wished to create its own army to foment insurrection in Ireland while the colonial ruler was otherwise occupied.

The IRB was now chiefly led by the veteran Fenian Thomas Clarke, and his closest ally Seán Mac Diarmada. This leadership recognised that given their conspiratorial nature and their small membership, they could not embark on such an effort alone or in an open way. Thus, Eoin MacNeill, a university professor and leading cultural Irish nationalist in the Gaelic League (and, notably, not a member of the IRB), was encouraged to write articles in support of the founding of a nationalist militia in separatist newspapers. Such was the response to MacNeill's writings that at a public meeting at Dublin's Rotunda on 25 November 1913, the Irish Volunteers, also referred to by their Irish name Óglaigh na hÉireann, were formally founded and thousands signed up. Inevitably, MacNeill was elected as chief of staff of the Volunteers at this meeting, but the IRB leadership, many of whom were appointed to the Volunteer Executive, regarded him as little more than a figurehead to be manipulated for their own ends. The Volunteers' aim, at least on paper, was to ensure the implementation of Home Rule, by military force if necessary, with this theoretically setting the stage for an armed confrontation with the UVF. In addition to the Irish Volunteers, a number of other nationalist militias were also active in this period, and regularly involved in drilling and training. These were the Irish Citizen Army, a small trade union militia led by the socialist-republican James Connolly; the republican boy scouts Fianna Éireann (translated as 'Fianna of Ireland'); and Cumann na mBan (translated as 'Irishwomen's Council'), the all-female auxiliary to the Volunteers.

Around April 1914, a Volunteer company was formed in Mitchelstown, and that summer leading organiser Colonel Maurice Moore reviewed the company and those in the surrounding districts, after which all members of the local AOH were encouraged to join the Volunteers.[52] It is more than likely that Lynch first joined the Mitchelstown Volunteers around this juncture and he would have been involved in their regular routine of drilling and parades.[53] Mitchelstown has been credited as being one of the first major towns in Ireland to form a local Volunteer corps, and, standing at the junction of three counties (Cork, Limerick and Tipperary), the town was also an important focal point for the development of the organisation in the surrounding countryside. By the summer of 1914, over 2,000 men were members across eight companies of the Galtee Battalion.[54]

John Redmond and the IPP regarded the new nationalist militia with both interest and suspicion, and soon successfully lobbied to allow for members of the party to be on the Volunteer Executive, where they formed a majority. Yet, however promising this new national organisation was, and it was certainly exciting for its members, the Volunteers distinctly lacked something the UVF seemed to have in abundance: arms and ammunition. In an attempt to remedy this situation, and arranged through the auspices of the IRB, landings of arms and ammunition took place in both Dublin and Wicklow on 26 July 1914. In Dublin, an attempt by the British military authorities to disrupt the Volunteers' activities and seize the arms resulted in three civilians being shot dead by the Scottish Own Borderers on Dublin's Bachelor's Walk. This clear contrast between the treatment of the Irish Volunteers and the UVF in similar circumstances by the British authorities did not go unnoticed, and outraged nationalist Ireland.

It was just two days later that an international development marked a distinct turning point in world history, altering the course of the increasingly heightened military and political situation in Ireland. On 28

July, the heir to the Austro-Hungarian throne, Archduke Franz Ferdinand, was assassinated by a Serb nationalist, resulting in Austria-Hungary declaring war on Serbia. What followed was the 'July Crisis', which saw the great powers of Europe dividing into two coalitions: the Triple Alliance of Austria-Hungary, Germany and Italy against France, Russia and Great Britain. The global military conflict that would become known in time as the Great War, and ultimately, in our modern-day parlance, the First World War, had now begun. For the leadership of the IRB, the old Irish republican maxim 'England's difficulty is Ireland's opportunity' now applied, but the leaders of constitutional Irish nationalism also saw a chance to improve their political fortunes.

By mid-1914, the IPP was on the cusp of extraordinary political success. The third Home Rule Bill had passed the House of Lords and was due to receive Royal Assent by King George V that September. Controversially, Redmond had reluctantly agreed in negotiations with Carson to the partition of six counties in the north-east of Ulster, a measure that Redmond's party assumed was temporary. In the event, the implementation of Home Rule was suspended for the duration of the European war, as it was generally assumed this would only last for several months. From July 1914, Redmond publicly called for Irish support for the British war effort on the continent, in the belief this would help in the establishment of a Home Rule parliament governing all Ireland once the war had concluded. Seeing members of the UVF flock to join the new 26th Ulster Division of the British Army, Redmond believed the formation of a distinct Irish nationalist division could only help the Home Rule cause. On 20 September, he appeared before a mass gathering of Volunteers at Woodenbridge, County Wicklow. In a speech in which he insisted the interests of 'the whole of Ireland' were at stake in this new war, he encouraged those present to 'go on drilling and make yourself efficient for the Work, and then account for yourselves as men, not only in Ireland itself, but wherever the fighting line extends, in defence of right, of freedom, and religion in this war'.

Redmond's call aroused the fury of many involved in the leadership of the Irish Volunteers, particularly elements in the IRB, who were already deeply aggrieved that Redmond's nominees sat on the Volunteer Executive. The result was a split in the movement, with over 170,000 joining the Redmond-aligned National Volunteers and the remaining rump of nearly 14,000 retaining the title of the Irish Volunteers, led by MacNeill. Over the course of the four-year conflict, 130,000 Irishmen volunteered for service in addition to the 60,000 already serving in the British Army. Of the volunteers, 24,000 of these originated from Redmond's National Volunteers.[55] At the outset of the conflict, no one could have imagined the death and horror that was to ensue and led to the deaths of an estimated 35,000 Irishmen serving in the British ranks.

In 1914, Liam Lynch identified as a supporter of Home Rule and was a member of the Mitchelstown contingent of the National Volunteers following the split.[56] Hanna Cleary remembered how Lynch's brothers Seán and James were also active in the National Volunteers in their home locality of Anglesboro.[57] Lynch's membership card for the Mitchelstown Company of the National Volunteers is still in existence, with 'Wm Lynch/Baldwin St/ Mitchelstown' scribbled on it.[58] His brother Martin recalled meeting Lynch at the mass review of the National Volunteers in the Phoenix Park in Dublin city on Easter Sunday, 4 April 1915. Lynch was one of 27,000 members who gathered in the Phoenix Park and marched to the Parnell monument on O'Connell Street, where Redmond took their salute.[59] Previous biographers of Lynch barely mention his earlier politics; O'Donoghue, for instance, only briefly refers to Lynch's involvement in the National Volunteers, saying that he joined the Mitchelstown Volunteers in 1914 and made 'an instinctive response to the appeal of soldiering, but he was politically immature'.[60] Lynch later derided his own involvement with the National Volunteers, claiming to his brother Martin that he was 'only wasting [his] time with the Molly Maguires'.[61] Tom Lynch insisted that his brother was 'surprised at John Redmond for recruiting [to the British Army]' and was only trying to find his political bearings in this period.[62] In 1922 Lynch remarked to one Sinn Féin organiser that had there been more effective republican propaganda distributed at the time, he may never have become a member of the Redmondite National Volunteers in the first place.[63]

Having completed his apprenticeship with Patrick O'Neill in 1913, Lynch had continued in employment at the Baldwin Street store for another year. He then got a job at Flavins, another hardware store in Millstreet, until he returned to O'Neill's in late 1914.[64] In January 1913, in a reference, O'Neill wrote of Lynch, 'I found him attentive and anxious to learn his business. As far as I know he is open and honest and I wish him every success.'[65] On 3 February 1914, M.J. Flavin wrote that Lynch was 'honest, sober and a good stock keeper'.[66] Following Lynch's second period of employment at O'Neill's, the owner wrote another reference, stating how he 'always found him attentive, interested in my business and most trustworthy ... I'd be pleased to know he is improving himself.'[67]

On 5 June 1914, Lynch's father, Jeremiah, died at the age of sixty-nine in the family home. The cause of death was given as 'cancer of nose' and Lynch's older brother Seán, who signed the death registration, is listed as being present at the time of death.[68] Lynch's personal reaction to his father's passing is not known, and there is no evidence for what kind of relationship he had with him. Lynch maintained a close relationship with his mother, returning to the Barnagurraha family home every Sunday until his later revolutionary activities intervened.[69]

In the autumn of 1915, Lynch relocated to Fermoy, where he worked in the hardware shop for Messrs J. Barry & Sons, Ltd, a prominent timber merchant in the town. O'Donoghue noted Lynch had by then 'acquired a sound knowledge of commercial life and was a keen student at Gaelic League classes'.[70] As one history of the town has noted, Fermoy was 'defined by its military barracks, which was one of the biggest in Ireland' by the early twentieth century – in fact, the town had two barracks. In 1806, the East Barracks was built on a 16.5-acre site and overlooked the town. In 1809, the West, or New, Barracks was completed. It was in Fermoy that an estimated 67,000 British troops were assembled before departing to face France's Napoleon in the Battle of Waterloo of 1815. Thereafter, for several decades, the troop presence was considerably scaled down in the town, according to the military needs of the time. Yet, whether in times of war or peace, such military garrisons 'were as valuable to a community as a major industry is today and they attracted considerable social activity from which the community benefited'. In Fermoy, officers and soldiers secured vital supplies from local businesses as well as spending money on luxuries and drink, which led to a wider variety of business being established in the town, including Barry & Sons. Fermoy 'grew, evolved and benefitted from the military presence, with which there was an almost symbiotic relationship'. Of note, it has been estimated that 140 men born in the locality of Fermoy died in the Great War; they were listed on a memorial stone unveiled in the town in 2006.[71]

The Gaelic revival was prominent too in this garrison town, with the presence of a very active branch of the Gaelic League. As noted by the writer William Bulfin in 1907, while the 'town was overshadowed by the barracks', the influence of the Gaelic League 'has stricken its roots deep into the soil'.[72] On Lynch's arrival in Fermoy, however, one of his nationalist outlets was no longer in existence: the National Volunteers. By 1915, this organisation had faded away as an active body in the area. However, Lynch remained fervent in his personal politics.[73] Still active locally was a company of Irish Volunteers. At this time, Hanna Cleary, who was involved in the female auxiliary Cumann na mBan, remembered Lynch opposing her association with these local Volunteers as he 'was convinced that we were favouring the Germans then'.[74] Cleary recalled an hour-long argument between them on a street in Fermoy, which continued as both 'headed for a couple of miles along the road, and then the tears came down his face then when I couldn't change'. Though defeated, a week later Lynch sent his godmother a copy of a book by Cardinal Mercier, the leader of the Belgian resistance to German occupation.[75]

What is striking about this episode is how Lynch was so adamantly opposed to the Irish Volunteers in his debate with Cleary in light of his later devotion to the republican cause. O'Donoghue made reference to Lynch's 'logical mind with a stubborn hardness at its core'.[76] This stubbornness was clearly a fixed aspect of his character long before the considerable shift in his political views in May 1916.

* * *

By early 1916, elements of the IRB found themselves on the cusp of leading a rebellion in Ireland. A seven-man Military Council was formed within the secret society, headed by Clarke and Mac Diarmada, who had spent the duration of the war thus far plotting an insurrection against British rule in Ireland. Secretly in control of the Volunteers, the IRB had additional forces in the form of Cumann na mBan, Fianna Éireann and the Irish Citizen Army. The proposed date for this insurrection was 23 April 1916 – Easter Sunday.

By Easter weekend, however, the IRB's plans had been jeopardised. Kept out of these plans until the last moment, Volunteer Chief of Staff Eoin MacNeill made a critical last-minute decision. A small arms shipment from Germany was due to arrive off the Kerry coast, providing much-needed arms for the insurrection. But, following detection, the ship was scuttled on Good Friday to prevent its seizure by the authorities. In response, O'Neill published a countermanding order for any 'Sunday manoeuvres' in the Sunday newspapers and dispatched men to deliver this message to local commanders. This left Volunteer units throughout the country in a state of confusion, and nothing happened on Easter Sunday. The IRB Military Council members, particularly Clarke, were incensed, but nonetheless decided to proceed with the Rising the following day. And so, on Easter Monday, 24 April 1916, nearly 2,000 members of the rebel forces marched into the centre of Dublin and took over key locations to the total shock of the British military and political establishments, as well as the wider Irish public. Alongside Volunteers, members of Cumann na mBan, Fianna Éireann and the Irish Citizen Army now formed the 'Army of the Irish Republic'. At noon, the commander-in-chief of this force, Patrick Pearse, stood outside the republican general headquarters at Dublin's General Post Office. There, he read a Proclamation signed by the members of the IRB Military Council declaring an independent Irish Republic and establishing its Provisional Government. The Easter Rising had begun.

A combination of logistical confusion caused by both the IRB's strategy and MacNeill's countermanding order resulted in little rebel activity outside the capital, with the fighting mostly restricted to Dublin.

And, realistically, there was no hope of any kind of victory once the British military responded with its greater resources and manpower, with much of Dublin city centre devastated by British artillery shelling and fires. Despite this, the surrender in Dublin of the Irish leadership to the British military garrison after only six days came as a profound shock to many in the rank and file of the Volunteers.

In the aftermath, it became clear that civilians made up the largest group of casualties, with over 500 dead. The declaration of martial law throughout the country by British Officer Commanding in Ireland General John Maxwell only heightened growing tensions, a situation exacerbated when both the RIC and British military began rounding up those suspected of involvement in the Volunteers and other nationalist movements, including those in many areas which had played no part in the Rising.

In the early hours of 2 May, one final dramatic, violent episode of the Rising played out three kilometres outside the village of Castlelyons, just south of Fermoy, when a local contingent of seven RIC officers attempted to arrest four male members of the Kent family. The four unmarried brothers, Thomas, Richard, David and William, who resided at Bawnard House on a farm of 200 acres, along with their widowed mother, Mary, had helped organise the Castlelyons Volunteer Company and were well known to authorities as members of the Cork Brigade of the Volunteers. The Kents had a history of political activities going back to the land agitation of earlier years, and Thomas had been imprisoned for two weeks in January 1916 following an arrest by the local RIC for illegal possession of arms. When the Easter Rising began, the brothers waited for a general mobilisation order for over a week. On 2 May, the RIC arrived on their property to effect their arrest, resulting in an exchange of gunfire between the two parties over the course of several hours. At its conclusion, RIC Head Constable William Rowe was dead. Following the brothers' surrender, Richard, the youngest, was shot by arriving military while trying to escape.[77]

Following the arrest of the Kent brothers, the residents of Fermoy were greeted with an unusual sight on the streets of the town that morning. Mary Kent was accompanied by RIC Constable King in an RIC vehicle, while behind them came a military horse-drawn cart carrying David Kent and the wounded Richard. Behind this, Thomas and William Kent were being escorted handcuffed through the streets by armed guard, both men barefoot. It was a humiliating sight and also, sadly, the last time the four brothers would ever be together.[78]

Watching the pitiful scene, as the Kents were rushed across the bridge over the Blackwater River, was a shocked Liam Lynch. Bearing witness to the Kents' arrest and seeing them paraded through Fermoy in such a manner seemed to incense Lynch deeply. His anger was surely cemented further by the knowledge that the youngest, Richard, died of his wounds, and Thomas was executed on 9 May. Florence O'Donoghue depicted a dramatic political shift in Lynch from that moment: 'That night he made a resolution and vow. He would, God helping him, atone, as far as the dedicated life of one man could atone, for the sacrifices of the martyred dead ... he would do his part in making reality the Irish Republic for which heroic men died.'[79] One may be inclined to deride this as a hagiographic flourish on O'Donoghue's part, but other first-hand accounts suggest Lynch's political conversion was indeed almost immediate. As he explained to Hanna Cleary:

> He was Nationalist until the day the British attacked the Kents ... and he saw Thomas Kent being brought out bleeding through the town of Fermoy, and his poor old mother ... They were barefooted. ... he said then that he would join up with the Irish Volunteers ... He said that when he saw the Kents going through Fermoy it was like a sword going through his heart.[80]

Two weeks later, Lynch met John Joe O'Brien, later active in the East Limerick IRA, as they were both heading along the road into Mitchelstown. Knowing him as a supporter of the IPP, O'Brien was shocked when Lynch remarked, in reference to the defeated Volunteer forces: 'We should all have been out. Every one of us should have been out there with them.'[81]

Tom Lynch would recall the influence of the Kents' arrests on his brother, something that Liam often referred to in the years thereafter.

Tom remembered how in 'quiet moments while on the run I often learned from him of the resolutions made that night [of the arrest of the Kents]. The smallest and easiest was to die for Ireland himself; but he considered this such a luxury, that he determined if possible to become worthy of it, by striking some telling blows … if he could be any means remain alive and hit, hit, hit at the age-long enemy, he would forgo the pleasure of dying for Ireland altogether.'[82]

On 3 May, mere days after the rebel surrender, the execution of the leading figures and commanders from the Rising began on the orders of the British military administration, headed by Maxwell. While much of the populace, particularly in and around Dublin, held little sympathy for the rebels during the fighting, the tide of public opinion quickly shifted with these executions and the illumination of the personal stories of the leading figures within the press, along with bitter controversies over specific episodes of British violence during Easter Week. In the aftermath, over 1,500 men were rounded up and taken to various British jails across the Irish Sea. Not all had been active participants in the Rising; indeed, many Volunteers outside Dublin had been confused about the orders and never turned out at all but were still arrested in the aftermath. As John Dorney summarised, the 'post-Rising repression, no matter how justified from a British point of view, could only explode the very fragile Irish nationalist consent for the existing state in Ireland'.[83]

Much of the writing on this period ever since has detailed the radicalisation of those who would make up the influx into the Irish revolutionary ranks after Easter Week 1916. Cahir Davitt, based in Dublin, recalled his inner emotional turmoil both during and after Easter Week:

> After a severe examination of conscience, I did not feel myself bound to participate and I had no inclination to do so. At the same time I felt like a deserter and was miserably unhappy. During the course of the week wonder at their insanity gave way to admiration for their courage and pride in the fight they made. Then came anxiety and apprehension as to their fate upon the surrender and eventually grief and futile indignation at the executions.[84]

Lynch soon yearned to meet someone who had fought in Dublin during the events of Easter Week 1916, from whom he could hear first-hand what had happened. To his surprise, while working one day in Barry's, a regular customer, a farmer from the Galtees, informed Lynch he had helped hide a man who was 'on the run' after the Rising on his family farm. Lynch asked to meet the man and, on doing so, was delighted to learn it was a neighbour of his, Donal O'Hannigan.[85] O'Hannigan, had played an active part in an episode in Louth during the Rising and, having now avoided arrest, was hoping to make it to the United States.[86] Lynch arranged for O'Hannigan to hide out in his family home in Barnagurraha for some time, and his youngest brother, Tom, on his return from college in Clonmel, also helped ensure the man's safety. Lynch frequently visited both men back home, and in the midst of their many conversations, in the words of O'Donoghue, 'there was only one subject upon which he [Liam] would talk – the Irish Republic'.[87]

Chapter 2

'We have declared for an Irish Republic' (1917–18)

MOST PRISONERS DEPORTED TO BRITAIN after the Rising were placed in Frongoch internment camp in north Wales. Though conditions were difficult, it allowed association among many of the surviving participants in the Rising, particularly those who would be key to the rebuilding of the revolutionary movement. One central figure in this was the west Cork-born Michael Collins, then twenty-five years old, soon to be recognised for his natural leadership and extraordinary organisational skills. Collins, along with other key figures such as Thomas Ashe, was central to the rebuilding of the IRB.

Back in Ireland, support organisations were set up to assist the dependants of the prisoners and those killed in the Rising, one notable group being the National Aid Association. Following the tide of change in public opinion, and after repeated protests and entreaties, the British government eventually released all prisoners from their internment camps and jails during late 1916 and in 1917. They returned to their local communities, often to excited scenes and a rapturous reception from supporters. In addition to the returning prisoners, those who were radicalised back home by the events of the Rising and its aftermath were now eager to sign up for the republican cause. Both these groups were essential to rebuilding republican organisations: Sinn Féin, Fianna

Éireann, Cumann na mBan and, of course, the Irish Volunteers, each of which began to navigate through the uncertain political landscape in Ireland after the Rising, with the Volunteers resuming recruiting, training and drilling.

Inevitably, given how emboldened he was by this new devotion to the republican cause, Lynch joined the newly organised Fermoy Company of the Irish Volunteers in early 1917, as did one Lar Condon. Condon recalled joining the Fermoy Company in February that year, and claimed, '[in Fermoy] there were no Volunteers there before that, only Gaelic Leaguers. Fermoy was a garrison town and there was little in the way of National spirit among the people.' Condon said those who formed this new contingent of the Volunteers were inspired by the example of the Kents. A crowd of around eighty to a hundred joined on the first night, Lynch among them. Condon noted that 'Clondulane, an industrial village about three miles to the East of Fermoy, supplied the backbone of the Volunteer Company.'[1] George Power remembered that those who signed up to the Volunteers were members of the local Sinn Féin Club, which had already been in existence for a short time. He placed the number of the 'small company' at about fifty.[2] Shortly thereafter, Liam O'Denn was elected captain, Liam Lynch first lieutenant and Lar Condon second lieutenant of the Fermoy Company. In addition to a company adjutant and quartermaster, there were four sections in the company, one of which was led by a resident of Clondulane, and soon-to-be close friend of Lynch's, Michael Fitzgerald.[3]

John Fanning, who also signed up early in 1917, recalled:

Regular drills and parades were held a couple of nights each week. Some of these were in the Sinn Féin Hall [in Chapel Square, Fermoy], while others were held in the fields in the vicinity of the town. The only drill carried out at this stage was simple foot-drill. The instructors were the Company officers who took sections in turn … very little activity took place in the open and new recruits were usually 'vetted' by the officers before being admitted to the Volunteers.[4]

Now in the ranks of the Volunteers, and in the role of first lieutenant, Lynch, in the words of O'Donoghue, 'took the first step which was a prelude to the ever-widening scope of his activities and responsibilities in the following year'.[5] He quickly took to the regular activities in the Volunteers, honing his organisational skills in service to the republican cause. Ever given to study, Lynch frequently turned to books on the second Boer War (1809–1902) and the Peninsular War (1807–14), which gave him insights into aspects of guerrilla warfare.[6]

Through his involvement in the Fermoy Company, he came into the acquaintance of several key figures with whom he was to become closely associated. George Power recalled that Lynch's previous associations in Fermoy 'were either colleagues in the business where he worked or other members of the commercial element in the town, most of whom lacked any sort of National outlook'. On joining the reformed Volunteers, Lynch then 'associated only with comrades in the movement'.[7] Lynch's routine on joining both the Volunteers and local Sinn Féin Club in Fermoy involved attending every meeting and parade, and, after business hours, going to the local Sinn Féin Club. Power recalled his initial impression of Lynch as 'very shy and retiring. It must have cost him a big effort at the start appearing in public parades in Fermoy with the Volunteers.'[8] Some in this new group of comrades were to become deeply valued friends in the years ahead, including George Power, Maurice 'Moss' Twomey and Michael Fitzgerald.

Power was born in 1896 in Fermoy, and his home on William Street was later used as an important intelligence hub for delivering messages under the guise of business-related communications to his tailor father.[9] In 1917, he was adjutant of the Fermoy Company and a key organiser in the town and its surrounding areas.[10] In these initial weeks of Volunteer activity, he remembered how '[w]eekly parades were held, and simple foot drill was practised. In conjunction with the Sinn Fein Club, the local villages were visited occasionally on Sundays, and joint parades took place with the company of the particular village visited. At this time no arms were available, but, in spite of this, the Volunteers were enthusiastic and serious.'[11]

Like the others, Maurice Twomey, often referred to as 'Moss', joined the Volunteers in 1917. Twomey, born in Clondulane outside Fermoy in 1897, worked at the nearby Hallinan's mill, a commercial hub of the area and initially began to organise a group of Volunteers who worked there.[12] On first meeting Lynch, during his employment in Barry & Sons, Twomey remembered 'a rather aloof, serious and retiring young man ... in a way very shy'. Given Lynch wore rimless glasses and dressed well, Twomey felt this shop assistant was 'a scholar rather than a man of action ... not at all the type of man one would imagine who would handle a gun and lead men into battle'.[13] He noted, too, Lynch's inclination for books about Irish history and his interest in the Irish language. Whatever his initial impressions of this quiet young man, Twomey was to become closely associated with Lynch in various capacities within the military wing of republicanism in the years ahead, and ultimately was deeply loyal to Lynch's memory throughout his long life.

One important friend and comrade Lynch made in this period was Michael Fitzgerald. Born in 1881, in the rural townland of Ballyoran on the main Fermoy to Castlelyons road, Fitzgerald was the only son of Edmund Fitzgerald and his wife Margaret (née O'Brien). Growing up, Fitzgerald was keenly aware of the activities of the local Land League, as his father worked as a gardener for over sixty years on the local Briscoe estate and also collected the tolls from the farmers who attended the monthly fairs. While Edmund is not said to have taken part in the Land League, his son's sole biographer, Thomas O'Riordan, alleged that he held patriotic principles. In his youth, Michael Fitzgerald took an interest in hearing direct accounts of the Fenian Rising in 1867 from locals, particularly the story of John McCarthy from Fermoy, who escaped to the United States after the Rising. Fitzgerald was remembered as 'a great admirer and exponent of Gaelic games' and was a keen participant in the Gaelic League in Fermoy. He also took part in organising events for the 1798 centenary in his area. By 1916, he was employed on the farm at St Colman's College in Fermoy town, thereby bringing him into contact with his future comrades in the Volunteers. Fitzgerald was also the secretary of the Clondulane branch of the Irish Transport and

General Workers' Union (ITGWU) and was quite popular in the role.[14] This contrasted with Lynch, who never had any interest in engagement with organised labour.

It seems that Fitzgerald and Lynch first met in 1914, beginning what is described as a 'lasting friendship'.[15] Lynch's brother Tom later commented on their closeness and said the two men shared their hopes and fears with each other and possessed a 'friendly rivalry'.[16] Fitzgerald was nearly a decade older than Lynch, and became a close companion whom Lynch looked up to, akin perhaps to a surrogate brother. Paddy O'Brien, who came to know Lynch well from 1920, remembered the latter frequently mentioned Fitzgerald as one of his 'idols'.[17] Fitzgerald seemed to project an air of maturity and authority beyond his years, and he was a figure of admiration for others in the brigade. Matt Flood, on joining the Fermoy Company, seemed in awe of Fitzgerald on their first meeting, and observed that Fitzgerald seemed to be 'almost an old man, though he was just over thirty at the time'.[18]

Lynch kept his friends to a close, tight-knit group, and others in the movement were left with the impression of a self-serious man who kept others at a personal remove. Séumus Robinson, later officer commanding (O/C) of the South Tipperary Brigade of the IRA, recalled his impression of Lynch:

> I felt that he ignored if not deliberately suppressed, as a waste of time and energy, his own sense of humour. Yet he must have developed a good sense of humour. No man could possibly have lived and worked so long and so much with so many of the Cork boys without being smitten by a reasonable dose of the contagion.[19]

Accounts from Lynch's closet comrades in Cork do bear out that he was not beyond joking and relaxing in their presence, but this was clearly something he reserved for those who knew him best, not for formal dealings with most of his peers.[20] Of Lynch's sense of humour, Moss Twomey admitted he 'rarely heard [Lynch] tell a funny story, but nobody could better than he enjoy amusing and funny stories and incidents when told by others'. Twomey remembered how he often saw Lynch 'throw up his hands and bring them down on the table laughing heartily'.[21] He also recalled that while Lynch 'smoked an odd cigarette' in company 'he could be classed as a non-smoker' and he rarely drank alcohol among his peers. Paddy O'Brien felt that, when he met strangers, Lynch 'was a great favourite with the people whom he came in contact with, and I can categorically say that nobody ever heard him utter a foul word'.[22]

✶✶✶

Until the outset of the conscription crisis the following year, Volunteer parades and drilling were regular throughout 1917.[23] Patrick Ahern, who joined the Fermoy Company on its re-foundation after the Rising, recalled that the drills and parades 'were held mainly in the fields in the vicinity of the town and sometimes in the Sinn Féin Hall. Most of the drill instruction was carried out by the officers of the company who took the various sections in turn.' Ahern recalled, too, that it was rather difficult to join the Volunteers at this juncture; new members were only accepted on the recommendation of existing members and membership proposals were usually vetted by the officers.[24] It is likely that, as first lieutenant, Lynch was central to this process.

In February 1917 a resurgent republican movement began to see electoral success in a series of by-elections, in constituencies normally won comfortably by the IPP. On 3 February, the Sinn Féin candidate Count George Noble Plunkett – father of Joseph Plunkett, one of the executed rebel leaders of the Rising – secured a seat in the North Roscommon constituency. On 9 May, a by-election in the South Longford constituency saw another surprise Sinn Féin win – following a recount – for imprisoned Volunteer Joseph McGuinness, who had been second-in-command of the Four Courts garrison during Easter Week 1916. On 10 July a by-election in East Clare saw Éamon de Valera win a seat for Sinn Féin, in what was the beginning of a long political career. The American-born de Valera was already becoming a figure of reverence within the movement and a rising leader. Having won the seat only several weeks after his release from prison, he was one of the few surviving commandants who had taken part in the Easter Rising.

As John Dorney has pointed out, these by-elections were fought on the same old restricted franchise, but this time Sinn Féin's success 'did not signify the protest of an emerging social group. Rather, they were a judgement of ... the failure of the IPP to deliver Home Rule, and an indictment of its increasingly unpopular pro-British and pro-War stance.'[25] As part of their election pledges, all elected Sinn Féin MPs operated on a policy of abstentionism and did not take their seats in the Westminster parliament. Given the heightened political activity during the by-elections and the visible presence of such support for both Sinn Féin and the Volunteers, public tensions in some areas increasingly became the norm.

Patrick Ahern, by then a first lieutenant in the Fermoy Company, recalled trouble during a torchlit parade headed by Lynch and the local Volunteers celebrating Joe McGuinness' election in Longford in May 1917. The parade marched up Barrack Hill (now Oliver Plunkett Hill), where the parading Volunteers were subjected to jeers and protests by 'separation women'. On the Volunteers' return down Barrack Hill, the parade was attacked by both women and British soldiers from the local garrison and became, in Ahern's words, 'a general free-for-all'. Lynch ordered the parade to 'stand fast and reform ranks'. The Volunteer company moved to 'the Square' and Lynch dismissed the parade. Ahern felt the whole incident gave 'an idea of the outlook and mentality of the majority of the people of Fermoy at this time'.[26]

On 27 June, *The Cork Examiner* reported on the homecoming of David Kent to Fermoy following his release from Lewes prison in Britain. According to the report, Kent received a rapturous welcome at a public meeting in Fermoy, where 'an admiring crowd of people ... shook hands with him, and wished him welcome home'.[27] The report noted that Kent looked relatively well, 'although he bears traces of the suffering under which he went'. A large procession was formed, including Volunteer companies from Glanworth and Castletownroche, as well as 'a large contingent from Mitchelstown ... and they included about 150 cyclists from that district'. Leading the procession was, of course, the Fermoy Volunteer Company, accompanied by women – likely Cumann na mBan – 'who carried numerous Sinn Féin flags and colours'. As a leading member of the Fermoy Company, Lynch was undoubtedly part of all these proceedings.

✷✷✷

Paddy Casey recalled first meeting Lynch when he worked at Barry's. By now, both were committed members of the Volunteers in Fermoy: 'I got to know him and talked with him a lot. Any spirit of nationalism to which I can lay claim came from him.' Casey approached Lynch in September 1917 about the possibility of forming a local company from students based at the nearby St Colman's College. Lynch 'agreed immediately it … would stir up a real love of Ireland among young college people'.[28] This willingness to sound out and consider ideas from other officers was an early example of the collaborative nature of Lynch's leadership.

During that month, the hunger strike of Volunteer leader Thomas Ashe and others in Dublin's Mountjoy Prison was dominating the national headlines. The Kerry-born Ashe, a charismatic leading republican, had led the Fingal Battalion in one of the most successful engagements of Easter Week in Ashbourne. On 25 September, he died after an effort to force feed him by the prison authorities, an action which would be condemned by the jury in the later inquest. His funeral, on 30 September, would provide the opportunity for an important post-Rising show of strength for the Volunteers. A large procession of over 30,000 marched to Glasnevin cemetery during the funeral. The death of a figure such as Ashe only over a year after the Rising was profoundly shocking to republicans and the wider public, with one Easter Week veteran remarking that Ashe's death 'was a second "Easter Week" in terms of the change of public opinion'.[29] The historian Maryann Valiulis has noted that not only was Ashe's funeral 'an impressive tribute and a symbolic statement', but 'it galvanised the Volunteer movement'.[30] It also brought to the fore another key individual with whom Lynch would closely associate in times of war: Richard Mulcahy. Mulcahy, originally from Waterford, had become active in Gaelic League circles in Dublin and, on joining the Volunteers, rose in the ranks to second-in-command to Ashe during Easter Week. Mulcahy had been imprisoned in Frongoch and assisted in rebuilding the Volunteers. Being the main organiser of Ashe's funeral now brought him to great prominence in the movement, and he became the O/C of the reorganised Dublin Brigade of the Volunteers thereafter.[31]

There is no contemporary record of Lynch's reaction to Ashe's death and funeral, but through the months of 1917 his devotion to the cause became more notable for his family. One anecdote made mention of the tendency during his return visits to Barnagurraha every Sunday, where he sat by the fireplace in quiet thought. His mother would then remark, 'Glory be to God … he is the queer visitor. I haven't got three words out of him.'[32] Liam and his younger brother Tom frequently discussed political developments and appeared to share much in common in terms of republican beliefs after Easter Week 1916.[33] In the existing family archive, there are nearly thirty items of correspondence over five years from 1917 from Liam to Tom. These reveal the thoughts and priorities of an eager young man swept up in the tide of a burgeoning Irish republican movement, but interspersed throughout are comments from Liam on various personal matters, such as his brother's progression through the priesthood.

The brothers shared many of their hopes and dreams for both themselves and Ireland's future. In a letter written on 10 October 1917, Lynch worried that his brother 'won't by any means take up for a diocese in England as you would then never have a happy time … Perhaps if our dreams come true we will be sending in a few years' time missionaries to China and elsewhere to preach the gospel in the same tongue as St. Patrick preached to the Gael.' He made mention of possibly visiting an old school friend, Jack Kiely, who was in the British Army, saying while he 'would like very much to see him … [he] would prefer to see him dressed as a soldier of the Irish Republic'.

Lynch's eye towards a likely pending fight against the British alongside his comrades in the Volunteers, not to mention his excitement at such a prospect, is notable. He recalled how Tom 'mentioned in your last letter to have me wait to mount the breach when the hour comes. I as well as thousands of others are preparing hard at times in the twilight to mount whatever breach is allotted to us.' Furthermore, in 'a few months to come we will be able to marshal an army next to none in quality, and by that time our oppressors will have none but cripples and pensioners, if we do not get what is our own at the peace conference we will have to fight for it'.[34] On 26 October Liam excitedly informed his brother: 'I was second-in-command over 67 Volunteers in a route-march last Sunday.' Liam confidently assured Tom that in 'the meantime we are to keep on drilling until the last man is gone'. He had tried to convince his old friend Jack Kiely to desert the British Army and join the Volunteers. Acknowledging the upcoming Sinn Féin and Volunteer conventions, Liam explained how every Volunteer throughout Ireland paraded the previous Sunday 'to break the law of illegal drilling' and told Tom only to 'mention friendly matters' in future correspondence for fear of the censor. As a sign of how much he was committed to his Volunteer activities, Liam pointed out to Tom that he was 'not as unrobust as you may think; but a rest would do me a lot of good'. He hoped there would be no arrests as the 'Volunteers want to practice drill and thereby help to gain Ireland her freedom'.[35]

On the same day as this letter was written, Sinn Féin held a much-needed convention of its members in the Mansion House in Dublin. Though the party as an organised body had no part in the Rising, the association of its name with non-mainstream nationalism led to the authorities and press inaccurately referring to the insurrection as the 'Sinn Féin Rising' or the 'Sinn Féin Rebellion'. This inevitably led to an influx of new recruits to the previously minuscule party – including the likes of Lynch in the Fermoy branch – and many actual participants of the Rising. De Valera was elected as the new president of the party, and Sinn Féin pledged that it would demand an Irish Republic at whatever peace conference took place among the warring powers when the current international conflict had concluded.

The next day, a much smaller event took place – a secret convention of the Irish Volunteers. The large number in attendance at Ashe's funeral had signalled the importance of a new central authority for the organisation. This led to the election of a Volunteers' national executive, in which the positions of director of training and director of organising were given to Mulcahy and Michael Collins respectively, and they also sat on the Volunteer Executive. Yet, perhaps the most important position was that given to de Valera, who was now made president of the Volunteers.[36] With his ascension to the top position in both Sinn Féin and the Volunteers, he was now the leader of the Irish revolutionary movement.

Lynch was certainly aware of these developments, but around this juncture he was likely more preoccupied with developments closer to home. On 29 October, *The Cork Examiner* noted the arrest of the Fermoy Company captain, Liam O'Denn, the previous Saturday. O'Denn had been arrested under the Defence of the Realm Act and charged with drilling. He was expected to face trial by court martial.[37] According to a report in the *Kilkenny People*, the Sinn Féin Thomas Kent Club in Fermoy passed a resolution on the Saturday after O'Denn's arrest, 'indignantly protesting against the arrest of one of our most valued and respected members … who was … forcibly dragged from his home on a charge of drilling the Fermoy section of the Volunteers at Cornhill on Sunday last …'. The resolution also highlighted O'Denn's contribution to the national cause.[38]

By 1 November, Tom appeared to be contemplating the prospect of a mission to Australia. Lynch encouraged him to go, as Australia was 'a fine country to live in, as well as being a wealthy country. Australia has scarcely anything to do with England, of course you are the best judge.'[39] On Volunteer matters, Lynch noted that he seemed to have evaded arrest for now, as 'they have not picked me up yet but I do not know the minute as I am all the time ready'. Lynch excitedly informed Tom that he had been promoted to captain of the company since the arrest of O'Denn, who was at that time in Cork City Gaol along with other Volunteers awaiting trial. In his description of these events, Lynch wrote a phrase in the midst of a long, somewhat meandering sentence that, to this very day, are unquestionably the most famous words associated with him (marked in bold):

O'Denn was taken from us last Saturday and lodged in Cork main prison where they are forty-seven in all now awaiting trial, or rather, court-martial by the enemy, but **we have declared for an Irish Republic and will not live under any other law**, when he left I was appointed Captain and commanded about 150 men last Sunday and indeed did drill and march ...[40]

The phrase does not appear to have come into regular usage in commemoration or have been firmly embedded in the popular memory of Lynch until the publication of O'Donoghue's *No Other Law* in 1954. It is sometimes misattributed in secondary works as a public statement or utterance by Lynch during the Civil War, but while variations of similar phrases abound in many examples of his surviving correspondence, this is the only example of him saying it as worded. Such comments remain important and instructive, even if only made in passing, as their use in such private exchanges helps to illustrate the formation of Lynch's Irish republican ideology at this early juncture.

In the same letter, Lynch relayed an anecdote of leading the Fermoy Company on parade through the town the previous Sunday under the watchful eye of the local RIC. Demonstrating a touchingly naive and youthful exuberance, he seemed excited at the prospect of his own arrest and observed how those 'in command are being picked up all over the country but we mean to keep going until there is only one left to drill another'. Lynch requested of his brother that 'the moment you hear of me write at once to console mother as I am only doing my duty to God and country'. He ended breezily with: 'I am just going off to a Gaelic dance for a few hours and may be to gaol in the morning if so it is in a good cause as we are quite confident of success.'[41]

On 9 November, Lynch congratulated Tom on taking on the Australian mission. He was, however, more concerned about a worried note from their mother, 'letting me know she was told that there was [*sic*] rumours of my arrest, I wrote her telling her no but that things quietened down again. ... I told her I was glad to do my duty to my country.'[42] Lynch recalled having marched the previous weekend with local Volunteers to nearby Ballyhooly, to mark the opening of a new Sinn Féin Club there. Ultimately, 300 Volunteers gathered from the surrounding areas, and he proudly recalled how he 'had the honour to be at their head'. On the Volunteers' return through Fermoy, Lynch sardonically remarked: 'we had nearly all the town marching at our side so you see even loyal Fermoy can be changed ...'

Lynch lamented the arrest of Captain O'Denn and also explained how the rumours as to his own arrest may have arisen. Arrested with O'Denn, Captain Martin O'Keefe of the Ballyhooly Company 'was dressed very much like me'. Then Lar Condon, Lynch's first lieutenant was arrested, which further puzzled Lynch: 'how he was taken in preference to me I cannot make out unless that they did want to take me ... myself and O'Denn were working in one house'. Lynch's disappointment was perhaps influenced by reports he heard of the prisoners' treatment. He seemed under the impression they were able to have 'a real good time ... they drill together everyday so they will be in top fitness when they come, in fact I would want to be there at least for a few weeks' training. They also hold concerts and mock trials every night.'[43] This was not the case, but Lynch's frustration and insecurity as to his own perceived lack of military training are clear in his remarks.[44] Both O'Denn and Condon were released sometime before Christmas that year after a short hunger strike.[45]

Through late 1917, Lynch was still attending Irish dances, or céilídhe, hosted by the Gaelic League at the town hall in Mallow – an important social outlet for him. Moss Twomey admitted that he did not remember Lynch participating much in the dancing or ever having stood up to sing a song.[46] Siobhán Lankford, later an important activist in Lynch's intelligence network, remembered how these functions 'had the reputation of attracting the most presentable young men'. Lankford remembered how 'Liam was tall, handsome and very distinguished looking ... we had many enquiries as to who he was.' Liam was 'teased relentlessly' about the female interest he attracted, while both Twomey and Power 'got a lot of quiet fun about the ladies' interest in him'.[47] O'Donoghue wrote of Lynch's appearance by this age as that of 'a big man, with regular, handsome features and an attractive personality'. As well as wearing rimless glasses, he had a 'steep brow and broad expanse of forehead' which gave him a 'scholarly appearance'.[48]

The female interest goes some way to explaining Lynch's attendance at these events, for in 1917 he first made the acquaintance of a young woman called Bridget, or 'Bridie', Keyes from Mitchelstown. His second biographer, Meda Ryan, described her as 'a vibrant, dynamic young girl' to whom he was immediately attracted.[49] Of note is that she was over five years older than Liam, her birth registration giving her birth date as 6 May 1887; she was from a rural family in the Kilshanny townland outside Mitchelstown.[50] Both the 1901 and 1911 censuses list her as living in the family home. By 1911, her occupation is given as draper's assistant.[51]

In early November 1917, writing to Tom, Lynch makes a rather touching comment on his growing friendship with Keyes and mentions how she could still be shy in approaching him. 'I am doing a great line these days but she keeps always at a distance at my tail, sometimes she walks after my pals.' Lynch jokingly added in a reference to censors watching his letters: 'my other lovers at Mallow must know all [of his Volunteer activities] before now'.[52]

Lynch and Keyes developed a growing attraction and connection to each other, which was often noted by Lynch's close friends as the relationship blossomed. She was to be an important emotional anchor in Lynch's life as his revolutionary activities grew in the times ahead. Their relationship was first detailed in Ryan's biography, while O'Donoghue referred simply to 'the love and prayer of a devoted lady [that] went with him through all the days of strife, constant and faithful to the end'.[53] O'Donoghue likely left Keyes unnamed out of respect because she was still alive in 1954 when his book was published. Her role in Lynch's life was never publicly revealed in her lifetime, and rare accounts of her suggest she was an intensely private individual. The relationship between her and Lynch was known only to a small circle and was later a surprise to those who saw Lynch as a self-serious and shy personality. Indeed, Seán Moylan, who later served under Lynch in the IRA, dismissed the idea that Lynch 'gave any indication of a concern for women'.[54] However, Moylan and Lynch were not personally close.

Tom remarked that Keyes was:

> A splendid, sincere quiet girl who claimed Liam as her own all
> through the fight, who burned lamps perpetually for his safety
> before a Sacred Heart statue in her room, and who mourned
> deeply at his grave as his fiancée. She was certainly unselfish for
> Liam had no love for any girl but Ireland alone. Perhaps it was that
> Liam placed his affection in no other girl that she persisted ... In
> our intimate conversation, he was emphatic that he'd never marry
> or think of it 'till Ireland was free.[55]

While Tom seems to imply the relationship was more one-sided, Lynch
would admit the importance of it to others, and throughout the period he
would make sometimes risky efforts to meet Keyes.

On 12 December, Lynch wrote again to Tom, assuring his brother
he had 'escaped arrest so far'. With de Valera due to visit Fermoy, Lynch
also talked about holding the Irish Convention.[56] The convention was a
failed attempt, instigated by British Prime Minister David Lloyd George,
to allow all nationalist and unionist parties involved in the Irish question
to come together and discuss the possible implementation of Home Rule
in Ireland. Sinn Féin boycotted the talks, which began in July 1917 and
ended with no result in March 1918. In his letter to Tom, Lynch was of the
opinion that 'the [British] government has forced the Convention into
accepting a measure of Colonial Home Rule' and 'things are looking still
brighter than ever in favour of our independence. England is well on her
knees at last'. He ended on a note of anticipatory fear of some sort of
encounter with the authorities, stating that 'four of us here do not know
the moment we may be arrested'.[57]

The 15 December edition of *The Cork Examiner* reported on de
Valera's presence in Fermoy the previous day. The paper noted him being
'escorted from the local Sinn Féin rooms by a procession of horsemen,
Volunteers, Cumann na mBan, etc.' De Valera gave a specially designed
flag to the Volunteers and began a speech by saying it gave him great
pleasure to present such a flag. Criticising the IPP in his remarks, de

Valera explained how 'Sinn Féin stood for true nationality as they wanted Ireland to be absolutely independent of England ...' One remark that would have resonated with Lynch was de Valera's observation of how many in their ranks had once been 'followers of the Irish [Parliamentary] Party when they had seen that the leaders of that Party had gone wrong'.[58] The presence of de Valera passing through Fermoy was likely something of a moment of awe for Lynch, although more in terms of de Valera's service in Easter Week and his status as leader of the Volunteers than as the paramount political figure in Ireland. Tom Lynch recalled that his brother was photographed in his Volunteer uniform at this event. Realising this may bring his attention from the authorities, Lynch rarely wore the uniform in the years ahead.[59]

* * *

The year 1918 was critical in the growth of the revolutionary movement, in both the political and military wings. Strangely, it is the one year of Lynch's revolutionary career in which it is difficult to illuminate his reaction to several important developments due to a lack of relevant sources. Tom Lynch recalled his older brother had suffered an illness through the winter of 1917–18, which he described as an 'attack of rheumatic fever', and suggested that Lynch used the period of recovery to return to his books to get a sense of military strategies and tactics.[60]

By the end of the previous year, the executive of the Volunteers had established a General Headquarters (GHQ). Its creation was a result of the progress the organisation had been making in rebuilding since the Rising, with the leadership satisfied at the progression of training and the maintenance of high morale and discipline among the ranks. The creation of a GHQ would allow for the co-ordination of the work of brigades throughout the country and provide a central command for the Volunteers, at least in theory. In March that year, the executive met to decide on membership of this new body. The make-up was as follows: Richard Mulcahy as chief of staff, Michael Collins as adjutant general and director of organisation, Seán McMahon as quartermaster general,

Rory O'Connor as director of engineering and Dick McKee as director of training. Maryann Valiulis has described the distinction between GHQ and the Volunteer executive: 'While the Volunteer executive remained in control of policy, GHQ was responsible for directing military activities.'[61]

In County Cork, 1917 had seen an unprecedented growth in Volunteer membership, and O'Donoghue made the claim that by the end of that year 'there was scarcely a parish without a local Volunteer company'.[62] By early 1918, the ranks of the Fermoy Company had swelled to around 100 men. Efforts were then made to source arms by raiding loyalist homes in the locality, which led to the acquisition of a dozen shotguns and half a dozen revolvers of various calibres. George Power remembered how the company made some progress in the production of crude canister bombs when a quantity of gelignite was acquired.[63] However, by 2 March, Volunteer GHQ prohibited all units from carrying out such raids, thereby closing one avenue of arms supply.[64]

The Cork Brigade leadership, among them Brigade O/C Tomás MacCurtain, realised that the organisation of the Volunteers needed perfecting further, with new companies across the county continually being organised.[65] MacCurtain had been on the founding Cork Executive of the Volunteers in December 1913. His organisational skills and dedication to the cause marked him out as a natural leader. Due to the confusion over the countermanding orders in 1916, both MacCurtain and his vice-O/C, Terence MacSwiney, had ensured that the Cork Volunteers did not 'turn out' for fighting – nonetheless both men, and many under their command, were rounded up and arrested in the aftermath. Released in December 1916, MacCurtain would be arrested again the following year but was released after a short hunger strike.[66] As time went by, he was to become a figure greatly respected by Lynch.

Early in 1918, the brigade leadership made the decision to create the Fermoy Battalion, the sixth of twenty battalions in the brigade at the time. The battalion consisted of the following companies: Fermoy, Kilworth, Araglen, Rathcormac, Watergrasshill, Glenville, Ballynoe, Bartlemy and Castlelyons. As per the procedure within the Volunteers, four leading officers were elected to oversee this new battalion: Martin O'Keefe as battalion commandant, Michael Fitzgerald as vice-commandant, George Power as quartermaster and Liam Lynch as adjutant.[67] Fitzgerald's biographer, Thomas O'Riordan, noted that both Fitzgerald and Lynch 'discussed every problem that confronted them, in the battalion and made many plans to improve the organisation in the area'.[68]

It was in this period that Lynch began to develop a routine he would maintain as he ascended to higher military rank, that of his tendency for frequent on-the-ground inspection and investigation of various areas under his command. In his role as battalion adjutant, Lynch visited one company per week. O'Donoghue made mention of how, on meeting the officers involved, Lynch made 'an intensive study of every problem they had to face, always urging the perfection of organisation, the intensification of training, and the acquisition of arms'.[69] This last point was to be a major issue for the battalion in the months ahead and deemed important to the maintenance of regular drilling and training, to say nothing of morale. Retrospectively, George Power was in no doubt: 'Lynch was the driving force in organising the battalion and in helping to develop the backward companies'.[70] This was to prove important with the onset of a major political crisis in Ireland.

**

As the war continued to rage, with unprecedented loss of life on the European continent, the British cabinet contemplated introducing conscription to Ireland by way of legislation in the Westminster parliament. (Conscription had already been introduced to Britain in 1915.) This became more paramount from 21 March 1918, after the German Army began a series of attacks along the Western Front which became known as their spring offensive. With the possibility of Irishmen being forced to serve in the ranks of the British Army, a wave of protest across Irish society saw the Catholic Church hierarchy, the IPP, Sinn Féin and the Labour Party participating alongside each other on public platforms. All were united in support of what was to become known as the 'anti-conscription campaign'. At an important meeting in the

Mansion House on 18 April, representatives of the numerous political parties made the following pledge: 'With all the responsibility that attaches to our pastoral office we feel bound to warn the Government against entering upon a policy so disastrous to the public interest, and to all order, public and private.' On 21 April, outside church Masses, thousands signed an anti-conscription pledge. Throughout Cork, both the Volunteers and Sinn Féin co-operated in ensuring these public signings were carried out.[71] This campaign of passive resistance gained momentum with anti-conscription rallies across the country, along with a major one-day general strike organised by the trade union movement on 23 April.

In April, Lynch temporarily left his employment at Barry & Sons in anticipation of full-time active service. Intriguingly, O'Donoghue wrote that Lynch ventured out to Bawnard House to tell David Kent of his decision, Kent clearly having become something of a mentor for Lynch since his joining the Volunteers. Lynch and his closest allies, including Michael Fitzgerald and George Power, began devising plans for the battalion response in the area should conscription be enforced. Lynch's absence from his employment resulted in frustration on the part of the local authorities in their efforts to locate him, with Barry & Sons being raided on three separate occasions. His employers ignored a request that on his return to work his employment be terminated 'as he was a disturbing influence on the town'. His absence from work ensured there was little risk of Lynch being rounded up in the so-called 'German Plot', invented by the British authorities to capture key leading figures in both the Volunteers and Sinn Féin in early May.[72] Tom later wrote that 'Liam was now cured of his desire for jail. Active resistance was the order and Liam now feared the idea of arrest ...'[73]

During May 1918, Liam Tobin arrived in Cork, to function as an organiser and give advice to Volunteer leaders in the county on behalf of GHQ.[74] The Cork-born Tobin had been active in the Volunteers during the Easter Rising and was interned in Frongoch until early 1917. At the time, he was an intelligence officer attached to the Dublin Brigade and a member of the IRB, close to Collins. He was also inspector for the New

Ireland Assurance Company, which he had co-founded with several fellow Frongoch internees, and he was able to travel freely in the province under this guise.[75] Tomás MacCurtain, as Cork Brigade O/C, was keen to have a strong intelligence network established throughout the brigade area, and Tobin was to assist and advise him. MacCurtain had already established an intelligence unit in Mallow, utilising female activists who worked in various business premises to safely store and transport Volunteer-related dispatches – often at great risk to themselves. A key operative in this network was Siobhán Lankford (then Siobhán Creedon), who worked in the Mallow Post Office.[76]

One Sunday evening in May, Lynch travelled by bicycle to meet Lankford and Tobin at the home of a sympathiser in Castletownroche. Lynch made arrangements with them for an intelligence link-up between Mallow and Fermoy. Important dispatches were to be sent by telephone under the guise of business-related messages to George Power's home. As Lankford explained: 'The Powers were tailors, and messages about suits, clothes and measurements would excite no interest in any phone tappers.'[77] Lankford would frequently work closely with Lynch in the years ahead and, as borne out in her own memoir, would prove herself a trusted ally and genuine friend. For all the purported shyness in his character, several accounts demonstrate that Lynch seemed to enjoy a number of close female friendships. Perhaps due to his closeness to his godmother Hanna Cleary, Lynch seemed at ease in the company of women of a similar age with whom the relationship was strictly platonic, such as Lankford and, later, Kathleen Barry Moloney.[78]

On the day Lankford first met Lynch, some of this group (along with George Power) attended a concert run by the Fermoy branch of the Gaelic League in Castletownroche that evening. In her memoir, Lankford wrote of an amusing episode that highlighted Lynch's sometimes self-serious and fussy nature. The concert was so amateurish that some of their group quickly left the venue, unable to contain their laughter. Lankford, meanwhile, found herself unable to leave as she was seated between Lynch and another Volunteer, Séamus Lankford (her future husband). She lamented how 'I had to sit through the whole concert to the muttered comments of these two perfectionists.' Both men 'saw nothing funny in the whole performance, nor did they see the desperate earnestness of the poor man who was trying to run the show'. This same man then 'made a long speech in which he sought to heal a breach in the local volunteer company. Liam Lynch was tense and he muttered savagely: "He has no right to mention these things."' Afterwards, Lynch complained, only to be informed that most of the usual, more competent Gaelic League branch performers were in fact currently in jail.[79]

Lankford's memoir is the reason Lynch has the nickname 'The Real Chief'. In an anecdote from the Civil War, Lankford mention a Cumann na mBan courier getting confused over meeting 'the Chief' – a nickname often used for Éamon de Valera. In her telling, Lankford explained, 'we called Liam Lynch the Chief, which he was, of the IRA'.[80] While Lynch was then chief of staff, there is mention in other accounts of him being called 'chief' by those under his command even before that appointment.[81] In her biography of Lynch, Meda Ryan misquoted Lankford's story, saying she called Lynch 'the real Chief'.[82] Of interest, this was used as the title of Ryan's biography and led to Lynch having a long-held posthumous association with the nickname.

It was during the conscription crisis that both Lynch's comrades and the Volunteer leadership came to recognise his considerable organisation skills.[83] At some juncture during the summer, MacCurtain met with Lynch and gave him instructions on what positions the battalion were to occupy in their area should conscription be enforced. In his assessment of this period, O'Donoghue felt that Volunteer GHQ 'appear to have been able to do no more than to indicate the broad policy ... of a general plan of resistance ...'.[84] It was to up to brigade leaders and battalion officers to respond to any local problems and difficulties, if need be, when conscription was enforced. Until the end of the war, the Volunteer leadership was anticipating some degree of military clash over conscription, no matter what tactics were endorsed by leading political figures. One notable article on the subject appeared in the Volunteer newssheet issued by GHQ, *An tÓglach*, on 14 October. Written by Ernest Blythe under the heading 'Ruthless Warfare', it stated that it 'would be desirable ... to eliminate all talk and thought of passive resistance'. Hence, if the British government 'decides on this ... then we, on our part, must decide that in our resistance we shall acknowledge no limit and no scruple'.[85] Lynch likely shared such sentiments.

Despite the threat of conscription and unlike in other areas, Con Leddy, O/C of the Araglen Company within the Fermoy Battalion, recalled little change in the number of members signing up locally at this time, 'as all those young men in the district who wanted to be Volunteers had already joined up'.[86] While a full-scale engagement with the RIC and British military was perhaps out of the question at this time, Lynch still sought to take the initiative come what may. Such an opportunity arose involving an attempted arms capture at the Castletownroche train station in May 1918.

Patrick Hackett, a local Fermoy man who worked in the Army Stores Section in Cobh, kept Lynch personally appraised of the movement of supplies, including arms. The army stationed in Fermoy Barracks received arms from the depot in Cobh: empty ammunition boxes were dispatched from Fermoy railway station to Cobh, usually then returning full within several days. In early May, Hackett informed Lynch of a large consignment of rifles and ammunition due to arrive in Fermoy. Lynch, along with Lar Condon and Michael Fitzgerald, began devising plans to hold up the train and seize the stores. Joining them in these plans were Liam Tobin and John Fanning, O/C of the Fermoy Company.

Careful arrangements were put in place, starting with hiring cars from a local garage under the guise of transporting people to a funeral. These cars were to be used to move the seized arms to planned dumps in Araglen. Lynch, along with the group of battalion officers travelled in the cars to a prearranged meeting point at Penny boreen, the site chosen for the transfer of the captured arms from the train. Volunteers from different companies were spread across the nearby area on scouting and lookout duties.

Fanning, along with a group from the Fermoy Company, proceeded to Castletownroche railway station. The plan was for two Volunteers to take up a position on the footplate of the arriving train and compel the driver to take the train to the Benny boreen. The other Volunteers were then to board the train as it moved out of the station. All proceeded according to plan until the train's arrival at Castletownroche. Fanning later explained that the Volunteer delegated to cut the cable wires when he heard the whistle of the train pulling out in fact cut the wires when the train pulled in. As a result, the train could not progress further and became stuck at Castletownroche.

Fanning realised it was too late to alter the plans, and so the action was called off, with the Volunteers quickly returning to their own areas. Adding to the disappointment of Lynch and the battalion leadership, it was determined by subsequent investigation that there had, in fact, been no army stores on the train. The arms actually arrived at Fermoy at 6 a.m. the following morning.[87] In spite of this, the operation was deemed good practice for future efforts.[88] Power later recalled how, during the conscription crisis, a 'train which was suspected of carrying ammunition between Mallow and Fermoy was held up and some .303 ammunition was obtained' – but he does not provide a date.[89]

By June, wary of the protest in Ireland, the British government had dropped its conscription plans. At this juncture, the tide of war had begun to turn in favour of the Allies. On 11 November 1918, an armistice signed between the Allies and Germany ended the war. Thus, the threat of conscription in Ireland dissolved, yet the ramifications of the crisis were enormous. Not least of these was heightened public sympathy with Sinn Féin and the republican cause, which was to prove vastly beneficial for the party in the general election on 14 December that year. The electoral franchise had also been expanded, by way of the Representation of the People Act 1918, allowing all women over the age of thirty, provided they owned property, to vote, along with all men over the age of twenty-one.

As part of its election manifesto, Sinn Féin continued with its policy of 'abstentionism'. Another key item on the party's manifesto was the promise to plead the case for recognition of an Irish Republic at the post-war conference with the winning powers in Paris in 1919. Also of note, as highlighted by Diarmuid Ferriter, was an item that was open to different interpretations: Sinn Féin's promise to 'use any and every means available to render impotent the power of England to hold Ireland in subjugation'.[90]

The Fermoy Battalion covered much of the constituencies of both Cork East and Cork North East, in which the respective candidates for Sinn Féin, David Kent and Thomas Hunter, were elected unopposed. These constituencies were two of twenty-five where Sinn Féin ran uncontested; there were 105 constituencies in total. Bearing this in mind, many of the Volunteers in the area were dispatched to other constituencies to assist Sinn Féin operations in campaigning for contested seats. John Fanning recalled Volunteers of the Fermoy Battalion assisting in Sinn Féin's election campaign in Waterford that December. Inevitably, given that Waterford was a traditional support base for the now late John Redmond, Volunteers guarding Sinn Féin political workers clashed with IPP supporters, just as they had done in a previous March by-election which the IPP had won.[91] Vice-O/C of the Fermoy Battalion, Lar Condon, recalled one dramatic episode during the March by-election, 'when about six of us were hemmed in by them at a polling booth in Manor Street, we would have got a very rough handling from them [the IPP supporters] only I had a revolver and fired a shot in the air. This cleared them back and we rushed through them.'[92] Such scenes were common during the electoral events in Waterford that year and clearly unforgettable to those involved, with one IRA commander later commenting years afterward that he met those 'who had served flying columns in Cork, Kerry and Tipperary, and they all told me that they would much prefer to repeat the service they had given in the IRA columns rather than serve in an election campaign in Waterford'.[93]

There are no accounts of Liam Lynch's presence alongside the Fermoy Battalion Volunteers in Waterford during either the by-election in March or the general election that December. In the election, Sinn Féin won an astonishing seventy-three seats across Ireland – almost seventy per cent of the vote, and one that completely annihilated the political power of the IPP, which was reduced to six seats. Of the political wing of the revolutionary movement, though Lynch had joined the Sinn Féin Club in Fermoy, this seemed to him more of a duty than something that truly appealed to him. As O'Donoghue determined, 'At no time did the political side of the movement appeal strongly to Liam Lynch. He was a soldier by instinct and temperament. He could have been a great priest, but he did not possess that flexibility of character which would have made him a successful politician.'[94] Indeed, as he became more embroiled in military conflict, Lynch expressed a distaste for Sinn Féin activists and elected members, and, as will be seen, a general disinterest in their activities often widely shared among much of the Volunteer membership.

One organisation that was of interest to Lynch was the revived IRB. In late 1918, he joined the organisation, and from there formed a 'circle', as its units were known, in Fermoy. He was subsequently elected the Fermoy circle's centre, which meant he would have had to take responsibility for making sure that regular meetings were held. As O'Donoghue noted, being the head of a small grouping of the IRB would have given Lynch little influence in the wider organisation, at least at this juncture.[95] But his respect for the institution of the IRB, undoubtedly rooted in his own family associations with the Fenians and his dedication to this enigmatic body, came second only to that of the Volunteers during his revolutionary activities.

Within the revolutionary movement at the time there was debate about the necessity of the IRB, given the existence of open organisations such as the Volunteers and Sinn Féin. Leading figures such as de Valera and MacCurtain had resigned their membership after the Rising, seeing little use for it in the radically changed political climate. Despite this, by the end of 1918, 350 IRB circles had a total membership of 3,000, with each circle forming the nucleus of a Volunteer company, the claim being that 90 per cent of the best Volunteers – such as Lynch – were in the IRB.[96] Mulcahy, as chief of staff of the Volunteers, saw no conflict of interest between the respective aims of the IRB and Volunteers; indeed, according to his biographer, he 'saw positive value in the mechanism it [the IRB] provided for escapes and intelligence contacts it established'.[97] Given that he joined, Lynch undoubtedly shared these perspectives on the IRB.

While the IRB operated in the shadows, the activities of the Volunteers would be more visible. Towards the end of 1918, Con Leddy,

O/C of the Araglen Company, approached Lynch about the possibility of raiding the local RIC barracks in his area. In response, Lynch 'remarked that it might be inadvisable to go ahead with the raid on account of the national unity then prevailing'. Leddy ruefully recollected how by 'the end of 1918 we had neither rifles or revolvers'.[98] Disappointed as he may have been, neither he nor Lynch could have realised how the year ahead would provide a chance for such a raid on Araglen's RIC barracks and, indeed, much greater military opportunities.

Chapter 3

'I have started something that will shake up these fellows' (1919)

FOLLOWING THE RESOUNDING VICTORY IN the general election the previous December, the elected Sinn Féin TDs – at least those who were not in prison – assembled in Dublin on 21 January 1919 for the first meeting of their underground, independent legislative assembly, Dáil Éireann (Irish for 'Assembly of Ireland'), which was to function as the single-chamber parliament of the Irish Republic. The inaugural meeting of the First Dáil took place, entirely in Irish, in the Round Room of the Mansion House, the residence of Dublin's Lord Mayor. The historian Michael Hopkinson believed this first meeting 'was concerned more with winning publicity for the cause, both at home and abroad, than with establishing a working legislature and government'.[1] Four key documents were read out and adopted at the meeting: a constitution, a declaration of independence (ratifying the Irish Republic declared by the provisional government in 1916), a 'Message to the Nations of the World' and the Democratic Programme.

As the small number of deputies met in the Mansion House that day, in the townland of Soloheadbeg in rural south Tipperary a group of Volunteers sprang into action. Led by Séumas Robinson, O/C of the Third Tipperary Brigade, this group of armed Volunteers ambushed and killed two members of the RIC who had been escorting two council workers in a cart containing 160lb of gelignite. Robinson and the

Volunteers, including Dan Breen and Seán Treacy, secured the gelignite and eventually distributed it to the brigade's battalions.

The most controversial aspect of this action – aside from it occurring on the same day as the first sitting of Dáil Éireann – was that it was completely unsanctioned by GHQ. Mulcahy and other GHQ members were deeply unhappy about it, given the public controversy it aroused. Mulcahy was of the opinion that 'people had to be led gently into open war'; years later, he complained how the incident was 'outrageously propagandised as a leading episode in waking up the country' and said that it was unfortunate it happened on the same day as the Dáil first met.[2] Robinson later recorded how he discussed the issue with his vice-commandant, Treacy, and did not request sanction because they would have to await an answer, which may have come too late. Retrospectively, Robinson felt the condemnation from the political wing of the revolutionary movement was hypocritical, noting that the Dáil's message to the nations of the world issued that day stated: 'The existing state of war between Ireland and England can never be ended unless Ireland is completely evacuated by the armed forces of England' – he took this to be a declaration that a state of war already existed between the Irish Republic and Britain.[3] Breen, meanwhile, said that Treacy told him 'we wanted to start a war, so we intended to kill some of the police whom we looked upon as the foremost and most important branch of the enemy forces'.[4]

By early 1919, the RIC was deeply disliked, and even hated, among sectors of the Irish population. The overall perception of the force across the country was that it was an armed wing of the British authorities in Dublin Castle, gathering intelligence on Irish nationalist movements and the overall populace, and it was inevitable that its members would become targets in the heightened political atmosphere. Already in April 1918, there had been an IRA arms raid on an RIC barracks in Gortatlea, Tralee, County Kerry – an incident that has rarely received historical attention despite a Volunteer being killed by one of the constables.[5] Despite this growing animosity, a position in the RIC was still seen as a respectable job, but although the ranks of the RIC were largely Catholic, most RIC inspectors were Protestant, causing one leading Sinn Féin figure to note 'that conversion to Protestantism was the key to advancement to that level'.[6] This almost certainly did nothing to help improve feelings towards the force. Of note, by 1919 the RIC had only around 9,000 men stretched thin over nearly 1,500 'huts' and 'barracks'.[7]

In any event, the outcome was that the Soloheadbeg ambush would be remembered and celebrated as the first military engagement of the Irish War of Independence. Historian John Dorney has pointed out that the retrospective 'symbolism of the events of 21 January was impossible to miss', with the same day seeing an Irish rebel parliament proclaiming a republic in the capital while Volunteers who claimed to be acting as the army of that republic took action against British forces.[8] For better or worse, the events at Soloheadbeg threw down the gauntlet to other Volunteer leaders, not least to Liam Lynch who by then had been given a new command, to pursue similar actions against British forces.

***

By the end of 1918, the Cork Brigade encompassed twenty battalions across the county, with a membership of around 8,000. The decision was made at GHQ to split the brigade into three: Cork No. 1, commanded by Tomás MacCurtain, encompassed Cork city and extended from Youghal to the Kerry border beyond Ballyvourney; Cork No. 3, commanded by Tom Hales, encompassed West Cork; and Cork No. 2, encompassed north Cork.[9] On 6 January 1919, at a house in Glashbee, Mallow, the meeting that led to the formation of the Cork No. 2 Brigade – also referred to as the North Cork Brigade – took place. In terms of territory, this new brigade extended eastward from the Cork–Waterford border near Tallow to the Kerry border at Rathmore, extending northward then from Milford and almost to Donoughmore in the south (see Map 1).

Presided over by MacCurtain, the meeting was attended by several officers representing most of the battalions in north Cork that this new brigade was to encompass: Fermoy (First Battalion), Mallow (Second Battalion), Castletownroche (Third Battalion), Charleville (Fourth Battalion) and Millstreet (Seventh Battalion).[10] For reasons

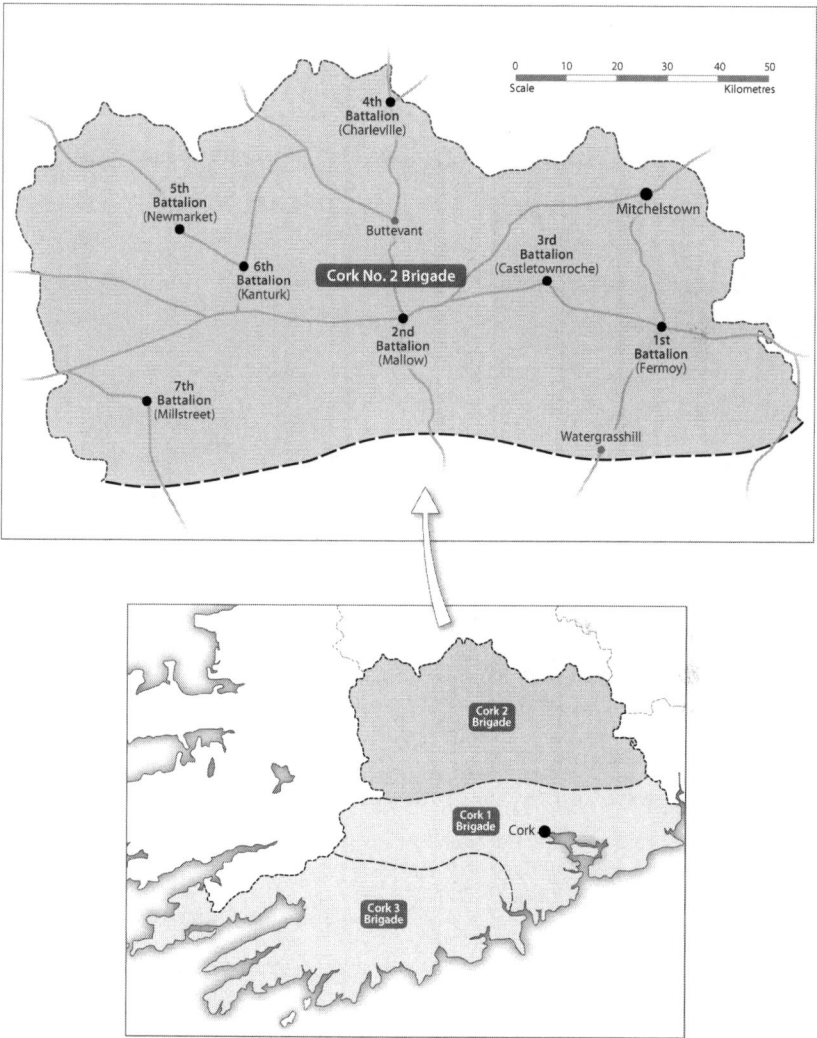

Map 1: The area encompassing the IRA's Cork No. 2 Brigade, also referred to as the North Cork Brigade. Liam Lynch was appointed O/C of the brigade on 8 January 1919. Following the beginning of the War of Independence on 21 January that year, Lynch remained in this position until his appointment as O/C of the IRA's First Southern Division in April 1921. The brigade area was altered in early July 1921, when it was split into two brigades, Cork No. 2 and Cork No. 4 (see chapter 5).

that are still unclear, the message to attend the meeting never reached the commandants of Newmarket (Fifth Battalion) and Kanturk (Sixth Battalion). The commandant of the Newmarket Battalion was Seán Moylan; George Power noted that he soon developed 'a longstanding prejudice' towards Lynch and resented his appointment as brigade O/C. Power implied that Lynch later had to travel to Newmarket to secure Moylan's support, which he did after some difficulty.[11] Moylan, like Lynch, hailed from County Limerick, but moved to Newmarket as a young man to seek better commercial opportunities. Also like Lynch, he joined the Volunteers in 1914 and founded the Volunteer company in Newmarket, where he was elected captain.[12] Whatever the nature of their relationship, Moylan was to become a valued commandant within the brigade area for Lynch, and, in time, he would gain his own sterling military reputation.

Florence O'Donoghue and other sources all agree that Lynch was elected unanimously as the commandant of the newly formed brigade at the meeting in Glashbee.[13] Others elected included Dan Hegarty as vice-commandant, Thomas Barry as quartermaster and Lynch's close comrade George Power as the adjutant.[14] Lynch was almost certainly delighted when his close friend Mick Fitzgerald became Fermoy Battalion O/C. The two men continued to work closely together, and Thomas O'Riordan wrote that from this time on, Fitzgerald 'devoted all the time at his disposal to training and improving the organisation.'[15]

George Power put the strength of the No. 2 Brigade in early 1919 at around 2,500 men, with limited armaments numbering about a dozen rifles, two dozen revolvers and about 200 shotguns.[16] In opposition to Cork No. 2 Brigade were brigades of the British 6th Division, commanded by Major General Sir E.P. Strickland, stationed in various fortified barracks, including Fermoy. The total military garrison of the area was made up of 4,300 soldiers of various ranks in five battalions that encompassed elements of the 6th Division's 16th and Kerry Brigades, along with two brigades of Royal Field Artillery and a machine-gun battalion. In the fifty-four RIC barracks throughout the brigade area, there were 490 armed members of the RIC who had all the normal advantages of the force, including an intimate knowledge of the area and its local populace.[17]

Lynch's brother Tom visited his older sibling at Barry & Sons not long after Liam's appointment as brigade O/C. Tom noticed that his brother was 'elated and happy', but Tom was personally frightened and nervous at the turn of events in the country since Soloheadbeg. He asked Liam if he was aware of 'the responsibilities and the heavy task' ahead. Liam replied confidently, 'I'll be able for it … 'Tis great scope.'[18]

In 1919, Lynch's brigade HQ was initially in Fermoy, which put him somewhat at a disadvantage given he was in a very eastern part of the brigade's territory, but it meant that, with the adjutant, Power, also based in Fermoy, much of the brigade correspondence for Lynch's attention was centralised. Power also began to develop an intelligence network from the town.[19] Dispatches to and from GHQ, along with communications from the westward part of the brigade area, were delivered by railway workers, who were often active Volunteers. Mallow railway station, in Power's words, 'was the vital pivot in distribution' – rarely did a letter to GHQ in Dublin take longer than two days to arrive. In reflecting on this period, Power paid tribute to cyclist Volunteers and members of Cumann na mBan in the area, who 'were always at hand, on the shortest notice, day or night' to deliver dispatches.[20]

Lynch was not deterred by his distance from other battalions in the brigade area, making sure every afternoon and Sunday to visit one of them; O'Donoghue wrote that such dedication was an example of his 'soldiery spirit' and 'missionary zeal'. Within several weeks, Lynch had made personal contact with almost every battalion officer under his command and met many Volunteers within the brigade area. O'Donoghue, from information provided by Lynch's contemporaries, wrote that those Lynch met at this time were 'impressed by his dignified, soldiery bearing, his sincere earnestness and intuitive understanding'.[21]

A notable aspect of Lynch's military leadership that soon emerged was something of a collaborative nature with those under his command. At this early juncture, Lynch initiated a system in which he accepted any written suggestions from Volunteers of any rank to improve the brigade and its activities in any area. At brigade council meetings, Lynch stuck to the programme, but he would discuss ideas and suggestions after the meeting had concluded and kept diligent notes.[22] P.J. Paul, who later served under Lynch in the First Southern Division, felt this approach was key to Lynch's appeal as the O/C and remembered how he 'became very fond of Lynch and had great confidence in him because, as well as inspiring confidence in his leadership, he always seemed grateful for any information he got, or for any assistance rendered, and in that way attracted loyalty to himself'.[23] Yet, one anonymous account written of Lynch's life criticised this collaborative approach and argued that his 'wish to discuss every officer's viewpoint' resulted in 'slowness of decision'. However, the unknown writer emphasised that Lynch was 'eminently suited for [the] position in which [he was] eventually placed'.[24] In O'Donoghue's view, during these early days Lynch was 'somewhat diffident in asserting his own views too forcibly ...', suggesting he took some time to grow into confidence in the role. In rare moments of anger, or sometimes excitement, during conferences with his men, those gathered would notice Lynch could stutter over his words.[25] An impression of social awkwardness can also be seen in Twomey's description of Lynch during formal interactions with his officers, where he says he was 'not a good conversationalist, in fact he found it difficult and a strain to express at any great length his ideas and wishes in words' – Twomey felt that, over time, Lynch was better at doing so in writing.[26]

Lynch also maintained frequent contact with fellow brigade officers within Cork and in neighbouring counties, such as Limerick, Waterford and Tipperary. From March onward, at great risk, he made semi-regular trips to Dublin to meet Mulcahy, Collins and others at GHQ headquarters.[27] Given he was still working in Barry & Sons during this time, not to mention still making his routine visits home to Barnagurraha, Lynch no doubt had to draw on reserves of tireless energy. While conscious of approaching conflict, he is described as having an overall 'happy disposition' in these early months of 1919.[28]

***

In looking at the development of the conflict over the course of 1919, the historian Michael Hopkinson felt the 'extremely limited and episodic nature of the hostilities ... scarcely merits the term "war"'.[29] While Hopkinson is correct, in that there is nothing on the level of violence that was to take place the following year, important developments did take place that were to define both the political and military trajectories of the revolutionary movement right up to the Truce.

Though it had formed a major plank in their election manifesto, the Dáil delegation achieved little success at the Paris Peace Conference that led to the Treaty of Versailles, as the Irish situation was deemed by the majority of those attending to be an internal British matter. In its opening weeks, the Dáil began the process of forming a cabinet, headed by President de Valera, and various ministries and departments. Michael Collins, in his capacity as Minister for Finance in the Dáil cabinet, began raising a Dáil loan in defiance of the British authorities. By June, de Valera had departed to the United States, to begin a lengthy American tour to raise money for this loan and also achieve recognition of the Irish Republic from the American government.

On 10 April, the Dáil issued a decree to the populace to begin a peaceful boycott of the RIC. Specific instructions to the Sinn Féin cumainn read: 'Avoid all social intercourse. No salutations. No social contact. If they attend, you leave. Avoid places where police known to visit, particularly public houses where they frequent.' Yet there was no public statement from the Dáil issued as Volunteer encounters with the RIC became increasingly more violent.[30]

Inevitably, with the beginning of military conflict, the relationship between the Dáil and the Volunteers became a point of discussion. On 1 April, at the first private meeting of the Dáil, Mulcahy, in his capacity as Assistant Minister for Defence, made a statement that while there 'was no explicit authority from the Executive ... to do so ... the implication must be accepted' that the Dáil had the authority over the Volunteers. That month *An tÓglach* stated that the 'Volunteers are the right arm of the Irish Republic, the men who can be trusted to carry out the will of the Irish Government with the readiness and effectiveness of disciplined men.' Although the relationship between the two bodies would not be formalised until the spring of 1921, with the onset of conflict, within the nomenclature of the revolutionary movement, the wider distributed propaganda and even among the Irish public, the Volunteers would become better known as the Irish Republican Army (IRA). From August 1919, all IRA members would have to take an oath of allegiance to Dáil Éireann, yet the debate about the Dáil's authority over the IRA would endure into the future.[31]

In Dublin, Collins oversaw the formation of an elite group of assassins, known as 'the Squad', within the ranks of the IRA. The main targets of the Squad were the detectives who made up G Division, the investigative body of the Dublin Metropolitan Police. By the end of the year, the Squad had shot dead up to four of them.[32]

John Dorney has noted that outside Dublin the guerrilla war as a whole 'developed haphazardly due to local circumstances'. From 1918 into 1919, most Volunteer actions tended to involve attempting to retrieve arms by raiding the RIC and on occasion the British Army.[33] However, in the initial weeks of 1919, some sought to take a keener initiative in their locality, which naturally included certain officers within the Cork No. 2 Brigade area. Con Leddy, O/C of the Araglen Company, again proposed a raid on the Araglen RIC barracks. On this occasion, Lynch was much more amenable to such an operation; he had probably been looking for just such a chance since Soloheadbeg. Mick Fitzgerald, as head of the Fermoy Battalion, which encompassed the Araglen Company area, was not only keen on the idea but wished to take direct part.

On a Sunday in late March, George Power and Lynch inspected the barracks, thereby putting the plans in motion for the morning of Easter Sunday, 20 April. On the same day, Lynch was to travel to Dublin for a GHQ meeting to report on developments in his brigade area. For him, the timing of this meeting could not have been better as it allowed him to demonstrate the capabilities of Cork No. 2 Brigade in such an operation and he was also keen to ensure the operation received GHQ sanction, albeit retrospectively.[34] On the Sunday morning, Lynch, anticipating the planned raid on Araglen Barracks, could not help but admit to Pax Whelan, O/C of Waterford No. 2 Brigade and also present at the GHQ meeting, that 'I have started something that will shake up these fellows.'[35]

While five of the six RIC men based in Araglen were attending Mass that morning, seven Volunteers, including Fitzgerald and Leddy, approached the barracks from the rear. As the only remaining RIC officer emerged from the rear of the building to collect water nearby, the seven men entered the barracks. On his return, the RIC officer was shocked to find guns drawn at him in the yard. He flung the bucket of water at the Volunteers and ran across the yard, while shouting that if he was armed 'he would blow their brains out'.[36] He was quickly captured by the Volunteers and surrendered. Fitzgerald, watching this from an upper window of the barracks, was greatly amused at the lone RIC officer's reaction. Three decades after the event, Leddy could still distinctly recall Fitzgerald's amusement at this episode: 'It was his [Fitzgerald's] happy day ... and perhaps his last happy day on this earth, although to suffer seemed to be a joy to him.'[37] Fitzgerald, whom the authorities suspected of taking part in the raid, was arrested by the RIC following a raid on his workplace in July 1919, when a quantity of ammunition was found. Since March of that year, the British authorities had all republican prisoners treated as criminals in the prison system. Fitzgerald was signalled out for particularly harsh treatment and spent the entirety of his sentence until the end of August 1919 in solitary confinement – such surroundings took a psychological toll on him.[38]

In the aftermath, the Volunteers seized six carbines, ten hand grenades, 400 rounds of .303 ammunition, a Webley revolver and twenty rounds of ammunition. Florence O'Donoghue claimed that the constable was so grateful for his good treatment during the raid that he refused to identify any of those involved. While likely true, he may also have been concerned about his continued personal safety.[39]

Mulcahy's reaction to the unsanctioned Araglen raid is unknown, but Con Leddy noted that Lynch informed Collins as it was taking place. The following day, Collins read of the raid in *The Cork Examiner* and showed it to Lynch. According to Leddy, Collins 'expressed his delight and asked Liam to convey his congratulations to all who took part'.[40] Following the GHQ meeting, Lynch was nonetheless disappointed to be given only a few revolvers and no rifles for the brigade.[41]

As the conflict progressed, Lynch built a close association and friendship with both Mulcahy and Michael Collins, the IRA's director of intelligence and, by 1919, also president of the Supreme Council of the IRB. Even decades after being on opposing sides of the Civil War, Mulcahy recalled Lynch as the most competent, reliable and inspiring of the IRA leaders in the south, referring to him as 'a lion of the resistance movement' during the 1919–21 period.[42] Mulcahy counted on him to set an example to other officers, even sending copies of Lynch's reports to them to demonstrate the procedures, methods and techniques that Lynch used. For Mulcahy, Lynch came to represent the ideal officer as the conflict progressed, due to his grasp of guerrilla tactics, his detailed reports, his maintenance of order and discipline amongst his men, and his regular contact with GHQ.[43] The two men shared several commonalities: they projected an austere, sometimes self-serious persona to those under their command, shared a forensic and diligent approach to their work and demanded high standards from their officers, all of which most certainly complemented their own strong working relationship.

Yet, Lynch's close association with GHQ throughout the conflict sometimes irritated those fighting colleagues who had mixed feelings about its role in overseeing the IRA, including Séumas Robinson.[44] Robinson noted with disdain that it 'was well known to me and to other Brigade Officers that G.H.Q. was Sanctum Sanctorum to Liam, that the Chief of Staff [Mulcahy] was its High Priest, and that Liam and all Cork were as the children of light to G.H.Q.'[45] Despite this, Robinson noted in the same remarks that he never doubted Lynch and the North Cork Brigade's considerable contribution to the fighting. However, Florence O'Donoghue believed Robinson's description of Lynch's relationship with IRA GHQ was unfair, and he said Lynch's dealings with GHQ were more 'not so much not to do anything without G.H.Q. sanction, as to carry G.H.Q. with him in any developments which he felt we were capable of undertaking'.[46] This view is supported by Lynch seeking retrospective sanction for the Araglen Barracks raid.

When Lynch was visiting GHQ in Dublin during the War of Independence, he occasionally stayed with the Delaney family at 71

Heytesbury Street, a regular hideout for senior IRA members during the conflict. There, Lynch frequently met other leading IRA figures, such as Mulcahy.[47] Hanna Cleary noted that while there Lynch also often used to visit Kathleen Clarke, Tom Clarke's widow.[48] Lynch's frequent contact with the Dublin-based GHQ, and its staff, gave him an appreciation of its strengths and weaknesses as a high command for a guerrilla army, particularly how it worked with IRA leaders far from the capital.

∗ ∗ ∗

IRA operations elsewhere in the country continued to grow more daring. On 13 May, members of the Third Tipperary Brigade and the Galtee Battalion of the East Limerick Brigade undertook a daring rescue operation at Knocklong train station in County Limerick. On a Cork-bound train passing through the station was Seán Hogan, a member of the Third Tipperary Brigade, who was being transported by members of the RIC to Cork for imprisonment. The eighteen-year-old Hogan had been on the run for some months due to his part in the Soloheadbeg ambush but had finally been captured at a house outside Clonoulty, Tipperary, some days earlier. While Hogan was rescued and spirited away by his comrades, in the aftermath of the dramatic shoot-out aboard the train, two of the RIC officers were killed and several of the Volunteers involved were wounded.

Two of these wounded Volunteers, Ned O'Brien and James Scanlon, were hidden in the Cork No. 2 Brigade area for a number of weeks, in a successful operation that spoke much of the strength of the brigade's organisation and intelligence. One night, Tom Cavanagh of the Fermoy Company, drove Lynch and the two recovering Volunteers from Ballyporeen to a residence in Ballydorgan, near Tallow. As they passed Moore Park Army Camp, the sentry demanded that the car stop. Lynch told Cavanagh to keep driving, so the sentry fired at the car, but they all escaped without injury. Cavanagh was struck by Lynch's determination during this incident.[49]

Yet, by mid-1919, Lynch still managed to make time for leisure, a sure sign that brigade activities were not overwhelming at this time. One

Sunday that June, Lynch and his brother Tom took a day trip to an old graveyard around Hyde Castle, just outside Fermoy. Of particular interest to both was the location of gravestones belonging to the Lynchs' ancestors, and they subsequently managed to find several. On their arrival, the two men noticed new memorials to those killed during the Great War, and Tom ruefully recalled how the brothers 'noticed all the inscriptions were Protestant in sentiment' and 'wished that the bones of our grandsires did not rest in this place among strangers'.[50] Tom recalled how they spent several hours exploring the cemetery before walking back to Fermoy by the early evening. As the brothers smoked, Tom recalled 'Liam half-wished to be buried there himself ... only for it being now in the hands of those who are alien in creed and moreover he couldn't rest so easy with so many "Heroes of the Great War" buried all round.'

Despite this brief respite for Lynch, the coming summer would see ongoing activity from the various elements of Cork No. 2 Brigade. Thomas Barry, the Fermoy Battalion's quartermaster, recalled how in 'the late summer of 1919 there was a general raid for arms. Imperialists' houses were raided with success. We pushed on the general organisation more extensively, especially arms drilling. Lynch's policy was to get the Brigade into a working machine before any active measures would be taken.'[51] Yet, despite this policy, for a number of weeks, Lynch was eager that the brigade embark on a larger and more daring operation. By July, he saw an opportunity for one.[52]

∗∗∗

Patrick Ahern of the Fermoy Company felt that being based in a town with such a large concentration of British soldiers made the acquisition of arms paramount for the local Volunteers, with which Lynch agreed.[53] In July, Lynch and George Power began actively discussing the possibility of attacking and disarming a party of British soldiers somewhere in Fermoy. Lynch approached GHQ to gain formal sanction for such an operation and, after some correspondence, permission was secured – provided casualties on either side could be avoided.[54]

Lynch had long noticed that a party of soldiers attended the Wesleyan church in Fermoy town, about half a mile from the barracks at the eastern end of the town. These soldiers could inadvertently help provide a major arms haul for the brigade.[55] Lar Condon recalled that one suggestion of Lynch's involved the occupation of several houses along the line of the soldiers' morning march, but he felt this would certainly be noticed. Condon later claimed he was the originator of the actual plan carried out, 'which was to have a few of us sauntering along and suddenly fall on the military when we would immediately be joined by a number of others who up to this point would, to all appearances, be just idling away the morning in town.'[56] Lynch agreed to his suggestion.

Several meetings were then held with officers of the Fermoy Company, and other companies of the battalion. Naturally, the Fermoy Company carried out the preliminary scouting work and submitted regular reports.[57] Ahern recalled the scouting work on the movement of the soldiers through Fermoy town:

> The movements of the Wesleyan Church party were kept under observation for about three months. The party usually marched in fours from their barracks via Barrack Hill, the Square and Patrick St. to Walkers Row – the site of the Wesleyan Church. The rifles were carried at the slope until the party were within a short distance of the church when the arms were changed to 'the trail'.[58]

One recurring debate between Lynch and his officers was whether the soldiers' guns were in fact loaded. A recent news report had made mention of an accident in Cobh, which saw a soldier on church parade injured by the discharge of a bullet from his own rifle.[59] Additional intelligence also indicated the guns were to always be loaded as per instructions. John Fanning, a member of the Fermoy Company, was sure the British soldiers had been given such an order because of an earlier attempt to disarm a soldier in the Castletownbere district.[60]

The final meeting on the proposed Fermoy attack took place two days before the planned date for execution, on Friday 5 September, and was presided over by Lynch. At this meeting, all the key details were agreed upon.[61] In the 1930s, Power provided 'a fairly full list' for the Military Service Pensions Board of the total number of Volunteers who took part in the operation, which came to about fifty-two. However, Power pointed out that if those who took part in the roadblocks nearby on the day were accounted for, it brought the number to sixty-five.[62]

Michael Fitzgerald was part of the main attacking party, although that was not always part of the plan. Condon recalled his surprise at Fitzgerald taking part, noting he 'was in bad form for he had a hard time in prison' – a reference to the psychological strain he had been under in solitary confinement. But Fitzgerald was seemingly determined to prove himself, and Condon noted how he 'had been warned to keep away but he fell in with us just as we got abreast of the Church Parade, only about ten yards from the Church door'.[63]

Leo O'Callaghan was to position his car on Patrick Street so that when the attack took place it would be behind the enemy party, ensuring their way back to the barracks was blocked. Lynch was in this car along with four others as O'Callaghan drove the vehicle close to the town gas works, which were to the east of the Wesleyan church on the opposite side of the road. O'Callaghan proceeded to drive his car slowly towards the military from behind. Just as they reached the church, he swung the car across the road to cut off their retreat. As Lynch and the other passengers emerged from the car, the brigade O/C blew a sharp whistle.[64] He then called on the military party to surrender, but the soldiers immediately prepared to resist, so the assigned Volunteers rushed the group. The confused struggle which followed, in which shots were fired, lasted for just over a minute.[65] Condon, part of the rushing Volunteers, recalled how, within seconds, he and the others of the Fermoy Company, 'fought the soldiers with sticks and the Araglen and Clondulane men joined in. We, the first three, had revolvers and we produced these'.[66] Ahern stated that the soldiers were only 'disarmed after a tough fight on the part of some'.[67] He referred to it as a 'short sharp tussle' involving the main attacking party, 'hangers on' and also the party who exited the car with Lynch.[68] In one highly dramatic moment, Lynch jumped for a rifle lying on the road but slipped and fell. As he briefly lay on the ground, a soldier rushed at him swinging a rifle-butt but was hit by a bullet.[69]

The sole casualty of the Fermoy arms raid – perhaps the same soldier who swung at Lynch – was Private William Jones, the first British military casualty caused by the Irish Volunteers since the Easter Rising. Jones was a twenty-year-old Welshman from Carmarthenshire. Tragically, he was due to be discharged that week so he could return home to be married.[70] Ahern estimated that several shots were fired in the melee, and three or four other British soldiers were wounded.[71] The Cork *Evening Echo* later reported that Jones was shot through the heart, while another British soldier was almost fatally wounded. A third soldier, a Private Lloyd, was shot through the neck, but later recovered. The paper also noted that 'others of the party were badly injured on the head by bludgeons' and alleged some of the Volunteers used the 'spokes of wheels as weapons'.[72]

Records of the number of arms seized in the raid varied, with claims of anything from fourteen to nineteen rifles, and possibly in addition one bayonet.[73] In any event, it was a major haul for the brigade in what was a mostly successful operation and the first major engagement members of the Volunteers had had with the British Army since the Easter Rising. In the immediate aftermath, most of the captured rifles were placed into O'Callaghan's car before he drove off with Lynch and his other passengers. Another car used by the Volunteers also took some of the captured rifles and several of the participants. The remainder of the Volunteers nearby quickly dispersed to their own areas on foot or by bicycle.[74] The arms were taken one mile across the county to a drain in the Kilbarry woods, where they were initially hidden.[75]

When O'Callaghan's car left Fermoy, the group realised that Lynch himself had been wounded during the raid. The wound did not appear to be serious and so elated was he at the success of the Wesleyan raid, Lynch actually joked about it.[76] On meeting his brigade O/C in the aftermath, Condon felt Lynch had been injured by 'possibly a wild revolver shot from one of our own men'.[77] The fact that Lynch's injury likely came from someone on their own side tended to be omitted from popular accounts of the incident.[78] Power later described it as 'a flesh wound in the shoulder

... How we didn't know, but the wound had the appearance of being caused by a rifle bullet ... a clean entrance and exit.'[79] It is a possibility that the source of the shot that injured Lynch was well known among the men who took part but played down in future accounts to prevent any embarrassment on the part of the Volunteer responsible. While the wound was not overly serious, it was deemed necessary for the Lynch to have it treated and get a degree of rest and recuperation that lasted for several weeks. Two days after the raid, Lynch, having been moved and tended to in several locations, was brought across county lines into the Waterford No. 2 (or West Waterford) Brigade area, and he rested in the home of the Kirwan family who lived beneath the Comeragh mountains.[80]

The *Evening Echo* reported that 'there is but one feeling of condemnation at the cowardly outrage' within Fermoy.[81] Aware of the heightening tension in the town, the Volunteers who took part were conscious that there had been civilian witnesses to the attack on the soldiers. That night, on the orders of the Fermoy Battalion's Intelligence Officer, Paddy Ahern, Volunteers painted the slogan 'Spies and Informers beware' on walls and paths throughout Fermoy.[82] Nonetheless, the arrest of twelve Volunteers occurred in the immediate aftermath – among them Fermoy Battalion Commandant Michael Fitzgerald and Vice-Commandant Lar Condon, in addition to Fermoy Company Captain John Fanning. Further arrests occurred a month later in Mallow, but only after RIC Head Constable Daniel Sullivan was dismissed for refusing to arrest the men due to lack of evidence.[83] For Fitzgerald and the others deemed responsible for the murder of Private Jones, it was the beginning of a lengthy period on remand until they were eventually brought to trial in April 1920. While charges against most of the men were later dismissed, September 1919 was the beginning of another lengthy term of imprisonment for Fitzgerald, and this was to have a tragic outcome in late 1920.[84]

On Monday evening, an inquest was held in the Fermoy Military Hospital into Private Jones' death. Over the course of the inquest, the jury heard evidence from various civilian witnesses and soldiers caught up in the attack. In what was to prove a controversial decision, the jury found a verdict of 'death due to a bullet wound inflicted by some persons unknown'. They expressed horror at the incident and expressed sympathy with the relatives of the deceased. Somewhat incredulously, RIC District Inspector Lewis, who represented the police, asked, 'Are you, then, of opinion it was not murder?' The foreman replied: 'We came unanimously to the conclusion that these men came for the purpose of getting rifles and had no idea of murder; that it was unpremeditated.'[85]

The jury's verdict was to have a dramatic impact in Fermoy that same night, resulting in reprisals on homes and business by members of the Shropshire Light Infantry based in the barracks. A reporter with *The Freeman's Journal* reported that the 'attack by the soldiers on the shops was obviously an organised one'.[86] The report detailed how the attack began with a soldier blowing a whistle, and then 'at intervals to rally his followers and direct their movements'. Soldiers, armed with hammers and other implements, smashed the windows of the shops. They were backed up by a crowd of civilians, who proceeded to loot the premises. One shop specifically targeted was a jewellery establishment owned by the foreman of the jury in the inquest into Private Jones' death. As alarm spread throughout Fermoy town, 'shopkeepers and their families, reinforced by neighbours, stood in the streets guarding their houses'.[87] The destruction continued until about 10.30 p.m., when additional military and RIC arrived. While the RIC dealt with the civilian looters, many said to be under the influence of drink, the offending soldiers were rounded up and confined to the barracks. Most of the looting ceased by 11 p.m., with some isolated incidents still taking place, with the additional British military forces now patrolling the streets with fixed bayonets. In the aftermath, it was estimated that about fifty to sixty shops were wrecked.[88]

The military historian William Sheehan, in his overview of the British Army in Cork during the period, has called the destruction after the Fermoy inquest an example of an 'unofficial reprisal', events which often took place at weekends after heavy consumption of alcohol by the offending British soldiers.[89] In this instance, Sheehan has argued that it was organised by rank-and-file members of the Shropshire Light Infantry, without influence or orders from senior officers, and directly targeted premises owned by members of the inquest's jury. He has also suggested that popular memory of the reprisal ignored the considerable role of civilian looters in the attacks on the shops – frequently referenced in newspaper reports – which, as will be seen, also occurred during a later reprisal in Fermoy in 1920.[90] Nonetheless, the events of the night did little for the long-term reputation of the British Army among the ordinary people of Fermoy. As a contemporary edition of *The Cork Examiner* noted, Jones' killing 'is greatly regretted in the district, but apparently the soldiers associate this outrage with its people, and … vented this spleen in a manner that will not improve the relations of the soldiers and the people'.[91]

The strong feeling among the townspeople was almost certainly not helped by Fermoy being placed under martial law by the British military. This order prohibited meetings, assemblies or protests 'within a radius of three miles of the RIC barracks in Fermoy'. The gathering of four or more persons was to be regarded as an assembly or meeting.[92]

In December, *An t-Oglách* featured what it called the 'dashing exploit' in Fermoy. The article, a reflection of the attitude within IRA GHQ, stated that the 'success of this daring feat illustrates the value and importance of speed and dash in military operations'. Somewhat tellingly, the article also admitted that, in terms of the reprisal visited on Fermoy: 'Abuse from the enemy is always welcome afterward; but it is difficult to find words strong enough to characterise those grovelling slaves of Irish nationality who, cringing in their cowardly souls, have joined in the enemy's vilification of the gallant raiders of Fermoy.'[93] George Power recalled being on the streets of Fermoy during the destruction carried out by the local British garrison. Somewhat coldly, he admitted in later years, 'candidly I was not very concerned as Fermoy being essentially a loyalist town 95% of the damage was done to loyalist houses. The smashing up was done by 200 to 300 soldiers in uniform accompanied by about four offices in civilian attire.'[94] At Lynch's request, Power personally met with him during his recuperation, at a location in Dungarvan within the Waterford No. 2 Brigade area, to give his personal account of the aftermath in Fermoy.[95]

As Lynch's period of rest and recuperation began, Jerry Kirwan cycled to Clonmel and brought news to Lynch's brother Martin that Liam was staying with him. The following Saturday, the brothers had a happy reunion in the Kirwan family home.[96] While Liam was delighted to see his brother, he was anxious that Martin may have been followed. Martin assured Liam he had been careful. Martin was pleased to see his brother was not bedridden and was dressed normally. Liam remarked to his brother that he tended to stay indoors during the day but walked the grounds of the house at night.[97]

In the Kirwan home, while recovering, Lynch found time to relax. Drawn to his typical reading material of Irish history, the ever-studious Lynch leafed through Michael Doheny's *The Felon's Track* – a favourite book of his.[98] Doheny had been involved in the 1840s Young Ireland movement, a participant in their doomed 1848 rebellion (of which the book was his account), and was later one of the founders of the IRB.[99] Pax Whelan, O/C of Waterford No. 2 Brigade, recalled how much Lynch enjoyed the Kirwans' library, and 'in it Liam was able to read for two weeks'. Lynch was to become very fond of both the family and their home, later telling Whelan, 'Someday I'll go back there … for a good rest and a good read.'[100] He would indeed get the opportunity to stay in the Kirwans' home again.

With renewed activity in the county by the British military authorities, Lynch voluntarily terminated his employment at Barry's in Fermoy.[101] He was now on the run and would remain so until the Truce.[102] Following his recuperation, provided he could avoid arrest, Lynch was determined to devote all his energy and time to the work of his brigade, which would enable him to be central to all decisions and activities involving everyone under his command. Until the close of 1919, Lynch toured much of the brigade area, being particularly anxious to visit battalions based in the west of his jurisdiction that he had earlier been unable to visit as frequently.[103]

Despite the heightened pressure from British forces in the area, Lynch still insisted on high standards and discipline across the brigade. In one instance, towards the end of 1919, he oversaw a restructuring of the Mitchelstown Company, having been annoyed by the continuous changes in officer personnel. The result had been not only company inactivity and no training, but also poor morale amongst the rank and file. Lynch proposed Patrick Luddy for company O/C, while Luddy instead suggested another man who had been active in the company since 1916. Under this proposal, Luddy would become first lieutenant. Showing as always that he was amenable to ideas from others, Lynch agreed, albeit reluctantly, telling Luddy that he 'would hold me responsible for the efficient reorganisation of the unit'.[104] In keeping with Lynch doing all brigade tasks to the letter, he approved the new appointments and promptly informed GHQ.

On 29 October, Lynch wrote to Tom and made mention of his recent meeting with their older brother Martin. In the careful code he and Tom sometimes used to get around the censor, he referenced the safe passage to the United States of Jimmy Scanlon and Ned O'Brien of the Knocklong rescue: 'Pleased that the lamps reached their destination alright.' On contact with the family in Barnagurraha, Lynch assured Tom that they 'hear from me at home now and then. Christmas won't be long coming now, when I do hope to see you.' Closing on a note of positivity, Lynch added, '"Keeping deadly cool" and having a great old life'.[105] On 13 November, a still exuberant Lynch wrote to his youngest brother: 'The Republic is now within our grasp, at the most eighteen months' – a sure sign of his greatly emboldened confidence since the Wesleyan raid. He made mention that 'my pals are locked up after being remanded eleven times. I expect them out again after first trial, as there is no evidence against them.' He also made vague, careful reference to the Fermoy arms haul and compared it with the most famed action by his childhood hero, Patrick Sarsfield, and the destruction of the Williamite siege train, jokingly remarking to Tom that he 'always thought Sarsfield made a daring ride ... but he burned the guns!'[106]

***

As 1919 ended, despite the heightened nature of such incidents as those at Fermoy in September, the conflict between the rebel Dáil Éireann and the ruling British administration in Ireland could not yet be truly defined as a 'war'. John Dorney has written that deaths in 1919 were relatively few and 'usually incidental to arms raids, arrests or riots' along with several targeted assassinations on Collins' instructions.[107] In addition, despite its considerable ambitions, Dáil Éireann had had a difficult first year in operation. In September, Dublin Castle declared the Dáil an illegal organisation, forcing it to operate underground. On 26 November, the authorities in the Castle issued further bans on Sinn Féin, the Volunteers, Gaelic League and Cumann na mBan. Being driven underground resulted in the Dáil having few meetings of its representatives; in fact, only eight were held, in secret, between September 1919 and July 1921.[108]

In the last weeks of the year, Lynch yearned to return home for Christmas, but worried the precautions needed to facilitate this would give undue anxiety to those at home. Nonetheless, Tom advised him at least to try.[109] Tom recalled his brother's somewhat uncertain return to Anglesboro for Christmas in an account published in Florence O'Donoghue's biography. It is a genuinely moving piece and provides a window into the two brothers' relationship, the closeness of the Lynch family and Liam's own state of mind by the end of 1919.

Tom wrote, 'Darkness set in and no Liam. The old home was so strange without him. We were all trying to be happy at supper, I was the only one to know he would surely attempt to come. How often I walked out into the darkness and listened sadly.' At 8.30 p.m. there was a knock on the door and, along with another Volunteer, 'Liam was waiting behind the pier of the gate lest some of the neighbours be in the house. At that time people had not learned to keep their tongues quiet.' Tom recalled that what followed was 'a great night. Three of us brothers watched the boreen, each his turn of an hour until dawn ... Nobody knew he was home that Christmas. After dark each night I strolled with him for hours down the old boreen, and he was happy. He would talk on one subject only – the Irish Republic.'[110] Seán Lynch later wrote how Liam felt confident enough to suggest going to Mass on Christmas morning, but his mother would not hear of it. Seán recalled how there were strict orders in case of 'a raid to keep away from the kitchen door and leave all doors and gates around the yard open'.[111] So excited were the brothers to see each other, none went to bed that night.

Nights and treasured times such as these shared between Lynch and his family were to prove increasingly rare during the difficult times that lay ahead.

Chapter 4

'I would not wish to be born in any other generation but this' (1920)

ON 2 JANUARY, LIAM WROTE to Tom from a safehouse within the brigade area and mentioned 'the people here as they are more homely than any I have ever met'. Liam jokingly insisted he was 'having a fairly good time here as a change from quiet life I was leading'. Incredibly, he had recently managed to attend a céilí, where he 'met a lot of the boys'. In a none-too-subtle allusion to his brigade activities, he hoped 'to have job soon as all are looking up for me. Our cause is going great guns lately certain of success in near future.'[1] It was impossible for him to disguise that familiar youthful exuberance, even as the conflict escalated.

Since being on the run following the Fermoy arms raid, Lynch never travelled through the brigade area unarmed except on his visits to Dublin and Cork cities. He later issued a brigade order requesting all officers on the run always to be armed and resist capture by the enemy. George Power remembered how, in the early months of conflict, Lynch had stayed at selected houses without guards, but with the continued fighting any safehouse where he temporarily resided was usually guarded by Volunteers supplied by the local company. From September of the previous year, Lynch's preferred mode of travel was with another officer by way of horse trap through each company area, with a cyclist scout some distance ahead.

Lynch had little patience with officers who took personal chances. Power recalled being scolded on more than one occasion by him for travelling by motor car on main roads, 'even for short distances'. He described Lynch as 'methodical, conscientious, and acutely conscious of his own responsibilities'.[2] Hanna Cleary recalled that Lynch still managed to make infrequent trips home to Barnagurraha; he would 'come home in the nighttime and he would be gone in the morning'.[3] During one visit to Hanna's farm, Lynch borrowed the writings of the radical James Fintan Lalor of the Young Ireland movement. His tendency for constant reading of his preferred literature did not let up even during this demanding period.

Some close to Lynch noticed his tendency not to find time to rest properly or even sleep well during these periods on the run. Power put this down to him being 'an exacting person' and often he woke Power during the night to discuss various brigade matters. Lynch would complain he could not sleep 'as his brain appeared to be on fire' – something that Power recalled as being typical of Lynch since he had first met him in 1917.[4] Paddy O'Brien, who knew Lynch from 1920, also recalled being woken up by him for similar reasons.[5]

Since the Fermoy arms raid, Lynch had been a key figure of interest to the RIC in the area. In a police-issued description of the men involved in the arms raid, Lynch was only one of two mentioned by name. The description of him was as follows: '28 year old age, fresh complexion, long thin face, 5 foot 10 inches in height, high cheek bones, smart appearance, light brown hair, wears gold rimmed glasses, rarely ever seen without glasses.'[6]

Given the poor RIC intelligence on Liam, Tom felt it was no coincidence that their family home was never raided during the conflict:

A few days after the affair the local peelers from Galbally called at the old home; but my brother [Seán] assured them that Liam would not dream of taking part in such a thing. The District Inspector of Police in Fermoy, some weeks later, told one of the priests very confidently that young Lynch was buried. 'A pity as he was a rather respectable type of young man.' It seems strange that in the preceding years they failed to identify the 'much wanted Liam Lynch' with the quiet mannered clerk at Barry's … Otherwise the old home would receive attention from the Tans.[7]

On 7 January 1920, Lynch travelled to Dublin and would not return to the brigade until 7 March, the longest venture he made to the capital in his lifetime. During these two months, Lynch was in frequent conferences with GHQ staff, particularly Michael Collins and Richard Mulcahy – strengthening the working relationship and the mutual respect he had with both men. Two men he also got to know better during this time there were Dan Breen and Seán Treacy, both on the run and hiding in Dublin since the Soloheadbeg ambush the previous year.[8] Treacy in particular, who had built up a considerable reputation within the IRA, became something of a figure of great personal admiration for Lynch.[9] In one amusing anecdote, Lynch invited Breen to accompany him to the dentist to have a tooth removed. He feared that he would unknowingly reveal IRA-related details while sedated and requested that Breen remain nearby. Lynch was pleased when Breen told him afterwards that he had been silent during the procedure.[10] Writing to his mother from Dublin, Lynch hoped she was

> not troubled about me … While I have my liberty, I will do all in my power against the enemy. They are now getting desperate in their last effort to hold their ground, but go they must. We are confident of victory. I would not wish to be born in any other generation but this. It is glorious to live at the present day.[11]

Lynch was present in Dublin for the important local elections of 15 January, which would see Sinn Féin candidates come to dominate 172 of Ireland's 206 borough and urban district councils. The arena of local government was to become an important means for Dáil Éireann to expand its jurisdiction, and rural local elections followed in June.

On 22 February, Lynch wrote to Tom from Dublin about how he was having 'a good time here so far even though things are desperate hot here. We are making it hot for John Bull these times.' He referred to the difficulty he and others had in being able to carry out duties due to the prospect of arrest, but stated that nonetheless his brother 'will be surprised to hear later some of the famous places I have been in since even where I write this now'.[12] On at least one occasion during this period he attended a play at the Abbey Theatre with Treacy and Florence Burke (née O'Mahony). Lynch would often stay with the latter's family in De Courcy Square in Glasnevin, the house once being raided when he was not present. On this occasion at the Abbey, because of a warning, he and his two companions left before the performance ended and the premises were surrounded by police and the military.[13]

During his stay in Dublin, Lynch was offered the post of deputy chief of staff of the IRA by Mulcahy but turned it down. There are few available sources that detail the circumstances of this offer. In one letter, Lynch mentioned to his mother that he could take the position any time he wished, but 'I intend on remaining in the country to help the boys while things remain at their present pressure'.[14] It was not the last time he would turn down a higher military position due to worries of letting down those under his command back in his brigade area.

On his return to Cork, Lynch wrote to Tom about what had happened on his journey back to brigade HQ when taking a train to Tipperary. He had 'got in with Tipp hurling team, I travelled direct with them carrying some of their togs'. Lynch referred to Tom trying to gather Liam's belongings at his Mitchelstown digs, where his brother could not locate his watch and a specific pair of glasses, as well as two of his favourite books, a biography of the 1803 Irish revolutionary Robert Emmet and *The Felon's Track*. He vaguely alluded to the larger picture, that he was in his current locale for 'some business to do in my own area for a few weeks. Hope to get to work permanent about Easter. Very busy presently in the Old Cause, keeping the ball rolling'.[15]

Brigade activities, along with the heightened attention of the authorities, prevented Lynch from contemplating a visit home to

Barnagurraha over Easter. He lamented this in a letter written to Tom on 31 March, but there was no doubt where his true priorities now lay:

> I hope that when next holidays come around the Republic will be a reality when all Irish men and women can move about in freedom as it is a God given right that every nationality should. We have driven the enemy at last to the breaking point in their final effort to hold on they are losing their sense ... they are bound to get it hot and heavy now.[16]

Lynch also commented on IRA activity in and around the area of the family home and expressed a hope 'that by now Galtees area is active again.'[17]

* * *

Since 1919, the standing of the RIC had greatly diminished in communities across Ireland due to targeted attacks and assassinations by the Volunteers and the boycott decree issued by Dáil Éireann. One RIC officer even reported, 'Several respectable Nationalists – not of course Sinn Féiners – told me that the people are in a state of terror from the Sinn Féiners and afraid to speak to, or have any communication, with the police.' Despite personal reservations, many in the populace were likely reluctant to report on their neighbours.[18]

From January 1920, IRA GHQ encouraged its forces across the country to attack rural RIC barracks. This usually involved a large group of Volunteers surrounding a barracks at night, with several policemen stationed inside. The Volunteers would fire on the building and often they would then attempt to set it on fire or blow it up with a crudely made bomb. Following the surrender, death or escape of the RIC men inside, the Volunteers would then acquire the arms and set fire to the barracks.[19] After the RIC began to withdraw from barracks, on 3 April, IRA GHQ ordered brigades all over the country – Lynch's Cork No. 2 among them – to burn these barracks in a further statement of defiance of the colonial police force.[20]

The resulting collapse in policing across the Irish countryside greatly diminished the authority of the British administration in Ireland. This was further damaged by the success of the Dáil courts system, which had begun following another decree issued by Dáil Éireann the previous June. These arbitration courts, alternatively called 'Republican Courts' or 'Dáil Courts', won great support from the public in settling matters such as land disputes. John Dorney has called the creation of this system 'a curious mixture of the revolutionary and the conservative' given that it required a boycott and replacement of the British justice system, but the new courts adhered almost exclusively to British Common Law and upheld the right to private property.[21] By March 1920, courts had been formed in twenty-eight counties. While they dealt with civil matters, IRA officers dealt with criminal matters in their capacity as members of the new Republican Police Force.[22]

It was in March 1920 that Lynch sought to utilise this court system in an early, often celebrated, example of the effectiveness of this new legal authority. On 27 November 1919, nearly £19,000 had been robbed from the bank at Millstreet by a group of armed men. Though the local RIC had made little effort to arrest those responsible, the British press had laid the blame for the crime on local IRA members. As the months passed with no arrests, Lynch became increasingly troubled that the perpetrators were yet to be found and that rumours persisted about the involvement of those in the revolutionary organisations.[23] In early March, he wrote to Gearóid O'Sullivan, GHQ's adjutant general, and explained how he had ordered the Millstreet Battalion to establish the facts of the case as far as possible. Having determined the particulars of the case, Lynch awaited orders from GHQ to proceed with the investigation. He noted of the men involved in the robbery:

> There are six in the gang, two of which are ex-soldiers and one who was counted a good Volunteer. All are a tough crowd, except this Volunteer … after getting in touch with Battalion O/C has left the country without any of this money for safety … These fellows are under Volunteer observation and are noticeable as they are

taking a little extra drink but not enough to give the game away. If handled at once we believe that most of the money can be got, even some which has left their hands ...[24]

Lynch had received intelligence that more raids on banks in the area had been planned by the same gang in the short-term and he determined, 'it is important that [they] be humiliated at once'. Having discussed matters with the battalion O/C, Lynch planned to travel to the area and personally investigate the case.

At this early juncture, Lynch explained to O'Sullivan that he planned to hand over the perpetrators 'in some way' to the local RIC. He asked for a suggestion as to what to do with the stolen money, which was estimated to be about £19,000. Lynch proposed either handing the money back to the banks, or perhaps, 'an order from you to put money into Brigade arms fund would be received with pleasure, but don't take this suggestion too serious [sic]'.[25] The events around the Millstreet investigation are often referred to as an example of Lynch's shrewdness and good decision-making in such a situation, which is certainly evident across several accounts. In the end, he seemed ready to take charge of the investigation himself, at least partly due to his frustration over lack of advice from GHQ. In another communication on 5 April, he expressed surprise that he still had not heard from GHQ with regard to instructions to carry out the investigation and arrest the perpetrators. Nonetheless, if there was further delay after a few days, Lynch had concluded he 'must act myself'. He proposed an immediate arrest and the seizure of the stolen money.[26]

The IRA's chief of staff, Richard Mulcahy, replied to Lynch three days later and explained that all the latter's dispatches related to the Millstreet robbery had only just arrived. Mulcahy had only just discussed the matter with Minister for Defence Cathal Brugha, and he instructed Lynch to have the local battalion commandant take charge. Mulcahy emphasised that everyone involved in the robbery should be arrested, the money returned to the bank manager and the men involved handed over to bank officials.[27] Lynch, however, appears to have ignored Mulcahy's suggestion on not taking command of the investigation and continued to oversee the investigation and subsequent arrests. He seemed concerned about criminal activity spreading in the brigade area if the perpetrators were not publicly apprehended and punished.[28] On 12 April, O'Sullivan wrote to Lynch and, in a likely reflection of a general GHQ view, assured Lynch he was 'glad you think it will be possible to bring the culprits to heel. I can understand the discretion necessary when they all happen to be local people.'[29]

From a safehouse in Drishanbeg, close to Millstreet, Lynch conducted a methodical investigation which impressed the local Volunteers. From the available intelligence, he quickly expanded the investigation beyond the locality of Millstreet and by 24 April had issued warrants for the arrest of ten men involved in the robbery. On the same night, members of the Millstreet Battalion, aided by members of the republican police, began rounding up a number of those involved. The arrested men were then held in several IRA safehouses, in the absence of any prison available to the IRA. At no point did the local RIC interfere. On 27 April, Lynch presided over a special court where members of the gang confessed. Five were sentenced to periods of deportation for five to fifteen years, while two were ordered to leave the brigade area.[30] One member of the gang, called 'Red' Hugh O'Brien, evaded capture. As late as mid-June, Lynch was forwarding photographs of him to GHQ to be circulated to the other brigades.[31] O'Brien may be the same unnamed individual who escaped in the aftermath of the Millstreet robbery referred to by Siobhán Lankford in her memoir. According to Lankford, this individual later joined the Black and Tans. Sometime later, she inquired of a Volunteer as to the man's fate, and he informed her that the man had in fact returned to Cork. When Lankford asked where the one-time bank robber was now, in a moment of gallows humour she was told, 'He's growing grass.'[32]

Though Lynch had overseen the return of the money to the bank, he was surprised when he was later contacted by the bank manager to claim the reward that had been offered. On meeting the manager, Lynch explained that any reward money would be used for purchasing arms and equipment for the IRA – he doubted very much the bank directors would want their money spent this way. Lynch was probably surprised by the bank manager's response: 'But my dear man … the directors are perfectly aware how you would spend this money; they have set it aside for your forces, and they will be highly honoured by your acceptance of it.'[33]

✱✱✱

March 1920 also saw Batt Walsh and Jeremiah Buckley, two prominent Volunteers attached to the Mallow Battalion, open their business premises, the Abbey Stores, in Mourneabbey adjacent to the abbey ruin. The Stores' location on the main Cork to Mallow road made this a convenient meeting point, and almost every day Lynch consulted officers from all over the brigade for updates at these premises. Once the meeting had concluded, he, along with one or two of his staff, would leave across the fields and head for nearby Clogheen or Monaparson.[34] The Abbey Stores remained a regular meeting point for Lynch and his brigade officers until they were raided in September 1920.[35]

On 20 March 1920, the war escalated with the assassination of Tomás MacCurtain at his home in Blackpool, Cork city. MacCurtain had a distinctive profile in the eyes of the British authorities in terms of his dual roles as lord mayor of Cork and O/C of Cork No. 1 Brigade. The killing was carried out by members of the RIC, in response to the shooting dead of an RIC constable by the IRA in the city the previous day. The action had, in fact, been unsanctioned by MacCurtain, who made clear his disapproval to those involved. However, as brigade O/C, he became a target for the authorities. Buried in Cork's St Finbarr's cemetery on 25 March, MacCurtain's funeral was attended by several thousand people, mostly delegations of the revolutionary movement, including Liam Lynch. On the day after the funeral, in a communication to IRA GHQ, Lynch noted how the IRA 'had 417 men at funeral of O/C Cork 1st Brigade yesterday. May God help his family, Cork county and Ireland to bear his loss. RIP.'[36] On 28 March, Lynch made mention of the funeral in a letter to Tom: 'I, and several like me, risked everything to see the last of a noble soldier'. He lamented that MacCurtain was 'one of my best friends in the cause and indeed I felt terrible over him. He was foully murdered by the enemy; but the hour is at hand when they shall rue the moment they did so.'[37] While Lynch certainly respected MacCurtain in his position as O/C of Cork No. 1 Brigade, he also felt gratitude towards him for recognising his talents; MacCurtain played no small part in Lynch being appointed head of Cork No. 2 Brigade. Lynch asked Tom to tell their brother Martin, 'I am A1 and still in the big push.' Elsewhere in the letter, he made mention again of the offer of promotion to IRA GHQ in Dublin: that there 'is a good position waiting for me any time I wish to take up same. I intend remaining in the country to help "the boys" while things remain at the present pressure.'[38] Following MacCurtain's death, his vice O/C, Terence MacSwiney, became lord mayor and O/C of Cork No. 1 Brigade in his place.

After Sinn Féin's success in the local elections of 1920, the arena of councils and corporations became another important means of electoral legitimacy for Dáil Éireann. Yet typically – given his own disinterest in political activism – Lynch never foresaw any involvement for himself at the level of local politics, unlike MacSwiney or the late MacCurtain. Hence, in March 1920, Lynch expressed surprise to Gearóid O'Sullivan that the 'officers of Cork No. 1 tell me that [their] Brigade Council has a veto on men put forward for District and County Councils.' Lynch felt 'we had enough … work' without involvement in such local electoral issues but admitted, 'still I believe this an important matter'. He awaited instructions from GHQ on how to proceed.[39] On 10 April, O'Sullivan responded to this point and assured Lynch 'there is no such order re: veto, and as you know we have got quite enough to do without interfering'. Furthermore, 'Cork city is peculiarly situated on account of its personnel with regard to the political machinery and no doubt the arrangements there suit them and does some good'. While O'Sullivan felt while it was 'important that persons selected and elected should hold our views in matters of national principle … All we can do is influence people … this … must not be taken away from our Volunteer work.'[40]

***

By early 1920, the British government was determined to regain ground after the collapse of the RIC in parts of Ireland. One means by which to do so was through extensive recruitment into the constabulary. The new recruits were mostly former British Army soldiers from throughout the United Kingdom, and the nature of the new force has been rightly described by Michael Hopkinson as 'speedy and ill-thought'. The fact that these men had no discipline and little training quickly led to their acquiring a notorious reputation. The RIC was augmented by the arrival of these new recruits to Ireland in March 1920. Due initially to the lack of available uniforms, the new members had to wear a mixture of green RIC tunics and khaki trousers, and thus gained a derisory new nickname from the populace: the Black and Tans.

In July that year, a further force was organised to complement the work of the RIC. Composed of veteran army officers, they were known as the Auxiliary Division (referred to as the 'Auxies' by many). The Auxiliaries were dispatched as companies to active IRA areas and were intended to function as a gendarmerie, a military force with law-enforcement duties. Though a separate component of the RIC – and with a different uniform – to the Black and Tans, the Auxiliaries then, and now, are often wrongly referred to as such. The actions of the Auxiliaries during the conflict were also controversial, with over forty incidents of wanton destruction ascribed to them. Although the Auxiliaries were recruited by the British War Office to aid the RIC, their relationship with both the RIC and the British Army, neither of whom had authority over them, was rather confused. A backdrop to the activities of both these deadly new sections of the RIC was the confused role played by the British Army stationed throughout Ireland. With its centralised militarised command, the army was often ill-suited for the passive policing role required by the collapse of British authority throughout much of the country.[41]

In a letter to his brother Tom on 19 April, Lynch commented on recent developments. On MacSwiney's election, he agreed with Tom that MacSwiney, whom Liam knew well, was well able 'to step into boots of old Lord Mayor'. In commenting on republican success in the local elections back home, Lynch expressed concern about the drift of young men towards getting involved in Sinn Féin rather than the IRA. In his view, there was 'a turn in politics in Anglesboro as elsewhere ... I hope the young men all over the country won't get it on the brain as this is only a secondary consideration to our movement.' He felt the 'army has to hew the way to freedom for politics to follow' – quite possibly his second most well-known statement in writing.[42] It is also a perfect, if brief, summation of his view of the importance of political activity in the revolutionary movement – behind that of any military activity by the IRA, which he thought must always be at the forefront.

Even with the conflict becoming more entrenched, Lynch felt 'we are facing fast for freedom at last, but the darkest hour is before the dawn. Hope the country will stick this terrible suffering.' Quoting a previous letter from Tom, in which his brother said, 'This generation is destined to witness the most glorious victory yet won ... or a defeat more black and bitter than in the last', Lynch admitted, 'my hopes are all with the former as I believe we cannot be beaten now'.[43]

On 30 May, despite his frequent fear of censorship, Lynch could not resist alluding vaguely to the recent arrest of those involved in the Millstreet bank robbery when writing to Tom: 'Millstreet business – Did you dream that it was I [who] got this in motion ... This case has set all Ireland on ...' Lynch promised his brother, 'hope in a short time to give you a full official account of Millstreet coup'. In a likely reference to the new Black and Tan force, Lynch noted, 'We have now double enemies, the last perhaps worse than the old.' Acknowledging the more ruthless nature of these adversaries, he claimed, 'bobbies have threatened to track us down to death, in fact we got a list on one having 22 down for execution including a priest'.[44]

*　*　*

By the summer of 1920, the brigade intelligence operation had vastly expanded and included the systematic observation of enemy movements and activities.[45] It was known by then that British Brigadier General

Cuthbert Henry Tyndall Lucas, commander of the British 6th Division's 18th Brigade, and two other army officers spent their leisure time fishing at the Blackwater near Clondulane. Lynch's brigade staff agreed it would be useful to capture the British officers' arms, particularly if they had an armed escort, but whether Lucas and his compatriots were armed or not, it was agreed that to capture these men could ultimately be a great morale boost for the IRA.[46]

Lynch, it seems, was eager to carry out the kidnappings when thinking of the current plight of his friend Michael Fitzgerald and others in Cork Gaol. He considered using the British officers as hostages, and felt that the proposed operation was entirely feasible and the officers a fair target. He based this decision upon reports of the routines of these senior officers coming and going from the two barracks in Fermoy.[47] During a meeting of brigade officers planning the operation, Lynch instructed Moss Twomey to further investigate Lucas' regular movements in the area. Twomey seemed initially to have had little luck, but was then astonished to learn from Lar Condon that Condon himself had 'been talking to [Lucas] one morning on the road to Kilbarry, where I passed him pumping a bicycle on the side of the road and he was speaking to me'. Condon, who noted Lucas' height at about six feet two inches, subsequently learned from local contacts of a pending fishing expedition that Lucas was planning.[48] On receiving news of this, Lynch fixed the date of Saturday 26 June as the day on which to proceed with the operation.[49] He selected Commandant Seán Moylan of Newmarket Battalion and Commandant Patrick Clancy of Kanturk Battalion to assist him and George Power in carrying out both the capture and transport of Lucas and any other officers with him. As had become standard since the Fermoy arms raid (on occasion to the dismay of his junior officers), Lynch put himself at the forefront of carrying out an operation in which he was a key strategist.

Several days prior to 26 June, Lynch and Power moved into the Fermoy Battalion area to make a final check that all arrangements had been made, including borrowing a Ford car from a local republican supporter. On the day prior to the operation, Volunteer scouts were posted to observe the various fishing pools in the vicinity of Fermoy. A report from Kilbarry, five miles east of Fermoy, confirmed General Lucas was fishing with two other officers there. They were attended by Lucas' personal servant.[50]

On 26 June, after a few hours' drive, the Ford car containing the Volunteers arrived at the location. Intelligence had determined Lucas' fishing lodge was located on the banks of the Blackwater.[51] The car's occupants were met by Condon and a section of men from Cork No. 2 Brigade, who were to assist in the capture. All Volunteers present gathered for a final discussion and instruction before the operation proceeded. The fishing lodge was a small structure surrounded by a low stone wall, and the initial intelligence indicated two British officers were present as Lucas' escort. Lynch determined the first task should be to capture the officers inside. He instructed Moylan and Clancy to lead the initial attack on the house.

Moylan and other men crept through a shrubbery, and then took cover outside the boundary wall at the front. Clancy, with his section, carried out a similar manoeuvre at the rear of the house. At the sounding of a whistle, the two sections charged through the front and back doors. Sweeping through the house, the Volunteers initially found only an old lady (the cook and housekeeper) and a young girl. Following this, Lynch ordered the men to take cover again and await developments. The Volunteers lay in the shrubbery for around an hour until they spied three men approaching the lodge. Two were tall, athletic men – clearly British soldiers – and the third was shorter and seemingly lighter – Lucas' personal servant. As the taller men went to the rear of the house, the servant walked in Moylan's direction. Moylan quickly took him into custody.[52] Both of the soldiers were captured in a similar way. Taken completely by surprise, none of the captured men offered any resistance.[53]

There was still no sign of Lucas and it was now late in the afternoon. Anxious for their plan to proceed, Lynch remarked to Moylan, 'We can't wait too long, we'll go and get him.'[54] George Power and Patrick Clancy decided to proceed in opposite directions along the river in the hopes of finding the absent general. As he began his search, Power proceeded through a small wood, where he ran into Lucas unexpectedly as the latter was making his way back to the lodge. Both scrutinised the other for a moment, then Power gave the order 'hands up'; Lucas complied immediately. Power disarmed him and marched the captured general back to the lodge.

Lynch and the others were still unsure as to the identity of the first two captured British officers. In an act of good faith, Power named the IRA men present and asked Lucas if he, in turn, had any objection to naming his comrades. Lucas replied, 'None', and identified them as Colonel Danford of the Royal Artillery and Colonel Tyrrell of the Royal Engineers. A wary Lucas then added, 'What do you propose to do with us?' The prisoners were informed that all three were to be held pending further instructions from IRA GHQ. They were also assured they would be permitted the means to communicate with their relatives.[55]

Lynch allowed the prisoners to have a meal at the lodge.[56] Lucas' personal servant was then released to carry a letter to the O/C at Fermoy Barracks. The letter notified the British military of the capture of the three officers and that they were being held as prisoners of war.[57] The British officers were then prepared for transport to a secure location in two cars, with Tyrrell in the Volunteers' Ford, and Lucas and Danford in the British officers' own motor car, which would be driven by Volunteer Owen Curtin. Lynch later admitted he did not want to tie the men's arms when he was moving them, perhaps due to their co-operation thus far, but in retrospect this was to prove a crucial mistake.[58]

Shortly thereafter, both cars approached the main Fermoy to Cork road near the village of Rathcormac. The first car containing Tyrrell, driven by Moylan, temporarily disappeared from view at a wide sweeping bend of road. Noticing this in the backseat of the rear car, Lucas and Danford started speaking together in Arabic. Following what seemed to be a pre-arranged signal, Danford sprang on Patrick Clancy, who was seated between him and Lucas, while Lucas grabbed hold of Lynch in the passenger seat. So sudden was the attack that both IRA officers were taken at a considerable disadvantage and almost immediately disarmed. The battle of Lynch and Lucas was recalled as 'particularly severe' given both men were athletic and over six feet in height.[59] Lucas grappled for Lynch's handgun, and Lynch later told Ernie O'Malley, 'Lucas nearly crushed my hand as we twisted the gun every which way.'[60]

Inevitably, as the four men thrashed about in such close quarters, the driver, Owen Curtin, had great difficulty in controlling the vehicle. Curtin, when he later listed his service as a motor driver for Volunteer work during this period, only briefly referred to his transport of these prisoners along the road 'until we met with a mishap'.[61] In fact, he lost control of the car and crashed into the roadside ditch; he was temporarily rendered unconsciousness.[62] Just as the car crashed, Lucas had managed to get on top of Lynch, and was still frantically trying to get the gun away from him when the door gave way. Even being unexpectedly thrown onto the road did not halt the physical fight between the two men, until Lynch managed to overpower Lucas, through his 'superior strength and fitness' according to Florence O'Donoghue. An exhausted Lucas ended the fight with a cry of 'I surrender.'[63]

Having overcome Lucas, Lynch noted that Clancy was in difficulty in his own skirmish with Danford. These two men had also continued their own fight onto the road, with Danford now throttling Clancy. Lynch raised his revolver and shouted to the British officer, 'Surrender or I shoot!' Danford ignored the request and maintained his grip on Clancy's throat, so Lynch fired. The bullet struck Danford in the face and he collapsed onto a shocked Clancy.[64]

Meanwhile, in the preceding car, Power had been keeping a close eye on the vehicle behind. When both Power and Moylan realised the second car had not followed them round the long bend, they retraced their route and found it ditched and the combatants fighting on the road. On stopping, Moylan removed his own prisoner from the car and kept him covered.[65] Moylan's later narrative for the Bureau of Military History differs from Power's in stating that, on arrival at the scene, it was actually Danford and Lynch who were engaged in a physical struggle on the roadside, while:

[The] little driver [Curtin] dived like a terrier on to the back of the big British officer [Lucas] who was on top of Clancy on the road, both struggling for possession of a gun. At that moment a shot rang out and the struggle between the Brigade Commandant and his opponent was over. ... The second combatant, seeing the game was up, threw up his hand.[66]

Whatever the order of events, and who exactly was fighting whom, the outcome as described was the same. After their arrival on the scene, Power recalled Lynch's angry demeanour for 'the abuse he showered on me for not turning back sooner'. Lynch, always self-conscious about his poor eyesight, was particularly upset that his glasses had been broken in the struggle.[67]

With the fight over, Lynch attended to a shaken Clancy.[68] Colonel Tyrrell, held by Moylan and Power, was permitted to attend to the mortally wounded Danford. Lynch decided that the now recovered Curtin was to contact a doctor in nearby Rathcormac to attend to Danford, while Tyrrell was allowed to remain at the scene and could consider himself released. Holding a hurried conference with the other IRA officers on the road, Lynch decided that Moylan and Clancy would take Lucas in the Ford, while Power was instructed to proceed east to Waterford and on to Dublin later that night in order to report the details of the capture to IRA GHQ personally.[69] But before he did so, he was to acquire a new pair of glasses for Lynch.[70] General Lucas was then handcuffed with no protest and his crashed motor car was left abandoned in the ditch. All the Volunteers now crowded into their Ford car, dropping Curtin off in Rathcormac to alert a local doctor.[71]

By 3 a.m., the party had arrived at the O'Connell home in nearby Lombardstown, where members of the Mallow Battalion were already holding another prisoner, the stationmaster of the Great Southern and Western Railway at Mallow, who had been arrested by members of the local IRA company for filling the jobs of those who had been dismissed for refusing to transport British soldiers and artillery on their trains.[72] Having assessed the situation, and deeming Lucas of more importance, Lynch ordered the immediate removal of the stationmaster to another location, unhappy that the Lombardstown Company had taken over guarding this man from the Mallow Company.[73]

John O'Connell, O/C of the Lombardstown Company, who was resident in the house, recalled how, when 'General Lynch's escort and prisoner entered the house ... two of the party were unknown to me, namely Lynch and the prisoner, Lucas – two very reserved personalities in my opinion. I did not even know captive from captor until the prisoner was put to bed.'[74] Michael O'Connell, John's brother, also a member of the Lombardstown Company, recalled how they secured the prisoner: 'General Lucas was now placed in the room ... and a strong guard was mounted. Great secrecy had necessarily to be maintained, and trustworthy men had to be selected for guard duty ... I well remember that General Lucas was the first person I saw playing "Patience".'[75] Lucas requested some alcohol and gave money to Michael O'Connell, who then bought a bottle of whiskey for him.

Power noted that once Lucas became resigned to his lot, he displayed no resentment to his captors. He remembered how Lynch and General Lucas 'had many interesting discussions on a variety of subjects, but mainly on military matters, during the course of his captivity'.[76] According to Power, during one of these discussions Lucas 'tried to point out the futility of the fight to Liam Lynch ... Here were the British at the top of their strength after winning one of the most important wars in history'. In Lucas' view, the IRA 'couldn't make a dint in [the British] armour and resistance was futile'. Lynch in turn pointed out to Lucas that in the Fenian tradition, 'the fight would help [inspire] others to fight later if we were beaten in the field'. Lucas 'tried hard to persuade Liam Lynch that the attempt of the Irish to fight or affect British policy was hopeless'. No one, apart from Lynch, was allowed to engage in conversation with Lucas.[77]

In the meantime, the reaction to Lucas' abduction was to prove deadly. Lynch seems to have been first alerted to a potential danger when Patrick O'Connell, then a student at St Colman's College in the town, returned to the family home on the first evening of Lucas' captivity. Patrick was unaware of the presence of Lucas in the home and did not recognise Lynch reading a book by the fire. He told his mother that 'the British Military were going to blow up Fermoy'. After a short conversation with Patrick on the developments in Fermoy, Lynch proceeded to the room where Lucas was being held. Lucas, at Lynch's direction, drafted a message instructing the soldiers under his command to carry out no reprisals in Fermoy in response to the kidnapping. Originally entrusting John O'Connell with the dispatch, Lynch then changed his mind and instead gave it to one of the other guards, not wanting to endanger the whole household if John was caught. The dispatch eventually made its way to the British garrison in Fermoy by way of a local priest. Following the departure of the messenger, at around 11 p.m., Lucas was moved to another house within the brigade area.[78]

Nonetheless, this effort at an intervention by Lucas was for nothing. His kidnapping had already resulted in an unfortunate response by the authorities. For the second time in as many months, a reprisal was visited on the town of Fermoy by the British military along with civilian looters, who aided the targeted destruction of commercial premises and residences in the town – the Sinn Féin Hall in Chapel Square was a specific target. There were reports of shots being fired in residential homes, and, in this instance, the soldiers were aided by men in civilian clothes and assumed to be officers. The reprisal began at 8 p.m., and a little after 2 a.m. a group of Volunteers engaged in a gunfight with soldiers in Mr Cole's jeweller shop, with some injuries inflicted on members of the British military. This seems to have brought the reprisal to an end.[79]

Two days after the kidnapping, in a brief message to Tom, Lynch lamented that his military activities prevented him from meeting his brother regularly, for 'as time goes on these days the more enemies are on my track. Thank God that I have been in the big push for the motherland, I think there could be no more sacred calling. Say a few prayers for me sometimes that I may be able to do my duty to God and Country.' He ended on a frustrated note, making mention of breaking his rimless glasses, 'so for heaven's sake, send me on by post my other gold rimmed ones which you must have taken out of my trunk and left at home'.[80]

Lynch arranged for Lucas to be moved to the West Limerick Brigade area on 29 June; however, the car intended to transport Lucas unexpectedly caught fire and had to be abandoned. As another vehicle was secured to move Lucas, Lynch had to assist in pushing the damaged car for two miles so that it could be left undercover to be removed from the district the next day. Lynch left for the Burnfort area on 30 June.[81] In the weeks ahead, Lucas was passed between various brigade areas, until he managed to effect an escape. There are indications that he may have been deliberately allowed to escape given the difficulty the Volunteers had in moving their high-profile prisoner. Ironically, on being picked up by the relevant authorities Lucas was unwittingly driven into an IRA ambush, which he narrowly survived.

Despite the prisoner's escape, the operation was a major propaganda success for the Volunteers. Though Lucas' seniority in the British military was exaggerated, it nonetheless caused considerable embarrassment to the British.[82] Despite the propaganda coup, however, Lynch felt the frequent moving around of the prisoner through brigade areas had not been especially to the IRA's advantage, and remarked to one contemporary, 'He [Lucas] must have learned a lot more about us than he should.'[83] Both Power and Siobhán Lankford felt Lucas and Lynch developed a mutual respect.[84] This is perhaps an overstatement, as there is no evidence Lucas ever referred to Lynch directly on his release. Nonetheless, he was keen to emphasise the generosity and basic humanity of his captors, and publicly stated he was 'treated like a gentleman by gentlemen' – which likely did little to impress the British military and political establishments.[85]

★★★

On 3 July, Lynch wrote to Tom that he had been 'offered a good position in Dublin at my own business this morning but will not take up for some time yet. Have promised my comrades to stick the game of soldiering for some time longer.' This is likely to be a reference to being offered the position of deputy chief of staff of the IRA again. While Lynch tended to avoid direct reference to brigade operations in his letters to Tom, he could not resist commenting at the end, 'John Bull should give in soon, at least Brigadier General Lucas thinks so.' In another remark on the IRA inactivity in his home area, he wrote, 'Any stir in Anglesboro and Galbally boys?'[86]

In another letter to Tom, on 4 July, Lynch worried that there was no prospect of seeing his brother any time soon, and still seemed frustrated at the lack of IRA activity in their native home: 'If Anglesboro does not hurry up and organise ... things are moving fast now.' Lynch referred to a recent day trip with Michael Collins and Harry Boland, and 'being out in Ireland's Eye', an island off the coast of Howth in north Dublin. Boland had recently returned for a brief visit from the United States, where he was centrally involved in Éamon de Valera's trip there. Lynch seemed fascinated by the dynamics in the Irish republican movement across the Atlantic and assured Tom there 'is no fear of a split in America as long as the young men at home stick to the one and only course. ... [Boland] gives glowing account of America.' Always optimistic, Lynch closed with the 'great hopes of us winning through this year. Anyway it is only a matter of time.'[87]

Even in the heightened activity of the summer of 1920, as far as possible Lynch maintained his inspections of the battalion and company areas of the brigade. After these inspections, Lynch, along with Power and Twomey would frequently stay at the Creedon family home in Clogheen, County Cork. Siobhán Lankford recalled how, on arrival, Lynch's reply 'to my mother's welcome was always the same. "Home again", he would say with his gentle smile.'[88] While being a hideout, the Creedon home was also a place of warmth and friendliness for Lynch. By that autumn, there was no prospect of him attending his usual social outlets of céilís or feiseanna with his peers in the brigade. While he seemed eager to progress with the Irish language, one fluent speaker suggested the best means to learn would be by spending three to six months in the Gaeltacht after the conflict was over. Lynch talked with Lankford of his efforts to improve, and remarked, 'Well I have done one thing anyway, I have got the girl to attend classes in Fermoy.' This was, of course, a reference to his infrequent courting of Bridie Keyes.

Lankford was struck by this mention of Keyes. Though Lynch 'was too shy to suggest it' himself, Lankford, along with George Power, organised for Keyes to visit the Creedon home when Lynch could be there. Power checked timetables and got in touch with Lynch's circle in Fermoy to arrange a suitable day. And thus, one 'fresh early autumn Sunday', Bridie

Keyes arrived at the train station in Mourneabbey, where George Power met her. Lankford remembered her as 'tall and pretty, very elegant in navy and white and like Liam, gentle and quietly spoken'.

After lunch, the couple walked alone in the family's glen, and later joined the Creedon family for tea. Lankford wrote of 'little talk during tea' among the group on the couple's return. When Power returned Keyes to the train station, Lynch went to work on documents in the family parlour. Lankford noted sadly that somehow 'the bright golden evening had lost its sparkle, and a feeling of deep sorrow stole over it'. When Power returned, she noted the usual 'bubbling laughter and teasing' that normally enlivened the two men's discussions was now absent. Lankford lamented on the parting of Lynch and Keyes and how 'these two wonderful people had postponed their happiness to serve Ireland's need'. Lankford felt Keyes had made a 'total' sacrifice, and 'was never to know the fulfilment of her dream of happiness but was to take her place with Sarah Curran' – the girlfriend of the martyred Irish revolutionary Robert Emmet – 'and all the generations of Irish women who stood aside for the cause of Róisín Dubh'.

Lankford implied in her memoir that this was the last time the couple met substantially. In truth, they continued to meet, though infrequently and often with long stretches of time in between, until Lynch's death. Lynch's second biographer, Meda Ryan, described brief periodic meetings between the two, during which Liam would regularly talk through his problems with her. Ryan mentions how these 'periods of intimacy went on for hours, eating into his time of sleep in one of his many hide-outs'.[89] As a precaution during these difficult days of conflict, the two went long periods without meeting, but, it seems, they did get engaged at a date unknown after the Truce in July 1921.[90]

***

Either on the night of 11 August or the morning of 12 August 1920, Lynch received an important communication mistakenly sent to him instead of the head of Cork No. 1 Brigade, Terence MacSwiney. The details of the content of this communication remain unclear, but the message was deemed urgent enough for Lynch to make swift arrangements to travel to Cork city to deliver it to MacSwiney. He was driven by Patrick McCarthy, then adjutant of the Mallow Battalion, and on arrival at a safehouse on Dublin Hill, Lynch requested that McCarthy venture into the city to make contact with MacSwiney.

McCarthy located MacSwiney at St Ita's, the school administered by his sister, Mary. MacSwiney agreed to meet Lynch at his office in City Hall around 7 p.m. As Lynch and McCarthy made their way into the city centre that evening, an increasingly wary Lynch at one point said to his companion, 'Keep out of step, Pat.' As McCarthy recalled, 'Although it was not too easy to do so we managed to stroll along without appearing to be "military minded".'[91]

That same night, a brigade council meeting of all the leading Cork No. 1 officers took place in one of City Hall's offices. It was an unusual venue for such a meeting, but its location was to facilitate MacSwiney, who was based there in his capacity as lord mayor. Florence O'Donoghue has inferred that a small group of IRB members were also to meet at City Hall that night, but neither MacSwiney nor Lynch was aware of that particular meeting.[92] Elsewhere in City Hall there was a Dáil Court session that took place that evening, but MacSwiney was not involved in this.[93]

While it is unclear what Lynch and MacSwiney discussed at their private meeting, or the nature of the message received, Lynch then joined MacSwiney and other Cork No.1 Brigade officers for their brigade meeting. McCarthy remained in the corridor outside, none the wiser as to what was being discussed. After a period of time, Lynch emerged from the room and made a surprising statement to McCarthy:

> After some time Liam came out and said, 'We are not going home tonight.'
> I said 'Why?' and he replied, 'We are taking on a job.'
> I then reminded him that we did not have arms and he said: 'Cork No. 1 will arm us.' Liam then re-entered the meeting room.[94]

Patrick McCarthy had little time to register his surprise that his brigade O/C had volunteered both of them for some sort of IRA action in the city before an alarm was raised. Corporation officials alerted MacSwiney and those at the brigade meeting that British soldiers had surrounded City Hall, obviously somehow tipped off about the meeting. McCarthy recalled what followed in those critical minutes:

> Terry MacSwiney, Liam Lynch and the other officers then left the room and joined me in the corridor. The whole party moved along several corridors until we were looking out on the Cornmarket end of the building. We then saw that the military had taken up positions in the Cornmarket so all avenues of escape were closed. Each member of the party then set about destroying any doubtful documents in their possession. Eventually the raiding party reached us and we were rounded up.[95]

The raid had come about because of an utter stroke of luck. An intelligence officer attached to the British 6th Division had found an item of post that apparently revealed the time and place of the meeting that evening.[96] Twelve men were arrested in the aftermath, with the remaining men allowed to leave City Hall. Florence O'Donoghue later accurately summed this action up as 'the most important capture of the war in Munster', with the British arresting most of the leading officers of Cork No. 1 Brigade and their O/C. All the men, expecting identification, ultimately gave their names and addresses, with two exceptions: Michael Leady, O/C of Cork No. 1's Fourth Battalion, and Lynch, who both gave false names. Lynch gave his name as James Casey, with an address at 25 Camden Street, Dublin, and that is how his name appeared in the prison record.[97]

Lynch feared he would shortly be identified, yet he confessed to a fellow inmate, Patrick O'Brien, that he had a more pressing worry. O'Brien was a lieutenant in the Liscarroll Company, who had been arrested the previous week. Like others, he was surprised one Sunday when attending Mass to see Lynch among the prisoners in the chapel.

On another morning, he met his O/C outside the compound exercise wings, where a concerned Lynch informed him that he still had on his person a map of the Cork No. 2 Brigade area, with all the battalions and companies marked on it. Lynch managed to slip the map to O'Brien without the nearby warder noticing. O'Brien later disposed of it by tearing it into pieces and flushing it down a toilet.[98] Having such documents on his possession was an instance of unusual carelessness by the normally diligent Lynch, which suggested he little imagined being captured in the dangerous environs of Cork city.

At this time in Cork City Jail, a considerable number of republican prisoners were beginning a hunger strike in protest at their treatment. According to Tom Crawford, one of the participants in the strike, there was a sympathetic warder who ensured there was a meeting between the party captured in City Hall, including Lynch, and the hunger strikers. The result of this was that Lynch and the other captured Volunteers agreed to join those already on hunger strike.[99] It was during his brief imprisonment that Lynch met his close friend, Michael Fitzgerald, now on the second day of a fateful hunger strike. There is little detail of what exactly the two discussed but, given his lengthy tenure in prison, Fitzgerald was an eager listener with regard to brigade developments. Those days in captivity were to be the last time Lynch was to see his friend alive.[100]

Yet, Lynch was not to share captivity with Fitzgerald and his hunger striking comrades for very long. He was released with others arrested in City Hall several days into his hunger strike. Apparently, intelligence later arrived at the jail from Dublin Castle revealing the exact identity of those in custody – but by then Lynch, under his false name, had already been released.[101]

Patrick McCarthy remembered how he and Lynch then spent one more night in Cork city, staying with friends, and, on receipt of *The Cork Examiner* the following morning, learned of the deaths of Volunteers Paddy Clancy and Seán O'Connell, both of Cork No. 2 Brigade, in Kanturk on 15 August. The two men had been shot by British forces while 'trying to escape' during a raid on their supposed safehouse. After travelling by car to brigade HQ at Mourneabbey, Lynch left immediately to the attend the funerals of both men, accompanied by his brigade quartermaster, Jeremiah Buckley.[102] Of note, Lynch wore a uniform to the funeral, a rare occurence in these years. His choice of clothing resulted in an unfortunate episode in the aftermath that served as a reminder as to why Lynch rarely wore it. Some weeks later, after the Mallow Barracks attack, British soldiers raided the home of the engineer of the Mallow Company outside the town, where Lynch had left the uniform. While arresting the unfortunate Volunteer, the uniform gave the soldiers the mistaken impression they had captured a leading figure.[103]

Of note, one curious find by this author is a portrait Lynch sat for in full Volunteer uniform at an undetermined juncture during 1920. Little is known about the circumstances behind this painting, or why he sat for it.[104]

Lynch was conscious of his sheer luck in his release and in not enduring a prolonged hunger strike. Some weeks later, while in position for a planned ambush involving his flying column, he engaged one of his officers, Matt Flood, in conversation. Lynch 'started talking and telling me yarns and he said to me, "You were never in gaol?"'

Flood replied he had never been in jail, and said to Lynch, 'If you were in gaol then you wouldn't be here.' Flood was bemused when Lynch described his accidental release from Cork City Jail weeks before and felt Lynch was 'chancing his arm' with the tale, though Flood was convinced when his brigade O/C insisted he had escaped: 'That's a fact.'[105]

Except on his visits to Dublin and Cork, Lynch tended to move around the brigade area unarmed. Yet, from August 1920, following his release, he instructed all his officers to be armed and issued orders to resist capture. Perhaps shaken by his brief experience of arrest, Lynch commented often to his comrades, 'If I'm taken, I'll never be taken alive.'[106]

In a letter to his brother Tom on an unknown date in September, Lynch made no secret of his relish at the good fortune that ensured his release. 'However the fresh air in the open is the business, and we have a better chance of making them pay the piper.' He lamented that those in prison were 'suffering terrible agony by the hunger-strike but I believe they will win through'. On MacSwiney, Lynch felt he 'could nearly wish that they would leave the Lord Mayor die, his death now would be worth a thousand later'.[107] Lynch was under no illusions as to MacSwiney's personal determination.

Early in the hunger strike, MacSwiney was deported to Brixton Prison in London. Given his high profile, placing him in a separate jail in the heart of Britain was, in retrospect, a bad move for the British. As Lynch began forming the brigade's first flying column, a bold new military initiative for his men, MacSwiney's hunger strike was to catapult Ireland's revolution into international headlines.

★

By the autumn of 1920, the British cabinet under Prime Minister David Lloyd George was still refusing, both publicly and privately, to admit to a state of war in Ireland. Nonetheless, on 9 August, the Restoration of Order in Ireland Act was passed by the Westminster parliament. Among various expanded powers now given to the British authorities in Ireland, courts martial could cover offences encompassing ordinary civil law and could implement the death penalty, while coroner's courts were replaced by military courts of inquiry.[108] With the British now having much more latitude to deal with the IRA, raids on homes and safehouses became more frequent, particularly in key fighting areas in Dublin, Clare, Cork and Tipperary. As a result, with IRA members no longer safe at home or in their places of employment – a situation Lynch would have related to since late 1919 – many now had to go on the run. Accordingly, IRA GHQ issued orders for the formation of active service units, or, as they are better known, flying columns: bodies of IRA Volunteers continually on the move and attacking key locations and personnel associated with the British police and military forces.[109]

Following his return from a GHQ conference in Dublin, just prior to his arrest in Cork city on 11 August, Lynch held a brigade council meeting at O'Callaghan's in Quartertown. The main order of business was to select several Volunteers from each of Cork No. 2's battalions to form its first flying column. Commandant Patrick Clancy was appointed column commander.[110] However, the start of the flying column's operations was delayed by both Lynch's arrest and the death of Clancy.[111]

Finally, on 15 September, the flying column assembled at a location at Badger's Hill, Glenville. Lynch and Power, his vice-commandant, took part in the two weeks' training.[112] Assisting in this training was Ernie O'Malley, a staff captain attached to IRA GHQ. Mayo-born O'Malley had been radicalised by the events of Easter Week 1916 and joined the Volunteers soon after. He was GHQ's key trainer and organiser for IRA units in Dublin, Clare and Tipperary.[113] Lynch had been requesting an organiser from GHQ to assist Cork No. 2 Brigade since March that year, 'even for four or five weeks to lecture officers, we would take good care of any of our friends on the run in Dublin if they come here'.[114] Though O'Malley, as a representative of GHQ, sometimes received a mixed reception on his arrival to fighting areas (as borne out in his memoir), he and Lynch developed a strong rapport and the two came to recognise in each other a fierce commitment and enormous belief in their cause.

O'Malley, in his brilliant, literary style wrote a vivid account describing Lynch when he first met him:

> Liam Lynch had a domed forehead. When he smiled I could see a row of large teeth; his face tightened quickly on his smile. He was quiet, but forceful and commanding. He tapped the table impatiently with his pencil at side issues and quickly worked through a large agenda. His eyes had large pupils which grew blacker and larger when he stammered in anger. He had a clear, well-organized mind.[115]

Lynch envisaged that eventually each battalion in the brigade would have its own flying column, with perhaps two or three of these combining for specific operations. In the interim, he intended to put the initial flying column of the brigade staff into action quickly.[116] O'Malley wrote that the initial brigade flying column counted twenty-four officers from the battalion staff, including Lynch and other officers from the brigade command.[117] Given that they were to be the quintessential force within the brigade in this phase of the conflict, Lynch had very specific ideas about how members of a column were to conduct themselves. William Regan, O/C of the Doneraile Company, recalled Lynch's instructions, given to each column active in their battalion:

> The instructions of the Brigade O/C regarding battalion columns were that when not lying in ambush, each column should carry out a regular schedule of training on its own during the day. At night the members of the column were to train the members of the companies in whose areas they were billeted. In this way he felt that an unlimited supply of trained personnel would be available throughout the brigade area at all times.[118]

Daniel Daly of the Rathcormac Company was tasked by Lynch with the job of arranging billets and transport for the column, with Daly's home initially functioning as one such base for up to twelve men including Lynch. Daly was itching to join the fighting men and 'made a special request to Liam Lynch to be permitted to proceed with the Column. Liam refused and said I was doing equally important work at home.'[119] Lynch also refused permission for married men in the brigade to join the column.[120]

The flying column initially billeted in locations around the townlands of Island and Greenhill.[121] Paddy O'Brien recalled that Lynch was 'apprehensive' about one aspect of the operation of the column, that of support from the local populace. Lynch admitted to him that he 'wondered how the people would react when asked to harbour men who were openly carrying arms'.[122] O'Brien observed how, given the abundance of food and shelter offered to members of the columns in the weeks ahead, it 'was a great relief to [Lynch], as he was of a very sensitive nature'.

With this first flying column of the brigade now established, Lynch and O'Malley sought opportunities. The two men inspected the road from Mallow to Cork city on foot. Convoys of lorries and armoured cars frequently passed in opposite directions along the road, with either armoured cars escorting lorries or two or three lorries travelling together. The men determined two good positions along the road for the placement of Volunteers for an ambush. However, these plans were put aside after a startling new development. O'Malley recalled, 'Whilst I was giving a lecture in a barn to officers that night, Liam was called outside. After the lecture he said, "The Mallow commandant brought out a young lad named Bolster, but I thought I'd wait until you were finished. He's working in the military barracks, and says he thinks it can be taken."'[123]

Central to this plan to attack the military barracks in Mallow were two members of the Mallow Battalion, Jackie Bolster and Richard Willis. Willis was attached to a painting contractor who had been carrying out works there since June 1920. Shortly after the work began, an opening for the position of a carpenter had arisen. Willis helped Bolster get the job, and it was then that the two men began considering the possibility of acquiring rifles and ammunition from the barracks. Both men mentioned the possibility to the leadership of Mallow Battalion several times, until their O/C instructed Bolster to meet Lynch at the column's base at Sheehan's farm in Mourneabbey.[124]

Lynch and O'Malley carefully questioned Bolster alone in a room in their safehouse. O'Malley noted that Bolster was 'tall, serious looking, a little nervous at first, but by degrees the nervousness wore off. He … was eager to speak.'[125] From Bolster, they established that nearly all the barracks arms were in the guardroom at certain times, and four or five soldiers were based in the guardroom at any one time. The soldiers based in the barracks were from a cavalry regiment, the 17th Lancers, who called themselves 'The Death or Glories', and numbered about forty or fifty. Along with one officer in the barracks, there was a sergeant major. One sentry was outside the main gate during the day, and eight or nine soldiers, along with the officer, took the horses out for exercise every morning. Bolster drew an outline of all the barrack buildings on a piece of paper, and Lynch asked him to examine the guardroom without attracting attention and return the following evening.

After Bolster departed, Lynch asked O'Malley for his thoughts and whether the young Volunteer could be trusted. O'Malley believed the proposed operation was 'simple enough' and on the matter of trust,

Bolster 'gave his information steadily'. Furthermore, O'Malley pointed out that 'two machine guns and thirty rifles are worth a risk. We often have men killed trying to capture a rifle.'[126]

In the course of planning the operation, Willis and Bolster saw an opportunity for a third Volunteer to be present within the barracks before the attack began. Several days earlier, the garrison O/C had mentioned the poor water pressure to Willis, who promised he would raise this with the clerk of works. Willis could leave the barracks on the day of the attack on the pretence of meeting this clerk, and then bring him inside the grounds. Seán Moylan at one point suggested that he pose as the clerk of works, but Lynch turned down the request. Paddy McCarthy of the Millstreet Battalion would instead fulfil this role.[127] The date agreed upon for the attack was the morning of Tuesday 28 September.[128]

Lynch instructed Leo O'Callaghan of the Mallow Company to secure the use of a Buick car, which the Mallow Volunteers had used on a previous operation. As O'Callaghan was a local, Lynch said he was holding him responsible for ensuring any material captured in the operation was dumped at a safe location.[129] Just prior to the operation, Lynch and O'Malley positioned Volunteers near the barracks, particularly in the nearby town hall, in case British reinforcements should arrive during the attack.[130]

That morning, Willis and McCarthy entered the barracks, where McCarthy got out his notebook and started looking at apparent repairs near the barrack gate. As they entered the guardroom, both men took note of the arms but were surprised to see seven soldiers there instead of the expected three. McCarthy proceeded to pretend to measure the guardroom as both men ran down the clock until O'Malley arrived at the barrack gate.[131]

Lynch, O'Malley and others of the column had been billeted in Mallow town hall since the early hours of the morning. As per the plan, O'Malley walked up to the front door of the barracks and knocked. Telling the sentry he had an envelope for the O/C of the barracks, O'Malley was admitted and the door shut behind him. As the sentry reached for the envelope, O'Malley managed to take the rifle from him and quickly unbolted the barrack door previously locked behind him.[132]

As the Volunteers rushed through the door, Matt Flood spotted how 'Lynch was making to be in first but someone gave him a shoulder so that he was about the fourth in' – undoubtedly a deliberate act.[133] Lynch's men may have been consciously attempting to stop their O/C putting himself directly in danger, a likely result of his wounding during the Fermoy arms raid. Close behind Lynch was his aide-de-camp for this operation, William Regan, the O/C of the Doneraile Company.[134]

Several of the Volunteers reached the guardroom and immediately held up the soldiers inside. Willis then looked through the doorway to see the sergeant major approaching. Willis fired, as did another of the Volunteers, and the sergeant fell wounded across the doorway of the guardroom.[135] Lynch then gave a prearranged signal and three motor cars commandeered by the Volunteers (including the Buick driven by O'Callaghan) were driven into the barracks. The arms haul consisted of two Hotchkiss light machine guns, twenty-seven rifles, a revolver, some pistols, 4,000 rounds of ammunition and a quantity of bayonets and lances.[136] The arms would benefit the members of the flying column; William Regan recalled how, prior to the raid, the column had mainly trained with fourteen rifles captured in the Fermoy arms raid in 1919, 'but the new capture strengthened the position considerably'.[137] Lynch instructed Regan to return the rifles to the 'home area' and he took them to Badgers Hill where they were 'dumped' by Denis Hickey, the O/C of the Glenville Company.[138]

As the Volunteers quickly left the barracks, there was an attempt to set it alight using bales of hay. The fire was quickly quenched by the soldiers, however, after the Volunteers' escape. Though no republican forces were killed in the attack, Lynch regretted the fact that the Lancers' sergeant major later died from his wounds.[139] Matt Flood of the column was struck, and perhaps somewhat bemused, by one 'humane' instruction of Lynch's during other operations of the column: 'if you could at all … don't kill. If you like that was a hard thing to do but he'd be happy if you could bring off a stunt without anyone being killed. That was the kind of fellow he was but he was strict as well'.[140]

O'Donoghue described what followed the attack on the barracks as 'the pattern now becoming familiar to the civil population ... a night of terror for the inhabitants of [Mallow] town'. Arriving from Fermoy and Buttevant Barracks, British soldiers, aided by police, burned and destroyed residences and businesses, along with Mallow town hall and the local creamery.[141] As the members of the column watched from a distance, the town buildings began to burn and Lynch remarked, 'Damn it, it's terrible to think of the women and children in there and the Tans and the soldiers sprawling around drunk, setting fire to the houses.' O'Malley felt that the column's initial elation at the success of their attacks on the barracks had 'ebbed away; we felt cowardly and miserable; in silence we journeyed on amongst the hills'.[142]

Nonetheless, the first action of the Cork No. 2 flying column could be considered a success. Despite persistence by the British forces in the area, the arms from the Mallow raid were never recovered.[143] Although aware of the cost for the ordinary townspeople of Mallow, Lynch was described as being 'jubilant' in the aftermath at the results for the column.[144]

✶✶✶

In the weeks following the Mallow attack, Lynch continued to seek out opportunities for the flying column, while encouraging this elite unit of fighting men to practise strong discipline. Matt Flood recalled a somewhat amusing encounter with his strict brigade O/C after he and other members enjoyed some leisure time one night: 'At the time we were training [after Mallow] ... Dick Willis, Jack Bolster and myself, wherever we got the few bob, went into the village on a Saturday night and had a couple of pints, that would be the most of it.'[145] As they were returning to the column's billets, Flood commented to Willis, 'Bejapus, Dick, if we met the big fellow on the road he'll smell it for sure.' Willis suggested the use of a sweet, which, as Flood recalled, 'were a very smelly sweet with a kind of perfume from them which could take away the smell of the drink. Well it was a good job we got them for well on the road back we met Lynch.'

Lynch regarded the three with suspicion, 'Where were you ... having a walk around? Getting to know the locality?'

'Yes,' Flood replied, but Lynch 'nearly had his nose in my mouth and I knew what he was on. I was standing to attention and afraid I'd be sent back. But that blooming sweet saved us.'

Despite this incident, Flood recalled that he got on well with Lynch during his time in the column and spoke fondly of his late O/C when interviewed for his own biography. His descriptions of Lynch in this period are well written, and his personal impression of the brigade O/C consistently show Lynch as a no-nonsense leader:

> He was a nice fellow to talk to but ... The signal when things were wrong for Lynch was, he had a habit of running his forehead above his glasses. Just across his eyebrows ... I can still picture him in that long sort of rain-coat he wore and his keen eyes peering through the glasses down the road looking for the approaching lorries. ... He was a very genuine man, strict in his habits and he didn't drink or smoke.

Flood's portrait of Lynch is one of the brigade O/C keeping his officers at something of a personal remove, but Flood had no doubt he cared for the well-being of those under his command. He was surprised to find that Lynch regularly guarded the men of the column as they slept in their hideouts. Lynch's difficulty sleeping continued throughout the height of conflict, which Flood felt may have been due to the personal strain of his military role: 'You could never tell whether he was feeling the strain of his responsibilities, but the only thing was you could meet him, whether it was telling on him or not ... late at night. I might go down and have a look at the sentries ... and I'd meet him along the way. He'd say, "What, can't you sleep either?"'

After an attack on another barracks was abandoned some days later, Flood was disappointed to have been unable to put his machine-gun training and the armaments taken from Mallow to use. On hearing of his disappointment, Lynch responded, 'Never mind Matt, we'll have a tune out of the gun next Monday for we are going to fix one up.' Lynch was referring to an impending ambush planned for Ballydrochane on 11 October.

Through the strong intelligence network in the area, Seán Moylan of the Newmarket Battalion became aware that two lorries belonging to a British military party regularly passed between the towns of Newmarket and Kanturk, four miles apart. Moylan convinced Lynch that a well-concealed ambush party could successfully attack this small convoy. As he took Lynch and O'Malley on an inspection of the proposed ambush site, all three observed the two military lorries – containing twenty-four soldiers altogether – pass by them.[146] Moylan was struck by a comment O'Malley made to Lynch, as they surveyed the proposed ambush area. When Moylan explained one aspect of the plan to O'Malley, the latter remarked to Lynch, 'Do you know, these country fellows are coming on amazingly.' Moylan found it enlightening, that O'Malley, from Dublin GHQ, regarded Lynch – as much a 'country fellow' as Moylan – being of 'intellect or experience ... on his (O'Malley's) own plane.'[147]

From 3 a.m. on 6 October, members of the flying column, including Lynch, gathered at the ambush site.[148] As they were waiting, Matt Flood noticed an old man with a horse and cart slowly making his way down the road and asked Lynch, 'Chief what about the old man there? If they come now, what's going to happen?' Lynch replied, 'He'll have to take his chance.'[149]

There were no civilians present when the ambush began, shortly after 11 a.m. To the surprise of those present, only one lorry appeared, which was blocked by a cart that the Volunteers had pulled out onto the road. After five minutes, they had killed the driver and wounded the rest of the party, who surrendered, suffering no casualties on their own side. The members of the column collected all the rifles, equipment and ammunition.[150] Lynch insisted that the wounds of the British soldiers be dressed. This act may have saved Moylan's life when he was arrested the following year as, on learning Moylan's name, one British soldier present at his arrest recalled his name from an account of the ambush's aftermath. Moylan felt this was the reason he was arrested rather than indiscriminately shot.[151] Moylan later noted, recalling the young driver dead across the wheel at the ambush, 'I am no soldier. I hate killing and violence. The thought ran through my mind, "God help his mother."'[152]

Less than a week later, there was a casualty who had a personal connection to Cork No. 2 Brigade. On 14 October, Liam O'Connell, a resident of Glantane in Cork, was killed during an ambush in Dublin city. A member of the IRA's Dublin Brigade,[153] he was also part of the O'Connell family whose home had been the first location where General Lucas was held after his kidnap several months earlier. O'Connell was buried in Glantane cemetery and Lynch spoke at the graveside. It was one of the few occasions he would ever speak in public. His oration included the following statement: 'We are here at the grave of one of our Volunteers whose young life is given for the freedom of Ireland. We will avenge his great sacrifice, and we will continue the fight until it's brought to a successful conclusion. Many more may follow Liam O'Connell before this country obtains its Independence.'[154]

Three days later, Cork No. 2 Brigade was to suffer a more seismic loss – one that was to be deeply personal for Lynch. On 17 October, the sixty-seventh day of his hunger strike, Michael Fitzgerald died in Cork City Jail surrounded by priests and nuns reciting the Rosary. Fitzgerald's biographer, Thomas O'Riordan, depicts a vivid scene:

> Fr. Fitzgerald [the prison chaplain] led the recitation of the fifteen decades of the Rosary. Relatives of the other prisoners knelt outside in the corridor joined in the responses ... voices of the huge crowd outside the gates could be heard as they also recited the Rosary. As Fr. Fitzgerald recited the second decade of the third rosary, one of the nuns turned around and said, 'He's gone.'[155]

Fitzgerald was thirty-eight years old.

After a memorial Mass in Cork City, closely watched by the British military authorities, Fitzgerald's remains were brought to Fermoy by members of the Fermoy Battalion. On the evening of 19 October, his coffin was placed in St Patrick's church to be taken for burial in nearby Kilcrumper cemetery the following day. Arrangements were made for Lynch to pay his respects on the night prior to the burial.[156] Matt Flood recalled Lynch's arrival that night: 'Liam Lynch arrived that night at the church coming with about twelve or fourteen of the column. I was just inside the door of the church, and he tipped me and said, "How are you keeping since?" and I said, "Alright."[157]

Two of the Volunteers unscrewed the lid of the coffin for their brigade O/C. According to onlookers, Lynch looked down on the remains in the coffin with a 'look of anguish and sorrow' and he clasped Fitzgerald's worn and emaciated hand. Fitzgerald's biographer gave a vivid impression of Lynch then emerging from the church and walking down the familiar streets of Fermoy, where 'he renewed a vow, not of vengeance against the tyrant responsible for the comrade's death, but that he would devote every moment of his life to secure the achievement of the aims and ideals for which he died'.[158] A number of Lynch's contemporaries were struck by his genuine, deep grief at Fitzgerald's passing. Flood, watching his brigade O/C in the church, felt if he 'ever saw sadness in a man's face it was in Liam Lynch's face that night'.[159] On his departure from the church, Lynch rejoined the flying column on the outskirts of Fermoy.[160] Lynch undoubtedly carried this personal loss deeply for the remainder of his short life; one of his final requests was to be buried with his late friend and comrade.

Lynch had already suffered a personal loss just three days before Fitzgerald's death, when Seán Treacy was gunned down by a British Secret Service member in Dublin on 14 October. Lynch had come to know Treacy well during his frequent visits to Dublin. Paddy O'Brien noted how the two men whom Lynch 'most frequently mentioned were Michael Fitzgerald ... and Seán Tracey ...' Both men, in O'Brien's view, were Lynch's 'idols, and I will never forgot how distressed he was when he learned of both their deaths'.[161] Not surprisingly, an enduring theme in Lynch's surviving personal correspondence from 1920 onward is the recurring idea of having to live up to the sacrifices of the patriot dead.

The hunger strike begun in Cork City Jail ended on 12 November, with nine survivors. Three men, including Fitzgerald, had died – the most high-profile being Terence MacSwiney, who died in Brixton prison in London on 25 October after seventy-four days on hunger strike, with Volunteer Joseph Murphy dying the same day after seventy-six days.

Murphy was twenty-five years old and, like Fitzgerald, was greatly eclipsed in historical memory by MacSwiney. MacSwiney's death dominated the headlines worldwide, bringing international attention to the revolutionary situation in Ireland. Ultimately, it proved a huge propaganda coup for the Irish revolutionary movement.

By the end of October 1920, Lynch had the brigade flying column demobilised, with each battalion taking up the formation and training of its own column. At brigade meetings and visits to the battalions, Lynch was closely attuned to the development of the columns, which would be involved in several successful actions in the weeks ahead. Castletownroche Battalion took part in an ambush at Labacally, near Glanworth, on 26 November, and then assisted the East Limerick Brigade column with an ambush in their own area, at Glencurrane near Lynch's birthplace, on 19 December. On 10 December, the Fermoy Battalion column took part in a successful ambush at Leary's Cross, near Castlelyons.[162]

On 22 November, the Millstreet Battalion column staged an ambush on an RIC patrol. Several members of the Black and Tans, along with Captain Patrick McCarthy of the Volunteers, were killed. McCarthy was a well-liked member of Cork No. 2 Brigade and had been active in the Mallow Barracks attack and at the Ballydrochane ambush. The night after the ambush, Lynch ordered flying column members to occupy key positions in Millstreet in case a reprisal took place in the town. The column dispersed the following day after a quiet night. When McCarthy was buried at Lismire on the same evening, Lynch took charge of the funeral procession. During the temporary occupation of Millstreet, Lynch remarked to Captain Con Meany of Millstreet, in reference to McCarthy's death, 'No matter who is killed or captured by the British now, thank God there are plenty of men left to lead and carry on the fight.'[163]

★★★

The closing months of 1920 were to see an unprecedented escalation of the wider conflict within Cork and beyond, which ensured that the

Irish conflict captured the attention of the international media, and saw martial law imposed in Cork, Kerry, Tipperary and Limerick. British raids and both official and unofficial reprisals became commonplace. On 20 September, in an event later known as 'The Sack of Balbriggan', much of the town of Balbriggan in north County Dublin was burned by British forces in response to the local shooting dead of an RIC head constable. Over 100 Black and Tans from the nearby Gormanston army camp burned residences and businesses, including the local creamery. A similar pattern of destruction was seen in other towns through to the end of 1920, but Balbriggan's proximity to the capital ensured it received major international press notice.

IRA actions were not found wanting either. On the morning of 21 November, members of the Dublin Brigade and the elite IRA unit 'the Squad' assassinated fourteen alleged British intelligence operatives around the capital in a series of co-ordinated operations (with a further operative dying in December due to wounds sustained on the day). In response, in mid-afternoon on the same day, military trucks containing both Black and Tans and Auxiliaries arrived at the grounds of Croke Park during a Gaelic football match between Dublin and Tipperary, under the auspices of searching for the perpetrators of the shootings that morning. British forces opened fire on the crowd of 5,000 spectators, killing fourteen and wounding up to 100 civilians according to some estimates.

A number of successful IRA ambushes on British forces took place, such as those near Rineen in County Clare (22 September), at Tooreen in west Cork (22 October) and near Kinsalebeg in County Waterford (1 November), with the most dramatic ambush occurring along a country road near Kilmichael village in west Cork on 28 November. It was there that Commandant Tom Barry led nearly forty IRA men of the Cork No. 3 flying column in an expertly co-ordinated attack on two Crossley tender lorries. During the ambush, the IRA suffered three casualties, while sixteen members of the RIC's Auxiliary Division were killed.

On the night of 11 December and into the following morning, the residents of Cork city were to witness the most dramatic reprisal by British forces in response to an ambush at Dillon's Cross in the city that day when one Auxiliary was killed. That night, members of both the Auxiliaries and British military began an array of attacks on the civilian populace across the city, which involved indiscriminate shooting, looting and burning. Local firefighters had to contend with British forces hindering their efforts to quell the fires, and in the aftermath over forty business premises and 300 homes were destroyed, along with City Hall and the Carnegie Library. Two unarmed IRA members were also taken from their homes and killed.

The end of the year would also see the British government enact a divisive political decision, with long-lasting consequences for Ireland. In an effort to appease Irish unionism, the government introduced the Government of Ireland Act, which passed in the Westminster parliament that November and became law on 23 December. The legislation – drafted by a committee headed by the unionist politician Walter Long, and with no Irish input – essentially created two Home Rule parliaments in Ireland. The Northern Ireland parliament was to have jurisdiction over six Ulster counties: Derry, Antrim, Down, Armagh, Fermanagh and Tyrone. After years of opposition to Home Rule, this solution was agreeable to James Craig and his fellow Ulster unionists, as in their view it ensured for them a government with a Protestant, unionist majority. Meanwhile, the Southern Ireland parliament would control the remaining twenty-six counties. The response of the Irish revolutionary movement and its underground parliament and army was to completely ignore the creation of the 'Southern Ireland' entity.

In the meantime, British forces were determined to obstruct IRA activities on a wide scale in Lynch's brigade area. In early October, Lynch was particularly aggrieved at one British incursion arriving northwards into his brigade area. Lynch ventured into the Tipperary No. 3 (or Tipperary South) Brigade area and met the brigade O/C, Séumas Robinson, at his headquarters. The meeting opened, according to Robinson, when '[Lynch] complained with what seemed to me to be a good deal of pent-up feeling and politely-supressed indignation that the South Irish Horse (a British Cavalry unit stationed at Cahir Military

Barracks) was continually raiding southwards into his Brigade area.'[164] Lynch informed Robinson 'in measured terms' that it was the latter's duty to put a halt to these raids coming from Cahir.

Robinson argued that neither he nor any of the surrounding brigades had the men and equipment available to prevent the incursions into the Cork No. 2 Brigade area. He sensed that Lynch realised the difficulties, but the Cork commander still insisted, 'You will have to do something about it.' Robinson agreed and pointed out the only way to deal with the situation was 'to combine at once sufficient forces on lines parallel to the British' – perhaps some sort of association of the three Cork brigades, East Limerick Brigade, and the Second and Third Tipperary Brigades. Robinson felt that together they would 'make an almost irresistible force'. He observed of Lynch's response to this proposal: 'Liam made no sustained argument … To Liam, unless a decision were legitimate, it could not be moral.' Lynch was understandably anxious for sanction from GHQ for such a proposal, which would be a drastic change in the military command of the brigades in the area. Robinson noticed Lynch 'quietly fidgeting with obvious impatience … and, in his usual quiet, strictly polite manner, his intriguing slight impediment of speech a little accentuated, he put his proposition, direct, unequivocally and with finality: "Will I call a meeting of Munster Brigade Officers, get their views and send a report to G.H.Q.?"' Robinson assured Lynch he was behind him.

Robinson was of the opinion their exchange was 'the germ of the idea of forming the [IRA] into large divisions' that was to begin with the proposed meeting early the following year. And while he did not realise it yet, Liam Lynch was soon to be thrust into an important, new role – a greater expansion of his already considerable responsibilities as O/C of Cork No. 2 Brigade. For Mulcahy and the IRA leadership, Lynch was to be a key figure in the IRA's campaign to step up its momentum in the face of increasing challenges.

Chapter 5

'That bloody shop assistant has been here' (January–July 1921)

THE FIRST SIX MONTHS OF 1921 saw the continued escalation of the military conflict in Ireland with resultant casualties. Between January and July, a thousand people would die because of political violence in Ireland; an average of forty per week.[1] At the year's outset, IRA brigades in key fighting areas, such as Cork No. 2 Brigade, continued to come under repeated pressure.

One of the most devastating losses for republicans occurred at Clonmult on 20 February 1921, when twelve IRA Cork No. 1 Brigade Volunteers were killed in a military engagement with the British; two more who were captured in the aftermath were later executed. Following the execution of Kevin Barry of the IRA's Dublin Brigade on 1 November 1920, the first such since the Easter Rising, executions continued apace into 1921. By July, the British had executed twenty-four IRA Volunteers. John Dorney has noted that the IRA's response to these killings often carried a 'dark logic'. For instance, on 28 February, six IRA members were executed in Cork city; the next day, six off-duty British soldiers were shot dead by the IRA.[2]

Against the background of an increasingly bloody guerrilla war, the first, faltering efforts at peace negotiations between the British government and the Dáil cabinet took place by way of intermediaries.

This convoluted process was beyond the knowledge of Lynch and many leading IRA figures, though over the coming months, as will be seen, Lynch became somewhat aware of them. At the start of the year, the possible outcome of these peace efforts, much like the ultimate course of the war itself, was uncertain.

✷✷✷

Following Lynch's discussion with Séumas Robinson at the end of the previous year, on 6 January, within the Cork No. 2 Brigade area at Glanworth, representatives of all three Cork brigades, Tipperary No. 2 and No. 3 Brigades and the East Limerick Brigade met in conference for two days. In an indication of his reluctance to take charge, Lynch asked Robinson to chair the meeting. A report was subsequently issued to GHQ with various suggestions. These included: shooting all enemy hostages on sight in response to a similar British proclamation, regular provision of medical and food supplies, and all present brigades to create their own flying columns which would be permanently on active service. On this last suggestion, Robinson recalled the reasoning for the creation of a larger operational flying column 'was the fact that the enemy posts were now all large ones' across the area of the southern brigades. Mulcahy and IRA GHQ, however, immediately turned down these suggestions.[3] Despite this, there emerged one positive, as Florence O'Donoghue, then adjutant for Cork No. 1 Brigade and present at the meeting, observed: the 'keynote of the conference was co-operation and mutual assistance between the Brigades.'[4]

Operational difficulties within the Cork No. 2 Brigade area were to endure. In early February, Lynch reported to Collins on the collapse of the intelligence network in parts of his brigade area: 'We are not picking up messages now as before … Fermoy, I must say is completely burst up … but we are making all efforts to regain our position.'[5]

On 15 February, a disastrous action occurred for Cork No. 2 Brigade during an ambush at Mourneabbey. Intelligence had been received that senior British officers were meeting at their divisional HQ in Cork. At a conference two days earlier, Lynch advised members of the Mallow

Battalion flying column to occupy a position along a road a mile south of Mourneabbey, hoping to ambush British officers being transported through the area in a convoy. Despite careful preparation, on the morning of the ambush the rifle and shotgun sections of the columns found themselves suddenly surrounded on three sides by British forces. The column had to beat a hasty retreat and the ambush resulted in the death of three Volunteers, with another dying of wounds and two later executed for their part in the ambush. Immediately, it was suspected that there was a spy within the ranks of the brigade and Lynch began an investigation, though their identity was to remain elusive for several weeks.[6]

On 2 March, Collins wrote to Lynch and expressed regret about the deaths at Mourneabbey. He added, 'I hope it will not be too long before you are able to make a settlement with the person responsible'.[7] On 8 March, Mulcahy asked Lynch to convey to the head of the flying column from him, 'my appreciation of his dash and decision in this instance'. Mulcahy suggested improved means of scouting and signalling to prevent similar losses in future.[8]

From March to May, most of the brigade's actions, such as sniping attacks and ambushes, were on a smaller scale, mainly in the west of the brigade area as the east was more heavily garrisoned by British forces.[9] Lynch was conscious of these heightened difficulties. On 19 March, he insisted to Mulcahy, following a failed ambush in the Kilbrack area, that there was 'a splendid fighting spirit in this area together with some good Officers, so we should have good results from them in the future'. Lynch insisted they had had 'very hard luck' as 'enemy now move seldom in this area and in large convoys'.[10]

Enemy numbers were not the only issue that could arise. On 4 March, Lynch reported to Collins that one flying column had lain in an ambush position 'with a machine gun for three days'. Then the local parish priest threatened to write to the nearby British garrison, so Lynch sent three Volunteers to confront him at his home but, ultimately, 'decided to drop the matter, as we believe he won't chance it again, the officers appearing in trench coats and full equipment may have had an effect'. Lynch requested further instruction from Collins on the matter and suggested ordering the priest 'out of the parish as we count him nothing less than a traitor. I see the difficulty, but we must meet it'.[11] Collins replied on 9 March and noted other brigade areas had suffered similar interventions by clergy: 'Very difficult to deal with – aren't they?' In a previous instance, Collins had given Cork No. 3 Brigade a similar suggestion to Lynch's but admitted, 'I'm inclined to doubt its efficacy'.[12]

On 10 March, Lynch and others were involved in a dramatic incident at a Newmarket column training camp on a farm in Nadd. Brigade HQ was based at the farmhouse, owned by Paddy McCarthy, with Lynch, George Power and Mossie Walsh billeted there. Given this fact, one member of the flying column and one local Volunteer were on guard duty together at Nadd Cross, with pairs alternating for set periods from nightfall until 8 a.m. Additional scouts were posted day and night at nearby vantage points.[13]

That Thursday morning, Tadg McCarthy (no relation to the owners of the farm), an engineer attached to the Mallow Battalion staff, was on guard with another member of the flying column and two local Volunteers. McCarthy recalled it was a wet and foggy morning. Despite the rain, he remained on duty at the crossroads, when, at 8.30 a.m., he caught sight of two military lorries as they appeared around a turn 150 yards from him. McCarthy later said that by the time he reached HQ, a farm labourer employed by the McCarthys had already informed Lynch and the others there of the impending raid.[14] George Power recalled it was a thatcher coming to fix the roof – it had been a particularly wet morning – who first informed him and Lynch of the raiding party nearby. Lynch burned some papers in the fire, then gathered up the rest. He was the first to leave the house.[15] Power felt their initial response to the danger was perhaps somewhat lax, as they did not realise how close the approaching soldiers were: 'Even then we didn't seem to think of it [as] very important for we were not in a great hurry. We got up, had a cup of tea, [and] took away the typewriter and correspondence. We went up first to the back of the house on to a hill.'[16]

As the group went along the cover of a hedge towards part of a boreen, one of the Volunteer scouts at Nadd Cross came up to them. Seán

McCarthy remembered how 'Liam Lynch stayed behind to talk to him and he was so angry that he felt inclined to shoot him [the scout] for no shot had been fired of warning ...'[17] According to McCarthy, Lynch had been aware of poor discipline in the Newmarket Battalion and had long felt the members of its flying column lacked discipline and were even inclined to drink. During their retreat, Lynch and the others engaged in a brief gunfight with British soldiers nearby, but the group managed to escape to the nearby farmhouse of a sympathiser. Ahead of the arrival of a local doctor at the farmhouse, Lynch assisted in treating the wounds of one of the party injured during the exchange.[18]

Though the brigade O/C was undoubtedly a prize target, George Power observed of Lynch in the aftermath, 'Liam Lynch wasn't shaken. It was hard to shake Liam.'[19] As the McCarthy house was being searched, the British realised how close they had come to capturing their chief prize. A resident in the house observed that when a British officer found Lynch's razor with 'Barry & Sons' on it, he remarked aloud, 'That bloody shop assistant has been here.'[20]

As with Mourneabbey, it seemed that British intelligence had accurate information that both Lynch and the members of the flying column were in the area.[21] In the aftermath, suspicion fell on a member of the Kanturk Battalion flying column, Michael Shiels. Particularly damning was a comment Shiels had made a few days before. While taking over guard duty one morning, he remarked to Leo O'Callaghan that the area would be ideal for an ambush. O'Callaghan found the remark strange: 'What would bring an ambush party here, they'd never find the place.' Shiels replied, 'You'd never know.'[22] O'Callaghan recalled of him: 'Something of a braggart, he was very fond of drink and, generally, was not popular with the unit. While he participated in the training activities of the battalion column he was always absent, on some pretext, when an engagement was due.'[23]

During March 1921, Shiels had been attached to brigade HQ at Nadd. He regularly went into Kanturk to draw his British Army pension, where he also frequented public houses. Michael Moore, the intelligence officer of the battalion, became aware that Shiels had called into the RIC barracks.

Moore sent a dispatch to the brigade HQ, but for some undetermined reason it never arrived. The raid took place the following morning and Shiels was spotted at the farmhouse in Nadd with the arriving British forces, wearing the typical uniform of the Auxiliaries. O'Callaghan later claimed Shiels disappeared after this and was never traced by the IRA, despite efforts in both England and the United States to locate him.[24] An intelligence report from later that year recorded the confession of one executed spy in relation to the elusive Shiels: 'Michael Shiels ... is an ex-soldier of about forty years. He is 6 feet high, a smart looking man, sometimes dresses in khaki and when in ordinary clothes wears a soft hat, collar and tie, sometimes wears glasses to disguise himself ... Shiels and I were keeping in touch with each other to give the game away on the Sinn Féiners.'[25] Among the brigade it was widely assumed that Shiels had passed on information that had led to British success at the Mourneabbey ambush.[26]

From then on, the brigade HQ moved between various locations within the Mallow Battalion area. Lynch and the brigade leadership agreed that, in view of the increased enemy activity, it was essential that all approaches to the Mallow district should be held in order to prevent a repeat of what had happened at Nadd. As Tadg McCarthy recalled, 'special steps were taken to ensure that all roads were trenched, bridges demolished and all enemy lines of communication cut. This work necessitated the constant attention each night of the members of the local Companies as well as members of the Column who acted as armed guards while the work of demolition and trenching was in progress.'[27]

On 19 March, Lynch put forward several suggestions to Mulcahy to obstruct enemy activity, indicative of his deepening frustration over the difficulties in brigade operations. He suggested poisoning the food of British cavalry horses or disruption of enemy supplies from the civilian population. Lynch felt that if this resulted in British forces having to 'force supplies from the people, it is alright, but then it will take time and men to do it'.[28] On information being supplied to the British military by ordinary civilians, Lynch wondered if 'we rigidly put in force that none of the civil population speak or communicate with them, it will break up their all-important Intelligence Department'. In his reply, on 26 March, Mulcahy promised to have the proposed poisoning of cavalry horses looked into. However, with 'regard to enemy supplies ... Don't do anything exceptional ... until you hear further from me. An opportune moment will probably turn up in the very near future for a widespread move on these lines.'[29]

A false rumour that was to endure from this period was that Lynch had died after suffering wounds during an IRA action at Milford near Liscarroll. Elements of British intelligence and the military seemed to believe the rumour right up until the handover of army barracks in early 1922.[30]

✱✱✱

Despite the earlier rejection of the suggestion of combined action by the southern brigades, the attitude of Mulcahy and GHQ now began to shift. In the face of British raids and military successes, Mulcahy understood the appeal of further decentralising the IRA by forming brigades into divisions. He later explained that the 'idea was that they could get on if they were driven to get on without us [IRA GHQ]'.[31] On 8 March, when replying to Lynch on other matters, Mulcahy wrote, 'we [are] sending a HQ representative to the south ... it has appeared for us for some time that it is necessary to create a Divisional Command in the south for the area'. He summed up his reasoning by stating that it was 'quite impossible to co-ordinate the work of the Brigades in that area from here and it is absolutely necessary the work be co-ordinated'. He closed with a proposal that would have immediately caught Lynch's eye: 'it is my idea that you will be appointed Divisional Officer in charge of the area with instructions to co-ordinate the work and to develop the Divisional Staff ... I want you to think over this matter and if you have any definite thing to say on it, I shall be glad to hear from you.'[32]

And yet, as with previous offers of greater military command, Lynch felt compelled to turn down his chief of staff immediately. Writing to Mulcahy on 12 March, he laid out the reasoning for his reluctance to assume this new role:

I hope you that you will not insist I should take over such an important command. This means being responsible for the war and I consider myself far from being able to fill such a position. … I thoroughly know my own area now, realise it is my duty to remain if possible with the brave fighting men here and give them my assistance in every detail while the enemy leaves me to do so.[33]

Loyalty to those under his command and recognition that his success as brigade O/C depended on his familiarity with the north Cork area underpinned his reluctance to take on this position, as before. Yet, Lynch was otherwise highly amenable to the proposal of the formation of this new division and recognised the 'absolute necessity for this immediately'. Echoing familiar past concerns, and his meeting at the end of the previous year with Robinson, Lynch felt brigades 'are often hard pressed by the enemy, while neighbouring Brigades are listening to the guns and do nothing, often perhaps allowing enemy reinforcements pass through unmolested'.[34] This last point was a very serious charge to put to the IRA's chief of staff about neighbouring brigade O/Cs. Lynch went so far as to suggest that British forces were doing their utmost to 'try and squash' Cork No. 2 Brigade and reiterated again his concerns about the other brigades' inactivity: 'we have too many gunmen on active service while some of our adjacent Brigades are inactive'.[35] No doubt, the recent incidents at Nadd and Mourneabbey were still fresh in Lynch's mind.

It is not clear from the existing sources why Lynch changed his mind about the new position. He was formally appointed without protest as the O/C of the new First Southern Division the following month. However, a change in his position within the IRB in this same period may help to explain his shift in attitude. On 20 July 1920, Tom Hales, O/C of Cork No. 3 Brigade, was arrested within his brigade area by British forces. Hales also sat on the IRB Supreme Council due to his position as head of the South Munster IRB Division, which encompassed Cork, Kerry and Waterford. In mid-March, with Hales in prison, Lynch was offered the opportunity to act as head of the South Munster centre, which he accepted. With Lynch now in a much more influential position within the IRB, he had authority over all IRB members who held rank across many of the southern IRA brigades.[36] Thus, the idea of taking leadership in a parallel military role over the southern brigades, and thereby possibly influencing the course of the conflict, was no doubt irresistible to Lynch and suited the purposes of those such as Mulcahy and Collins who no doubt sought Lynch for this position. Even beyond the Truce in June, for the remainder of the year Lynch was reorganising the IRB within the South Munster Division and increasing membership.[37] John Joe Rice, then vice-commandant in Kerry No. 2 Brigade, believed the IRB Supreme Council thought it could easily influence Lynch. Rice was later impressed, in light of events at the end of 1921, that that was not the case.[38]

On 13 April, Mulcahy wrote to Lynch, and formally informed him he had been appointed Divisional Commandant of the First Southern Division. He instructed Lynch to form a divisional staff 'at the earliest possible moment compatible with you being in a position to know and select the best possible officers'.[39] Lynch was to submit the names of the proposed officers to GHQ for ratification, to include a vice-commandant, adjutant, quartermaster, engineer and intelligence officer. Mulcahy also informed Lynch that further divisional commands north (four) and south (two) were being created. The brigades under Lynch's new division included all three Cork brigades, all three Kerry brigades, both Waterford brigades and Limerick West Brigade, comprising just a little under 31,000 members in total.[40]

Thereafter, Mulcahy instructed O'Malley to organise a meeting of all relevant brigade officers in North Cork, announce the formation of the new First Southern Division and appoint Lynch as the divisional commandant. Ahead of the meeting, Lynch and some of the Cork No. 2 staff met O'Malley on Claragh Mountain near Millstreet. O'Malley had recently escaped from Kilmainham Gaol, and Lynch presented him with a gift on their meeting: a photograph of O'Malley issued by the British authorities. Lynch remarked to him, 'I must say you look a murdering tough.' He then filled his comrade in on recent developments involving the brigade.[41]

The meeting on the formation of the division and Lynch's appointment took place on 24 March, at a hidden location at Kippagh within the Cork No. 2 Brigade area. For some, it did not have an auspicious start. Tom Barry, the celebrated O/C of Cork No. 3 flying column, felt it began on a rather 'depressed note', given that representatives of only five of the nine brigades chose to attend. O'Malley, who presided at the meeting, read out at length a document issued by GHQ detailing the reasoning behind the formation of the division, which raised the ire of both Barry and the much-esteemed O/C of Cork No. 1, Seán O'Hegarty. Both men rounded on O'Malley as the GHQ representative, with O'Hegarty delivering 'ten minutes of a telling and hard-hitting talk' related to his own complaints about GHQ, particularly with regard to the lack of fighting in inactive areas and the supply of arms.[42] While O'Malley privately agreed with O'Hegarty's issues over arms, he noted that Lynch 'was getting annoyed' at the intervention.[43] After O'Hegarty spoke, Lynch was formally appointed O/C of the First Southern Division.[44]

For some, this initial conference or those thereafter would be the first time they encountered Lynch during the conflict, although his reputation already preceded him among his contemporaries. Con Casey recalled his first encounter with him, at the division-formation meeting. He was 'very impressed with Lynch. You know his appearance, priestly and ascetic … At the same time, he was a strong disciplinarian.'[45] P.J. Paul, O/C of the East Waterford Brigade, too, 'was very impressed by Liam Lynch … He seemed to be very sincere, very earnest and to have all the qualities of leadership.'[46] Despite being dissatisfied with the division-formation meeting, Barry admitted he was already impressed with Lynch's reputation before their first meeting at the March conference: 'He was a terrific worker, and never seemed to relax, day or night, from his military duties.' Barry was, however, left with the impression that Lynch was stubborn and not receptive to new ideas, but admitted that he shared this characteristic with many leading IRA officers, including Barry himself. (Of note, this is a departure from those who emphasised Lynch's collaborative nature in the earlier phase of the conflict.) Barry also picked up on something of Lynch's social awkwardness and felt he was 'not very fluent in discussion, and when angry or excited, would stutter slightly'. Yet, Barry recognised him as 'a man of the highest personal standards' and an ideal choice for the new divisional O/C.[47] With this new position and his seat on the IRB Supreme Council, Lynch was now the most influential IRA leader outside GHQ – a testament to the respect and esteem felt for him in the IRA.

Despite this, Lynch immediately ran into difficulties when trying to create a divisional staff, due to the initial reluctance of brigade O/Cs to let go of some of their officers.[48] In the end, though, Ernie O'Malley recalled that all the O/Cs ultimately co-operated despite complaints about losing some of their best men.[49] The new First Southern Division staff included Florence O'Donoghue (formerly Cork No. 1 intelligence officer) as divisional adjutant, Joseph O'Connor (formerly quartermaster of Cork No. 1 Brigade) as quartermaster and Patrick Coughlan as divisional engineer. Further appointments followed in July, with Liam Deasy (formerly O/C of Cork No. 3) as vice-divisional O/C and Tom Barry of Cork No. 3 Brigade as divisional training officer.[50] O'Donoghue, in his biography of Lynch, recalled how he had 'known Liam since 1917. Now I came into continuous and more intimate contact with him on being appointed adjutant to the division.'[51] O'Donoghue's time working with Lynch was to last a little over a year, but his O/C was to make a considerable impression on him that was to last for the remainder of O'Donoghue's life.

George Power was put forward as a possible replacement for Lynch as commander of Cork No. 2 Brigade. Power, however, argued that he was too inexperienced for the role, so, after some discussion, it was suggested that Seán Moylan of the Newmarket Battalion should take over command. Moylan was an obvious candidate, having recently overseen two rare successes for the Brigade: an ambush at Tureengarriffe (28 January), then another at Clonbanin (5 March). Power was ultimately to take over as brigade O/C when Moylan was captured on an enemy raid and imprisoned in Cork's Spike Island a little under a month later.[52]

On 1 May, Lynch wrote to Mulcahy in his first communication to the chief of staff as commander of First Southern Division. Apologising for the delay in replying to several communications, Lynch hinted at how much his agonising over his decision seemed to distract him: 'Delay in replying to the several matters mentioned owing to I not fully made up my mind as to Divisional Command. I now thank you for appointing me to such a Command which I will do my utmost to fill.'[53] In reflection of his usual due diligence as a military commander, Lynch informed Mulcahy of his intention to visit all brigades within the divisional area as soon as possible, and then 'go into calibre and working of each in detail and issue such Orders as may be required'. On 5 May, in a communication mostly concerned with general suggestions for the new divisional command, Mulcahy wanted to 'wish you the greatest of success and good luck in your new command'. Mulcahy again demonstrated the esteem in which he held Lynch: 'I cannot tell you how grateful I am, personally, for the way in which you are thus shouldering what I know is a very great burden. I am fully alive to the responsibility on us here to help you in every way, and we are giving a considerable amount of thought by the means best we can do it.'[54]

Not long after the division's formation, Lynch asked Jamie Moynihan, attached to the Cork No. 1 Brigade, to identify a suitable house in which to set up an HQ in the Baile Mhúirne district, a central point of the division. Moynihan recommended a safe farmhouse in Gortyrahilly. In his memoir, he claimed the parish of Baile Mhúirne was one of the safest in Cork following the Cúil na Cathrach ambush on 25 February.[55] Given its centrality in the divisional area, and with little movement of British forces through there, it was the ideal location. Moynihan noted how 'Lynch immediately undertook responsibility for the administrative and supply problems for this huge Volunteer force, which meant the involvement of lorry drivers, railway workers, travellers, shop workers, public house and post office workers, not to mention many others who could help in getting dispatches to their destinations.' Lynch, as always, recognised that a strong intelligence network was key to any IRA success – and under his new command, such a network was to be on a grander scale beyond the familiar confines of the brigade area of North Cork. Maurice Walsh from Mitchelstown was Lynch's principal staff officer, and Moynihan recalled how from divisional HQ in Gortyrahilly both Walsh and Lynch 'put in motion an intricate system to co-ordinate what was happening in the different brigade areas' – this including keeping written orders to a minimum and in code.

Lynch was keen to familiarise himself with the entire divisional command and, as he had promised Mulcahy, made a point to visit all the brigade areas immediately as his first task. Over a number of weeks, Lynch, along with O'Donoghue, travelled by horseback, pony and trap, and even by boat (across the Rivers Lee and Blackwater), to meet the various battalions and commandants. Lynch reviewed every detail he could in terms of each area's security, intelligence network, training and general organisation – and issued orders for any changes and improvements he saw as necessary.[56] As Moynihan observed, in these months before the Truce, 'Lynch's life … was an endless labour of planning, organising and inspection of brigades'.[57]

One such plan, which may perhaps have been easier in earlier times of conflict, had to be abandoned. Around summer, a proposal for the establishment of a divisional training camp was dropped on the advice of Tom Barry. Barry felt it would be dangerous to have so many senior officers in one place and that it could jeopardise the fighting in the south-west of Ireland should the camp be discovered and the entire leadership captured.[58]

* * *

Throughout the duration of the War of Independence, country mansions and rural 'big houses', often belonging to members of the unionist Protestant ascendancy, became a target for the IRA. Attacks initially took the form of raids for arms and ammunition, since the IRA recognised that shooting was one of the favourite leisure pursuits of the aristocracy.[59] However, from the spring of 1920, these houses and mansions also became targets in counter-reprisals and, hence, faced total destruction by the IRA, particularly as the violence began to heighten in early 1921. In his study of attacks on these structures in the period, Terence Dooley has written how, for the IRA, 'country houses were regarded as highly politicised targets because of the loyalism of their owners, who openly proclaimed same'.[60] Over the course of the period, over a hundred such buildings were destroyed across Ireland.[61]

In April, not long after becoming First Southern Division O/C, Lynch issued orders in response to British reprisals involving the destruction of ten houses of republican supporters and allies across the north Cork area.[62] On receiving word of these reprisals, O'Malley remembered how Lynch's eyes 'blackened with rage' and he said, 'I'll bloody well settle that; six big houses and castles of their friends, the imperialists, will go up for this. I don't know what GHQ will do – but I don't give a damn.' Lynch and O'Malley then selected six targets and issued the relevant orders for these counter-reprisal actions to the battalion O/Cs in their respective areas.[63]

Lynch's comment to O'Malley on potentially defying IRA GHQ in issuing such an order was particularly striking, but was indicative of Lynch's greater confidence in acting on his own accord. From this juncture, one can see a notable shift in tone in his correspondence with Mulcahy, with Lynch now more forceful in putting forward his own suggestions as to IRA conduct during the conflict and in his commentary on other matters, such as the taking and shooting dead of hostages held by the IRA.

In April 1921, IRA GHQ issued an order concerning the shooting dead of suspected spies: 'communication to the Enemy of information concerning the work ... of the Republic is an offence ... and in the ultimate is punishable by death'.[64] Over the course of the conflict, the IRA would shoot 180 civilians as 'spies and informers', mostly across the brigade areas of Cork, especially that of Cork No. 1. At the time, this led to fears within IRA GHQ that some of the executions of suspected spies were based on flimsy evidence.[65] In the historical writing since, there have been accusations of religious sectarianism by the IRA towards the Irish Protestant community during this period as a motive in such incidents. For example, historian Peter Hart has suggested the IRA deliberately targeted members of the Protestant community as 'in their view Protestant unionists were traitors'.[66] Others, such as John Dorney, have pointed out that Irish republicanism as an ideology was non-sectarian, and the revolutionary movement itself included several prominent members of the Protestant faith. Inevitably, those loyal to the British crown (and hence, informers) tended mostly to be Protestants within the unionist minority, but Dorney has also noted the sectarianism prevalent in Ulster during the conflict and in isolated incidents elsewhere involving the IRA, including in Cork.[67]

In terms of Lynch's views on members of the Irish unionist community, on 4 May he wrote to Mulcahy with a particularly dramatic suggestion, which is indicative of his emboldened confidence in his role as divisional O/C. Lynch suggested that, in future, the IRA should shoot a local loyalist for each republican prisoner executed in the divisional area: 'It is proposed to notify the loyalists to this effect, and by doing so we hope to get them to prevent the enemy from shooting our prisoners.'[68] Lynch explained his reasoning here was 'in view of the fact that in the Cork No. 2 Brigade area, where the enemy burned houses as a reprisal, we burned loyalist houses as a counter reprisal, with the result that the local loyalists approached the enemy authorities immediately asking them for God's sake to stop the reprisals'. Hence, in terms of Lynch's cold logic, the shooting dead of loyalists in the area would result in other loyalists doing 'their best to have the shooting of our prisoners stopped in order to save themselves'.

On 7 May, Mulcahy replied to Lynch, and urged him to 'hold your hand until you hear further in this matter from me.'[69] Perhaps fearful of the impact of any British response, given IRA GHQ was then involved in plotting the burning of Dublin's Custom House on 25 May, Mulcahy explained that there was a 'possibility that it might be thought inadvisable to have any definite change of policy in this matter appear within the next fortnight or three weeks'. Furthermore, he expressed scepticism as to what 'exactly has been the result, as far as you can see, of the approaches made by local loyalists to the Enemy authorities with a view to getting them to stop reprisals against property. It does not seem to me that it has had any results'.

On 10 June, Lynch sent an emotive response, pushing back on Mulcahy's reluctance and determined to get the chief of staff to see the merit in his proposal:

We higher officers are expected to lead the rank and file and I for one look to GHQ and the Government for definite action in this matter. If the enemy continue shooting our prisoners then we should shoot theirs all round and they should be told so. If a day is fixed for such an action and the whole Army act together from that [day] forward, I am sure the enemy will quickly change its policy.

All lives must be considered sacred and indeed, we would all wish to be chivalrous but when the enemy continue such an outrage, let it be a barbarous war all round. Anyhow, whatever action is taken, let it be Official and working all round if possible.[70]

On 5 July, Lynch wrote to Mulcahy and claimed success by way of house burnings and shooting of spies, and thus, 'with the enemy ... tired of the game as they have more or less stopped official executions, they have realised that they have lost far more than us within that period'.[71] He claimed these actions had demoralised British forces across the divisional area, 'while on the other hand it has only steeled our rank and file to increased action'. Lynch pointed out that British forces 'now seem to have adopted torture and urgent execution in place of official sanction'. He requested advice from Mulcahy on reprisal killings of hostages held by various brigades and slightly rebuked his chief of staff on the recent peace negotiations, which he seemed informed on: 'You may like to hold your hand until this peace move is over, but peace during executions seems ridiculous. Hostages should not be held any longer if we are not to use them when a case arises.' In any event, the onset of the Truce in July halted the need for Mulcahy to make a final decision on their back-and-forth on this matter.[72]

Despite this, two days after the Truce, Lynch sent two reports to Mulcahy on the murders of two Volunteers and seemed keen to revive the idea of reprisal killings if war broke out again: 'This deserves the drastic action suggested by me to you ... Percival and his Essexes being a regular murder gang deserve no quarter and shall get none.'[73]

One case of reprisal killings that remains controversial to this day is the shooting dead of Mrs Mary Lindsay, a unionist landowner, and her chauffeur, James Clarke (himself an Ulster Protestant), whilst held in captivity by members of the Cork No. 3 Brigade. Lindsay had been identified as someone who passed information to the British military authorities about the planned Dripsey ambush on 28 January 1921. On a road between Dripsey and Coachford, an IRA ambush party were surrounded by the British Army and a number of them were wounded and captured. Lindsay and Clarke were kidnapped by the IRA and held hostage until the execution of five of the IRA Volunteers involved in Dripsey, and then the two were summarily executed and buried in a hidden location sometime in mid-March. On 12 July, Mulcahy wrote to Lynch and included a copy of a letter from a sister of Mrs Lindsay requesting information. Mulcahy reminded Lynch that an order had been issued for Mrs Lindsay's release on 9 July but, having noted that she was dead, Mulcahy requested an 'early report of the circumstances concerned with her demise'.[74] In Mulcahy's own papers, there is no copy of a reply to his request, so Lynch's thoughts on the matter, which occurred before he became O/C of the First Southern Division and gained command over Cork No. 3 Brigade, remain unclear. The previous November, while still O/C of Cork No. 2 Brigade, Lynch had issued an order related to the discovery of female spies, and its contents reveal how the tenor of conflict changed in only a few short months. If found guilty, Lynch advised that instead of execution, the women involved should be 'ordered to leave the country within seven days … only consideration of her sex prevents the infliction of the statutory punishment of death'.[75] To date, it has been determined that three women were shot dead as accused spies by the IRA over the course of the War of Independence.

✶✶✶

In these weeks, the political wing of the revolutionary movement was preparing for the British general election to be held on 24 May 1921. These were to be the first elections held following the passage of the Government of Ireland Act, and within Ireland they were elections for the new parliaments of Northern and Southern Ireland.

Though Dáil Éireann did not recognise partition, nonetheless the election would again be used to demonstrate its considerable electoral mandate among the population. All 128 candidates in the new jurisdiction of 'Southern Ireland' were returned unopposed, with 124 seats won by Sinn Féin (and four by unionists representing Trinity College). The candidates put forward by Sinn Féin included prominent IRA officers such as Seán Moylan, Seán Mac Eoin and Eoin O'Duffy. Surely an esteemed commander such as Liam Lynch should have been among them?

In fact, Lynch was under consideration to be put forward. Around late April, or early May, an East Cork Sinn Féin Commission was held to select another Dáil candidate to contest the forthcoming general election alongside the two existing TDs, Tom Hunter and David Kent. Lynch had in fact been the third selected election candidate, subject to him providing word of his acceptance of the nomination. When no acceptance arrived, a majority on the commission put forward Séamus Fitzgerald, then involved in the local Dáil courts, instead. Fitzgerald was subsequently elected. Lynch later told Fitzgerald he never received any request to stand, 'but was quite satisfied' that Fitzgerald had been elected.[76] In contrast, Liam Manahan, a Sinn Féin organiser, remembered that Lynch refused outright to be put forward – his own personal preference would have been for Lynch to run.[77]

Lynch's disinterest in participating as a candidate reflected his continued lack of regard for the political side of the revolutionary movement.

***

Inevitably, tensions arose across Lynch's new divisional command over various issues, especially with those from neighbouring brigades to Cork No. 2 who were not used to his style of command. In late April, Lynch proposed a restructuring of the command of the three Kerry brigades, which was to include the appointment of new commanders to each. He was particularly aggrieved at the command of Kerry No. 2 by Paddy Cahill (who did not even regularly attend divisional meetings). An additional proposal of Lynch's partly involved splitting up the Sixth Battalion area of Kerry No. 2 Brigade and moving two company areas – Glencar and Glenbeigh – into that of Kerry No. 3. The meeting in which Lynch put his proposals forward took place at Brackhill, a townland in Kerry. Dan Mulvihill, an IRA Volunteer whose home was the site of the meeting, gave an amusing anecdote of the lengths taken to disguise Lynch, a 'wanted man', on his way to the meeting: 'Liam got the pants and coat of a brother of mine. I can still see him holding the pants under his armpits.' Nonetheless, despite this comical scene, the discussion that ensued at the meeting was described as 'explosive'.[78]

Seán Scully, vice O/C of the Sixth Battalion of Kerry No. 2, was particularly aggrieved at the proposed deposing of Cahill and told Lynch at the meeting that he 'felt that it was no time for new experiments in organisation and thought that Cahill was making a good job of things'. Scully asked Lynch why Cahill was being replaced. In a demonstration of his impatience over the matter, Lynch got suddenly 'very angry' at Scully's query and snapped, 'It is an order.'[79]

After the meeting, in frustration at the exchange, Scully tendered his resignation as vice O/C to Lynch in objection to the breaking up of the battalion. He was told afterwards that Lynch regretted the incident at the meeting, had ordered that Scully's resignation was not to be accepted and ultimately left the entire Sixth Battalion intact under Kerry No. 2. Decades later, Scully discussed with Cahill the purposes of this meeting, and Cahill's explanation indicated the complexities between the IRA and IRB in 1921. Cahill, who in 1921 was head centre of the IRB in Kerry, claimed that Lynch was following a policy – directed by IRA GHQ – to take all IRA brigades out of IRB centres' control. However, in his witness statement to the Bureau of Military History, Scully admitted he was unable to make sense of Cahill's statement, as more members of the brigade were sworn into the IRB after the Truce, not to mention the fact that the IRB Supreme Council, on which Lynch sat, later accepted the Anglo-Irish Treaty.[80]

One aspect that has dominated discussion of the closing weeks of the War of Independence is the level of arms and ammunition which the

IRA held at this point. One intriguing historical controversy that arose three decades later was Lynch's part in conveying the perception to IRA GHQ that the IRA would soon run out of arms and ammunition. Lynch had long held concerns about the lack of ordnance while O/C of Cork No. 2 Brigade. On 8 March 1921, in a comment labelled 'private' at the end of a message, Lynch wrote to Collins of the worryingly low supply of ammunition and arms within the brigade: 'Will soon be in a bad way for .303 as we have been in hard luck for capture of same recently. Please say a few words in the matter, also a few rifles at once ... about 1000 rounds ... will be appreciated.'[81] On 15 March, Collins assured Lynch, 'With reference to the little note you sent me regarding shortage of a certain commodity ... if it can be done it will be done ... within a very short time.'[82]

Of bitter disappointment to Lynch was the collapse of a deal to import arms from Italy in early May. This had been in development since January, with Lynch involved in various GHQ and southern conferences on the matter in his capacity as brigade, and later divisional, O/C. The plan was so far along that a number of landing and distribution points for arms and ammunition had already been determined across several of the southern brigades.[83]

In 1926, in the first published (not to mention state-sanctioned) biography of Michael Collins, Piaras Béaslaí briefly referred to the fact that: 'at this time [in May] ... Liam Lynch, and other Southern IRA officers, went on a deputation to GHQ, in Dublin, to state that, owning to the shortage of arms and ammunition, and enemy pressure, they were unable to continue the fight'.[84] Béaslaí's remark, which does not cite any documentation in reference to this, was controversial, although Béaslaí himself may be considered an authority, given he was the IRA's director of publicity at the time. In his memoir, Tom Barry was dismissive of the statement, and claimed not only that no such deputation took place in May but also that Lynch never visited Dublin between April and the Truce in early July.[85] Florence O'Donoghue also disagreed strongly with Béaslaí, not only through his own research on the matter but also because he had no personal recollection of this, despite working closely with Lynch in the IRA at this time. O'Donoghue was so determined to settle the matter in his biography of Lynch that he published in full a letter from Béaslaí on the disputed statement. Béaslaí informed O'Donoghue he made the statement on Lynch in his biography of Michael Collins 'in good faith' and added he was 'not in a position, nor have I any desire, to contradict' O'Donoghue's views, saying O'Donoghue was in a 'better position' to get to the truth. Béaslaí assured O'Donoghue he had 'no desire to disparage Liam Lynch or anybody else' and pointed to the aforementioned March correspondence between Lynch and Collins to show arms worries were a genuine concern of brigades in 1921.[86] This author shares O'Donoghue's view that such a visit by Lynch to IRA GHQ in May to convey such arms and ammunition supply issues did not occur.

John Dorney has written that whether by mid-1921 the IRA could have 'broken British will or been crushed remains a contentious issue'. He has pointed to a captured report of May 1921 highlighting the overall weakness of the IRA, which was down to 2,000 active fighters in the field, who held 569 rifles and 477 revolvers, with only twenty rounds per weapon. Nonetheless, considerable efforts continued to import new weaponry, such as a batch of Thompson machine guns that arrived in Ireland in July. While the IRA faced ongoing obstacles, its resolve had not diminished and the prospect of a long fight ahead for its members endured in the summer of 1921.[87]

***

On 10 July, at Dromhane, Lynch presided over a brigade council meeting of Cork No. 2 in his capacity as divisional commander. At this meeting, Lynch announced he had decided that the existing Cork No. 2 Brigade had become too unwieldy, and so a new brigade would be established. Paddy O'Brien, from Liscarroll, was to head this new brigade as O/C.[88] What would be designated Cork No. 4 Brigade would include the Mallow, Millstreet, Newmarket, Kanturk and Charleville battalions. With Waterford No. 1 (West Waterford) and No. 2 (Waterford City) brigades now merged into one, the Lismore Battalion of Waterford No. 1 was absorbed into Cork No. 2 Brigade. The new Cork No. 2 consisted of the Fermoy, Lismore, Castletownroche and Glanworth battalions. George Power retained the position of brigade O/C.[89] In a communication the previous month, Lynch had explained to Mulcahy that his old command, Cork No. 2, was 'far from being compact and owing to numbers and activity of enemy, communications are causing serious trouble'. Lynch was well aware of the talent and capabilities of those within the brigade area and felt these two Cork brigades could now 'be very much intact and officers can be got from for both staffs ...'[90] The actual division of Cork No. 2 officially took effect a week after the July meeting.[91] Yet, a far more important development was to occur on the very same day of the brigade council meeting.

At some point on 10 July, while at divisional HQ, Lynch received an order to implement the ceasefire from 11 July in the area overseen by the First Southern Division.[92] The order, signed by Mulcahy, and distributed to all IRA commanders, read in part, 'In view of the conversations now being entered into by our government, with the government of Great Britain, and in pursuance of mutual understandings to suspend hostilities during these conversations, active operations by our troops will be suspended as from noon on Monday, 11th July.'[93]

The Truce that was to end the Irish War of Independence was the result of infrequent contacts since the end of 1920 between intermediaries representing the British government and the Irish revolutionary movement. By the time it was agreed, the British had realised that unless more extreme measures were taken they had arrived at a military stalemate with the enemy, not to mention having to contend with a critical press both at home and abroad. Among the terms of the Truce was the cessation of all military activities by both the IRA and the British military while more serious negotiations were pursued at a political level. All executions and arrests of IRA members and those involved in the revolutionary movement would cease, and the IRA would not have to surrender arms. As Pádraig Óg Ó Ruairc has written in his forensic survey of the Truce, its terms 'were far more favourable to the IRA than ... the British government ... and this represented a significant gain for the Irish republicans.'[94]

The closest to a first-hand account of Lynch's immediate thoughts on the Truce was Moss Twomey's mention of Lynch accepting the Truce in the spirit of it being 'a breathing space' and 'an opportunity to perfect organisation and training'. Twomey felt the Truce came like a 'bolt from the blue', as no effort was made to prepare the IRA for the cessation of fighting.[95]

Two days after it came into effect, Lynch departed Gortyrahilly to return to the family homestead in Barnagurraha. Before his departure, he told Jamie Moynihan he was delighted to be able to visit his parents and family in safety with no military conflict in the near future. The prospect of a pending marriage to Bridie Keyes was also on Lynch's mind. In his memoir, Moynihan wrote that Lynch's 'sincere hope was for a final settlement so that his days "on the run" would come to an end and Bridie and himself could at last settle down and have a future together. Sadly, he did not live to realise that dream and ambition.'[96]

Chapter 6

'Thank God I am left alive to still help in shattering the damned British Empire' (August 1921–March 1922)

ON 11 JULY, LIAM LYNCH had the First Southern Division HQ transferred to Glantane village, south-west of Mallow, given it was more central to his overall command. This move, likely planned before the Truce, demonstrated that a lull in the fighting would not prevent Lynch from maintaining high standards in his division, and he was determined to see this reflected throughout the command structure. Lynch issued orders for the formation of camps, which would entail a week's intensive training overseen by staff officers.[1] Moss Twomey remembered how Lynch 'took literally the opportunity the truce afforded to perfect Volunteer training and organisation and general efficiency'. Twomey observed how 'Lynch directed and took the keenest interest' in this. He took very few holidays and had little free time.[2] Liam Deasy, in his memoir, wrote that the Truce brought 'no relaxation to Lynch, much less any kind of celebration. His one concern was how long it might last so that he could improve and enlarge the existing units and be ready for the continuation of the war which seemed to him quite inevitable.' Lynch indicated to Deasy that he felt this respite from fighting would only last three to four weeks and from then on operated under the assumption that some six months of training had to be accomplished in this time frame. Deasy saw how in this period 'Lynch drove himself relentlessly and expected a similar dedication from his staff', which Deasy felt 'they more than fulfilled' along with 'their full and local co-operation'.[3]

Three weeks after the Truce, Joe O'Connor, the divisional quarter-master, had a vacant house in Glantage fitted out to the standard of a divisional headquarters. Deasy recalled how the house quickly saw 'a constant stream of communications ... dispatched and received. Visiting officers were calling frequently with reports or for further orders.' The only break in the flurry of clerical activity all week, was when Lynch would call a halt on Sunday and suggest a walk in the countryside to those present. Sometimes, too, Lynch, Deasy and others would travel by train or car to brigade council meetings or carry out inspections of various battalions within the divisional area.[4]

Lynch was to be continually preoccupied with discipline among the troops in the relative peace of the closing months of 1921. In a communication to Mulcahy, he demanded action by the Dáil over the 'demoralising and poisoning' of his Volunteers by their consumption of drink, by way of the illegal brewing of poteen. Reports of excessive drinking by IRA members across the country in this period regularly reached members of the Dáil cabinet and IRA GHQ.[5]

***

Despite what he may have inferred to Jamie Moynihan on the news of the Truce, Lynch's trips home remained infrequent. On 22 July, he wrote to his mother from divisional HQ in one of his few surviving letters to her. He acknowledged the previous rumour of his death and that three months had passed since his last communication to her, but was 'indeed surprised when I heard from Tom as to your fear of me, I all the time thought you were aware of my safety ... The last letter wrote to you ... I did indeed think it would be last as enemy ... often close on my trail.' Lynch assured her of his well-being: 'Thank God I am left alive to still help in shattering the damned British Empire. I am living only to bring the dreams of my dead comrades to reality and every hour of my life to now is entirely devoted to same.'[6]

Despite the changed military situation, Lynch felt that 'even though Truce is on we are still at high pressure'. He observed that through 'the war I have got to understand so much of the human being when peace comes I would wish for nothing more than hide myself away from all the people that know me or even follow my dead comrades'. Bidding his mother farewell, he closed with: 'I do hope to see you and all the lads before hostilities resume but same is doubtful.' He was not alone in anticipating the resumption of military conflict.

Yet not long after this letter, Lynch managed his first trip home since the Truce. On Saturday 6 August, Michael O'Connell, a Volunteer of Cork No. 2 Brigade, had a chance encounter with Lynch on the railway platform in Lombardstown. O'Connell had a personal connection to his divisional commander. His family home in Lombardstown was where General Lucas had been held on his first night, and the funeral of his brother Liam in late 1920 had been one of the few occasions when Lynch spoke in public. O'Connell later wrote a detailed account of his meeting with Lynch, which is informative as to the latter's mindset after the then-recent political developments.

On boarding the train, the two men talked until they reached Mitchelstown. There, Lynch persuaded O'Connell to go for a drink in a saloon bar in the town. At the bar, Lynch explained that he was on his way to his family homestead in Barnagurraha, and asked O'Connell to accompany him as a bodyguard. O'Connell seemed confused by the request and asked Lynch if he was sure of the necessity. Lynch replied in the affirmative and asked O'Connell if he was armed.

Staying at a location in Mitchelstown, Lynch left O'Connell for a few hours to visit Bridie Keyes. The following morning, both received a lift to Anglesboro church in time for Mass. After Mass, O'Connell was introduced to members of Lynch's family, including his mother, Mary. The Lynch matriarch noticed O'Connell's black armband. 'Did you, too, lose somebody in the fight for Irish freedom?' O'Connell told Mary of his brother's death in Dublin, to which she replied, 'it was a terrible time for all of us' and referred to the Providence of God. O'Connell then accompanied Lynch on a visit to the home of his uncle John Lynch, the old Fenian, in Kildorrery. He was struck by the resemblance between uncle and nephew. Following this, the two returned to Mitchelstown that evening.

As they settled in for the night, O'Connell asked Lynch how he felt 'things were likely to work out' in reference to the Truce and the possibility of the resumption of conflict. 'The politicians will defeat us', Lynch replied. O'Connell was surprised by such a blanket statement in reference to all politicians within the revolutionary movement. He asked Lynch 'what authority the politicians could possibly have, seeing that the army was making the fight' – his comment completely sidestepping the idea that the Dáil held nominal authority over the IRA. Lynch seemed to pick up on this, explaining, 'that was not the way it would be; that the army would be subservient to the representatives of the people'. Lynch added 'it would be for the people to decide'.[7]

Paddy O'Brien felt that Lynch's tendency to rarely relax during the Truce was due to him not having 'much faith in the politicians'. Lynch said to O'Brien on one occasion, 'I am afraid they [the politicians] are not strong enough and there is the danger that they will let the country down.'[8]

If this is to be taken as a true snapshot of Lynch's political thinking in the initial weeks of the Truce, events in the months ahead were almost certainly to do little to shift his attitude towards those involved in Sinn Féin and Dáil Éireann.

✳ ✳ ✳

The Truce-period IRA faced an array of challenges during this relative peacetime. Chief among these were accusations and counter-accusations between the IRA and British military that the other side was violating the terms of the Truce. Within Lynch's divisional area, the British disputed the idea that they had to recognise IRA liaison officers in a part of the country that was still under martial law.[9] Writing to Mulcahy on 19 July,

Lynch complained that the British 6th Division's 17th Brigade did 'not recognise our liaison officers as army officers'. Lynch was also disturbed that the 17th Brigade still insisted on carrying out training and route marches; one march had taken place the previous day from Cork city. For Lynch, it was 'a very serious matter for us if hostilities again commence … under no circumstances should we allow [the enemy to train] outside their barracks'.[10] On 22 July, Mulcahy replied to Lynch and assured him that the issue of recognition of their liaison officers had been resolved, but enemy training 'cannot be interfered with by us'. If any of the 'training operations are regarded as provocative', it would be formally dealt with between GHQ and the British.[11]

During this time, there was a temporary breakdown in the relationship between Lynch and one of his divisional staff, Tom Barry, over the latter's position as IRA liaison officer to the British in Cork. Barry accused Lynch of not being satisfied with his work in attempting to address the difficulties with the British, and he felt that neither man could work with the other. A bemused Lynch assured Barry that this was not the case, and Mulcahy backed Lynch to the hilt over the matter. Unbeknownst to Lynch, Barry resigned his liaison and First Southern Divisional positions because of the disagreement, before withdrawing the resignations. Mulcahy commented to Lynch that he felt Barry was the problem, due to his 'vanity' along with his 'petulant and childish' nature.[12]

Despite anticipating a resumption of war, Lynch admitted to some personal relief at the break in the fighting. In a letter to his brother Tom dated 22 August, something of a relaxed tone is reflected. Lynch told his brother of his 'hope this Truce will last some time as I am anxious to get a few more days at home'. President de Valera and Chief of Staff Mulcahy both visited, for a week and three days respectively; they were taken on a tour of the divisional area, and companies and columns were inspected. Lynch ensured both were taken to various ambush sites, surely a moment of great pride for him, particularly as this was Mulcahy's first visit to the area as IRA chief of staff.

Lynch regaled his brother with a story of an incident near Ballinhassig the previous week, in which the car he was travelling in was stopped by

Black and Tans accompanied by a district inspector. Lynch and his driver were taken to the station at Bandon, where Lynch 'demanded the right as an Irish Army officer to use my own transport without an enemy permit, as well as they do without our permits'.[13] Lynch was held in the station's cell from 6 p.m. to 1.30 a.m., when, after several phone calls including to Dublin Castle, he and his driver were eventually released. In an amusing passage, Lynch confessed to Tom of having 'enjoyed the time with the Tans and D.I. as the Truce feeling prevailed all round and we discussed the possibility of again meeting them face to face in a clash of arms'.

Lynch's expectation of a resumption of fighting was reflected in a communication to Mulcahy on 23 August, when he returned to a familiar worry – that of ammunition and arms: 'Can GHQ in a reasonable time make up for shortage of revolver ammunition, otherwise such activity cannot hope to go on. Grenades in plentiful supply will of course ease the situation ...'[14] (Though a breach of the Truce, IRA GHQ continued to import munitions until December 1921.)[15]

On 30 August, Liam wrote again to Tom of how it was 'now impossible for us to have a few days together at home, which I thought certainly would not be so ... All this week is taken up by an already heavy programme.' On his heavy workload, Lynch remarked 'I don't know how it is that I would not spare a few days off, but somehow I would consider it a National aim when there is work to be done.'[16]

Another of the Truce-period issues that arose was the flurry of labour activity across Ireland. Historian Conor Kostick has written that large swathes of Irish workers 'saw the Truce as an opportunity to raise their demands'. The British feared the rise of militant labour and the workers' seizure of factories in much of the country following the collapse of their authority, and one RIC county inspector was concerned enough to report, 'generally speaking the Truce is headed towards a sort of Soviet government'. Kostick has argued such fears were not without foundation and has pointed to a lengthy workers' occupation of a bakery mill in Bruree, County Limerick, beginning at the end of August 1921.[17] To Mulcahy's discomfort, the Truce period-IRA regularly had to engage with labour disputes and the resultant strike activity. Inevitably, as Maryann

Valiulis has pointed out, issues of class and nationalist outlook often arose with the IRA's involvement, with labour leaders frequently claiming the IRA were anti-union and anti-working class. The ITGWU went so far as to claim employers regularly used the 'IRA to protect their petty interests against their employees, under the pretence of safeguarding National interests'.[18]

On 13 October, Lynch forwarded a report to Mulcahy on a farm-labourer dispute in Cork, with his own additional comments. He addressed a major worry of GHQ that, despite the array of strikes, he himself did not 'see any danger of this "sporadic warfare" [labour activity]' and 'in my experience there is no ground for insinuation that employers and farmers' sons are using Army for their petty interests'. Overall, Lynch felt union organisers were 'antagonistic to Ireland's National demands … We cannot allow any civil organisation to interfere with Army especially at a time when enemy is making desperate efforts to crush us.' In Lynch's experience, 'certain organisers try to put Labour above Freedom, this may go on for some time'. Lynch felt most of the dispute could be settled 'if there is a body set up to arbitrate on same'.[19]

While it can be assumed the studious and well-read Lynch had a basic understanding of labour thinking and possibly Marxist literature, statements such as these reveal he held no overwhelming sympathy for ordinary workers in such strikes and disputes. Late 1921 was not the last time he would engage in such matters or make his views on them clear.

∗∗∗

While the IRA prepared for renewed conflict, the politicians on both sides focused on building towards some sort of settlement. In late July, at the request of David Lloyd George, de Valera met him at Downing Street in London in a series of discussions that would set up the parameters of the Treaty negotiations. Liam Deasy later admitted that he and his IRA contemporaries, including Lynch, only had a 'passing interest' in such political developments. At the time, their main purpose was 'building up our forces for some kind of confrontation that seemed inevitable'.[20] On 26

September, Lynch wrote to Tom, and responded to a joke in a previous letter where his younger brother had said the saints were looking out for him. In response, Lynch admitted, 'I don't know ... about that free pass from St. Patrick, my position looks well from outside'. Returning to what was becoming a recurring theme of his correspondence, Lynch felt 'were it not that I continually think of my dead comrades and the glorious cause we fight for it would be more than impossible sometimes to carry on'.[21]

Attempting to assuage any doubts his brother might have had about political developments, in Lynch's view, Tom:

> may rest assured that our Government as well as the Army is out for the Republic anything less ... we are and must be prepared to fight to the last for that. In justice to the yet unborn as well as to the dead past we have no other authority but to fight on, a fight thank God which never for generations seemed more hopeful than now ...[22]

Lynch admitted to Tom he was keen to socialise as much as possible, given a pending return to the fight, and hence, it was his 'intention to go to a Republican dance in Milltown on Saturday night, not for amusement but just to meet all the boys and perhaps girls ... I may have a poor chance of seeing them again'.[23] More than likely inferred in this is hope of an increasingly rare meeting with his fiancée, Bridie Keyes.

Not all Lynch's attempts to maintain discipline in his division ran smoothly. On 21 November, in response to an enquiry from IRA Adjutant General Gearóid O'Sullivan, Lynch complained that not everyone saw the necessity of maintaining company parades in various brigades, though 'in several Brigades in this Area such is the rule at present'. Lynch felt during the Truce that it was necessary 'that our companies have a half day for parade ... To develop the soldiery spirit and general efficiency and to hold the present necessary discipline'. He felt the parade schedule was frequently disrupted by a 'few employers who may not be too willing to give way on this matter'. Lynch suggested that O'Sullivan issue a memo defining parade times for a few hours on Sunday and one evening after dark, with officers to 'acquaint any necessary employers' as to this schedule.[24]

Around this time, de Valera, in his capacity as Dáil president, asked Minister for Defence Cathal Brugha for 'a list of things that the Sinn Féin Clubs might do to help your Department, the idea being to incorporate all into a circular to be sent out by Sinn Féin Headquarters to all Cumann'.[25] The question was asked of several divisional commanders, and Lynch issued a lengthy reply. It is a fascinating document and reveals much of Lynch's ideological thinking in the use he saw for the political wing of the Irish revolutionary movement and how he regarded it during the previous years. It also highlighted areas of war he regarded as crucial to improve on should conflict with the British soon resume.

Lynch felt that if war were to begin again, it could mean a dramatic new role for Sinn Féin activists: 'Sinn Féin Clubs could form a second line of resistance, and be at the same time a kind of Army Service Corps for the Army, organising … financial support … food supplies, billeting, clothing and boot supplies, general transport, care of sick and wounded'. He cited a surprising example from the recent global conflict: 'England during the world war is a striking example of what a mighty force the civil population is in wartime if organised on definite lines. They had all towns and villages doing their utmost assisting the various organisations.' Lynch concluded that without this assistance, 'the Empire would have gone down in the world war'.[26]

With considerable disdain, he concluded:

> We must admit that all civil organisations, County Councils, District Councils, Corporations, Urban Councils, Sinn Féin Clubs and all other organised bodies were an absolute failure during the last phase of hostilities, if [anything] they were a burden on the Army, why even the civil Government failed. Had there been a highly organised system the results would have been far more effective.[27]

Lynch was quick to praise the 'general spirit, morale and assistance given by population to Army', particularly during the last phase of the recent conflict, but felt it could have been more given 'a definite method of administration' – clearly in his view neither Dáil Éireann or Sinn Féin provided this from January 1919 to July 1921.

In the same document, Lynch also discoursed at length on making a considerable effort at 'striking the enemy at his strongest point – his army – therefore we should smash up all his [government] machinery ... harassed in every way and made impossible, when he cannot govern'.[28] This particular point is important to note in light of Lynch's tactical outlook during a prolonged phase of the Civil War, discussed later.

There is no evidence of a reply to Lynch's lengthy memorandum in the existing archive. Yet even a brief consideration of his assessment of Sinn Féin, republican political activists and the revolutionary movement's use of Dáil Éireann and the local bodies during the War of Independence (not to mention popular public support enjoyed by the Dáil) shows it is unduly harsh. However, this disdain and lack of appreciation for these political bodies was typical of leading IRA figures at this time, particularly for those like Lynch who had seen such success (often first-hand) as a guerrilla commander, and it seemed a logical trajectory from his earlier political thinking. There is no suggestion that by late 1921 the political work of Sinn Féin or the bodies of Dáil Éireann interested Lynch. There is something of his view in Todd Andrews' memoir of the period, who recalled that, as a young IRA Volunteer, 'I regarded the Dáil as merely an adjutant of the IRA, a weapon to help make [British] government impossible ... The Departments of the Dáil ... were to me mere ancillaries to the militant core of the Movement. My only aim was to break the connection with England. To do that I believed force was the only way.'[29]

✳ ✳ ✳

During the Truce, Lynch made increasingly frequent trips to Dublin and was a regular guest at Barry's Hotel on Gardiner Row, which would be used as a base for IRA officers in 1922. Annie Farrington, the then-owner, recalled of his frequent presence, 'Liam Lynch was a marvellous character and the other lads used to warn us not to say anything flippant before him, as he was very religious, and they looked upon him as a saint.'[30] Indeed, Barry's Hotel came to be considered such a regular home for Lynch in Dublin that, following his death, his mother visited the premises. Annie remembered, 'After Liam's death … his mother came to see us and wanted to find out everything we knew about Liam. She went to see the room he had occupied. She wanted to walk in his footsteps she said.'[31]

On 11 November, Lynch wrote to Tom in a buoyant mood, which suggested the break from military conflict was heartening for him. He admitted being 'delighted with my run home, especially with all the Limerick friends I met at Ballylanders races. Perhaps my welcome home depends on the Peace situation, but war or peace I am always the same.' He complimented Tom on the 'clear view you take of the Irish situation, you would do fairly well playing my game.'[32] As always, he valued his brother's counsel deeply.

That month would see Minister for Defence Cathal Brugha embark on an ambitious scheme for a reorganisation of the IRA. A decision was made at a cabinet meeting on 7 November that Brugha was 'to take steps to give immediate effect to … recommissioning of the Army'. New commissions were then to be offered to all IRA GHQ staff and divisional commanders. Mulcahy and those in GHQ were to receive the rank of commandant general, giving them the same rank as the divisional commanders, and all would be subordinate to Brugha in his ministerial capacity.[33] The reorganisation was something of a pet project for Brugha – the product of long-time tensions between his ministry and GHQ, and his often turbulent relationship with Mulcahy.[34]

Most divisional commandants accepted their new commissions, including Frank Aiken of the Fourth Northern Division, Michael Brennan of the First Western Division and Seán MacEoin of the First Midland Division. Dan Hogan, of the Fifth Northern Division, accepted only after consultation with Mulcahy.[35] Lynch did not give his answer to Brugha until early December – and it was an outright refusal:

> I feel that the Commander-in-Chief and his Staff cannot do their
> duty when they are not placed in a position to do so. I may have

the wrong views of the duties of a Commander-in-Chief and Minister for Defence, if so, I will put up with the result. I painfully realise the consequences of the present relations between Cabinet and GHQ Staff, therefore I cannot act blindly in the matter and be responsible for waging war in the most active area of Ireland. I hold GHQ responsible for directing general operation policy, at the present moment when war may be resumed at short notice ...[36]

Maryann Valiulis has pointed out that Lynch's reply demonstrated both support for Mulcahy's position and reluctance to tamper with a formula that, in the view of Lynch and other divisional commanders, had worked so well previously during the conflict.[37] A subsequent meeting on 25 November between GHQ and the Dáil cabinet did not conclusively solve the matter, but ultimately Brugha's scheme came to nothing – lost in the rancour over the subsequent divisions over the Treaty. Of note, the date of the communication in which Lynch gave his refusal was 6 December, the very same day the newspapers announced the signing of the Articles of Agreement between the British cabinet and the Sinn Féin delegation in London.

***

Since the Truce on 9 July, the IRB had become, in the view of one member, James Hogan, 'a rather remote, unreal and shadowy kind of organisation' to the ordinary members of the IRA. Indeed, even before the end of the conflict, Hogan observed, with the IRA 'taking the whole burden of the national fight on its back, it was absorbing and assimilating the IRB'.[38] Florence O'Donoghue, himself a member, wrote that although the IRB's activities during the War of Independence were 'nominal', the organisation was important in that 'it bound a group of men into a historic and respected brotherhood which evoked loyalty of the highest order' without undermining the IRA itself.[39] Events now propelled the organisation to the forefront of developments within the revolutionary movement, with Lynch a key player.

As the negotiations for a treaty with the British, which had started in October, continued apace, the plenipotentiaries appointed by the Dáil to go to London for talks, headed by Collins and Arthur Griffith, made occasional return visits to Ireland to brief de Valera and the rest of the cabinet. Collins, in his capacity as president of the IRB, was also keen to keep the IRB circles informed. During November, he attended a gathering of all IRB centres in Munster, which Lynch, O'Donoghue and Deasy attended in their respective capacities as divisional centre, Cork County centre and divisional secretary. It was at this meeting that Lynch was officially elected divisional centre in south Munster, having held the position temporarily since March.[40] Just prior to entering the meeting, Collins informed the three that 'there would have to be some sort of compromise in the current negotiations in London'. Digesting this, Lynch told Collins not to tell those at the meeting as it would 'blow up'. Deasy recalled that Collins did not do so and was 'enthusiastically welcomed' by the IRB delegates; no 'difficult questions' were introduced to the meeting. Later, in the throes of the Civil War, Deasy would often think back to that meeting and ponder what may have happened if Collins had ignored Lynch and told all present 'a Republic was not on the cards'.[41] O'Donoghue recalled that Collins promised to keep those present at the meeting updated on any developments.[42] It is intriguing that Lynch was conscious of how talk of a compromise could impact the republican faithful even at this early juncture, but he certainly underestimated how personally devastating he would find such a compromise when it came about.

On 3 December, during a recess of a pivotal Dáil cabinet meeting, Collins sent a copy of the proposed agreement between the Irish and British delegations to the IRB Supreme Council. Since his arrival in London, Collins had kept the Supreme Council, which included Lynch, updated on a week-to-week basis on the progress of the negotiations.[43] In his unpublished memoir, Seán Ó Muirthile referred to his dealings with members of the Supreme Council during these critical weeks. Late on 3 December, at the Gresham Hotel, ten of the fifteen members of the Supreme Council, including Lynch, were presented with the draft copy of the Treaty. (Collins was not present, then attending a cabinet meeting at the Mansion House). Ó Muirthile observed how each Supreme Council member 'sat round, each with a pencil and notebook, and noted the different points as [he] read from the document'. The major items of the Treaty draft of contention being the oath to the British monarch, the matter of the British military retaining three coastal ports of the Irish Free State, and the matter of partition. O'Murthile highlighted Lynch's contribution to the meeting, given his later opposition to the Free State forces during the Civil War. Lynch, then, was 'a man held in great esteem by Collins ... the most respected of Collins' Southern friends'.

Lynch apparently 'first took up the oath question' and following a discussion among the other members, 'put into words an Oath that he himself would accept and what he thought would be acceptable to the Volunteer mind'. Lynch was assisted by both Eoin O'Duffy and Gearóid O'Sullivan in this drafting, and in O'Muirthile's words, 'in the framing the alternative oath we felt that the Volunteer point of view ought to be sufficiently safe through these three officers'. A critical item in this revised oath was its first part professing an oath of allegiance to the Irish Free State, its second part an oath 'to the faithful to His Majesty King George V ... in virtue of the common citizenship'. Again, like in Deasy's account, Lynch seemed aware some degree of compromise was necessary.'[44]

John Regan has suggested this perhaps imbued Collins with the hope that the draft Treaty had the genuine endorsement of the entire IRB Supreme Council. If that was the case, theoretically, under the IRB oath and constitution, all grassroots members would fall into line.[45] The reality, however, was to be quite different.

After weeks of intense negotiations, on 6 December 1922, at Downing Street, the Sinn Féin delegation and their British counterparts signed the Articles of Agreement, otherwise known as the Anglo-Irish Treaty. The plenipotentiaries were no doubt under a degree of pressure and duress, as British Prime Minister David Lloyd George had threatened 'an immediate and terrible war' in Ireland if they did not sign. The Treaty allowed for the creation of an Irish Free State, a self-governing British dominion consisting of twenty-six counties of Ireland. The border of Northern Ireland would remain untouched until a promised Boundary

Commission would consider its alteration. Most controversially, the mention of the British monarch in the oath of allegiance remained, which had to be taken by all who sat in the parliament of the new Irish state.

Collins and Griffith admitted to their Dáil cabinet colleagues the pressures they were under in London, but they were steadfast in their acceptance of the Treaty settlement. For Collins and the cadre of the revolutionary government that supported him, the Irish Free State was a means to eventual, and total, independence from Britain: the 'stepping stone' argument. However, while Collins and Griffith were prepared to compromise, the final document had not been referred to the Dáil cabinet as agreed with de Valera. As a result, de Valera made the first major public break among the ranks of the revolutionary movement, declaring as President that he would not support the approval of the Treaty in Dáil Éireann. Disagreement over the terms would lead to further breaks among the political and military wings of the Irish revolutionary movement. From the outset, Lynch made it clear where he stood.

The closest we have to a first-hand account of Lynch's reaction is from a later interview with Moss Twomey, who observed how he 'was shocked and taken by surprise'. Twomey recalled that Lynch had met Collins on the Saturday before the latter's return to London, ahead of the signing of the Treaty, and on meeting Twomey in Fermoy the following Monday, Lynch informed Twomey, based on the conversation with Collins, that he understood the Treaty negotiations were going to be broken off. Lynch had planned to issue an order to alert the entire Southern Division that war with the British was to resume. On reading of the signing of the Treaty in the newspapers on the morning of 6 December, Lynch told Twomey 'all that had been done, all the sacrifices made had been betrayed'.[46] While it is certain that, as a member of the Supreme Council, Lynch had anticipated some degree of compromise, in his view the final agreed terms as signed were too far from the republican position and what he himself was willing to accept.

During the critical days after the document was signed by the plenipotentiaries, Lynch moved quickly as head of the First Southern Division to make clear his public opposition. On 10 December, at

Lynch in Fermoy Barracks. The most famous photograph of Liam Lynch, seated at a desk in Fermoy Barracks during 1922. Taken by local photographer Patrick Stritch, Lynch apparently had to borrow a Volunteer officer's coat, having rarely worn such a uniform. (© Cork Public Museum, Cork)

Mary Lynch. Liam Lynch's mother, with whom he was close. After leaving home, Liam continued to visit every Sunday until restricted by his Volunteer activities. (Private collection)

Jeremiah Lynch. Liam Lynch's father and a veteran Fenian. (Private collection)

Right: **Fr Tom Lynch.** Liam's youngest brother, with whom he was particularly close. (Private collection)

Below: **Liam with two brothers.** Liam, standing right, alongside his brothers Tom (standing left) and Martin (sitting) in a studio photograph taken around 1918. (Private collection)

Studio photograph. Liam Lynch on the cusp of the War of Independence. (Private collection)

Liam Lynch's scapulars. It is not surprising Lynch wore these, given that he was a devoted Catholic. After the bishops' pastoral condemning republican forces in September 1922, Lynch distinguished between the views of the hierarchy and his own faith, and still regularly prayed. (Courtesy of the National Library of Ireland)

Marching with the Volunteers. Three months before the Volunteer split, the Mitchelstown Volunteers march through Ballyporeen town, County Tipperary, in 1914. Liam Lynch can be seen just about to pass the laneway. (Derby collection)

National Volunteer membership card. Dating from roughly 1915, this Volunteer card of Lynch's is from the time he was a member of the National Volunteers. At this point, Lynch was a supporter of Home Rule. (Courtesy of the National Library of Ireland)

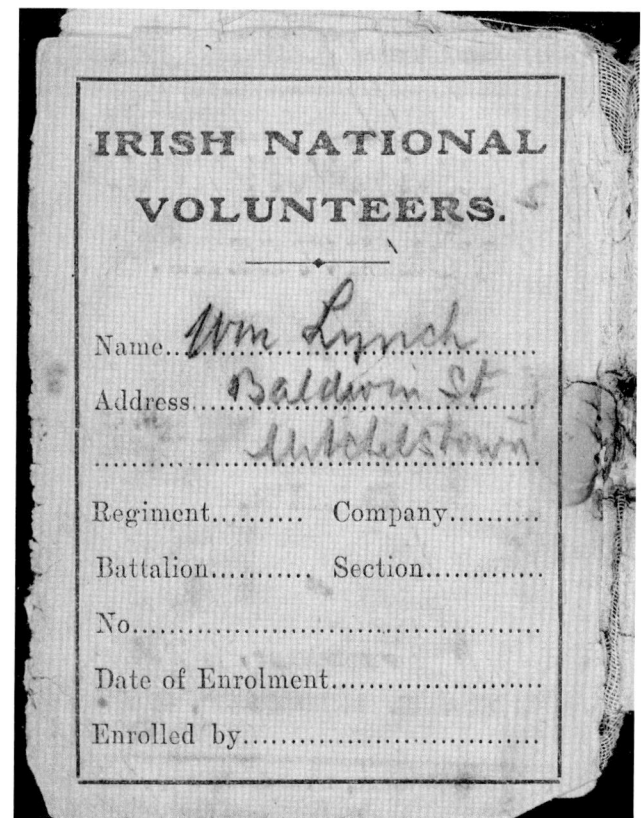

Arrest of the Kents. On 2 May 1916, the arrested Kent brothers were brought through the streets of Fermoy by British soldiers following a dramatic shootout at their family home, the only major incident in Cork during the Easter Rising. Pictured between the uniformed RIC are Thomas and William Kent respectively (Thomas was later executed). Being a first-hand witness to this very scene radicalised Liam Lynch in the republican cause. (Courtesy of Bill Power)

Richard Mulcahy. As chief of staff of the IRA, Mulcahy developed a mutual respect with Lynch. Even though pro-Treaty during the Civil War, he later called Lynch 'the lion of the resistance movement' between 1919 and 1921. (WikiCommons)

by the enemy, but we have declared for an Irish Republic & will not live under any other law, when he left I was

'We have declared for an Irish Republic and will not live under any other law.' The most famous phrase associated with Liam Lynch, this was never uttered as a public statement during the Civil War as often assumed, but instead was a comment in a letter to his brother Tom dated 1 November 1917. (Courtesy of the National Library of Ireland)

George Power. A Fermoy resident, Power knew Lynch from his early days in the Volunteers. He would become both a trusted ally and close friend of Lynch in the IRA's Cork No. 2 Brigade. (Courtesy of Barbara Scully)

Moss Twomey. Twomey first met Lynch when the latter worked as a quiet shop assistant in Fermoy, little realising how much regard he would have for Lynch as an IRA leader. He remained devoted to Lynch's memory until his death in 1978. (Courtesy of Brian Hanley)

Michael Fitzgerald. Fitzgerald was an important comrade and close friend for Lynch within the ranks of what became Cork No. 2 Brigade. His death on hunger strike in October 1920 devastated Lynch, who, while dying, would request to be buried with Fitzgerald, 'the greatest friend I ever had on this Earth'. (© Cork Public Museum, Cork)

General Lucas kidnap. The kidnapping of British General Cuthbert Lucas engineered by Lynch and Cork No. 2 Brigade created a media sensation. The distinctly unimpressed Lucas is pictured centre here in a famous 'proof of life' photo, surrounded by four Volunteers: Paddy Brennan, Michael Brennan (standing, left to right), James Brennan and Joe Keane (sitting, left to right). (© Cork Public Museum, Cork)

Siobhán Lankford (née Creedon).
Lankford was an indispensable
operator in Cork No. 2 Brigade
intelligence network, from her
position as a postal worker in
Mallow. She would also become
close friends with Lynch, and he
and other brigade officers frequently
stayed at her family home. (Courtesy
of Éamon Lankford)

Cork No. 2 flying column members. Members of the Cork No. 2 flying column at a
training camp in Liscarroll in 1921. Front row (from left): Joe Moran, Leo O'Callaghan,
Jack Cunningham, Seán Breen. Back row: Jeremiah Daly, Fr J. Pigott, Tadhg Burns,
M.C. O'Connell and Dan Burns. (© Cork Public Museum, Cork)

Lynch and the 1st Southern Division. Liam Lynch (pictured, front centre), with some staff and brigade officers attached to the First Southern Division pictured outside the Mansion House ahead of the reconvened Army Convention on 9 April 1922.

Front row (left to right): Seán Lehane, Tom Daly, Florrie O'Donoghue, Lynch, Liam Deasy, Seán Moylan, John Joe Rice, Humphrey Murphy.

Second row: Denis Daly, Jimmy O'Mahony, George Power, Michael Murphy, Eugene O'Neill, Seán MacSwiney, Dr Pat O'Sullivan, Jim Murphy, Moss Donegan, Gerry Hannifin.

Third row: Jeremiah Riordan, Michael Crowley, Dan Shinnick, Con Leddy, Con O'Leary, Tom Hales, Jack O'Neill, Seán McCarthy, Dick Barrett, Andy Cooney.

Fourth row: Tom Ward, John Lordan, Gibbs Ross, Tadhg Brosnan, Dan Mulvihill, Denis McNeilus.

At back: Con Casey, Pax Whelan, Tom McEllistrim, Michael Harrington.

(© Cork Public Museum, Cork)

Éamon de Valera. While Lynch praised de Valera, the political leader of republicanism, as 'the first to rebel' against the Treaty, the two men were to have an increasingly turbulent working relationship during the Civil War. (WikiCommons)

Truce committee. Outside the Mansion House, 4 May 1922, before a meeting of the 'Truce committee'. Left to right: Seán MacEoin (pro-Treaty), Seán Moylan (anti-Treaty), Eoin O'Duffy (pro-Treaty), Lynch, Gearóid O'Sullivan (pro-Treaty) and Liam Mellows (anti-Treaty). (© The Brother Allen Collection at the Military Archives)

Republican propaganda poster. No republican-occupied territory was ever formally established by Lynch as 'the Munster Republic' during the Civil War. Yet, ordering the anti-Treaty IRA to hold much of the south under the Limerick–Waterford line was a central plank of his strategy in the conflict's opening weeks, as this propaganda poster demonstrates. (© Trinity Digital Collections, item no. 77a: https://digitalcollections.tcd.ie/concern/parent/sn00b059h/file_sets/9p290b94g)

THE ARMY OF THE SOUTH

Is United under Liam Lynch

in Defence of

THE REPUBLIC.

Men of Dublin

WHERE DO YOU STAND?

With the English Allies

Or with a United South of Ireland ?

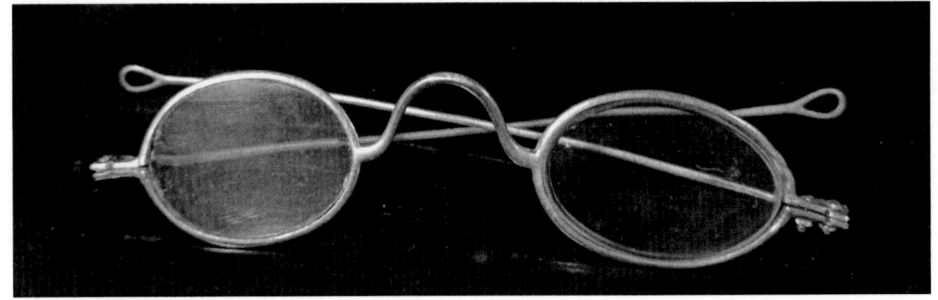

Liam Lynch's glasses. A pair of glasses belonging to Liam Lynch, allegedly worn at the time he was shot in the Knockmealdown mountains. (Private collection)

Scrapbook portrait. This extract is from a scrapbook, possibly family-owned, and shows a striking and rare portrait of Liam Lynch. (Private collection)

Couch Lynch was laid out on in Nugent's pub. After being mortally wounded, Lynch was laid out on this couch in Nugent's pub in Newcastle, County Tipperary, before being taken to Clonmel military hospital, where he later died. (Courtesy of John Foley)

Lynch lying-in-state. Lynch lying-in-state among family and supporters before his funeral. Directly behind the Cumann na mBan guard of honour in front of the coffin are Lynch's fiancée, Bridie Keyes (left), and mother, Mary Lynch (right).

(© Cork Public Museum, Cork)

Lynch's funeral cortège. Liam Lynch's coffin passing through Mitchelstown on the day of his funeral. The tricolour is emblazoned with the letters 'IRA' and both Lynch's cap and belt are atop the coffin. (Private collection)

Memorial tower, Knockmealdown mountains. Unveiled in 1935 on the site where Liam Lynch was shot, this memorial tower remains a regular site of commemoration. (Courtesy of John Foley)

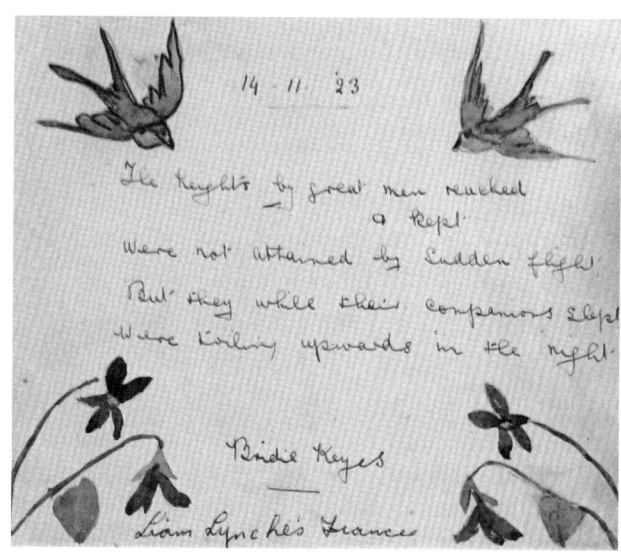

Bridie Keyes at a commemoration. Bridie Keyes, Liam Lynch's fiancée, looks at the camera at a commemoration in Kilcrumper, some time in the mid-1920s. Liam's mother, Mary, stands to the right. (Private collection)

Memorial poem. 'The heights of great men reached/& kept/were not attained by sudden flight/ But while their companions slept/were toiling upwards in the night.' Extract from 'The Ladder of St. Augustine' by Henry Wadsworth Longfellow, copied and illustrated by Bridie Keyes in memory of her fiancé. (Private collection)

Liam Lynch's uniform. The uniform worn by Lynch when he was shot. His boots were repaired by Jerry Kirwan several days before the fateful venture up the Knockmealdown mountains. (© National Museum of Ireland)

Portrait. Liam Lynch sat for a painting in full Volunteer uniform some time in 1920. The circumstances behind the creation of this little-known work are enigmatic. (William Sheehan (1894–1923), portrait of General Liam Lynch (1893–1923), 1920, oil on canvas, 77 x 61 cm, NGI.4014, National Gallery of Ireland Collection; photo © National Gallery of Ireland)

divisional HQ, Lynch held a meeting of the divisional staff officers and all brigade commandants to discuss the terms of the Treaty. At the end of the meeting, a resolution was issued to be transmitted to the Dáil cabinet: 'The Treaty as it was drafted is not acceptable to us as representing the Army in the 1st Divisional Area, and we urge its rejection by the Government.' This resolution was part of a longer communication signed by Lynch and the divisional leadership detailing their rejection of the Treaty. It was tempered with criticism of specific terms of the settlement and suggestions for substitutions.[47] Such an approach by Lynch and the other southern IRA leaders betrayed their fundamental lack of political acumen, not to mention their own political naiveté as to how the negotiations had played out and the impossibility of now renegotiating the terms after the fact.

It was in this atmosphere that Lynch attended a meeting of the IRB's Supreme Council in Dublin later that same day, in which the Treaty settlement was discussed. In the debate that ensued among the fifteen members of Council, eleven voted for the settlement with four against, including Lynch.[48] Following this meeting, the council issued a statement in which it urged 'that the present Peace Treaty between Ireland and Great Britain should be ratified'. However, in reflection of the growing division among IRB members, those who were also elected TDs in Dáil Éireann were 'given freedom of action in the matter'.[49] While this implied the decision of the council in support of the Treaty was unanimous, there was one dissenting member: Liam Lynch. Two letters he wrote in the two days thereafter, one to Florence O'Donoghue and the other to his brother Tom, are pivotal in revealing his feelings on the developing situation.

On 11 December, from Dublin, Lynch wrote to O'Donoghue that while others voted against the Treaty with him, in his own arguments he felt he 'stood alone' at the Supreme Council and that the Southern Division now 'seemingly stands alone' in the IRA. Lynch accepted the inevitable, that the Treaty would probably be approved for ratification by a majority in the Dáil, but he intended to stand by his own personal rejection of the Treaty even if the rest of the Southern Division did not. He made clear to O'Donoghue, however, that 'I do not recommend immediate war' – a return to fighting the British – 'as our front is broken, which our leaders are responsible for'. With the Treaty now almost certain to be ratified, Lynch anticipated that those who voted against 'will fall in and act on decision of majority, the same must apply to the [IRA] or we are lost'. Lynch asked O'Donoghue, in his capacity as divisional adjutant, to provide a list of rifles and ammunition, perhaps in preparation for a potential return to hostilities with the British. He closed with a strong sentiment towards Collins: 'I admire Mick as a soldier and a man, thank God all the parties can agree to differ.'[50]

On 12 December, Lynch wrote to Tom, opening with the assurance that 'my attitude is now, as always, to fight on for the reorganisation of the Republic. Even if were to stand alone I will not voluntarily accept being part of British Empire.' Nonetheless, looking ahead to the Treaty debates in Dáil Éireann, Lynch's primary personal concern, especially in the period ahead, was the prevention of a split. He hoped this concern would be shared across the Treaty divide, realising the days ahead were crucial: 'What ever will happen here on this week of destiny we must and will show a united front. Thank God that we all can agree to differ. Majority of the Dáil will stand by majority no matter what side, the same will apply to army. Therefore, there will not be disunity as in the past.' Lynch knew the Treaty would split opinion, but at this juncture, in the interest of unity, hoped it could be possible to maintain a political and military front to the British and maintain the Irish Republic.

Surprisingly, Lynch showed an appreciation of the supposed merits of the settlement and seemed to carefully favour its ratification, which demonstrated he had been listening to some of the arguments articulated by Collins. Throughout the letter to Tom there is the sense of Lynch attempting to sell the merits of the settlement to his brother and perhaps also to convince himself. While not emphasising how he himself helped shape the proposed oath at Supreme Council level, Lynch felt the Treaty did not ask for allegiance to the British Empire, 'only to be faithful to it'; instead they must be faithful to whatever new constitution took shape. He stressed that Tom 'must realise the humiliating position of Great Britain to accept us on equal terms when she has no more authority than

us and the other states of the [Commonwealth].' Somewhat echoing the
arguments of Collins and his support base that the Treaty was a means
to eventual Irish independence, Lynch stressed any acceptance was 'only
a question of the best means to smash her for Ireland's freedom's sake'.
That said, if the Treaty proved not to be such a stepping stone, even if 'we
must temporarily accept the Treaty[,] there is naturally another lap to
freedom and we certainly will knock her [Britain] off next time'. While
he acknowledged 'de Valera was the first to rebel' against the settlement,
Lynch added, 'Speeches and fine talk [do] not go far these days ... what
we want is ... to use the most effective means at our disposal.'[51] In already
making clear the opposition of the leadership of the First Southern
Division, Lynch would have known the use of this important body in the
IRA was one such means.

In light of his own firm republican position, Lynch still wished to
distance himself from one former ally: 'Sorry I must agree to differ with
Collins. That does not make us less friends. If the war is to be resumed he
will again surely play his part as before and that better than some of the
Irish diehards.'[52] He may not have been in Collins' camp, but remained
loyal to his friend and was frustrated – not for the last time – with some
of the more intractable republican opponents of the Treaty. Lynch was,
nonetheless, optimistic for the future, closing the letter to Tom with: 'we
can scarcely realise what a fine country Ireland will be when freedom
comes'. This optimistic note suggests he did not anticipate the considerable
fissure that would tear the revolutionary movement in two.

Despite the views of a majority on the IRB Supreme Council, this
secret society – so closely aligned in membership and activities to that
of the IRA – began to split over the settlement. The early statement of
one Cork circle that the Treaty was 'utterly at variance with the principles
of the IRB and treason to the Republic established in 1916' is just one
indication of the stark split in the organisation.[53] How much influence
the IRB Supreme Council held over the vote of IRB members who also
served as TDs in Dáil Éireann, remains a considered debate.[54] Lynch's
view of this is irrefutable, given that he told his brother he suspected the
majority in the Dáil would vote in the Treaty's favour.

On 14 December, the fractious Dáil debates on the Treaty began. At some point during these proceedings, Lynch was invited, along with other leading IRA figures, to watch the debates, which were held at the UCD buildings at Earlsfort Terrace. This was more than likely Lynch's first opportunity to observe the workings of Dáil Éireann. While it is not clear on which days he attended, or which of the famous speeches or exchanges he witnessed, Liam Deasy, who attended along with Lynch and Florence O'Donoghue, remembered all three of them finding the experience 'unforgettable and most distressing' as the national revolutionary movement came apart in front of them.[55] The intense rancour of the politicians undoubtedly did little to improve Lynch's already poor opinion of Sinn Féin and the Dáil.

In the period ahead, Lynch was to adopt a twin-track approach during attempts to heal the rift across the revolutionary organisations. Firstly, he sought to prevent the dilution of the Irish republican ideal and pushed for a situation whereby, in the absence of the Dáil or IRB, the IRA would represent the interests of the existing Irish Republic. Secondly, in consideration of this, he emphasised that unity within the IRA was a paramount goal and that some sort of accommodation with his former comrades who now represented the pro-Treaty position was vital, given the prospect of a return to war with the British was always looming.

Given that Lynch was the commandant of the First Southern Division, and a member of the IRB's Supreme Council, any attempt to bridge the divisions over the Treaty would have to involve him in a central role. He almost certainly realised this.

✱✱✱

The First Southern Division's public rejection of the Treaty, the first by any body of the IRA, was to prove an awkward development for GHQ, not least for Mulcahy, the IRA chief of staff, who himself supported the settlement. On 12 December, a frustrated Mulcahy wrote to Lynch following the issuing of a notice to all TDs in the Cork No. 1 Brigade area by its O/C Seán O'Hegarty, reiterating the rejection of the Treaty by the staff of the First Southern Division and reminding all TDs that 'it is your duty to support this demand. To act otherwise would be treason to the Republic to which we have all sworn allegiance.'[56] Mulcahy complained that it was 'a most irregular interference on the part of the O/C'.[57] O'Hegarty, in private correspondence with Mulcahy, refused to apologise and explained that it was important Dáil deputies be aware 'in plain terms of our attitude towards these proposals'. Brugha, on being informed of the affair by Mulcahy, felt it was 'intolerable that military men as such should interfere in matters of this kind. The officer should be severely reprimanded.'[58] However, it does not appear that Mulcahy took any action, being worried he would upset the entire rank-and-file of the First Southern Division.[59]

On 3 January 1922, Mulcahy demanded an explanation from Lynch after O'Hegarty's men disrupted a meeting of pro-Treaty farmers in late December. Mulcahy advised suspension or disarmament of the section of the Volunteers responsible for the incident but made clear he was 'quite satisfied' to leave the matter to Lynch.[60] Lynch merely forwarded O'Hegarty's report on the incident to Mulcahy, stating it 'speaks for itself'. Furthermore, he advised against suspending or disarming insubordinate officers, as those in the First Southern Division 'realise that the Government, GHQ Staff and the Army in the rest of Ireland outside the Southern Division and Dublin Brigade have outrageously let them down'. Lynch felt that when the Irish Free State came into existence, IRA GHQ would be responsible for discipline 'which I have grave fears will be hard to maintain'.[61]

O'Hegarty risked drawing further ire from GHQ when Volunteers of Cork No. 1 destroyed a printing press in the process of production of a pro-Treaty pamphlet[62] and later abducted a journalist, moving him to a secret location in Cork.[63] On 6 January, Lynch replied to Mulcahy's requests for an explanation. The following statement would likely have done nothing to alleviate Mulcahy's worries over Lynch's divided loyalties:

> It is with deep regret that I have to acquaint you that while at all times I shall do my utmost to carry out your orders, maintain general discipline and above all insist on Truce being maintained

I cannot carry out any order against IRA principles during the present Treaty negotiations when our principles stand [in] danger of being given away by our unthankful government.[64]

On 7 January, the Dáil finally held a vote on the Treaty, with sixty-four TDs voting in favour of and fifty-seven against the settlement, the majority carrying the day as Lynch had predicted. With much of Irish civil society, the Catholic Church hierarchy and most of the national press throwing their support behind the implementation of the terms of the Treaty, the anti-Treaty contingent of republicans was to face enormous obstacles in voicing opposition.

On 9 January, the night Griffith was elected president of the Dáil, there was a meeting in the Mansion House of GHQ staff and divisional commandants, with Cathal Brugha and de Valera present. The meeting was called by Mulcahy to discuss unity among the IRA, now split over the Treaty.[65] Brugha began with a direct appeal for unity, calling for 'discipline and the presentation of a united front' and insisted 'that something good would come of it'.[66] Mulcahy asked for recognition of the authority of Dáil Éireann and for recognition of Mulcahy himself as the new Minister for Defence. Eoin O'Duffy was to be the new IRA chief of staff. Lynch then responded, and a somewhat unfortunate, though still memorable, contribution followed. Oscar Traynor, O/C of the Second Eastern Division, explained that 'when it came to his [Lynch's] turn to present his views on the proposition [he] broke down so completely that it was only with difficulty that his views, which were against the proposition, could be ascertained'. Traynor, who was to have several dealings with Lynch in the months ahead, was left with an 'impression of Liam Lynch … that he was rather highly-strung and on occasions inclined to excitability in debate'.[67] Traynor elaborated further in an interview with Ernie O'Malley: 'Poor Lynch began to cry when he stood up to speak. He wasn't accepting either instruction from present Minister for Defence or the later Minister for Defence and that justice and righteousness were greater than discipline. He spoke in jinky sentences … Mulcahy bowed his head whilst Lynch was crying. We felt awkward and shocked at Lynch.'[68]

Frank Aiken, O/C of the Fourth Northern Division, also recalled Lynch's emotional contribution. While Traynor was disparaging in his recollections, the more sympathetic Aiken recalled how Lynch made 'a most impressive speech … at the meeting, although he broke down in the course of it'. Aiken recalled the 'general drift of it [the speech] was, that a disastrous position had been reached in the Army and that this was the end of unity' – an obvious counter to Brugha's initial appeal. Aiken attributed Lynch's obvious emotion to him being 'very deeply moved and [that he] seemed to feel disappointment that was almost despair'.[69] Even at this early juncture in 1922, Lynch was already very distressed at the prospect of an IRA split – and could do little to hide the personal toll it was taking on him. His contribution may not have encouraged others, such as Traynor, that he was capable of negotiation and navigating such future meetings. At the meeting's close, de Valera appealed to all present to do nothing to widen the breach in the IRA. Mulcahy repeated what he had said in the Dáil, that the IRA would be maintained as the army of the Republic.[70] This was not the last such conference to end with such a hope.

On 10 January, a conference was held of IRB members by the IRB Supreme Council, which encompassed the division and county centres of the whole organisation. The purpose of the conference was to prevent a split in the organisation over the Treaty, an abnormal circumstance in that such a meeting was outside the remit of the IRB constitution. Florence O'Donoghue recalled how 'on both sides the issue was debated with commendable objectivity and restraint'. Much of the ensuing debate reflected that previously played out in the Dáil. On this occasion, Lynch and Collins, in O'Donoghue's view, were 'the principal protagonists of the two opposing viewpoints. Admiring and respecting each other, but each apparently immovable in his own conviction, they wrestled with the grim threat of disunity.' To those present, Lynch was 'one of the voices listened to with attention and respect'. Nonetheless, the conference ended with nothing more substantial than an exchange of views and a decision to reassemble at a later date.[71]

Lynch was not alone within the IRA leadership in opposing the Treaty, his views being shared among key officers. This group, along with divisional commandants, such as Ernie O'Malley, and members of the IRA GHQ, such as Rory O'Connor (director of engineering) and Liam Mellows (director of purchases), now began to organise following the Dáil vote on the Treaty. On 10 January, likely after the IRB conference, this group met to formulate an anti-Treaty policy to keep the IRA a purely republican organisation. In the view of this group of IRA leaders, the IRA should revert to having an Executive as their authority, instead of Dáil Éireann, as had been the case with the Irish Volunteer organisation prior to 1919. Support for the current Dáil was contingent on it being a representative body that upheld the Irish Republic. At this meeting, Lynch declared his decision to cut off the First Southern Division from the authority of IRA GHQ.[72] This was a departure from the statement issued by the First Southern Division on 10 December, in which the leadership made clear the opposition to the Treaty but had suggested changes. With the Dáil having voted on the Treaty, Lynch now realised the situation had changed in only a few weeks.

The following day, Minister for Defence Mulcahy received a communication from those members of IRA GHQ and divisional and brigade leaders who were opposed to the Treaty. Lynch, along with figures such as Liam Mellows, Rory O'Connor, and Ernie O'Malley, had added his signature to this pivotal document. It requested the holding of an Army Convention for the purpose of passing a resolution which stated: 'That the Army re-affirmed its allegiance to the Irish Republic. That it shall be retained as the Army of the Irish Republic, under an Executive appointed by the Convention. That the Army shall be under the supreme control of such Executive, which shall draft a Constitution for submission to a subsequent Convention.'[73]

Mulcahy responded carefully two days later, reminding the signatories that 'the Dáil as a whole is the elected Government of the Irish Republic, and that supreme control of the Army is invested in it'. Therefore, the proposed resolution 'to change the supreme control of the Army is entirely outside the constitutional powers vested in the Dáil'. Clearly in his view the authority of the Dáil must remain paramount. While he did not dismiss outright the idea of a convention, Mulcahy nonetheless promised to make the arrangements to meet and discuss the matter with each member of the group over the next few days.[74] This was to be the beginning of a very delicate balancing act on Mulcahy's part in placating both these newfound opponents and his colleagues in the Dáil cabinet.

As promised, Mulcahy did attempt to meet individually with each of the signatories of the communication in an unsuccessful effort to get them either to drop or delay the idea of a convention. One Mulcahy biographer insisted that Lynch's opposition to the Treaty had impressed on him the gravity of the situation, as Lynch previously had not been considered one of the extremists. Mulcahy also felt personally aggrieved about Lynch's involvement due to their mutual respect and closeness.[75] On 13 January, Lynch rejected Mulcahy's request for a meeting on the developing situation: 'No purpose will be served by meeting me after 10.30 tomorrow as I must take united action with signatories.'[76] Though the pair's dealings had been decidedly mixed since the signing of the Treaty, this was the first serious break in the strong working relationship the men had cultivated over the previous three years.

On 16 January, two weeks after the vote on the Treaty, Lynch wrote to his brother Tom. He made reference to the increasingly bitter arguments playing out in public and in private, 'as you say a hotter fight than pre-Truce days'.[77] Lynch felt Tom could 'rest satisfied that the IRA will save the situation. Time will tell whether Lloyd George has got the best of the Irish Nation or made a big mess of himself.' Still optimistic, Lynch recognised that 'people have been stampeded owning to war weariness and threat of extermination by enemy, in cooler moments they will really realise that indescribable spirit of nationality and again stand up with their heads high'. He closed with looking forward to seeing Tom that weekend following a dance fundraiser for republican prisoners in Milltown.[78]

On 18 January, Rory O'Connor, elected the chairman of this group of anti-Treaty IRA leaders, wrote to Mulcahy in response to his earlier written reply to the letter of 11 January demanding an Army Convention. O'Connor made it clear that a convention would be held by the signatories regardless of Mulcahy's wishes. However, in a sign of how precarious the situation was already becoming within the IRA, he assured Mulcahy of assistance during the British military evacuation from what would become the jurisdiction of the Irish Free State: 'we repeat our desire to co-operate with you in hastening the evacuation of the country by enemy troops, but to that end the signatories can only act on orders issued by you and countersigned by me'.[79] O'Connor's message may have spurred a meeting on 18 January between IRA GHQ officers and divisional commanders at which Mulcahy presided. The outcome of this meeting was the formation of a Council of Four, consisting of two of the signatories who had demanded an Army Convention (Lynch was not one of them) and another two from the remaining divisional officers. To ensure the 'Republican aim shall not be prejudiced', this council was to act as an advisory body for the IRA under the chief of staff. This proposed arrangement was to hold for two months, when the Army Convention would finally be called. Until then, all IRA officers were to assist in the British evacuation.[80] This council was the first example of one of the many formulas proposed or adopted over the months ahead in order to stave off a civil war that neither side wanted.

In the meantime, the institutions of the new Irish Free State began to come into being. On 12 January, Mulcahy reported to the Dáil cabinet on arrangements for a military force loyal to the government – formed from the ranks of the IRA – to take over certain barracks, chiefly Beggar's Bush in Dublin. Clothing and general maintenance for this force would come from the funds of the new Provisional Government of the Irish Free State. This was the genesis of what eventually became the National Army of the Irish Free State from pro-Treaty IRA units loyal to the Provisional Government. At the time, however, these plans were not made public due to issues over the rejection of the Treaty by many within the wider ranks of the IRA. Despite this, key anti-Treaty IRA leaders soon got wind of the military build-up in the weeks following, with O'Malley realising this new pro-Treaty army of Irish recruits would be used by Mulcahy and Collins 'for their own purpose and slowly our men would either be absorbed or would return to their farms, businesses or universities'.[81]

On 14 January, a meeting of the Southern Ireland parliament, set up under the Government of Ireland Act, took place, which was necessary under the terms of the Treaty. With the refusal of their anti-Treaty opponents to recognise this body, the only Sinn Féin representation was of the pro-Treaty TDs elected the previous year, in attendance for the first (and only) time. They then elected a government and begin transferring political powers to the Provisional Government of the Irish Free State. Pro-Treaty TDs held ministerial portfolios in the cabinets of both the Dáil and that of the Provisional Government, the biggest difference being that Griffith held the position of Dáil president while Collins held the position of chairman of the Provisional Government.

Alongside this build-up of the political and military institutions of the Irish Free State, there were burgeoning protests over the Treaty. On 12 January, Cumann na mBan became the first organisation of the revolutionary movement as a whole to reject the settlement, its Executive overwhelmingly voting against it. Meanwhile, after considerable debate, the Sinn Féin Ard-Fheis held at the end of February staved off a wider debate on the Treaty, as fissures in the political wing of the revolutionary movement rumbled on alongside those in the military wing.

***

Efforts to maintain IRA unity were complicated by the speedy British Army withdrawal from the jurisdiction of the Irish Free State in early 1922, and the subsequent handover of barracks. Initially, it was agreed that those barracks in areas controlled by anti-Treaty IRA would be occupied by them, with no interference from Provisional Government forces. Large areas were still under the command of anti-Treaty IRA forces, such as Lynch's First Southern Division, which inevitably meant large segments of the jurisdiction of the Free State were potentially outside the control of the Provisional Government.[82] On 17 February 1922, the handover of Mallow Barracks, the scene of the successful arms raid in September 1920, took place. Lynch, appropriately enough, marched at the head of the Volunteers involved in the handover, accompanied by Dick Willis and Jack Bolster. It was a proud day for Lynch.[83] Liam Deasy, who was present, was struck by what a 'contrast it was for Liam Lynch to now lead a company of armed Volunteers through the streets of Mallow to cheering crowds with the British guard at the barracks' entrance presenting arms as he passed in'.[84] Later handovers would not be so straightforward.

The Mallow Barracks quickly became the divisional HQ.[85] The rumour the previous year of Lynch's death persisted, as he discovered when dealing with a British officer during the handover. On signing his name during the formal process of the handover, the British officer said to Lynch, incredulously, 'You're not Liam Lynch.'

Confused, Lynch replied, 'I am surely.'

'We heard that you were dead long ago.'

'Really, how did I die?'

'Of tetanus we were told.'[86]

On 19 February, Éamon de Valera was the lead speaker at a republican rally at Grand Parade in Cork city, at which other noted political figures, such as Cathal Brugha, Liam Mellows and Countess Markievicz, also spoke. An advertisement ahead of the rally said Lynch was to attend, along with other noted Cork IRA luminaries, such as Tom Barry and Tom Hales.[87] While it is not clear from the subsequent reports if Lynch attended the rally, had he been present he would have heard de Valera tell the gathered crowd that 'any attempt by Irishmen to disestablish the Republic … or to commit the Irish people irrevocably to the acceptance in advance of the proposed new [Irish Free] State … is an obvious betrayal of Ireland's interests and is not to be tolerated'.[88] As the political face of opposition to the Treaty, de Valera was to become more controversial in the weeks ahead for his public pronouncements, such as the suggestion that it might be necessary for the IRA to 'wade through Irish blood' to achieve freedom. However, while a figure of respect to them, in truth de Valera had no influence over the anti-Treaty IRA leadership in this period.

Despite the growing tensions, Lynch ensured that the IRA within his jurisdiction continued to follow any direction from GHQ regarding the breaking up of labour strikes, which had continued into 1922. In February, Lynch was involved in settling an occupation of mills by workers in Mallow. Lynch, after consultation with the Dublin-based leadership of the ITGWU, asked the workers to leave or he would order IRA members of the First Southern Division to remove them.[89] On 8 February, the Mallow Mills Workers Council issued a statement concerning Lynch's direct request for the council to end their occupation, which had been started by instruction of the same ITGWU leadership. The statement explained that they 'had never any reason to doubt Commandant Lynch's word, and we ask every Irish worker to realise how we have been stabbed in the back'. The council also informed all members of the union, 'that our Dublin leaders [of the ITGWU] are no longer tolerated but treated as traitors to our case'.[90] A subsequent report in the *Irish Independent* noted a strike at the Clondulane mills was settled similarly the day before.[91] There is no commentary from Lynch on these strikes in the existing archival material, but in following these instructions Lynch showed he was content to follow the pro-Treaty GHQ direction in such matters – a reflection of his lack of interest in the politics of organised labour.

On 6 March, from division HQ in Mallow, Lynch wrote to his brother Tom. He sarcastically referred to rumours that he had recently married: 'I presume they are satisfied at home by now that I was not married, while my whole time is required by Old Ireland it won't be wasted otherwise.' Clearly the prospect of marriage to Bridie Keyes was still some way off. In a particularly moving passage in this letter, Lynch expressed how his younger brother's letters sustained him in these troubled times, indicating the closeness they shared and how much he valued his brother's opinion: 'Your notes give me great courage, to carry on even against terrible opposition and you generally strike the individual points at issue.' Lynch expressed a desire for a life away from IRA activities, given he 'had tried to resign several times during the past few months but same would not be accepted'. He thought nothing of the 'lofty position' he was now in as head of the First Southern Division, as 'at the moment I am fed up of Army and people, and were it not for Ireland's sake alone I would drop out of things, I know my services at moment are sorely needed'.[92]

He seemed sceptical of any civilian support for the IRA in opposition to the Provisional Government given the current politician situation, ruefully reflecting on experiences during the previous conflict: 'At any rate I don't give a damn about the people when it comes to praise, or notoriety and they are making the hell of a mistake if they think I forget their actions during the War. I remember at one time in the best areas where it was next impossible to find a bed to lie on.' Looking towards the prospective general election, Lynch felt that in 'the past I made the most of every situation that arose … and will continue to do so. I will do my best at elections to keep Ireland from handing away the Republic and at least the portion of her birthright.' What his 'best' would constitute is not clear, but Lynch seemed optimistic that even if 'we [the anti-Treaty republicans] fail at the elections I hope to have the army united under an Executive and giving allegiance to any party of government. If we the army stand together – which it will – we can save the country and the Republic.'[93] Consistent in Lynch's thinking during these months, was the idea that the bonds of comradeship across a unified IRA were the only means by which to repair the split over the Treaty.

A crisis that started at the end of February, however, showed how unlikely Lynch's hope of a unified army was. Limerick city, regarded as a key military base due to its position on the River Shannon linking control of the Munster province and the western coast, was the setting for a clash between pro- and anti-Treaty forces. It began when pro-Treaty forces from the First Western Division led by Michael Brennan marched into the city and took over evacuated RIC barracks, in contravention of the agreed deal and to the fury of the local anti-Treaty forces from the IRA's Mid-Limerick Brigade. The situation escalated when the pro-Treaty IRA took over evacuated military barracks the following week. In response, Ernie O'Malley arrived in the city with forces from his Second Southern Division to augment the anti-Treaty Mid-Limerick Brigade. A dramatic armed stand-off ensued, with the respective forces occupying various buildings and locations across the city, for the first time making civil war between the respective factions of the IRA a real possibility.[94]

On 10 March, Lynch and Oscar Traynor, the head of the IRA's Dublin Brigade, were called to a meeting at Beggar's Bush Barracks, arranged by Limerick's mayor, Stephen O'Mara. Lynch and Traynor came to an agreement with pro-Treaty IRA figures such as Collins, Mulcahy and O'Duffy over the escalating situation in Limerick. The local Mid-Limerick

Brigade forces would occupy most of the barracks in the city, with a small pro-Treaty military force occupying one police barracks. Lynch and Traynor then ventured to Limerick to get both O'Malley and Tom Barry, leading the anti-Treaty forces, to accept the agreement. Traynor recalled that he and Lynch 'had an awful job with Barry … We had to try and impress on Barry there would be fighting at some point'.[95] In a letter afterwards to his brother Tom, Lynch made no secret of his disgust over the situation and towards both sides involved. He displayed little patience for the more extreme on the anti-Treaty side and clearly viewed himself as a moderating figure. In his view, the 'stunt in Limerick was all gas, a disgrace to both sides especially the Limerick and Tipp men. Thank God I was used to bring pressure to bear at absolutely the last moment on GHQ to save slaughter in the streets of Limerick. Had it happened the Nation was for ever disgraced'.[96]

In the interim, conferences were begun between pro- and anti-Treaty IRA leaders, which delayed the holding of the proposed Army Convention, in an effort to find an agreed IRA position on the Treaty. (The Convention was originally scheduled for 24 February but was then moved to 26 March.) Florence O'Donoghue, who accompanied Lynch to many of these in Dublin, recalled the atmosphere at these meetings 'was one of goodwill and genuine, mutually-shared desire' to prevent civil war by unity within the IRA.[97] Furthermore, O'Donoghue noted that Lynch maintained friendly relations with Collins and Mulcahy, indicating the great esteem in which all three held each other.[98]

On 15 March, just prior to a cabinet meeting, Mulcahy and Gearóid O'Sullivan, the IRA's adjutant general, met with Lynch and suggested an alternate wording to the resolution for the Army Convention, in which the IRA: 'reaffirms the allegiance of the Army to Dáil Éireann'. The proposed resolution suggested that if the situation were to change with a general election, a commission could put forward 'proposals for associating the IRA with whatever Irish government is then in authority'. In turn, the resolution ensured the IRA would 'disclaim any intention of setting up a military government, as opposed to any government elected by the people'.[99]

Lynch informed the two men that this new proposed resolution 'wouldn't do'. While the intention of the Convention was to address control of the IRA, he insisted the IRA 'will not interfere with the Provisional Government or any government elected by the people', but it is likely this did not really assuage the worries of the government representatives.[100] In notes from a meeting later that day with the divisional commandants, Mulcahy noted how Lynch stated, given broken promises, that the Provisional Government 'can't possibly have an election' any time in the near future without specifying the consequences if it did.[101]

Mulcahy worried that a convention would result in an IRA that would reject the authority of the Provisional Government and may even attempt to set up a military government. In light of these concerns, shared throughout the cabinet, the holding of the Convention was banned. Mulcahy held a meeting with disappointed IRA divisional commandments, including Lynch, after the cabinet meeting that led to this decision. While Mulcahy attempted to convince the group it was for the best, Lynch and others complained that previous promises had not been kept.[102]

On 18 March, even in the midst of extraordinary political ill-will on both sides, a second IRB conference took place at 41 Parnell Square. The purpose of the conference, in the words of a letter distributed to the IRB county centres, was for 'dealing exclusively with the attitude of the [IRB] Organisation to the Treaty'. Florence O'Donoghue, who was present, wrote of the meeting taking place in an atmosphere that, 'although strained, was still dominated by the spirit of the organisation'. The strains between the opposing sides were almost certainly due to the cabinet banning the holding of the IRA Convention, and that Convention going ahead despite this. The proceedings of this IRB meeting were similar to the previous one, with Collins and Lynch again the chief proponents of the opposing views. Collins insisted the Treaty would allow the country to achieve full independence, while Lynch expressed the view that if the people accepted the Treaty, the Volunteers should revert to their original status under an Executive. This executive would then create a constitution requiring full allegiance to the Republic until it was achieved.[103]

In O'Donoghue's view, 'although the Supreme Council itself was, by a large majority, in favour of the Treaty, they would have been quite unable to carry any endorsement of their action at the meeting'. He felt a vote at that meeting would have shown a majority of IRB members against the Treaty, but the body present had no sway on decision-making within the organisation according to the constitution of the IRB, as final authority lay with the Supreme Council. The conference adjourned amidst these tensions in a heightened political atmosphere.[104]

As the situation continued to accelerate, on 20 March, at a meeting of the First Southern Division in Mallow, Lynch was surprised by the arrival of Minister for Defence Mulcahy and Chief of Staff O'Duffy.[105] Recalling this incident, Moss Twomey was of the view it 'was an indication of the importance they attached to the decision which the Divisional Council would take' in attending the Convention.[106] Mulcahy and O'Duffy put forward a proposal to select from among the divisional and brigade commandants a Council of Eight to 'frame definite proposals for associating the IRA with the government elected by the Irish people'. If this council's proposals were agreed, then they would go before the Dáil cabinet. Lynch and O'Donoghue, in their capacity as divisional O/C and adjutant respectively, responded a day later with agreement to the formation of this council, with two caveats: 1) If the proposals of the Council of Eight were to go before the Dáil cabinet, as a goodwill gesture, the planned Army Convention was to be delayed from 26 March until 18 April; 2) Recruitment into the new police force, the Civic Guard, was to be discontinued.[107] Put before the cabinet, this last ditch effort by Mulcahy and O'Duffy to stave off the Army Convention collapsed, as Collins and Griffith refused to entertain Lynch and O'Donoghue's caveats.[108]

On 22 March, four days before the planned Convention, Rory O'Connor, as the public face of this group of anti-Treaty IRA officers, held an improvised press conference. O'Connor explained the republican position in holding the Convention and stated that 'if a government goes wrong it must take the consequences'. In response to a journalist asking if O'Connor was proposing a military dictatorship by the body of the IRA he represented, O'Connor flippantly replied, 'You can take it that if you like.'[109] Todd Andrews, in his memoir, said of this that O'Connor 'spoke too much, particularly as he had no delegated authority, culminating in a bad political gaffe'. Andrews noted that long before the rise of Hitler in

Germany or the horrors of Stalin's rule in Soviet Russia, the connotation of a military dictatorship to ordinary Irish people was that they were liable 'to be pushed around on the whims of young IRA commanders'. For the young Andrews, a breakdown in IRA discipline was much more of an issue than the prospect of an IRA military dictatorship, which he admitted at the time did not bother him.[110] Retrospectively, Moss Twomey felt it was very hard to say how much of the anti-Treaty side O'Connor's view then represented, but he 'doubted if it accurately represented Lynch's views at that moment'.[111] Andrews later pointed to the fact that a motion proposing a military dictatorship by the IRA was defeated at the Army Convention.[112] Nonetheless, O'Connor's careless remark was a gift to the propaganda of their opponents in the Provisional Government.

The long-mooted IRA Army Convention was held at the Mansion House, Dublin, on 26 and 27 March. By this juncture, Lynch's division accounted for 33,550 Volunteers, an increase of 3,000 since April 1921 due to recruitment and prison releases. (The overall number in the IRA at this point was estimated to be 112,650.) It was later determined that those present at the Convention represented about 64 per cent of the IRA.[113] Thus, fifty-four delegates from Lynch's First Southern Division – amounting to over a quarter of the total number of 211 – attended and voted on the resolutions. The following resolution was passed unanimously: 'That the army reaffirm its allegiance to the Irish Republic. That it shall be maintained as the army of the Irish Republic under an Executive appointed by the Convention. That the army shall be under the supreme control of such Executive which shall draft a constitution for submission to a Convention to be held on 9 April.'[114]

On the second day of the Convention, a temporary IRA Executive of sixteen was formed and elected Liam Lynch as chief of staff.[115] Florence O'Donoghue, who attended, remarked that the 'Convention itself was [otherwise] uneventful'.[116] An intelligence report issued to Mulcahy about the developments at the Convention noted that on the second day officers of the First Southern Division took over the Clarence Hotel at Wellington Quay – this was to function as Lynch's occasional base of operations on his visits to Dublin during the following critical weeks.[117]

At 6 Gardiner's Row the following day, the constitution drafting sub-committee – made up of members of the new Executive – began their work. Joe O'Connor of the Dublin Brigade's Third Battalion was on this sub-committee. He was initially surprised to find representatives of the First Southern Division not present, but was not 'anxious as word was sent that they were meeting all the delegates from that Division prior to their departure for home'.[118] Lynch arrived later with the other members of the First Southern Division who held seats on the Executive, and the new chief of staff immediately introduced an early and particularly heated division among the ranks of the anti-Treaty IRA.

O'Connor was shocked when Lynch and his division's Executive members 'threw the first bombshell amongst us by stating they were dissatisfied with their number of representatives and adding that the Dublin units had too many seats on the Executive. This was a most unfortunate thing, and I am convinced we never got over the shock'.[119] Another attendee, Oscar Traynor, also felt Lynch derailed proceedings, at a critical time when unity among their forces was so important. Regarding Lynch's objection, Traynor felt it was 'an astonishing way to begin a meeting for he [Lynch] brought the matter up before we had begun to consider anything'.[120] Traynor, while pointing out to Lynch that the time to have objected to any of the Executive nominees would have been during the Convention, resigned from the Executive and suggested a nominee from Cork take his place. O'Connor similarly resigned.

Work on the new constitution continued apace, while the matter of Executive nominees would be resolved at the reconvened Convention in April.[121] While he may have felt personally aggrieved at the lack of his division's representation on the Executive, Lynch was operating with a degree of strategy on the nominee issue. He explained his reasoning to a sceptical Tom Maguire, O/C of the Second Western Division: 'There are three men whom I want on the Executive, if I can get them elected. They are Tom Hales, Florence O'Donoghue and Liam Deasy.' While Maguire was sure they were good men, in retrospect he noted ruefully that, in his view in light of their actions during the subsequent Civil War, neither O'Donoghue or Deasy managed to 'prove themselves'.[122] As well as the three men being trusted subordinates, Lynch maybe hoped his chosen nominees could be a moderating influence on the new Executive, as he was already wary of how certain republican elements had escalated the situation in Limerick in early March.

On 31 March, Lynch wrote to his brother Tom with something of that familiar youthful exuberance from his earlier days in the Volunteers. He was confident that with the holding of the Convention in defiance of Mulcahy's ban, the IRA had 'started to put an end to the Free State and general disgraceful compromise and we mean now to see it through'. Lynch estimated that about 85 per cent of the IRA stood against the Provisional Government. As for the ordinary people, they 'must hold what we won for them even if they cannot immediately and in a smooth manner mark progress to freedom.' While not altogether as optimistic as in recent previous letters, Lynch acknowledged that while he and his closest allies were 'run entirely off our feet these times … all is going tip top at the moment'.[123]

On 9 April, the Convention reconvened to adopt the new constitution and elect the new Executive. The constitution reverted the authority of the IRA to the Executive and appointed an Army Council of seven members who would function as a decision-making body when the Executive could not meet. In turn, the Executive would vote on a new chief of staff, who could form his own staff. Elections were then held for the sixteen-member Executive, to which Lynch, Deasy and O'Donoghue were elected. Again, the Executive elected Lynch as chief of staff. O'Donoghue later lamented that this new Executive was never a cohesive body, that it 'never fused into an effective unit. It never had a common mind or a common policy'.[124]

This lack of unity among the anti-Treaty section of the IRA was to greatly hamper the efforts of Lynch in the weeks ahead. In addition, the overall political situation was now more complex, with Lynch now the leader of a separate section of the IRA to the pro-Treaty element headed by Eoin O'Duffy, which continued recruitment and training. Becoming chief of staff was undoubtedly a proud moment for Lynch and indicative of the esteem he was held in among his comrades, yet the challenges ahead were enormous.

Chapter 7

'Would we could even get back all our glorious dead' (April–June 1922)

ON THE NIGHT OF 13 April 1922, on the instructions of the anti-Treaty IRA Executive, three to four hundred members of the Dublin Brigade seized the vast Four Courts complex on the quays as their main base. Almost certainly conscious of the charges of military dictatorship a few weeks before, Rory O'Connor, the most public face of the new anti-Treaty Executive, in an interview, clarified 'the occupation of [the Four Courts] should not be taken in any way as a coup d'état nor did it indicate the beginning of a revolution' but merely the need for a new base of operations for the IRA forces to which O'Connor was associated.[1] The symbolism of this action the day before Good Friday, so close to the anniversary of the Easter Rising (the Four Courts having been a rebel garrison in 1916), surely did not go unnoticed in the Provisional Government. There is no account that details how central Lynch was to the planning of this move, but it must be assumed he approved as chief of staff of the anti-Treaty IRA. It is worth surmising that, given Executive members such as O'Connor and Mellows were in Dublin and Lynch's base of operations was in Cork, Lynch's influence on events may not have been as considerable as he may have liked.

A concern and sense of lawlessness began to prevail throughout the country, heightened by the continued takeover of barracks by anti-Treaty

IRA units. Bank robberies by anti-Treaty forces looking for funds began to be a recurring concern for Free State authorities. In one controversial move, Rory O'Connor ordered the destruction of the printing press of *The Freeman's Journal* due to that newspaper's perceived pro-Treaty stance. In the weeks ahead, the anti-Treaty forces were also accused of killing off-duty British soldiers in the capital, but their most controversial action was the killing of thirteen members of the Protestant community on charges of suspected spying for the British within the Bandon Valley in west Cork. Accusations of sectarianism on the part of members of the Cork No. 3 Brigade involved have endured in the decades since. However, at the time, Tom Hales, O/C of the Cork No. 3 Brigade, condemned the action, while Tom Barry, Seán Moylan and Liam Deasy ensured armed guards were stationed at the homes of Protestants in the area. There was no public statement from Lynch on the action, though it occurred within the First Southern Division's area and, as their commandant, it can be assumed that he approved of Moylan's and Deasy's efforts to dampen tensions in the area. Florence O'Donoghue, while not referring to a specific event, questioned how many anti-Treaty IRA actions in the period leading up to the Civil War were undertaken without the knowledge of the anti-Treaty leadership, claiming, 'Things were done and ordered to be done without the knowledge of all the members, sometimes without Liam's knowledge.'[2]

✷✷✷

After Lynch's death, one former comrade penned an anonymous tribute in a republican periodical and recalled encountering him in the Four Courts during this time. It is a striking portrait of the state of exhaustion Lynch tended to work himself into during these difficult months: 'I saw him in the Four Courts snatching a moment for his lunch in company with his staff. His pale, long face was traced by his dark lines, his voice was tired out, his eyes were brilliant and sunken, all denoting he had been cruelly overworking himself … he never lost his temper and was always sympathetic to his subordinates and cheered them in their worries.'[3]

From his office in new Four Courts HQ, Lynch wrote to Tom on 18 April and came across as exuberant about recent developments: 'We have at last thrown down the gauntlet again to England through the Provisional Government, we stand on the Republic established in '16 and reaffirmed by the Irish people at the elections.' Lynch anticipated a military response from some quarter and admitted 'not knowing the hour we will be attacked by machine gun and artillery', though the IRA could depend on 'a well armed garrison of 150 men … or any part of the country when support will come in any numbers'. In light of recent developments, he was

> absolutely convinced that the Free State was sent to its doom by our action last week and come what may the Republic must live. Even if the people and a small percentage of the army are against us for the time being, days or at least weeks will justify our actions when the Irish people can again come forward erect before all nations of the world.[4]

Lynch admitted that it was sad 'to risk having to clash with our old comrades but we cannot count the cost, however I hold we need not shoot them down to maintain our cause'. Lynch closed with a lament that 'so many true and tried' supported the Treaty, but he anticipated they could return to the republican fold later, and when that occurred, 'we in Ireland will have to be really pure this time'.[5] As ever, his attention was towards a renewed war with the British alongside comrades on both sides of the Treaty divide.

Now firmly embedded as a garrison, Lynch and those residing in the Four Courts made the most of it. On 19 May, ever conscious of army standards, Lynch complained to the garrison commander about general sanitation and cleanliness within the complex: 'Scarcely any disinfectants are being used even in the lavatories and the corridors are very often not swept. The entrance to this block is usually in a most untidy condition.'[6] At one point Volunteer Con Casey remembered Lynch coming to him with the request, 'Come along and act as my escort while I get my hair cut'. Casey recalled how Lynch was 'always so meticulous about his appearance and dress'. Heightening the surreal nature of this episode, on arriving at the barber shop a surprised Casey recognised a former RIC detective sergeant from Tralee among the waiting customers.[7]

The attempts to form some sort of unity continued. On 19 April, at 41 Parnell Square, the final IRB conference of the pre-Civil War period took place. Twenty-seven IRB members were present, including Lynch, Collins, Harry Boland, Eoin O'Duffy, Diarmuid O'Hegarty and Florence O'Donoghue. With the two banned Army Conventions and the seizure of the Four Courts and key buildings in the capital having taken place since the last meeting, O'Donoghue remembered how the 'atmosphere of the meeting was tense and explosive'.[8] One observer noted 'hot and long words' between Lynch and Collins over the proposed Free State constitution, which was supposedly of a republican character to appeal to anti-Treaty sentiment.[9] As both chairman of the Provisional Government and head of the IRB Supreme Council, Collins was central to the drafting of the new Free State constitution. Collins said that the constitution would be available in two to three weeks and put forward the suggestion that it could be used as a basis for army unity. Lynch firmly rejected this, saying he – and presumably the section of army he led – would not wait for a draft constitution that may not alter their position, unless it was a republican constitution as Collins promised. Otherwise, Lynch 'would have to take action'.[10]

Florence O'Donoghue then put forward a proposal that the IRB members present appoint a committee of six – three from each side – 'to try to find a basis of Army re-unification and report back to a further meeting of the body then assembled'. Despite hostility from the pro-Treaty element, Collins, after a few minutes' discussion, decided to allow the appointment of such a committee. For the pro-Treaty camp, Diarmuid O'Hegarty was to lead this contingent, and nominated Seán Ó Murthille and Martin Conlon; for the anti-Treaty side, Florence O'Donoghue was chosen to lead, and he nominated Joseph McKelvey and Lynch. (It is unclear from O'Donoghue's account why he was to nominate the other two, given Lynch sat on the Supreme Council.) This committee met four times with few results, and Lynch was disappointed that no guarantee emerged from the pro-Treaty side for a settlement that would maintain the independence of Ireland or for a republican constitution. O'Donoghue noted how Lynch was determined at this juncture to find 'some policy, which would, without dishonour [to the anti-Treaty side], avoid civil war'.[11]

***

Far from the jurisdiction of Lynch's First Southern Division, the six counties of north-east Ireland had been a hotbed of unprecedented violence from 1920 to 1922. As the new state of Northern Ireland, which encompassed these counties, came into being from mid-1921, the Catholic minority found themselves in a hostile environment ruled by a unionist government headed by Prime Minister of Northern Ireland James Craig and backed by their state forces in the form of the Royal Ulster Constabulary bolstered by the all-Protestant paramilitary 'B' Specials. Horrific waves of sectarian violence were unleashed before and after this new state's formation, mainly in Belfast and impacting on the Catholic nationalist populace. This raised the ire of Collins and the Provisional Government, and impelled Collins into direct discussions with Craig. The two so-called Craig–Collins pacts that resulted (the first on 2 February, the second on 30 March) did little to alter the situation, as swathes of Catholic refugees fled across the new border into the new Irish Free State.

Following the second Craig–Collins Pact, IRA activity reduced in Northern Ireland throughout April. The IRA often found it difficult to operate there during this period, given the hostility of much of the Protestant majority that made up the populace. As these pacts resulted in no obvious changes to the situation on the ground in the area of sectarian violence, plans for a joint northern offensive by the two sections of the IRA began. While Collins was genuinely concerned for northern Catholics, he also perhaps saw the advantage of such a proposed offensive, in that it could help unify the divided IRA. The full details of the planning for this offensive remain obscure due to the patchy archival material available, and a full exploration of this episode in the lead-up to the Civil War, and its ramifications, is beyond the context of this study, save for how it pertains to Lynch. As historian Michael Hopkinson has noted, the proposed northern offensive remains 'a very sensitive and controversial subject because of the mistrust, secrecy and confusion involved, and its ... total failure'.[12] One can conclude that Collins was involved in a rather dangerous juggling act, attempting to satisfy his pro-Treaty colleagues, their anti-Treaty opponents, and the British and Northern governments.

Given his stature in the IRA, Lynch was a chief planner along with Collins for the proposed offensive, which was to take place on 19 May.[13] It was to involve the united IRA hitting targets across Northern Ireland to destabilise the new state and potentially overthrow the unionist government. The 'northern offensive' saw units from counties such as Cork and Kerry given arms and munitions in the Four Courts before being sent to the border. One of the few episodes of any note that resulted were the gun battles along the Donegal/Fermanagh border in late May and early June, between the British Army and the IRA (this being the last time both pro- and anti-Treaty IRA Volunteers fought alongside each other), with the latter suffering an outright defeat. However, ultimately, Collins called the northern operation off and, in response to a violent crackdown by the Northern Ireland government, northern IRA Volunteers fled across the border, with many joining the ranks of the pro-Treaty IRA, which became the National Army of the Irish Free State.[14]

In one surviving communication, Lynch blamed the pro-Treaty IRA GHQ in Beggar's Bush for the abandonment of the offensive and for issuing confusing orders. A central component of the northern offensive involved the pro-Treaty IRA swapping their British-supplied weaponry with the anti-Treaty IRA, so if IRA members were captured in the north they would not be carrying such weaponry. Lynch was disgusted when in one instance Eoin O'Duffy complained that anti-Treaty republicans were too slow in responding to arms requests. Demonstrating the convoluted nature of the political situation at the time, he replied that officers attached to his own First Southern Division were 'detained for a week or so at Beggar's Bush [pro-Treaty IRA GHQ] ... were ordered home to their own areas after being so urgently required ... for the North. It is very easy to judge where the responsibility lies for the situation that now exists.'[15]

Surprisingly, within the northern divisions there was little issue over the Treaty – except within Belfast, which was encompassed by the IRA's Third Northern Division. On 8 May, Seamus Woods, the O/C of the pro-Treaty Third Northern Division, wrote directly to Lynch. He complained about the lack of any outcome in the negotiations to unify the IRA, given from 'our point of view in the North it is unfortunate the final stage of unity has not been reached'.[16] Woods was aggrieved about a split within the Third Northern Division, particularly as he estimated that 90 per cent of the IRA had opted to remain with the pro-Treaty GHQ and 'in view of the fact that war conditions exist there, I consider it is up to you to issue orders to put your [anti-Treaty] following to fall in line with the majority, and to fight under one command.' Woods implored Lynch to arrange a visit for both him and Eoin O'Duffy to the Third Northern divisional area, and pointed out that in his view his O/C, Joe McKelvey, who leaned anti-Treaty, no longer had support within his former command.[17] There is no suggestion that Lynch replied to this communication or took Woods up on his request. As historian John Dorney has noted, by June, it was clear any attempt at unity within the IRA 'on a shared hostility to the partition of Ireland could not be sustained'.[18]

***

In the midst of this troubled, uncertain political atmosphere, Lynch was looking forward to his brother Tom's ordination in Thurles. On 1 May, he wrote to Tom and promised to do his very best to attend. On recent political developments, he did 'not wish to dwell too much on the present situation with you as your thoughts should be mostly in another direction until ordination'. However, he was still supremely confident, and, should events turn to open warfare, the IRA leadership was 'absolutely convinced of wiping out the supposed Free State, but we don't mind giving it a slow death, especially when it means the avoidance of the loss of life and general civil war'. Lynch recognised the uncertain political situation for the republican forces and that 'counting weeks from now seems very strange to a soldier. However as long as Irish Nationality is not temporarily sold all goes well for me ... Pray that God may direct us again in direction for final victory.'[19]

On 3 May, a deputation of five anti-Treaty IRA officers was admitted to a sitting of Dáil Éireann at Earlsfort Terrace. Seán O'Hegarty, the formidable O/C of Cork No. 1, addressed the assembly. He had emerged as a surprising opponent to civil war, though he remained opposed to the Treaty. Though this delegation was organised outside the authority of the anti-Treaty IRA Executive, the Dáil proved amenable to hearing O'Hegarty and his wish to prevent military conflict between the former opponents. As a result, a Committee of Ten of both pro- and anti-Treaty IRA officers was appointed (Lynch was not included) to determine if some degree of army unity could be found.

On 4 May, in this spirit of aspiration for unity, and in recognition of the spate of minor incidents that had arisen between both sides, a truce was declared between the pro- and anti-Treaty wings of the IRA, with the announcement of this signed by Lynch and O'Duffy. According to the text of this truce, it was in place 'with a view to giving representatives of both sections of the Army an immediate opportunity to discover a basis for army unification.'[20] The meeting was held at the Mansion House, where Lynch, O'Duffy and others were photographed beforehand. (The accompanying newsreel revealed a jovial scene between pro- and anti-Treaty opponents, with Lynch even showing a rare smile for the cameras.) On 8 May, Lynch and O'Duffy released a further statement ordering an indefinite continuation of this truce, so the Committee of Ten could see the work through to completion.[21] However, on 10 May the Committee of Ten reported to the Dáil that they had failed in their efforts to find a basis for unity. Though their meetings continued until 16 May, this was another effort at finding some sort of compromise that came to nothing.

While perhaps men such as Collins and Mulcahy still held a degree of respect for Lynch even at this juncture, despite their widening differences, not everyone within the pro-Treaty IRA held this view. J.J. O'Connell, nicknamed 'Ginger', observed Lynch up-close in these uncertain early months of 1922. O'Connell was deputy chief of staff of the pro-Treaty IRA, having previously served as the IRA's director of training.[22] In an unpublished memoir, he wrote of Lynch that he was one of 'the most constant callers' at the pro-Treaty IRA GHQ in Beggar's Bush Barracks. O'Connell observed how Lynch 'had very great influence with certain members of GHQ', which O'Connell found hard to understand given Lynch was 'a man hostile to the [Provisional] Government'. He felt 'the secret of Lynch's influence at GHQ can be explained on IRB grounds', because those within the pro-Treaty GHQ 'like myself ... had not any such influence at all'. In his dealings with Lynch, O'Connell realised: 'Gradually one got to feel that one was up against a stone wall, and that Lynch and what he stood for were being given a free hand. And as it fell out all the efforts to placate Lynch were unravelling.' O'Connell, a key member of GHQ, regarded Lynch with suspicion during these endless weeks of negotiation between the two sides of the IRA, and his summation of Lynch is telling:

> Personally I was never inclined to underrate Lynch. I regarded him as a distinctly formidable opponent, who would have to be fought sometime – unless it was made clear to him that he could not fight with any hope of success ... One southern officer, who knew Lynch intimately, agreed with me absolutely in my estimate of him.[23]

On 20 May, Lynch wrote to Hanna Cleary from the Four Courts HQ. Cleary was at that time a leading Cumann na mBan officer in the Anglesboro area.[24] Lynch's firm tone indicated an ongoing debate between the two on the merits of republican strategies, and one is reminded of the earlier, intense political debates between them in 1915, when they also differed. Lynch assured Cleary, who though firmly anti-Treaty was fearful for civil war, 'that there is no one more upset than I am that past comrades should now be shooting one another down'. Furthermore, he felt there 'can be unity if all forces will uphold the established republic now as in the past. It is too degrading and dishonourable for the Irish people to accept a treaty which brings them within the British Empire even if it were only for a short period.' In his view, the 'torture and general suffering gone through, especially during the last few years in upholding the republic would be in vain if the Free State is accepted. Surely the hundreds of our comrades did not die for this or the living go through such torture.' He admitted having 'hopes that the pro-Treaty people have seen the error of their ways and they will come to terms they will not let down the Republic'. Again, Lynch made clear more than anything that he wished to avert any sort of civil war, considering the events in Limerick in March.[25]

On 12 May, Lynch wrote to O'Duffy and complained about the lack of progress in negotiations between both sides of the IRA since their truce announced on 4 May. He lamented that 'no satisfactory effort has been made to discover a basis for Army unification', and, in a striking example of the growing distrust on both sides, accused those on the committee on O'Duffy's side of 'not being willing to discuss the vital matters at issue'. Lynch requested a meeting to discuss the outstanding concerns. If not, 'negotiations must cease if a definite understanding for agreement is not reached'.[26] This lack of enthusiasm for the ongoing truce was also felt by the pro-Treaty side. A lengthy surviving memorandum kept by the pro-Treaty side lists 'a review of some of the breaches of the pact' committed by the anti-Treaty forces.[27]

Mulcahy recorded brief minutes of a meeting between himself, Collins, Lynch and Deasy on the evening of 14 May to work through the outstanding differences. He wrote with bemusement: 'Long talk as if there was [sic] no difficulties.' An impatient Collins left after a suggestion from Lynch and Deasy that 'we should get down to actual facts'. There was general agreement that the truce between the pro- and anti-Treaty factions of the IRA could only last another twenty-four hours.[28] Nonetheless, it seems to have endured.

There were some positive signs civil war could still be prevented. Despite the failure of the Committee of Ten, following a conference, on 20 May, de Valera and Collins signed a controversial pact ahead of the election on 16 June. The pact stipulated that Sinn Féin would campaign as a coalition of pro- and anti-Treaty candidates. Following the election, in which they hoped to win an overall majority, this would theoretically result in an evenly balanced coalition government of pro- and anti-Treaty Sinn Féin figures, and was another effort to use politics to stave off a military conflict. Despite his reticence in this regard, Lynch was enthused at the supposed newfound unity this caused in the revolutionary movement, and confidently remarked to an IRA commander in Limerick, 'Collins was back with his own crowd ... and he would definitely remain that way.'[29]

In the midst of all this, Lynch was still planning to attend Tom's ordination. Ahead of the event, he wrote to Tom about making arrangements to bring their mother, other family members, some of his fellow IRA officers and even two sympathetic priests 'who have been special friends of mine during the war'. Lynch warned Tom that all the IRA members 'will turn up in uniform so I hope you will not be fed up with our military appearance'. He assured his brother that he did not 'forget saying a few prayers these times for you. I am certain some mysterious hand directed me through danger during all the escapades of the war otherwise it would have been impossible to get out of many certain trips. Thank God I am yet alive for Ireland's sake and that I was given the opportunity to assist her.' He also expressed hope at renewed negotiations between pro- and anti-Treaty IRA officers following the pact. Lynch seemed conscious of the tensions between the British cabinet and the Provisional Government due to the pact, and admitted 'a lot depends on the present negotiations in London [over the pact], the trouble there shows the satisfactory arrangement on our side'.[30]

These renewed IRA negotiations referred to by Lynch continued into the first week of June. While he remained central to such discussions, and was certainly not as extreme as O'Connor or Mellows in his position, his contributions demonstrated little deviation from the standard republican position. In one memorandum, he was still insisting that 'the IRA be maintained as the Army of the Republic under the control of an Independent Executive'.[31]

The basic make-up of the proposed unified IRA leadership – which was to be a combination of both pro- and anti-Treaty IRA leaders, a concession that Mulcahy was willing to accept – was a major stumbling block. On 7 June, Lynch wrote to Mulcahy that while new proposals from the latter's side had been accepted by the Executive, the personnel proposed by the pro-Treaty side for this new IRA GHQ were unacceptable. Lynch explained that the anti-Treaty IRA Executive was agreeable to a minister for defence representing the IRA and for Mulcahy to remain in the position, unless the next Army Convention decided otherwise. However, the anti-Treaty IRA Executive insisted on filling the position of chief of staff, although it offered other key positions to the pro-Treaty leadership. If this proposal was not agreed upon, the Executive would press for an IRA Convention on 18 June.[32]

On 8 June, Lynch wrote a note to Mulcahy that if it were agreed that Lynch be chief of staff in a unified IRA and in light of the proposed election pact:

> I am prepared to guarantee ... that I will do my utmost to maintain ... stability and will not endeavour to overthrow the administration of the government to be formed as a result of the elections of 16 June even though Mr. de Valera or any of his party do not become members of that Government, this guarantee to cover the period during which the constitution is being considered ...[33]

On 10 June, Ernie O'Malley wrote his own communication to Mulcahy in his capacity as secretary of the anti-Treaty IRA Executive. He reminded Mulcahy that the chief of staff position must be filled by an officer of the 'Executive forces' and that the Executive was agreeable to Mulcahy remaining in the position of minister for defence, at least until the 18 June convention. O'Malley suggested that the positions of adjutant general, quartermaster general and director of publicity be filled by pro-Treaty officers, while other suggested officer positions were agreeable to the anti-Treaty side. However, in a blunt addendum to his communication that was not present in Lynch's communication of 7 June, O'Malley made it clear to Mulcahy that 'these negotiations cannot be prolonged' after noon on 12 June.[34]

In a reply to O'Malley on 12 June, and in reference to Lynch's earlier letter, a clearly impatient Mulcahy insisted that the pro-Treaty side 'have gone in this matter as far as it is possible for us to go' in terms of the proposed make-up of a unified IRA of both pro- and anti-Treaty IRA officers. He made clear that any proposals from his side 'must not fall short of those we represent either in ability or patriotism; and these proposals have been inspired by a hope that we would be met in a spirit not less generous then our own', and reminded O'Malley about the 'very great national responsibility that rests upon us'. Mulcahy ended with the suggestion that the situation could only be left to whatever new coalition government was formed from the upcoming election.[35]

Tom Lynch was ordained on 11 June and the two days of his brother's absence from duty to attend was the longest such period since the Truce.[36] It was to be Lynch's final respite before the outbreak of a new conflict.

On 14 June, by majority vote, the anti-Treaty IRA Executive passed a resolution that announced the cessation of all negotiations on army unification with the pro-Treaty side. It vowed 'to take whatever action may be necessary to maintain the Republic against British aggression', while making clear no action would be taken against soldiers on the pro-Treaty side.[37] The text of the resolution was personally handed to Mulcahy in his capacity as the chief representative on the pro-Treaty side by Rory O'Connor and Ernie O'Malley on 15 June. However, only Lynch, Deasy and Moylan on the Executive actually remained in favour of these proposals. A stark split now took place among the anti-Treaty IRA ranks.

Also on 14 June, perhaps in light of little progress made with anti-Treaty republicans and one-time comrades, Collins made a speech in Cork repudiating the electoral pact with de Valera and urging the people of Ireland to vote for whomever they considered the best candidates.[38] The general election took place on 16 June and, after the results were fully counted, showed a decisive victory for the pro-Treaty Sinn Féin candidates and the other parties that supported the Treaty, such as Labour and the Farmers' Party. On the same day as the election, the proposed new Free State constitution was published in the newspapers. Due to pressure from the British cabinet, it contained little of a republican character that would appease the anti-Treaty side and maintained the controversial oath of allegiance.

Could Lynch have changed course with this electoral outcome? Though promoting the establishment of a republican democracy was central to Lynch's republicanism, as the political scientist Bill Kissane explained, 'evidence of a strong constitutional strain in the anti-Treaty thinking is not quite the same as an acceptance of the popular will as a deciding factor in national affairs'.[39] Even a sympathetic biographer such as O'Donoghue conceded Lynch had something of an 'utter indifference to public opinion provided his own actions [in his view] were just and honourable'.[40] Lynch even admitted to his brother that he worried little about wider Irish civil society turning against the anti-Treaty republicans as 'I always way [sic] my conscience when too many are on my side.'[41]

Lynch, like much of the republican military and political leadership by mid-1922, simply could not accept that the results of the election provided the pro-Treaty side with a legitimacy grounded in popular support. For the anti-Treaty republican leadership, the pro-Treaty victory in the election, and their claim that it confirmed their right to rule, simply confirmed their bad faith, particularly in light of the rejection of the pact. In the firm view of Lynch and other anti-Treaty republicans, both the Treaty and the 1922 general election results were the products of a British threat of resumption of war in Ireland made by David Lloyd George to the Sinn Féin plenipotentiaries in December and were, therefore, entirely illegitimate.[42]

The night of the election, Lynch wrote to Tom. He seemed deeply saddened over the turn in events and to have little faith that the much hoped-for unity within the IRA was possible: 'Well Tom, the situation generally is beyond anything I could any longer hold out hope for ... I always held out hopes to the last, but really all are blighted now ... I feel all my life's work has been in vain. Surely this is a terrible way to feel. Would we could even get back all our glorious dead.'[43]

***

While the election votes were being counted, increasingly doomed attempts at IRA unity had continued. Joseph O'Connor of the Third Battalion, Dublin Brigade, noted that while there 'were many strong men on the IRA Executive ... we failed to produce one extra-strong man to rule the others' – clearly, in his view, Lynch was not such an individual.[44] On 18 June, the third IRA Convention was held at the Mansion House to clarify the IRA's position, and Lynch strongly advocated the proposals for army unity as agreed with Mulcahy and other pro-Treaty leaders. This was despite, in Moss Twomey's recollection, Lynch's own disillusionment over the proposals.[45]

Relations between the divided republicans at the convention further soured following Tom Barry's introduction of a motion to declare war on Britain and give British forces seventy-two hours' notice to evacuate Ireland. Barry's thinking, shared by much of the republican leadership (though not Lynch), was that a renewed war with Britain could bring unity to both sections of the IRA. When the motion was defeated, a stark and unhelpful division arose among the anti-Treaty republican ranks as civil war loomed. The component parts of this division were led by Lynch on one side, who advocated the unity proposals, and by Rory O'Connor on the other, representing the body of the anti-Treaty IRA in the Four Courts, who advocated the resumption of war with Britain. In the aftermath of the vote on the controversial motion, with 103 delegates for the motion versus 118 against, O'Connor led a walk-out of the minority contingent back to the Four Courts. O'Donoghue, who sided with Lynch, recalled how the convention broke up 'in gloom and confusion'.[46]

Joseph O'Connor, who supported the war motion, was chairing the convention when the vote rejecting the pro-war faction's motion passed, and he recalled how after the events of the convention he was 'a physically sick and disgusted man'. O'Connor went to the Four Courts the following morning and hoped to get permission for a further meeting of the Executive, but when he arrived a new development did little to alleviate his mood. On entering the building, 'the sentry showed me a photograph of the officers of the First Southern Division, and stated he was instructed to refuse entry to any of those in the picture. I tried to get the person responsible for this, but failed.' Although O'Connor succeeded in getting permission to hold another meeting of the Executive, Lynch refused to enter the Four Courts, aggrieved at the instruction barring him and other First Southern Division members from entry. The subsequent meeting was held at 6 Gardiner's Row and 'was frigid and it was decided to take no action'.[47]

Liam Deasy noted the irony that by that point Lynch 'was not considered sufficiently extreme by some of his colleagues'.[48] Twomey remembered that Lynch 'took no action whatever which would in any way cause a clash, even of opinion, with them. But he felt very despondent over the whole situation'.[49] Deasy further noted how leading republicans in the faction led by Rory O'Connor 'could see no good in Michael Collins, Dick Mulcahy and Eoin O'Duffy'. While perhaps somewhat understandable given the pro-Treaty stance of those men, Deasy was struck that this distrust extended to the faction led by Lynch, who were then 'regarded as being well intentioned but failing in our stand to maintain the Republic'. Deasy did not take this to heart, as while 'we [Lynch's faction] were regarded as moderate, we felt that our policy was consistent and meaningful'.[50]

On the night of 19 June, Joe O'Connor was shocked to find a 'convention' being held in the Four Courts by those who had organised the walk-out at the Mansion House. As the official chairman of the IRA Convention, he protested, being particularly aggrieved at a proposal by those present for a war council of seven to be set up. O'Connor pointed out that if this happened, there were going to be three armies operating in this part of Ireland. An argument ensued, until the intervention of Cathal Brugha (now just an ordinary IRA Volunteer, but still a figure of respect) resulted in an agreement to refer the matter to yet another IRA Convention to be held in the Four Courts. Following this, Lynch and the First Southern Division officers started attending meetings at the Courts again but, with the agreement of the Executive members in the Four Courts garrison, the duties of chief of staff passed from Lynch to Joseph McKelvey.[51] McKelvey, who remains historically something of an elusive figure, had been O/C of the IRA's Third Northern Division and a member of the IRB. Though most of his division had gone pro-Treaty,

McKelvey was firmly aligned with the anti-Treaty IRA. Likely due to his status within the IRB and IRA, and particularly his defence of northern Catholics during the sectarian violence in Belfast in 1920, he was a figure of considerable respect among his comrades, making him ideal for the role in the eyes of men such as O'Connor and Mellows.[52] In the event, his appointment in Lynch's place as chief of staff did nothing to quell the increasingly bitter meetings of the anti-Treaty Executive in these pivotal days, which were, according to O'Connor, 'often far from satisfactory and we seemed to be unable to reach decisions. Thus, the Rory O'Connor element was doing one thing and the Lynch party something different. Mellows … was not the kind … to force a decision.'[53] However, a dramatic series of events would soon eclipse the squabbles among the anti-Treaty IRA leaders.

On 22 June 1922, Sir Henry Wilson, former chief of the Imperial General Staff and security advisor to the Northern Ireland government, was assassinated in central London. His two assassins were London IRA Volunteers: Richard Dunne and Reginald O'Sullivan. Both were British Army veterans (O'Sullivan had even lost a leg in the Great War) and members of the IRB. While the British Secret Service concluded that Dunne and O'Sullivan acted independently of the IRA Executive in the Four Courts, numerous accounts assert that Collins secretly ordered the assassination in light of Wilson's relationship with the northern government.[54] What is certain is that Lynch was unaware of the operation until it occurred. In conversation with one Volunteer in the aftermath, he remarked how unfortunate it was that O'Sullivan did not possess two sound legs.[55] Lynch and many of the anti-Treaty leadership did not realise the full ramifications the Wilson assassination would have – the British cabinet demanded the Provisional Government act against the anti-Treaty IRA garrison in the Four Courts, having deemed them responsible for Wilson's death.

Another action with considerable consequences for the anti-Treaty IRA at this time was an attempt by some of the Four Courts men to enforce the Belfast boycott, originally overseen by Dáil Éireann during the War of Independence. This scheme was a boycott of businesses and firms in Belfast, in protest at the sectarian violence against the Catholic populace in Northern Ireland. The economically damaging embargo had been lifted as part of the Collins–Craig pacts, but the anti-Treaty IRA attempted to reimpose it. On 26 June, Leo Henderson led a party of IRA Volunteers in a raid on a premises on Dublin's Baggot Street, due to this firm continuing to do business in Belfast. Henderson was arrested by Free State forces, so Ernie O'Malley devised a retaliation – the kidnapping of General J.J. 'Ginger' O'Connell, now deputy chief of staff of the pro-Treaty IRA. O'Connell was abducted outside his girlfriend's home that evening, and O'Malley personally telephoned Eoin O'Duffy in Portobello Barracks to inform him of this.[56]

The anti-Treaty forces in the Four Courts assumed a prisoner exchange would follow, but the Provisional Government cabinet, which met on the afternoon of 27 June to discuss Wilson's assassination and O'Connell's kidnapping, viewed the latter episode as a direct challenge to their authority. Following the cabinet meeting, Mulcahy alleged that Collins said to him, 'I think we'll have to fight these fellows' – likely a reference to just the anti-Treaty IRA garrison in the Four Courts.[57] Collins' decision may have been affected by his knowledge of the split in the anti-Treaty IRA ranks and a lack of awareness, as will be seen, that the rift had begun to heal.[58] With pressure from the British cabinet to respond to the continued occupation of the Four Courts, O'Connell's kidnapping now presented an opportunity to act.

Unbeknownst to many on the pro-Treaty side, by this point a form of rapprochement had begun among the anti-Treaty republicans. Several days before Henderson's arrest, Lynch, while in the Clarence Hotel, had received several visitors from the Four Courts garrison. Moss Twomey later distinctly recalled a long meeting between Lynch, Mellows and McKelvey.[59] In his memoir, Deasy recalled getting a phone call in Mallow from Lynch on the morning of 27 June, instructing him to come up on the next train to Dublin. Lynch 'emphasised that the matter was of the utmost importance, hinting that there was an approach from the IRA leadership in the Four Courts.'[60]

Meeting Deasy at Kingsbridge station, Lynch informed him that they were proceeding immediately to a meeting at the Four Courts. Deasy later wrote how, on arrival there, McKelvey and Mellows met them and took them to a room where they discussed matters until after midnight. Deasy was later unable to recall the full details of the meeting, but the ultimate outcome was 'our army was reunited and Liam Lynch had resumed his office as the commanding officer'.[61]

Joseph O'Connor, in his witness statement, has referred to this as a formal meeting of the anti-Treaty IRA Executive, with Lynch present, beginning at five o'clock that day. O'Connor expressed surprise that, at least in his presence, no mention was made of Henderson's arrest and the subsequent kidnapping of O'Connell the previous day.[62] As the Executive meeting ended, O'Connor was informed that all pro-Treaty IRA members had been confined to their barracks. O'Connor duly informed Lynch, who surmised, 'I suppose it is in connection with the arrest of Ginger O'Connell' and told him to let McKelvey know.[63] From this account, Lynch did not seem overly worried.

On the return of Lynch and the others to the Clarence Hotel that night, Deasy recalled that Lynch informed divisional officers 'we had healed the split between ourselves, the Executive members, and the garrison of the Four Courts. He added that he had resumed his role of Chief-of-Staff … if the Free State Army were to force a Civil War the re-united anti-Treaty forces would resist by every means at its disposal.'[64] Unlike Deasy, Twomey remembered no discussion of Lynch's return to the chief of staff role, but he made clear 'they had made great progress to fix up with people in the courts that night and Liam Lynch was in great humour'.[65] Even if no formal decision was made regarding Lynch resuming the role of chief of staff, it seemed to Lynch and his allies that such a process was under way. In his biography of Lynch, Florence O'Donoghue, in recognition of this confusion, ultimately concluded, 'how far these talks had taken [Lynch] towards a resumption of his post as Chief-of-Staff is unimportant, for it is clear that the differences which split the Executive … were being healed … It was the wish of every member of the Executive that he should resume his post, and there is no doubt he would have done so in any event.'[66]

With this rift among the anti-Treaty contingent of the IRA now seemingly healed, Lynch was almost certainly exuberant at recent developments, and perhaps now on a path to the unity among former comrades that he so greatly desired. By all accounts, the ramifications of O'Connell's kidnapping were of no immediate concern to him and he seemed to little fear a response from the Provisional Government. In their room at the Clarence Hotel, Lynch and Deasy continued to discuss recent events. Despite Mellows' and McKelvey's fears that preparations being made by pro-Treaty forces in Dublin presaged an attack on anti-Treaty forces, Lynch and Deasy were confident there was no immediate danger for the Four Courts garrison.

Eventually, Deasy drifted off to sleep. It was around 2 a.m. on Wednesday, 28 June 1922.[67]

Chapter 8

'How could all our dreams have been so blighted' (June–October 1922)

AT AROUND SIX O'CLOCK THAT morning, Liam Deasy was roused from his sleep by Lynch.

'Do you not hear the shelling?' Lynch asked his shocked comrade, 'The Free State army has been bombarding the Four Courts for two hours ...' Both men sat in silence for a while as they listened to the shelling of the Four Courts, too stunned to speak.[1] In the early hours of the morning of 28 June, Mulcahy had directed members of the pro-Treaty IRA to train two eighteen-pounder field guns on the Four Courts across the River Liffey. When the 180-man garrison under the command of Rory O'Connor and Liam Mellows refused a call to surrender, the bombardment began at 4.07 a.m.[2] The eighteen-pounder guns had been supplied to the Provisional Government by the departing British Army garrison commanded by General MacCready.

Thus came about an abrupt and definite end to the weeks of near-endless, convoluted negotiations and debates between the former comrades. The increased hardening of stances on both sides of the Treaty divide had now been brought to their logical conclusion. The ultimate result of the artillery bombardment of the Four Courts was to firmly unite the disparate factions of the anti-Treaty IRA. This was summed up best by O'Donoghue, who later wrote, 'nothing was more certain to solidify Republican opposition than this crude bludgeoning'.[3] A council of war of anti-Treaty officers was now imperative, but Deasy felt due 'perhaps to our optimism and over-confidence that war was such a remote possibility, no proper plans had been drawn up'.[4] This lack of forward planning was to greatly hamper the entire republican military effort from the outset of the conflict.

At the hastily arranged meeting in the Clarence Hotel, Lynch assembled a group of key First Southern Division officers, including Liam Deasy and Seán Moylan, along with other key figures such as Cathal Brugha and Éamon de Valera. All present agreed to resist by military force the Provisional Government's attack on the IRA Executive's garrison.[5] Instead of aiding in the fighting in Dublin, and with no military plan drawn up, the First Southern Division officers opted to return to their local commands and defend their areas, with Lynch setting up a GHQ in the south.[6] Dorothy Macardle claims Lynch sent a message to the besieged IRA Executive members in the Four Courts 'telling them that was he was going to rouse the country'.[7] Confusing matters as to when Lynch actually returned to the position of chief of staff, Moss Twomey later claimed it was at this pivotal meeting at the Clarence Hotel.[8]

Following the Clarence Hotel meeting, a republican proclamation was issued on behalf of the entire IRA Executive declaring war on the Provisional Government and its army, further underscoring the unity of all anti-Treaty republican forces. Moss Twomey and several others drafted this statement, which was to become unofficially known as the 'Four Courts Proclamation'.[9] Other accounts have vaguely identified Lynch as one of the principal authors, and it is likely he had some degree of input into and advice about the text.[10] Signed with the names of all those on the IRA Executive, copies of this proclamation were distributed throughout the capital during the subsequent fighting in Dublin and published in a republican newssheet. The document addressed 'fellow citizens of the Irish Republic' and told its readers, 'The fateful hour has come. At the dictation of our hereditary enemy, our rightful cause is being treacherously assailed by recreant Irishmen.' This proclamation was a lengthy call to arms for the Republic modelled on the 1916 Proclamation, though notably, unlike that document, there is no mention of a republican form of government to be created.

As the attack on the Four Courts raged, Lynch and the southern officers quickly departed the Clarence Hotel. Moylan later recalled that the general view, among those present, 'was that each man should try immediately to get back to his own command'. Lynch initially suggested his group should try and hire a car, but after several attempts they failed to do so. Ultimately, they opted to travel by train from Kingsbridge station.[11] Lynch's group arranged transport in two jaunting cars from the hotel to the station. Not far from the Clarence, they were held up by a pro-Treaty IRA patrol led by former Squad member Liam Tobin. What was to transpire over the next few hours reflected the atmosphere of considerable uncertainty amongst both sides as to who exactly to regard as the enemy – even with fighting now begun. Tobin's patrol escorted the group to Wellington (now Griffith) Barracks, where Lynch was separated from the others to have a private conference with General Eoin O'Duffy. O'Duffy, chief of staff of the pro-Treaty forces, was soon to oversee the South-Western Command, the area to which Lynch and his officers were headed.[12]

In private conference with Lynch, O'Duffy asked him what he thought of the situation in the capital. Lynch's reply was brief: 'I think ye're all mad.'[13] This remark seemed to imply to O'Duffy that Lynch was referring to both sides, and that Lynch himself would remain neutral, along with the entirety of the First Southern Division. In this respect, O'Duffy may have felt Lynch's presence in the south-western territory could have a limiting effect on the spread of the Civil War, and he let Lynch and the Southern officers go as a goodwill measure. It is possible that Lynch was deliberately vague to ensure a swift release.[14] (There is no evidence to suggest O'Duffy was aware of Lynch's return to the role of chief of staff of the anti-Treaty forces or the production of the recent proclamation.) Deasy found the whole incident puzzling, especially as he was not questioned despite being the second-highest ranking officer after Lynch in the First Southern Division. He did have a general, friendly conversation with O'Duffy before his group's departure, however.[15] Seán Moylan, who later questioned Lynch about the exchange, certainly believed their release was chiefly due to O'Duffy's misunderstanding of the 'mad' remark.[16]

After a journey by train, Lynch and his group reached the town of Castlecomer, County Kilkenny that evening by car, where they were met by a pro-Treaty IRA patrol which then resulted in what Deasy remembered as 'a very embarrassing incident'.[17] Lynch and the anti-Treaty southern officers were invited to a meal at a nearby barracks as a friendly gesture – which Deasy implored Lynch to accept given how long they had been travelling – and there, 'whatever tension may have previously existed quickly melted away. We spoke freely of the war with regret.' Parting near midnight, one of the pro-Treaty IRA officers asked Lynch's group to sign a piece of foolscap 'as a token of the friendship and camaraderie generated during our visit'. Lynch, Deasy and the others did so before they parted.[18]

The result of these two seemingly friendly encounters with pro-Treaty IRA representatives in the opening hours of the conflict was a statement by the Provisional Government, later published on 22 July 1922 in their *War News*, in which it was claimed Lynch was released by O'Duffy 'on giving his word of honour that he disapproved of the policy of the Irregulars, and would not assist them'.[19] The signatures of the anti-Treaty officers at the Castlecomer Barracks were later presented as evidence that the IRA officers were to keep their word to O'Duffy and remain neutral.[20] As with O'Duffy, it is possible Lynch remained deliberately vague at Castlecomer as to his intentions. However, he was vehement about these accusations of bad faith. 'I gave no promise of any kind,' he insisted, notably distressed, in an exchange with Robert Brennan several days later in Mallow. 'They wanted me to, but I refused. How can they tell such lies?'[21]

Both episodes, particularly the one in Kilkenny, were to betray Lynch's own political naiveté in the presumed goodwill of his new opponents, and their willingness to exploit this. In the days ahead, he was to be similarly outmanoeuvred in a much more dramatic fashion.

✳✳✳

In the familiar surroundings of the barracks in Mallow, Lynch established his first temporary base for his GHQ. There, on 29 June, he held a meeting of all available leaders of the IRA Executive. The meeting led to a unanimous agreement to gain control of the Shannon crossing by quickly capturing Limerick city. As Paddy O'Brien noted, it was Lynch's intention 'that by isolating the south and cementing it, the Provisional Government forces could become frustrated and so relent their holding'.[22] On 30 June, Lynch issued a statement to all anti-Treaty IRA units stating that communications had been 'established with all Southern, Western and Eastern Divisions, and a united plan of action [was] being carried out'. He expressed the hope of 'rapid progress towards complete control of the West and Southern Ireland for the Republic' and assured IRA fighters that the Dublin Brigade had control of the situation as the fighting in Dublin continued.[23] The historian Calton Younger surmised that, on arrival in Mallow, Lynch possibly assumed that the position of his forces in Dublin would become untenable, and his move to Cork probably suggests that he preferred to operate in territory with which he was more familiar.[24]

The army negotiations prior to the outbreak of civil war had left Lynch and other senior figures with little time to prepare a solid military strategy for the anti-Treaty IRA in case of war. Now operating on a considerable degree of improvisation, Lynch viewed the counties of Cork, Kerry, Waterford and parts of Limerick and Tipperary – encompassing much of the First Southern Division area – as essential in the formation of a significant block of territory that would be fully occupied by the republican military resistance. This would be bounded by the 'Limerick–Waterford line', which ran through Tipperary, Golden, Cashel, Fethard, Clonmel and Carrick-on-Suir and could be defended by republican forces, at least in theory. However, as O'Donoghue has rightly noted, holding this territory would prove difficult for the IRA in light of their lack of heavy artillery and machine guns as well as its long, undefended coastline.[25] Moreover, it was less a defensive line that was established; more depended on the anti-Treaty IRA holding their local positions across this area – sometimes referred to as Lynch's 'Munster Republic'. In the view of this author, Lynch's ambitions for this Limerick–Waterford line remain a somewhat misunderstood aspect of his strategy during the Civil War, as no territory was ever formerly established as an alternative state known as the 'Munster Republic'. The term is found nowhere in contemporary IRA correspondence and was never used by Lynch.[26] The confusion perhaps arises from Lynch's recurring claim of holding the south for the Republic, and republican propaganda referring to an 'army of the south', as well as the adoption of the 'Munster Republic' phrase retrospectively in histories of the period. His intention in establishing this defensive line is clear: to maintain this territory for anti-Treaty republicans as a bulwark against the establishment of the authority of the Provisional Government in the entirety of its new jurisdiction.

Following the surrender of the Four Courts garrison, fighting between the forces of the anti-Treaty IRA and pro-Treaty IRA played out in Dublin city centre from 30 June until 5 July. The fighting ended with a clear win for the latter, with anti-Treaty volunteers surrendering and hundreds imprisoned in the aftermath. One of the most notable casualties was Cathal Brugha, who was fighting in the anti-Treaty IRA ranks.[27] Séumas Robinson, second-in-command of the Second Southern Division, was bitterly disappointed that Lynch did not send more aid to the capital and compared it to the wider country not turning out for the Easter Rising.[28] Joseph O'Connor spoke for many in the IRA leadership in the capital when he later recalled of those behind the Limerick–Waterford line: 'They were doing well, but what a pity it was we lost those first few days in Dublin.'[29]

On 3 July, a parting of the ways arrived for Lynch and one of his most valued officers, when Florence O'Donoghue wrote to Lynch and offered his resignation as adjutant general of the First Southern Division and from the IRA. In his moving letter of resignation, O'Donoghue said that he felt 'there is nothing in the circumstances of the origin of the present conflict which could justify me in taking part in it'. He made clear that his sympathies were entirely with Lynch, 'but my judgement convinces me that out of Civil War will come, not the Republic ... but a prolonged struggle in which the best elements in the country will be annihilated or overborne'. Only if the British took up arms could he return to the

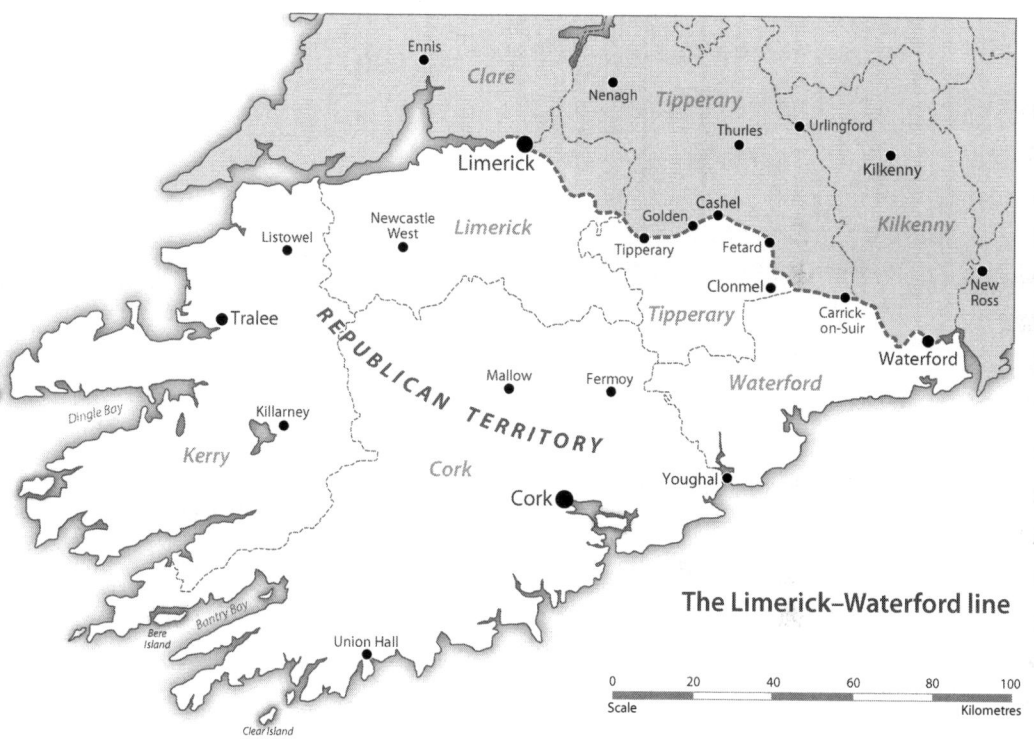

Map 2: At the outbreak of the Civil War on 28 June 1922, Liam Lynch immediately ventured to the First Southern divisional area and set up his initial HQ in Mallow. In the first few days of the conflict, he devised a loose strategy for the anti-Treaty IRA forces to hold the territory south of 'the Limerick–Waterford line' for republicans and prevent the movement of pro-Treaty forces. This area is sometimes wrongly referred to as the 'Munster Republic', a term never used by Lynch in existing IRA correspondence; it is a retrospective term used as a short-hand reference for this territory.

fight. In any event: 'As I cannot wish you success I will hope your work will in its result help to bring us nearer to the ideal we all have at heart.'[30] O'Donoghue later claimed that Lynch told him some months after his letter of resignation that he continued to leave O'Donoghue's position of adjutant general vacant in the hopes he would return.[31] Though O'Donoghue left the IRA with feelings of goodwill towards Lynch, the tenor of their dealings in the months ahead was to be quite different.

✶✶✶

In the initial weeks of fighting, Robert Brennan observed of Lynch, 'He was a strange young man to be at the head of a rebel army ... His looks, bearing and presence might have belonged to a single-minded, devoted priest ... without any training or experience, he had discovered in himself wonderful military qualities.' Yet, Brennan realised Lynch's 'heart was not in this fight of brothers. There had been something glorious and holy in the fight against the British, but now ...'[32]

Lynch began a pattern over the coming weeks of frequent movement between republican territories in order to consolidate headquarters in each key area. On 4 July, he went to Limerick city, where anti-Treaty IRA forces from Cork and Kerry already occupied key positions, to set up a headquarters at New Barracks.[33] At the outbreak of conflict, the Provisional Government cabinet had recognised the danger of the anti-Treaty IRA taking the city, and ordered Michael Brennan of the pro-Treaty Western Division and Donnacha O'Hannigan of the pro-Treaty Fourth Southern to move their forces into Limerick. For the second time in as many months, Limerick city was threatening to become a key battleground. This was not lost on General Brennan, who realised that 'whoever held Limerick held the south and the west'.[34] Brennan's overriding worry 'was that Lynch would attack me before they [additional pro-Treaty IRA forces] turned up, because we couldn't last ... I had to keep him talking to keep him from attacking.' Brennan's central fear was that if Limerick was under the IRA's total control, this created a 'solid block against the Treaty forces' through the provinces of Connacht and Munster, as was exactly

Lynch's intent. This, in his view, could allow Lynch 'to rush strong bodies of men to intervene in the Dublin fighting'.[35] Indeed, at an anti-Treaty IRA Executive meeting in October, Lynch, in a report on the fighting, admitted that the Limerick truce negotiations held up a 'plan for clearing of Posts right up to Dublin'.[36]

O'Hannigan, meanwhile, was an old comrade and former neighbour of Lynch, who had commanded the East Limerick Brigade during the War of Independence and had already had a near-altercation with the IRA. O'Hannigan's forces had occupied Ashford Castle in Mayo and found themselves surrounded by the anti-Treaty forces in the area in the days previous. Lynch, according to Deasy, felt 'any leniency [towards O'Hannigan] might seem an abuse of his authority in favour of a personal friend'. Nonetheless, he took Deasy up on his offer to work with the local anti-Treaty commander to find a solution. Following Deasy's intervention, O'Hannigan and his men departed the area still bearing arms. Deasy felt Lynch's 'happiness and satisfaction' over the peaceful resolution were very much evident, and that, at this juncture, he and Lynch 'were now of one mind in our efforts to find some way to end a campaign which we felt was going to destroy a solidarity which was the only hope of peace'.[37] No doubt the feelings of goodwill Lynch felt had been engineered between him and his old comrade motivated initial truce negotiations with O'Hannigan a few days later in Limerick city.

Lynch, at this point, felt the best solution to neutralise the pro-Treaty military forces was by ensuring the theme of all agreements was that neither side would attack the other.[38] In this respect, he was responsible for a degree of subtle deception, since, as Hopkinson noted, Lynch's efforts at an agreement in Limerick were 'an attempt to consolidate Republican control of Munster and to limit the spread of the war'. This could also have paved the way for an agreement with the Provisional Government.[39] The agreement that was reached on 7 July, as O'Donoghue noted, was representative 'of what was in the minds of officers like Lynch and O'Hannigan, old comrades in the fight against the British but now on opposite sides in civil conflict'.[40] One of the terms was that both sides would confine themselves to designated areas in the city. Most crucially, the IRA would ensure an 'abstention from attack on Comdt. General Hannigan's Forces'. This was despite the fighting taking place elsewhere in the country between pro- and anti-Treaty military forces.[41] A subsequent agreement clarified the retention of certain barracks and outposts by both sides.

Lynch and Hannigan agreed 'to these conditions in the practicable certainty that National peace and unity will eventuate from our efforts and we guarantee to use every means in our power to get this peace'.[42] A cover letter from the two men made clear their intention to meet Brennan of the pro-Treaty Western Division in the hopes he would accept these terms.[43] As Hannigan and Lynch negotiated with Brennan, Eoin O'Duffy was concerned enough to dispatch General Dermot McManus to Limerick to cancel Hannigan's agreement.[44] On arrival, McManus made his displeasure clear to Lynch in a letter: 'I have definite instructions that no such agreement even if signed could be admitted by GHQ and these Officers had no authority whatever to enter into such agreement.' McManus added that on 5 July he had instructed both Brennan and Hannigan that no further meeting was to take place, yet both sides still met. Furthermore, as the commanding officer on the pro-Treaty side McManus would 'herewith reserve full liberty of action and I have made certain dispositions to protect any posts in the City and their communications'.[45]

In any event, despite McManus' instructions, Brennan and Lynch came to a subsequent agreement on 7 July that was rather vague and muddled in detail. The agreement, signed by both, called for a conference to be held 'in the interests of a united Ireland' between leaders of the pro- and anti-Treaty military forces 'as soon as Séan MacEoin can be got into the area'.[46] McManus reluctantly conceded to this agreement between Brennan and Lynch, provided 'there is no change in the military situation here'.[47] Brennan meanwhile had to contend with suspicion from both his superior officers and the Provisional Government. He later said that neither he nor O'Hannigan felt Lynch 'had the slightest intention of ending "this fratricidal strife" except on the basis of imposing his views on his opponents'.[48]

Lynch himself judged the agreement to be a success, writing in one report on the situation that 'we will control from the Shannon to Carlow in a day or two'. Retrospectively, some of Lynch's allies on the anti-Treaty side felt the agreement was less tactical manoeuvring on his part and more indicative of their chief of staff's distaste for civil war.[49] Lynch nonetheless gained a short-term propaganda victory with the publication of the agreement, which apparently did nothing to assuage the fears of the Provisional Government cabinet that Brennan could not be counted on to remain loyal.[50]

Whether Lynch's primary objective was to use the Limerick agreement to seek greater terms with the Provisional Government was rendered moot, as the signing of the final agreement proved to Brennan his stalling tactics had worked. By not securing a key bridge into the city, the anti-Treaty IRA had allowed a considerable number of pro-Treaty forces with their arms to enter Limerick during the period of negotiations.[51] O'Donoghue noted that the final Limerick agreement was signed on the same day that the Provisional Government began a major recruitment drive for the new National Army among the populace, evidence in his view that 'Government policy had determined to destroy that section of the Army which refused to accept the Treaty.'[52] It seemed like fighting between the two sides in Limerick was only a matter of time.

In the meantime, Lynch had to deal with the concerns of the city's main civilian representative, Lord Mayor Stephen O'Meara. Their correspondence revealed regular, polite and even helpful exchanges, with Lynch in frequent agreement with O'Meara as to the maintenance of law and order in the city during a relative peace (Lynch being under the assumption for the most part that his agreed truce would endure). On 8 July, O'Meara implored both sides to allow a return to normality in the city, suggesting the returning of surplus commandeered goods, payment for goods retained, as well as the removal of barricades and evacuation of buildings.[53] In reply, Lynch assured O'Meara that his quartermaster general was ensuring the return of any stores of no use to his side, and though giving no guarantee of payment for stores retained he would 'see that a receipt is given for every article commandeered by us'. Lynch expressed his belief that the pro-Treaty military forces were evacuating buildings and removing barricades, and said he had issued orders for those under his command to do the same. At the end of the message, he suggested 'closing of Public houses at 7pm each evening and until further notice, in this I will actively co-operate'.[54] O'Meara agreed by telegram to this suggestion.[55] This exchange revealed that Lynch was determined to ensure the republican side was not held responsible for any outbreak of anarchy during the truce period.

Yet, the already precarious situation was not to endure. On 11 July, Brennan sent a message to Lynch informing him that the fragile truce was broken following the killing of a pro-Treaty soldier in the city. Lynch had, by then, moved his headquarters to Clonmel.[56] It was there that Robert Brennan found him in an office 'putting the finishing touches to a flagged map showing the territory held by the rival forces'.[57] Séumus Robinson, also met Lynch on his arrival there, and began a 'despairing effort to get Liam to command the whole Army, to march on Dublin and cut out the cancer before it spread. Couldn't move Lynch.'[58] The exchange between the two men was to be an early indicator of dissatisfaction from a leading IRA officer at Lynch's decision-making as chief of staff. More robust disagreements from others of similar republican pedigree to Robinson were to follow in the months ahead.

With the end of the truce, conflict broke out in Limerick with a series of engagements between pro- and anti-Treaty forces across the city over the period 11–21 July. Lynch, from his new base, attempted to monitor the situation by keeping up frequent communication with his officers in Limerick.[59] On 13 July, the third day of fighting, Lynch issued his first communication to all anti-Treaty forces since it started. He began the message with a defence of the reason behind the fighting as the 'agreement reached in Limerick city … has now been broken by the Free State officers who signed it'.[60] Not for the last time in the Civil War, Lynch assured those under his command that the anti-Treaty IRA as a whole held the initiative: 'GHQ is in close touch with the O/C Operations … Our troops hold the initiative now.'[61] In communications to officers based in other areas, Lynch made reference to the importance of Limerick. On 15 July he wrote, 'If Limerick is won it will take us a long way to upholding of Republic.'[62]

Despite this, Lynch ordered a general withdrawal of IRA forces from the city by 18 July, with Deasy suggesting 'he [Lynch] must have realised the futility of opposing artillery in street fighting.'[63] Lynch made a grim prediction to Ernie O'Malley, then over the Eastern Command, of what lay ahead after the republican loss in Limerick: 'The second agreement reached at Limerick has been broken by the enemy … I believe … we will eventually have to destroy all our posts and have to operate as of old in columns.'[64]

Tom Kelleher of the IRA's Cork No. 3 Brigade was disgusted at the decision-making of his senior officers, and later reflected ruefully on this outcome. He could not see the sense in the strong IRA force being 'disbanded into small and ineffective groups', particularly in light of the initially small number of pro-Treaty troops based in Limerick. In Kelleher's view, 'Liam Lynch and Liam Deasy were simply not up to it, but neither was our headquarters staff in Dublin. We were allowed to fragment in the countryside when we should have throttled the Staters in the early months of 1922.'[65] Connie Neenan, also of Cork No. 3, was not sure if Lynch and Deasy were completely to blame; he felt ultimately the anti-Treaty IRA units had ended up in 'a tight situation. In the end we had no chance against them [the pro-Treaty forces]. Retreat became inevitable.'[66]

The second crisis in Limerick was the last instance in which Liam Lynch would be central to a peace or a truce effort during the Civil War. As much as Lynch himself had an ulterior motive in trying to maintain a base of republican territory, the betrayal by Brennan and other pro-Treaty military figures was to result in him never contemplating such negotiations again. To Lynch, Limerick was the culmination of a long series of collapsed negotiation efforts, which he believed were the result of his military opponents' bad faith. In one communication to Deasy that September, Lynch concluded that, in retrospect, from the republican point of view: 'Before hostilities opened we had too much of this humbug, which was very much to our disadvantage.'[67] Lynch emphasised this point further to Deasy the following February: 'The enemy has adopted numerous intrigues ... First: letting down the Republic, secondly breaking Pact and numerous others such as the Limerick agreement.'[68]

An alleged remark Lynch made before the fighting in Limerick would have an unfortunately long shelf life following an interview Eoin O'Duffy gave to *The Freeman's Journal* on 24 July 1922. O'Duffy, eviscerating the tactics of the republican forces, claimed Lynch said to Hannigan, 'The people are simply a flock of sheep to be driven any way you chose.' While this author has highlighted statements Lynch wrote which were dismissive of politicians and political activity, none were put so bluntly as this statement, if it was ever said at all. Yet, the remark would unfortunately endure into Lynch's obituaries and at least one major historical study of the period as an example of the anti-democratic stance of republicans.[69]

***

At the outbreak of the fighting in Dublin, at the meeting held at the Clarence Hotel of the anti-Treaty IRA officers, it had been decided that each division would act on its own, given that GHQ had been based in the Four Courts.[70] As chief of staff, Lynch quickly changed his mind on this approach, creating three commands: a northern and eastern, commanded by Ernie O'Malley; a western, under the command of Michael Kilroy; and a southern, commanded by Liam Deasy.[71] O'Malley worried about his unfamiliarity with the area under his command, feeling that all 'I could see was the futility of the order. I did not know the officers or men ... and I knew little of the physical nature of the new command.'[72] Deasy, too, was not over-enthusiastic about his assignment, but 'accepted ... without question and ... [was] quite satisfied to continue serving under Liam Lynch's leadership'.[73] Yet, having to continually improvise strategy and restructure commands during the fighting did little to help the IRA.

Utilising considerable capital and resources, the Provisional Government continued its major recruitment drive to the new military force, swelling its ranks. From this juncture began the final transformation of the pro-Treaty IRA forces into the National Army of the Irish Free State. Resigning as chairman of the Provisional Government, Michael Collins established a War Council of Three, consisting of himself as commander-in-chief, Mulcahy as chief of staff and O'Duffy as assistant chief of staff. (Collins later received sanction from the Dáil cabinet headed by Griffith for this self-appointment.) Determined not to distinguish Lynch's IRA as the sole possessor of the name, or refer to them as republicans, Provisional Government propaganda dismissed their anti-Treaty opponents as the 'Irregulars' – a term Lynch came to loathe – while republican newssheets countered, less successfully, by calling this new force 'the Green and Tans'. While the National Army forces grew considerably, sometimes facing such raw recruits gave the IRA an advantage, most notably during the republican stand at Kilmallock in the south of Limerick, where veteran IRA Volunteers commanded by Deasy held out across a defensive line against 700 National Army soldiers for several days. However, the sheer scale of the National Army's resources were laid bare by their coastal landings at Fenit and Tarbert in Kerry on 2 August, and in Passage West in Cork on 8 August; Cork city fell to the Provisional Government just two days later. Waterford city had already been taken by 19 July following a National Army advance. All of this ensured a total collapse, of Lynch's 'Limerick–Waterford line'.

In looking at Lynch's correspondence from these critical weeks, there is a little evidence of him planning a grand strategy to retain this republican territory. In truth, he could do little more than advise, encourage and direct units to critical areas. Shortly before the National Army took Cork city, in reference to this, Lynch informed O'Malley, 'Bodies of our troops have been rushed to these places to delay and contest their advances' – thereby suggesting this was little conceived as a possibility until it occurred.[74] On 6 August, concerning the landing in Fenit, Lynch merely expressed the hope to Deasy that their forces could halt the National Army advance.[75] In truth, Lynch held more enthusiasm for a new strategy.

While the IRA abandoned or were forced to flee their barracks and positions, they were encouraged to set fire to them and destroy other infrastructure to slow the advance of the Provisional Government, and return to the strategy of guerrilla flying columns. With such deliberate acts of destruction, and not for the last time, there was little indication that Lynch gave much thought to how this might impact on republican sympathy and support among the local populace. Retrospectively, with the loss of territory and barracks, some republicans were later to feel this moment should have marked the end of the Civil War.[76]

Robert Brennan later recalled an incident that gave a telling insight into Lynch's character at this time. A group of captured pro-Treaty IRA soldiers had been brought into Mallow Barracks and Lynch insisted the prisoners were to share the same meals as their captors and freedom of the barrack grounds, and not be interrogated about troop movements. As Brennan explained, Lynch was 'ashamed to think they would give their chums away'. On this, a frustrated Moss Twomey, Lynch's adjutant, remarked to Brennan, 'All very magnificent … but it's not war. We're losing because the fellows are not fighting. We're firing at their legs.'[77]

It was likely around this time that the most famous photograph of Lynch was taken, the only one known of him wearing some sort of officer's uniform. The cropped version is better known; the full version depicted a uniformed Lynch sitting relaxed, with his arms folded, at a table in the yard of one of the Fermoy barracks. Patrick Stritch, who took the image, was a well-known professional photographer based in Fermoy. He later explained to his son Richard how he took the photograph during the Civil War, and Lynch had to borrow an officer's uniform for the portrait. Instead of the relaxed, slightly hunched Lynch in the image, the more usually reproduced cropped version gives the impression of a determined military leader sitting upright with a steely gaze.[78] This version has been endlessly printed in the century since, in many books and much commemorative material, and also adorned the covers of the first two biographies of Lynch.

✳✳✳

Before the loss of republican territory in the south-west, Lynch had begun to encourage the use of widespread guerrilla tactics among his forces. The day before the fighting in Limerick city began, with an eye to hostilities then petering out around the capital, Lynch seemed to realise the situation in Dublin was lost for the IRA. He wrote to O'Malley from Clonmel on 10 July, 'Press guerrilla tactics in Ireland as used against common enemy.' Lynch lamented the Dublin Brigades were 'so hard pressed' but luckily IRA forces 'lost no time in clearing up the situation' in the south.[79] Following the loss of Limerick, Lynch concluded to O'Malley that the 'military policy must be guerrilla tactics as in late war with common enemy, but … it can be waged more intensely'. Lynch noted in the same communication that it was only in his former First Southern Division area where guerrilla tactics were not being employed, due to the necessity of trying to maintain territory there.[80] That approach on the part of forces in the south was soon to change as, not for the first or last time in the conflict, Lynch was to have his plans disrupted by hard realities on the ground.

With the National Army encroaching, on 11 August Lynch instructed his garrison to abandon Fermoy Barracks and for the buildings themselves to be burnt. Siobhán Lankford stood with Lynch and the other men in the barrack square and recalled witnessing the sad sight. At that moment, Dan Mulvihill, an intelligence officer in the Kerry Brigade, began to sing: 'It was a heart-breaking moment. Suddenly Dan Mulvihill's voice rang out in the popular aria from Verdi's *Il Travorte* [sic], "Home to our Mountains". Appreciation of Dan's performance flashed on every face, and the dejection of the hour was somewhat lightened.'[81]

The destruction of Fermoy Barracks followed the general pattern in towns as the National Army advanced through the south-west, with departing republican forces controversially destroying barracks and buildings, such as Kilworth camp and Mitchelstown castle, to prevent their use by the enemy. Bridges, too, were a target, in one estimate thirty-two in Cork alone. John Borgonovo has observed that virtually every town in Cork was isolated due to the impediment of major and minor roads by republicans due to trenches and blockage by fallen trees. Borgonovo concluded this road wreckage was 'by far the most successful and well thought-out aspect of the IRA defence …'[82] Yet, it ultimately created local animosity from the local population due to the economic woes that resulted.

It was a cruel irony that the last town held by IRA forces in the country was Fermoy, where Lynch had grown to prominence in the movement. The departure from, and the destruction of, its barracks did little to alleviate Éamon de Valera's worries, who, in his personal diary, recorded that day in Fermoy as 'one of the most if not the most miserable days I ever spent. Thoughts! Thoughts!' That evening, while walking in a field at a hideout in Mallow, de Valera began to seriously doubt the prospects of a republican military victory, remarking in the same diary, 'The men dead and gloomy – just holding on. How long will it last?'[83] Former MP William O'Brien, when visited by de Valera, complained to him about the destruction of the railway viaduct over the Blackwater at Mallow and pointed out that not many locals in the areas had been against the republicans until then. De Valera apparently agreed and expressed the worry that the general Irish public would begin to regard the anti-Treaty IRA as 'bandits'.[84]

In the absence of a physical headquarters, Lynch put into operation a 'Field GHQ' remaining constantly on the move through various counties in the weeks ahead. Part of his thinking behind the operation of a GHQ on the move through the fighting territories is indicated in a telling communication to de Valera. Lynch realised that a major failing in the operation of Mulcahy's GHQ's during 1919–21 was that they fell 'absolutely out of touch with the country and gave no assistance whatsoever and further more kept the country Units from having definite co-operation and contact'. Lynch wished to avoid a repetition of this with his own GHQ. His final comment in the communication revealed he was not given to reflection on past military mistakes: 'there is no use in looking backwards but it is well to bear these things in mind'.[85] Inevitably, its role as a central command for the IRA was to have mixed results.

De Valera began to become a somewhat unwelcome guest at Lynch's Field GHQ during this time, and the first strains in the relationship between him and Lynch began to take hold. David McCullagh has pointed out that de Valera's increasing unpopularity with Lynch himself was often lost on the pro-Treaty side and many of its leading figures overestimated de Valera's influence on the IRA during the conflict. Eoin O'Duffy, for instance, referred to Lynch as a 'tool of de Valera'.[86] Even decades after the Civil War, Mulcahy was convinced that Lynch, his star officer, would never have been drawn into the fighting of the Civil War 'if the reaction of de Valera to the Treaty had been different or even if de Valera had stopped short of approving the use of arms by the Irregulars'.[87] Mulcahy and O'Duffy were perhaps well-meaning in wanting to believe their old IRA comrade was led astray by a wily politician, but such views deny Lynch his own agency and do not reflect his true dealings with de Valera.

✸✸✸

Not surprisingly, as the fighting to maintain the republican territories intensified, this led to questions from within the IRA leadership who were unsure of the path ahead. A frustrated Ernie O'Malley wrote to Lynch on 21 July, 'Could you give me an outline of your Military and National Policy as we [in the Eastern Division] are in the dark here with regard to both?' O'Malley's concern was that he and his staff 'might do things which would interfere with the general plan' – the implication being that O'Malley himself was unaware of the existence of one.[88]

Picking up on this, a condescending Lynch replied to O'Malley in a memorandum, dated 25 July, 'Is it necessary to state that our National policy is to maintain the established Republic?' In his view, Lynch felt that, following the attack on the Four Courts, 'we [the IRA] are finished with compromise or negotiations unless based on recognition of Republic' – which to him was synonymous with full Irish independence. Lynch went on to explain, 'we have no notion of setting up a Government, but await until such time as An Dáil will carry on as [the] Government of Republic without any fear of compromise; in the meantime no other Government will be allowed to function'.[89] Whatever his previous feelings about the political institutions of the Republic, Lynch seemed to foresee a future role for both a working parliament and government – however vague. But this was no detailed political policy, and Lynch's lack of movement on this matter was to frustrate his allies in the weeks ahead.

O'Malley sought direction on republican political policy from the IRA Executive member Liam Mellows, who had been imprisoned in Dublin's Mountjoy Prison since the capture of the Four Court's garrison in the opening days of the conflict.[90] Mellows was inclined towards a socialist-themed political programme on the part of republicans, and this is reflected in drafts of his 'Notes from Mountjoy' proposals. Additionally, he was fiercely critical of the military leaders' dismissal of political matters. This led Lynch to remark on Mellows: 'I fear his ideals prevent him from seeing the same military outlook as others at times.'[91] While Mellows' proposals have held great appeal among Irish political leftist circles in the last century, at the time there was no interest among Lynch and the IRA leadership for them.[92]

At least one push for a republican political programme came from an external body. Roddy Connolly, the then-leader of the Communist Party of Ireland, met Lynch at the temporary GHQ in Fermoy on 26 July 1922. Connolly lobbied for the formation of a republican government in Cork city that could advocate a democratic programme which people could get behind. Keenly aware of Connolly's avowal of socialist ideals, Lynch felt the latter's proposal was a dubious one for 'getting Labour behind the Republicans'. Ultimately, Lynch mentioned the proposal at his staff meeting in Fermoy the following day and dismissed the matter.[93]

The minutes do reveal that the possibility of consulting Roddy Connolly and a trade-union official, Eamonn Lynch, on creating a labour department within the IRA was discussed. The labour historian Emmet O'Connor has drawn attention to this, along with a meeting in August 1922 between communist activists and two prominent IRA figures (one possibly being O'Malley) to explore the possibility of a joint alliance between Irish communists and the IRA.[94] However, whether this was in relation to Irish communists aiding in gun-running or providing some sort of financial support, O'Connor concluded, 'there is a coincidence of republican and communist sources ... the link remains tantalisingly incomplete'.[95] In mid-December, writing to Todd Andrews, Lynch seemed to refer briefly to having 'some information as to Russian matters', but he did 'not see any use in bothering any further in this direction'.[96] Lynch had no interest in an alliance with either the Irish, or wider, global, communist movement – as O'Connor acknowledges.[97] For whatever reason, an alliance with communists tied to Soviet Russia, or the Soviet state itself, was ultimately abandoned by the IRA.

In one instance of support for workers' strikes, Lynch expressed approval of train workers who refused to repair an armoured train republicans had damaged, and he hoped 'they will continue in this attitude'.[98] But there is little in the surviving formal correspondence that suggests Lynch planned to utilise organised labour to assist in the IRA's military efforts.

✱✱✱

Moving through the southern counties with members of his Field GHQ, Lynch issued Operation Order No. 9, headed 'Organisation and Activities of Active Service Unit', which was in keeping with his intentions for the tactics of his forces. Admitting to 'attacks of the enemy in superior numbers', Lynch laid out, at length, how active service units should operate in following guerrilla tactics.[99] Senior officers were sceptical of the return to tactics so familiar during the 'Tan War' period; O'Malley retrospectively felt that the retention of republican territory from the outset should have been paramount.[100]

It is perhaps likely the widespread adoption of these tactics in the weeks ahead was more the result of on-the-ground necessity for the surviving IRA columns than a strict adherence to the instructions of their chief of staff. It is also arguable that the encouragement to resort to these time-proven methods was to be Liam Lynch's sole innovation as a military commander during the Civil War. Moss Twomey later perhaps summed it up best, when reflecting on this critical period, that his chief of staff 'had redirected the energies of his forces into the type of activity of which he was a master. But the future looked gloomy and the road long and hard.'[101]

On 18 August, Lynch wrote a handwritten memorandum to O'Malley, which covered his assessment of the recent territorial losses for republicans – it was a telling communication in summing up his relish at the return to the familiar tactics of the previous conflict. Lynch noted how 'the situation was a peculiarly difficult one for 1st Southern Division' in the last number of weeks. The 'great odds' faced at Kilmallock, and the National Army landings along the Cork and Kerry coasts, had resulted in the withdrawal of republican forces. Now, with 'guerrilla tactics resorted to everywhere … it was impossible to concentrate sufficient forces at any one front to defeat [the enemy] completely.' Lynch felt it had been difficult for flying columns to organise immediately, with the focus on the destruction of barracks and removal of stores, but that 'has now been overcome'. He pointed out the success of guerrilla tactics in Kerry – 'our men are fighting splendidly there' – and the subsequent National Army evacuation of Farranfore and the retreat to their base in Tralee. Lynch insisted to O'Malley that within Cork 'and elsewhere the organisation of columns everywhere is complete, and extensive operations will begin immediately'. Overall, Lynch was 'thoroughly satisfied with the situation now'.[102]

Four days after he composed this message, the greatest success of Lynch's new military strategy would come. On 22 August, Michael Collins – commander-in-chief of the National Army, president of the Supreme Council of the IRB and someone Lynch once considered a valued ally and great friend – was killed during an ambush on his military convoy in the West Cork countryside. From a military standpoint, the operation was not only a validation of the use of guerrilla tactics but a considerable success for the IRA men involved. At the time of the convoy's arrival, those in place for the ambush had begun to break up and depart the area on the orders of Collins' old comrade Tom Hales. Commenting on the report of the ambush sent to him by Deasy, Lynch congratulated the men involved and considered 'this a most successful operation … against such odds'. (He nonetheless expressed surprise and disappointment that no consideration was given to the laying of mines to halt the armoured car in Collins' convoy.) On the death of his old comrade, Lynch remarked, 'Nothing could bring home more forcibly the awful unfortunate national situation at present than the fact that it has become necessary for … former comrades to shoot such men as M. Collins who rendered such splendid service to Republic in the late war against England.'[103] In a communication to O'Malley, Lynch again expressed genuine regret for Collins' death, but, thinking in wider military terms of the impact on the National Army forces, expressed hope that 'Collins' death will probably alter their outlook and effect his higher Military Command. Collins' loss is one which they cannot fill.'[104]

Speculation over the events at the site of Collins' death, Béal na mBláth, has endured since, moving into the realm of conspiracy theory. Exploration of the various details of this ambush and its aftermath is beyond the context of this biography, but there have been numerous suggestions that Collins may have been in the area to meet key IRA figures, perhaps to seek an early end to the conflict. There is no contemporary documentary evidence to suggest Lynch was aware of or encouraged such discussions, in keeping with his stance on peace negotiations since the loss of Limerick city. De Valera, now no longer with Lynch's GHQ, had been escorted through the area by members of the IRA on the day previous to Collins' death. Lynch, still around the Fermoy–Glanworth area, had warned Deasy 'not to give Dev any encouragement' in his stance on ending the war, the latter having apparently realised republicans would never achieve victory.[105]

In Lynch's response to Deasy's report, he is clearly very proud of the fact that the ambush party successfully killed Collins. This and the brevity of his remarks on the death of his late comrade, whom he held in considerable esteem, may seem unusual, even callous, but one must note they come from Lynch's formal military correspondence. His feelings beyond the scope of these official dispatches were likely more complex. Todd Andrews – who was in Lynch's company as an adjutant for much of the latter's final weeks – noted how, in conversation, Lynch regarded the loss of Collins as a tragedy and hugely consequential for the republican side.[106] This complexity in the response to Collins' death was indicative of the reaction of many anti-Treaty republicans at the time.[107]

✳✳✳

By 15 September, one republican newssheet claimed the total number of attacks on Provisional Government forces was 467. Particularly damaging assaults had been made on these forces in at least thirteen counties. In addition, twenty posts or barracks had been captured, along with a substantial amount of guns and ammunition. The capture of Kenmare by republicans on 9 September, and Ballina three days later – just before the Third Dáil met – was particularly embarrassing for the Provisional Government. In September, pro-Treaty sources admitted that guerrilla tactics had been successful. Provisional Government troops controlled little more than the towns in the areas of fighting, and the stability of those was threatened by frequent IRA raids. Nonetheless, large areas of the midlands saw little guerrilla activity, with IRA flying columns more active in remote areas such as mountainous regions in south Kerry and west Mayo. This led to a military stalemate that existed until December, reflecting the limited nature of republican successes.[108]

Further contributing to Lynch's growing optimism was his appointment of Tom Barry as Operations Officer, Southern Command, following Barry's easy escape from Gormanston internment camp in September. Lynch placed a high value on Barry's skills, writing to de Valera, 'He is most capable and by far the best in Ireland.'[109] Lynch's confidence was to prove justified to some degree in the closing months of the year. Barry, along with column leaders from the Cork brigades and a force from the Second Southern Division, organised a combined attack on several southern Free State posts in late December. All were taken, with Barry himself leading an attack on Carrick-on-Suir, seizing over 200 rifles and two machine-guns.[110]

However, as historian Eoin Neeson has noted, the 'limited successes of localised guerrilla tactics seem to have blinded anti-Treaty commanders to the fact that they were merely local actions, that the Provisional Government now had control of the country at large ... the anti-Treatyites could not win.'[111] Lynch himself was prone to looking at the conflict through the prism of a brigade commander over his own command area, instead of considering, as a commander-in-chief of the overall forces, how such localised efforts impacted the big picture. It was a striking failure in

Lynch's military thinking for the duration of the Civil War that, decades later, still frustrated and bemused his one-time senior officers in their recollections.

Unsurprisingly, Lynch was quick to praise guerrilla operations to his officers throughout September and October. He told Deasy of an ambush in which the 'gallantry displayed by our troops on this occasion, was undoubtedly splendid'.[112] Lynch frequently encouraged innovations on the part of his forces. In one instance, he encouraged Deasy to pursue armour-plating for cars: 'everything possible must be done to try and get this plating. There is no doubt with some of these cars many posts held in Towns could be captured.' He also suggested the development of mortar bombs in the same communication.[113] In a separate communication, he remarked it was 'a pity that Mines are not being made more extensive use of … Their use in these places would make the enemy less anxious for raiding in the Country'.[114] That none of these ideas was ever widely adopted across the increasingly fragmented republican resistance did little to deter Lynch from trying to find new military innovations, as the final months of the conflict were to prove.

Lynch's dispatches, however, were not without criticism of anti-Treaty IRA operations. When commenting on the burning of a barracks at Rathfarnham to O'Malley, he delivered a lengthy critique of the tactics used: 'The fact that the attacking party walked into the enemy sentry would appear to show that the party had poor local Intelligence'.[115] Even at the height of the fighting, Lynch was conscious of poor conduct on the part of IRA officers. Having noted an occasion when two pro-Treaty officers were shot dead whilst boating on a lake in Killarney, he asked Deasy to ensure that he issue 'instructions that there will not be a similar reoccurrence of acts of this kind. We cannot expose certain enemy acts if our troops shoot their troops in this manner'.[116]

A frequent preoccupation was weak efforts at fighting in certain counties, as his Field GHQ surveyed the activities of republican forces first-hand. Passing through Kilkenny in early November, Lynch wrote to his adjutant general, Con Moloney, 'I found County Kilkenny very poor; in fact, I would say it is our worst area in Ireland.' Lynch noted that

'Officers and men most enthusiastic but little leadership from Brigade. A number of rifles given to staff would be well accounted for.'[117] Lynch, in one instance, went so far as to transcribe a whole article from *The Irish Times* to O'Malley. In the article, the writer expressed how pleasantly quiet the landscape had proved during a recent drive from Dublin to Wicklow, despite the military conflict. The area discussed was under O'Malley's command, and Lynch sardonically remarked, 'I hope since this article was written that steps have been taken which will make "Joy Riding" not so pleasing in the future.'[118]

England, as a new arena for fighting, also came to nothing for republicans despite an anti-Treaty IRA presence there, to Lynch's continued frustration. Pa Murray was appointed as O/C Britain in September 1922, a position for which he held no enthusiasm.[119] Mass arrests of over 100 anti-Treaty IRA Volunteers there through March 1923 further frustrated republican efforts, leading Murray to offer Lynch his resignation, which Lynch refused to accept.[120] He hoped Murray would come to 'realise our big difficulties here and that will you give all the co-operation possible'. The communication was written one day before Lynch's death.[121] Following on from the failed joint IRA action in 1922, the new Northern Ireland state also represented a potential theatre of war for the IRA. Yet republican strategy there remained confused, and military actions were highly limited against the backdrop of continued widescale sectarian violence.[122] Lynch was certainly little helped by the fact that Frank Aiken of the pivotal Fourth Northern Division of the IRA initially took a neutral stance – he was later appointed head of the Northern Command.

Deasy was of the opinion that he and other senior officers were more alert than Lynch to the lack of military success as the war progressed. He felt that two major factors prevented such success following the adoption of guerrilla tactics: first, the people 'were no longer enthusiastically with us as in the earlier fight … they were unwilling to face a renewal of [war] conditions when there was an alternative of peace, even at a price'; second, 'the reluctance of so many Volunteers to face up to the harsh realities. They seemed to have no heart in the fight'.[123] (Of interest, however, in June 1922, Deasy had written a lengthy memorandum for Lynch endorsing the use of guerrilla tactics.)[124]

Yet O'Donoghue wrote that 'behind [Lynch's] determination and optimism there was grief and heartache'.[125] This can be seen in a letter Lynch wrote to his brother Tom on 16 September. The letter is in stark contrast to Lynch's positive commentary in his military dispatches, and a raw honesty comes through in this communication. Lynch dramatically stated, 'The disaster of this war is sinking to my very bones when I count ... the general horrors of civil war.' Feeling resigned that the fight would continue, Lynch wrote of 'being hopelessly let down by ... former comrades-in-arms'. These former comrades had 'stooped to lower methods than the British, including murder gangs ... propaganda'. On this note, Lynch expressed his hope that future generations 'will have written for them the full details of all the traitorous acts'. The letter ended on a starkly despairing note: 'Who could have dreamt that all our hopes could have been so blighted.'[126] Though brief, what is clear from this letter is Lynch's distaste for the conflict, indicative of what he truly felt. Notably, there is little talking up of victory for the republican forces, despite what he continually reiterated to his officers in official correspondence. Far from assuaging any fears of his brother, Lynch felt his forces must 'fight to the bitter end before we allow the nation to dishonour itself'.[127]

✶✶✶

Since the March convention, the IRA Executive had held authority over the anti-Treaty IRA forces, at least in theory, but after the conflict started, there had been only one brief meeting of just eight members of this body, at Lynch's temporary Fermoy headquarters on 15 July. Lynch kept a keen eye on the progress of the conflict at his staff meetings, so 'complete control of the Republican forces may be said to have rested with him, in so far as it was possible for any one man to exercise authority in the circumstances'. Moreover, Lynch does not appear to have desired any change in this position.[128] At least one previous writer felt Lynch's refusal to convene a meeting of the IRA Executive in the initial period of fighting gave 'the impression that Lynch was succumbing to the lure of power'.[129]

However, there were genuine practical considerations when considering the convening of such a meeting. Lynch noted to O'Malley in August that travelling to proposed Executive meetings 'must be now almost impossible and dangerous' for Executive members.[130] Moreover, Lynch may not have been alone in his reluctance to hold an Executive meeting. Con Moloney admitted to O'Malley that he personally wished the Executive would only meet once the Civil War was over – though he was strangely reluctant to commit his reasoning for this to paper.[131] Yet sometime during September, perhaps after noting inactivity in certain areas, Lynch changed his mind. On 1 October, he announced to O'Malley the holding of an Executive meeting, which ultimately took place in a secret location near Tipperary town on 16–17 October.[132] The meeting was significant in that it was the first opportunity for all Executive members to meet since the war began and to take stock of the progress of the conflict. Of particular interest at this meeting, was the formation of a five-man army council consisting of Executive members Lynch, O'Malley, Deasy, Tom Derrig and Frank Aiken. This body was to function as the Executive when the latter was not in session.[133] Pressure from several key figures, such as Éamon de Valera, was to see the creation of another entity from this Executive meeting: the Republican Government.

Frank Aiken of the Fourth Northern Division, no longer neutral since August, was one of those wary at the lack of any sort of civil control of the IRA on the republican side. He left no doubt as to the reason why, later recalling, 'Lynch's attitude to civil control in the autumn of 1922 before the set up of the Republican Government was I think that he did not desire any change from the existing position in which the [IRA] Executive had complete authority. I know that he was not as conscious of the need for civil control as I was.' Clearly, Aiken felt the situation had changed dramatically since the early months of 1922 and the wrangling over the holding of the Army Convention. When he had joined the republican side early in the conflict, Aiken had at first refused a position on the Executive – which was perhaps essential given the area under his command – unless steps were taken to ensure some sort of civil authority was set up.[134]

Two major developments in September and October 1922 hastened the pursuit of a more definite political policy by Lynch and his allies on the Executive. Firstly, in September, the much-delayed first meeting of the parliament of the Irish Free State took place, styling itself the third Dáil Éireann; it began a debate about whether the elected anti-Treaty TDs should attend and recognise the body.[135] Then, in a major blow to IRA support, Cardinal Logue and the archbishops and bishops of Ireland issued a joint pastoral on 10 October. It focused on the question of legitimate authority and charged republicans with 'refusing to acknowledge the Government set up by the Nation' while choosing 'to attack their country as if she were a foreign power'.[136] Todd Andrews, who joined Lynch's staff several months later and was surprised to see his chief of staff still regularly prayed, noted Lynch's personal response was that there was a difference between the beliefs of the Roman Catholic Church and the politics of Irish bishops.[137]

Both of these developments made the formation of an alternative government imperative in the views of Lynch and the IRA leadership. As Calton Younger summarised, the IRA Executive had realised in September 1922 that if 'the Republican cause was seen to be in entirely military hands it was in danger of being discredited. It needed to be set in some kind of constitutional framework.'[138] These practical considerations, certainly when conveyed by others, swayed Lynch more than any previous entreaties by O'Malley, Mellows or even de Valera. Concerning de Valera, Lynch was perhaps reluctant to involve him in a more prominent role in the republican leadership. Andrews recalled O'Malley receiving a letter earlier in the conflict in which Lynch informed O'Malley that de Valera wanted to attempt to end the Civil War, recollecting 'that if he did Liam Lynch was to repudiate him'.[139] It must also be borne in mind that Lynch, as often noted, was both a reluctant public figure and one not sympathetic to the political wing of the republicans during the previous period of hostilities. This made him extremely unlikely as an individual to be able to shape a political programme for republicans in the midst of conflict.

Regarded as the political leader of the anti-Treaty faction, de Valera
was the crucial individual in the creation of the new body. As the conflict
entered into the more drawn-out guerrilla warfare phase, he was keen to
meet the IRA Executive to ensure the development of a political policy.
De Valera's entreaties and a subsequent memorandum to Lynch led the
latter to raise the former's proposal for the formation of a Republican
Government at the IRA Executive meeting in October. De Valera's
primary concerns were threefold: offering an alternative to the Free State
parliament as the legal successor to the second Dáil Éireann, providing a
rallying point for republicans and gaining access to funds raised for the
Republic in the United States.[140]

On 17 October, the assembled Executive adopted a resolution
calling upon 'the former president of Dáil Éireann [de Valera] to form
a government, which will preserve the continuity of the Republic'.
The resolution further stated that the Republican Government was
to negotiate with the governments of the Irish Free State and Britain,
provided the outcome 'does not bring this Country into the British
Empire'. Almost certainly conscious of the debates that convulsed the
Irish revolutionary movement after the Treaty, the resolution ended
with the caveat: 'Final decision on this question to be submitted for
ratification to the Executive.'[141] Clearly, Lynch was determined that any
influence held by politicians was to be a limited while fighting with the
enemy continued. And, as the main actor on the republican side, the IRA,
through its Executive, was to have the final say on whether the fighting
would conclude. With this in mind, it is not surprising that the creation
of this body, far from uniting the interests of politicians and militarists on
the republican side, instead, as Hopkinson noted, 'only served to paper
over divisions'.[142]

Lynch sent on a copy of the meeting's resolution to de Valera and
added, 'I hope to see you in the near future with other Members of the
Army Council the many matters arising out of the correspondence [sic],
and to draw up an Agreement as to Army Control, and its relations with
Republican Government.'[143] Both men were certainly anxious about this,
but for very different reasons. For de Valera, it was clearly a desire to use

his position in this new Republican Government to influence the war situation in his exchanges with Lynch. For instance, one month after de Valera was installed as president, Lynch suggested that the 'question of preventing all amusement during the war through the country should be seriously considered'. In a handwritten note on de Valera's own copy of Lynch's suggestion, likely for draft reply, de Valera wrote, 'There is no use taking on too much work of this kind. The Army in my opinion has quite enough to do in other directions.'[144] In contrast, Lynch had his own ideas about the influence of this new political body and its chief representative, which led to strains in his working relationship with de Valera. Further correspondence demonstrated how Lynch kept a careful eye on the nature of how this supposed government functioned. Historian Bill Kissane has noted that the 'process of [republican] government formation revealed de Valera's limited influence on the IRA leadership during the war'.[145]

Lynch, from the outset, began to subtly undermine de Valera's plans for this new body. For instance, on 23 October, de Valera submitted to Lynch, for ratification by the Army Council, the names of six republican deputies for ministerial roles in the new government. One was IRA Commandant Liam Mellows as minister for defence. Given that Mellows was in Mountjoy Prison, de Valera suggested that Lynch, in his capacity as chief of staff, instead function as minister for defence.[146] Replying, Lynch asked de Valera to reconsider as he already had a very public role as the IRA chief of staff. As a result, Lynch claimed, any 'unnecessary Proclamations to be signed by me as [as minister for defence] would not, I consider, be as effective as signed by somebody else.' Lynch added that placing him at cabinet level – in a politician's role, though he was unelected – could facilitate 'the usual "Dictatorship" propaganda by the enemy'. Nonetheless, Lynch ended the communication saying he was willing to act in a 'temporary' capacity, 'owing to present abnormal Government and general situation – on Cabinet and then only because of my position as Chairman of Army Council or as C/S'.[147] Sensing Lynch's reluctance, as a compromise de Valera suggested instead that he as president, and Lynch as chief of staff, sign any necessary documents and the defence position remain vacant while Mellows remained in prison.[148]

This arrangement between both men was to extend even to the instance of certain public statements, such as a lengthy one exhorting members of the new National Army to desert and assist the IRA.[149] Interestingly, Lynch's adjutant general, Con Moloney, thought it a good idea to have Lynch at the cabinet table, and wrote, 'it would have been wiser I think' – he likely meant Lynch could act as a check on the republican ministers.[150]

De Valera's effort to convince Lynch to take on the position of minister for defence was almost certainly a none-too-subtle effort to bring Lynch under his political authority. Had Lynch taken on the ministerial role, he would have been expected to adhere to collective cabinet decisions. Lynch's agreement was always unlikely, given that from the outset he regarded the Republican Government as occupying a strictly subordinate role to his authority, in keeping with the earlier resolution at the IRA Executive meeting that led to the government's creation. His role of IRA chief of staff during the Civil War, for the first time, gave Lynch a more heightened public profile and a further reticence to take on a political role. In this period, Lynch revealed to de Valera his reluctance regarding this change of status: 'I have always tried to avoid entering public life but up to now I could not avoid this in my army position.'[151]

A more forceful point of disagreement between the two men was the proposed appointment of Robert Barton as minister for economic affairs. Barton was the one cabinet choice of de Valera's that Lynch could not approve of, given his role as one of the signatories of the Anglo-Irish Treaty (though he later joined the anti-Treaty side). As Lynch explained, 'acting for whole Army and counting him [Barton] part responsible for present loss of life of our Officers and men I could not [support his nomination] and bear any responsibility to them afterwards'. Lynch informed de Valera, 'I am not looking for a strong man for the post ... I am keen on a man that will be looked up to by army and all Republicans who at the same time can always realise certain terms the Irish Nation could never accept.'[152] The fact that adherence to republican ideology was paramount for Lynch when considering cabinet positions, and not necessarily the nominee's capability for a specific ministerial role, revealed much about his regard for the utility of such a government. In reply, de Valera noted

Lynch's objections.[153] Nonetheless, he went ahead with the appointment of Barton, who was on the list of ministers that appeared in an IRA proclamation announcing the formation of the Republican Government on 28 October.[154]

Ultimately, the functioning of this Republican Government, as an attempt to enforce republican political authority, was to be a complete failure. It faced an array of obstacles and functional issues, among them imprisoned cabinet members and no financial resources, while de Valera was forced continually to appease IRA interests.[155] The government's most visible action was the issuance of public statements on anti-Treaty policy, but even this was a difficult task in a climate where the pro-Treaty side controlled the national press.[156]

Yet there is no evidence that the difficulties of the Republican Government greatly exercised Lynch. In March 1923, he actually admitted to Todd Andrews that he had not been in favour of the IRA setting up an alternative government as he feared de Valera would seek a compromise peace.[157] In this respect, by placing the Republican Government under the control of the IRA Executive from the outset, a move which allowed him to keep a tight rein on de Valera and the republican deputies, Lynch was able to live with the existence of this institution regardless of its weaknesses or potential uses.

For Lynch, one such potential use was that the government provided the impression of a functioning 'political' republican body to those unsuspecting of his real treatment of the institution. These included potential financial benefactors, such as Clan na Gael leader Joseph McGarrity in the United States. Lynch stated to McGarrity, in a boldly false claim, that, since the Republican Government's formation, 'Government departments are functioning as heretofore and the people are now in the same position as in last war.'[158] Several months after the government's formation, Lynch insisted to one senior officer that the republican 'position now would be a bad one were it not that the Govt was formed months ago … Do you seriously mean that Republican Government should not have been formed?'[159] In this instance, Lynch was responding to that officer's stinging criticism of the Executive's decision to form the government.[160]

As such, it should be read as a self-justification rather than an enthusiastic endorsement of the role of the Republican Government. Even this sort
of confused expression of praise for the institution was extremely rare on
Lynch's part.

On 28 October, Lynch wrote to Tom after the conclusion of an
Executive meeting. He was conscious of his brother's imminent departure
to Australia: 'I am sure you are now counting the few happy days left among
the friends before leaving the dear old country'. Lynch told his brother he
had 'great hopes' of being able to spend a few days with him, but that 'this
civil war goes on' and to take such time off is 'a thing almost unknown to
me'. He wrote that the recent Executive meeting 'was a splendid review
of the actual situation all over Ireland. We are now absolutely confident
that the Free State is beaten and that it is only a matter of time when
they must give in'. Lynch then made a curious mention of the grave of
their long-dead brother Jeremiah, who had been buried in London in
1904 following a drowning accident. He explained to Tom how he had
'requested the O/C London [Pa Murray] to visit Jeremiah's grave' to tell
him the condition. Murray had reported that the grave was 'very well
looked after' and 'there is a lovely Celtic Cross with Gaelic inscription on
it'. He also offered to show Tom the grave should he be passing through
London, but Lynch acknowledged such a venture for his brother was
probably not possible.

Lynch closed the letter with the hope 'to see you again before your
long journey, and your very long absence from Ireland'. This was to be
Lynch's final letter to Tom, who later inscribed a note at the end of the
document stating that he never did get to see his beloved older brother
again.[161]

Chapter 9

'Fight on to the last man'
(November 1922–March 1923)

IN LATE 1922, LYNCH TURNED his interest to reviving the IRB as another bedrock of support to boost republican fortunes. Since the outbreak of the war, the IRB had been inactive. Writing to Liam Deasy on 7 November 1922, Lynch suggested a meeting of all IRB centres and the IRB Supreme Council, to 'have the latter now definitely account for its action in sanctioning Treaty, account of each member in waging war on Republicans so that whole organisation can remain intact and get rid of all guilty members'. If the Supreme Council refused this request, Lynch then proposed, in his capacity as a Supreme Council member, a meeting of all anti-Treaty IRB members. He admitted towards to the end of the letter, however, of having 'little hope of such a meeting'.[1] In late December, Deasy, in reply, agreed with Lynch: 'I do not think it is possible to get the adjourned meeting convened ... the Treaty party being in a majority will prevent this'.[2] Writing to Joseph McGarrity, Lynch made reference to how 'Rank and file ... of Organisation [IRB] kept their allegiance, but majority of Governing Body [IRB Supreme Council] went wrong. This matter will be righted at first opportunity, but the war at the moment is putting many difficulties in the way'.[3] Lynch continued to toy with this idea in early 1923, even attracting interest from Florence O'Donoghue, who had remained neutral during the conflict.[4]

Around this time, it appeared that these rumours of republican efforts to revive the IRB reached Seán Ó Murthuile and his associates in the National Army, and in response, through early 1923, they led their own initiative to revive an IRB sympathetic to the Free State. At this juncture, Ó Murthuile was still secretary of the IRB.[5] It is unclear from the existing primary evidence exactly when and why Lynch's IRB initiative was abandoned, but after early 1923 no further correspondence from him survives on the matter. It is likely that other overwhelming concerns (the 'many difficulties' mentioned by Lynch to McGarrity) took precedence. Nonetheless, Todd Andrews noted that as late as March 1923, '[Lynch] indulged a persistent hope that the pre-Treaty unity could be restored through the IRB'.[6] This is certainly a different idea to that discussed with Deasy months before. In any event, it is intriguing that Lynch sought to use another political body – albeit, a conspiratorial and clandestine one – to revive republican fortunes and perhaps bring an end to the conflict.

Lynch looked for other means of promoting the republican message, in addition to using the Republican Government, such as through the realm of propaganda. In early August 1922, he had written to his assistant chief of staff, Ernie O'Malley, about a redesign of the tricolour flag given its use by the pro-Treaty forces: 'Owing to the abuse of the Tricolour flag by Free Staters during the present hostilities, it has been decided that the Republican Flag, which has been used by us, will bear the letters "I.R" on white of the tricolor [sic]'. Lynch then pressed O'Malley to order that such a flag be flown in each battalion area under his command.[7] Of note, in December 1922, Lynch attempted to revive his proposal to GHQ in late 1921 that Sinn Féin members should serve as a service corps for the IRA, which does not appear to have come to fruition.[8] Surviving correspondence from autumn 1922 shows Lynch also regularly engaged with Seán McCarthy, IRA director of publicity, and Erskine Childers, IRA director of propaganda (with Childers attached to the publicity staff), on crafting a republican message to be disseminated through propaganda to both republicans and the general public. Lynch implored McCarthy to frequently promote killings of republicans by National Army soldiers:

'See that Publicity is especially given to this whole enemy Murder-gang campaign generally in the hope of stopping it.'[9]

Prior to his capture by members of the National Army on 10 November, Childers had attempted the production of a republican propaganda newssheet as a means to counter the national newspapers sympathetic to the emerging Free State. Lynch was very congratulatory of Childers' efforts, having noted in early September: 'The contents of *An Phoblacht* are very satisfactory; I wish we could only have it or something similar circulated all over Ireland. Enemy propaganda and the Press are playing havoc with us when we have no means of counteracting it.'[10] Writing again to Childers, Lynch stated, 'I regard the issue of a special paper for the Army as a vital necessity' and suggested which divisions could distribute the paper.[11]

Childers later expressed his unhappiness at working in the publicity department; he wished to offer his services instead to the First Southern Division as 'an older man among the crowd who has had military experience'.[12] Unsurprisingly, this earned a slight rebuke from the adjutant general, Con Moloney, on behalf of Lynch, who replied, 'From the tone of your note you appear to be pretty sick of the way the Dept. has been functioning. I'm not surprised at that but I think it would be a pity if you definitely left the Dept.'[13] Lynch and his staff clearly saw great value in Childers remaining with the publicity department and clearly perceived a significant role for him in the period ahead.

The potential propaganda value of the plight of republican prisoners was seen by Lynch as another means of rallying support. In December, he encouraged Cumann na mBan activist Kathleen Barry (later Kathleen Barry Moloney) to become secretary of the Irish Republican Prisoners' Dependants' Fund. Barry, older sister to the martyred Kevin, had been active in the organisation since the beginning of the Civil War and had been involved in the fighting in Dublin. She was a trusted ally of Lynch and travelled up and down the country on her bicycle distributing relief to families of republican prisoners, as well as messages for the chief of staff.[14] Lynch seemed personally close to Barry and his surviving correspondence with her demonstrates a genuine warmth, and sometimes a surprisingly playful, perhaps flirtatious, tone. Lynch seemed to feel she was unhappy at the new appointment and insisted she 'blame the President for the decision. I, of course, am glad you had not to stick that job in the South for the winter; picture doing forty-mile cycle spin these mornings.'[15] He insisted it was important she take up the position, as when 'all men on active service as well as in jail realise that their [departments] are well seen after, their moral will be kept up'. Lynch gently chided her, 'I could abuse you for that first note you sent when being transferred from South but it was better let you get over that bit of temper.' In replying to Barry's complaints about her comrades, Lynch noted, 'your remarks as to "neurotic" girls, I am afraid won't get me to include you in such a list'. He added 'Mother was enquiring for you recently, she seems to have a great wish for you.'[16]

An overriding concern was the establishment of a new permanent base for Lynch's GHQ, which had been moving in the field since August. O'Malley, who was head of Eastern Command, wished that Lynch would set up his base of operations in the capital.[17] At the end of August, Lynch had admitted to O'Malley a preference for just that, but at the time he felt his Field GHQ was of more use in the south.[18] Then, on the second day of the Executive meeting in October, Lynch had talked privately to O'Malley and admitted he was considering moving the Field GHQ to Dublin.[19] He felt having Dublin as a base could improve communications and contact between the various commands.[20] This was undoubtedly influenced by his experiences working with IRA GHQ under Mulcahy during the War of Independence.

Lynch arrived in Dublin at some point in early November.[21] His new GHQ was located in a mansion called Tower House, based in the then-countryside of Santry in north County Dublin. The large house had originally been built as a school two centuries earlier, becoming known as 'Tower House' later when it became a place of residence. By 1922, it was the property of a family of republican sympathisers called the Fitzgeralds, who were prosperous merchants operating in Dublin city. Three sisters – Nora, Kat and Nan Cassidy – resided in the house with the Fitzgerald family. All three assisted in the transportation of vital dispatches to Lynch and his GHQ staff. This was achieved by way of 'The Brown Bread' shop owned by the Fitzgeralds in the city centre, to which dispatches were sent by IRA units across the country. From there, the Cassidys would bring them to Tower House. The following day, they would bring replies to these dispatches for couriers waiting at 'The Brown Bread'. Aungier Street church also functioned as a location for the sisters to receive messages to bring back to the secret IRA GHQ.

From November until February, Lynch was a regular guest at Tower House, along with GHQ staff, including Moss Twomey as his adjutant and Madge Clifford, a prominent Kerry-based Cumann na mBan officer, as his secretary. Twomey was also chief staff officer, in which role he was assisted by Seán Brunswick. Other senior IRA figures who regularly stayed in Tower House during that period included Frank Aiken (Fourth Northern Division), P.J. Ruttledge (the Republican Government's minister for home affairs) and Tom Derrig (assistant adjutant general until becoming adjutant general on Con Moloney's capture in January). The residence had a large secret room, which ensured regular GHQ staff meetings could be held there. Florence O'Donoghue noted the 'ingenuity and resource' of Kit Cassidy in particular, who ensured all the rooms were given a normal appearance in case of a raid. There only appears to have been one of these during Lynch's time there.[22]

Unfortunately, two days after Lynch's arrival in Dublin on 5 November, O'Malley was arrested following a dramatic raid on his own headquarters in the city. Given the various positions O'Malley held, Lynch was forced to reorganise the Command and GHQ staff.[23] Moreover, Lynch's position in the capital was to place him at a severe disadvantage in terms of being able to determine the progress of the conflict. His lack of direct involvement in critical fighting areas began to contribute to an even poorer understanding of the overall strength of the anti-Treaty IRA. Most fatefully, Lynch had little foresight into, or appreciation of, the lengths to which his pro-Treaty opponents would go to maintain their new political and military power.

✻✻✻

The fateful Army Emergency Powers Resolution had been passed by
the Free State Dáil Éireann on 27 September. It allowed for Free State
military courts to be set up, with powers of execution for offences such
as carrying arms or aiding in attacks on pro-Treaty military forces. These
military courts came into operation on 15 October, while an earlier
offer of amnesty to republicans in return for the surrender of arms and
acceptance of the authority of the Provisional Government was generally
ignored. This legislation, in the words of historian Michael Hopkinson,
'represented a turning point: it ushered in a harsher period of the war'.[24] As
the military commander of the republican forces, how Lynch responded
greatly impacted the events that followed.

Strangely, at the IRA Executive meeting in October, discussion of
the recent passage of the legislation appeared to have been brief. With
regard to the possibility of reprisals should any executions take place, the
meeting minutes stated, 'Nothing definitely decided … Decided to wait
until such time as our men were deported or anyone shot for bearing
arms'.[25] Ernie O'Malley, in attendance, later felt that while all present were
anxious to discuss proposed IRA actions in the event of executions, at
that juncture 'it was thought too remote a possibility'.[26] Perhaps, even at a
sub-conscious level, with the conflict still raging, hope remained for the
communal bonds of any previous comradeship to win through.

There had been some pressure to respond immediately to the passage
of the legislation. In one instance, a proposal from within the Dublin
Brigade involved two members going to a golf course in Greystones and
shooting members of the Provisional Government cabinet, such as its
chairman, W.T. Cosgrave, who regularly played there. Seámus Fox, of the
Dublin No. 2 Brigade's Sixth Battalion, recalled that 'Liam Lynch said it
was murder. He set his face against it …'[27]

Events dramatically accelerated with the capture of Erskine Childers
at Glendalough on 10 November. Lynch's initial response, at least to de
Valera, was to play down any concerns at this development. In what could
be perceived as a remarkable lack of foresight, Lynch wrote to de Valera,
'I am not sending warning to the enemy for the present, as I feel Childers'
sentence is not going to be extreme; later if we have definite Intelligence

we can act.'[28] On the morning of the day Lynch wrote this, the Provisional Government cabinet had approved the execution of four young Dublin-based IRA officers in Kilmainham Gaol, but it is not clear at the time of the communication if Lynch was aware of this development.

On 24 November, Childers was executed before a firing squad at Beggar's Bush Barracks. Lynch recognised the considerable loss of the talented and capable Childers, and wrote movingly to his widow, Molly, that it 'must have been a proud consolation to you to know that he did not falter but was true to the last, dying as he had lived, a heroic and dauntless soldier in the cause of Irish Freedom'. On their former allies, Lynch added that they 'are fools to think that killing Irishmen and women because they refuse to take an Oath of Allegiance to the King of England will accomplish their masters' purpose. It will fail now as it has always failed.'[29]

Yet from the outset, Lynch was considerably shaken at the commencement of executions of republicans on the part of the Provisional Government.[30] Once again, the lack of an advance strategy was to hamstring the IRA, yet Lynch was determined there must be a swift response. His approach would reveal a considerable ruthlessness on his part. The day after Childers' execution, he reminded de Valera of the IRA Executive's decision to execute all members of Dáil Éireann who voted for the 'Murder Bill'. (Though Lynch indicated this was a firm, unanimous decision, this is not in line with either the contemporary Executive meeting minutes or O'Malley's later account that the matter was not discussed in depth.) Anticipating de Valera's reluctance to agree, Lynch claimed the officers of the IRA's Dublin Brigade had been pushing for 'drastic action' on the introduction of the legislation. However, it was now Lynch himself pushing for such action and he made it clear that he was 'not taking strong views of Officers into consideration but taking the only action proper to deal with this mad action of enemy.'[31] A resigned de Valera responded to Lynch that, despite his doubts, 'I can see no other way to stop these others and protect our men, I cannot disapprove.'[32]

Lynch submitted a letter of protest to 'the speaker of the Provisional Parliament of Southern Ireland', Michael Hayes. In the letter, he reminded

Hayes that 'every member of your Body who voted for this resolution by which you present to make legal the murder of soldiers are equally guilty … an equal number of your body are to be shot at sight'.[33] Lynch had drafted and issued General Order No. 10 to all IRA O/Cs, requesting the execution of all pro-Treaty army members and officials involved in the executions.[34] The subsequent Operation Order No. 11 dealt specifically with those involved in the passage of what was referred to as the 'Enemy Murder Bill'. Its text stated, 'All members of [Provisional] Government who voted for Murder Bill will be shot at sight'. The order also called for the destruction of the homes of all those in parliament who had voted for the legislation, as well as those of their civilian supporters.[35]

On 28 November, Lynch wrote directly to Thomas Johnson, the leader of the parliamentary Labour Party, and referred to executed republican prisoners as 'a great proportion … drawn from the ranks of Labour'. This was no latter-day conversion to class politics, but a cynical attempt by Lynch to appeal to Johnson's sympathies.[36] The events that followed would brutally encapsulate the bitter nature of the conflict.

On 7 December, former Cork IRA commandant and pro-Treaty TD Seán Hales was assassinated while getting into a horse-drawn coach in Dublin city. In the same incident, pro-Treaty TD and Deputy Speaker of Parliament Pádraic Ó Máille was wounded. In response, in the early hours of 8 December, the cabinet of the Free State government ordered the reprisal execution in Mountjoy Prison of the four members of the IRA Executive imprisoned there since the fall of the Four Courts – Rory O'Connor, Liam Mellows, Joseph McKelvey and Richard Barrett. In defending the dubious legality of this on the same day in the Dáil, Minister for Defence and the National Army's Commander-in-Chief Richard Mulcahy cited Lynch's threat against members of the parliament as a reason for its necessity. Mulcahy reminded the deputies present that Hales had been killed whilst on his way to attend the very parliament in which they now sat.[37] In a dark irony, only two days earlier, a year after the signing of the Treaty, the Irish Free State had come into legal existence. In early 1923, Lynch wrote to one IRA officer that the 'Hales incident was most unsatisfactory, as we all wished that O'Maille should have been dealt with' – likely indicative of the true target of the attack. Furthermore, Lynch 'wished that he [Hales] would have been the last to be dealt with'.[38]

The proposed burning of the houses of politicians and supporters was also to have mixed results. A particularly tragic and disastrous instance involved the death of seven-year-old Emmet McGarry. Emmet was the son of pro-Treaty TD Séan McGarry, and was in his father's home when republicans burnt it down on 10 December.[39] De Valera later said to Lynch that he personally felt that 'the loss of the little boy prevented the rising up of the tide of feeling' towards the executions of republicans.[40] In response, Lynch coldly replied, 'McGarry's case was very unfortunate but it is the fortunes of war.'[41] Similarly, when the honorary secretaries of Cumann na mBan wrote to Lynch expressing their upset over the incident, Lynch had Tom Derrig reply on his behalf, making clear 'it is not our policy to expose women and children to danger. The McGarry case was most unfortunate and regrettable but we do not see that any blame attaches to our men under the circumstances.'[42]

With this considerably more ruthless approach to the conflict, Lynch explained to the worried de Valera that the 'I.R.A. in this war as in the last wish to fight with clean hands, but when enemy has outraged all rules of warfare ... we must adopt severe measures or else chuck it at once.' Furthermore, de Valera should not interpret this new approach as an 'eye-for-an-eye' policy.[43] Whatever his disinterest in the political side of the republican resistance, Lynch recognised, in his keeping de Valera informed, the value of a united movement. In reality, de Valera could do little but support Lynch, but their private correspondence from this juncture was to reveal growing disagreements as the conflict progressed.

Historian John Regan has argued that Lynch's threat to shoot politicians 'was the first and last military initiative that the anti-treatyites formulated which had any real chance of advancing the war in their favour ... A policy of assassination such as Lynch proposed could undermine the regime not by defeating the army but by circumventing it.'[44] Yet, the lack of a series of assassinations of pro-Treaty figures following that of Hales revealed, according to Hopkinson, Lynch's 'reservations about the implications of his own orders'. Furthermore, there was a general concern among the anti-Treaty forces that more reprisal killings could only result in further executions of imprisoned IRA members.[45] This arguably showed not an increasing distaste with the conflict but an erosion of trust in Lynch's vision for the conduct of the fighting. As events were to prove, this erosion of trust was to become even more pronounced in the early months of 1923.

***

Following the collapse of the Limerick truce, Lynch was, unsurprisingly, dismissive of further peace efforts by various civil bodies and non-military figures throughout the remainder of 1922 and was not centrally involved in any of these.[46] Indeed, in one memorandum to Moss Twomey, Lynch revealed his frustration that approaches from intermediaries were made to his subordinates, rarely directly to him.[47] Twomey felt the general attitude among the IRA at this time was that while 'things were very bad' they should 'cave in on the best terms one could get'. Twomey's impression of Lynch, meanwhile, was that he 'thought that negotiations would get us nowhere, if we were [beaten] we were [beaten]'.[48] In early September, Lynch remarked to Deasy, 'I do not believe the moment has arrived for negotiations, just yet, unless Free State see futility of their actions. Our position is vastly improving every day. We are all of course anxious for Peace as early as possible.'[49]

Just how Lynch foresaw the end of the conflict, albeit on terms dictated by republicans, is telling. In a communication on 15 December, de Valera expressed concern as to the 'ultimate results' of the then-current use of reprisal tactics by the IRA. He warned Lynch not to 'expect such a victory as will enable us to dictate terms, or simply a stalemate in which the others will be glad to come to meet us as far as they can'.[50] Lynch, in response, was sober-minded as to what he believed the anti-Treaty forces could achieve in the field: 'I do not expect we will gain a position to dictate terms to the enemy ... but I do believe we can force them to a position to recognise that Ireland's independence cannot be given away. Personally I believe there must be peace with the common enemy [Britain] at same time as with Free State.'[51] Here was Lynch in a firm admission to the political leader of the republican resistance that there could be no military victory over pro-Treaty forces. He further expanded on these points to de Valera in a communication on 28 December:

> We cannot hope to completely overthrow the enemy unless the unforeseen happens ... What I hope for, and am definite will secure, is to bring the enemy to the position of bankruptcy ... He will then realise his general position and have to stand with us in upholding our independence. He is certainly in a better position now than heretofore in putting our national ideals up to the common enemy.[52]

On possible negotiations on republican terms with the 'common enemy', i.e. Britain, Lynch had potentially offended his president by not suggesting a role for de Valera and his Republican Government in such a scenario, further demonstrating his dismissal of it and of the role that de Valera represented.

These remarks are a nuanced – if notably not public – position on the prospects of a republican victory on Lynch's part. It suggests that the chief of staff aspired to, or at least accepted the likely necessity of, a vague alliance with the pro-Treaty side against the British. Lynch's idea of independence remained nothing less than the Republic, and he adhered to the approach agreed by the IRA Executive in October of not agreeing to any settlement that left Ireland within the British Empire. From the existing evidence, there is no suggestion Lynch contemplated a dilution of this idea central to the republican position.

One of Lynch's wishes was to bring the Free State government to the point of bankruptcy and this aim is apparent in his orders to destroy important infrastructure within the jurisdiction, such as railways. Hopkinson has argued this was the most successful aspect of republican military policy during the Civil War and, although the main intention was to disrupt the movement of National Army troops, it also had enormous economic ramifications for the wider populace. The first few months of the war had seen the destruction by the IRA of railways in South

Tipperary, north Louth and the Silvermines area of County Limerick. Lynch complained of a patchy implementation of this policy overall among his forces, and said in one communication that 'a hundred bridges blown up was just as effective a blow … as a hundred barracks blown up'.[53] Nonetheless, by August, all routes to the south and south-west were non-functioning, forcing the Free State government to create a Railroad Protection and Maintenance Corps to carry out emergency repairs that September. A report by the following January referred to railway lines having been damaged in 375 places and forty-two engines having been derailed in the war thus far. As in earlier instances, there was little consideration by republicans of the economic and social consequences for the local populace.[54]

Lynch at this time saw no end of the conflict in sight, having written to his mother in late December that he had 'not much hope of an early ending as our present enemy still insists on dishonouring the nation by forcing her into the British empire'.[55] Much like the earlier correspondence with his brother Tom, Lynch's private despair over the conflict is revealing.

The downturn in republican fortunes by December 1922 had revealed the limits of success for the anti-Treaty IRA in military fighting against the pro-Treaty forces. By the year's end, Lynch's forces had lost all chance of any considerable future military success in the Civil War, even if that was not yet obvious to Lynch himself. He and other republican leaders still profoundly underestimated the manner in which the continuing conflict made the personnel of both the government and military of the Irish Free State ever more entrenched and determined to preserve the new political dispensation under the terms of the Anglo-Irish Treaty. In addition, at this point a new and unexpected threat to Lynch would come to the fore. In the new year, his authority would be challenged directly by the emergence of more considerable peace efforts coming chiefly from within the IRA itself.

***

Florence O'Donoghue observed that by January 1923, 'the Republican forces … had lost that essential moral constituent of success' in light of the successful establishment of the Free State and the lack of wide support for republicans.[56] Hopkinson has further noted that the first few months of 1923 showed how 'large-scale military activity was impossible' given the limited nature of their arms and finance. Demoralisation among the republican resistance was also heightened due to thirty-four executions of republican prisoners by the end of January.[57] Among republicans it was felt the anti-Treaty IRA was 'rapidly exhausting its resources', as there were more republicans imprisoned by the Free State government than fighting in the field.[58] Many IRA commanders had doubts about the prospect of continuing a military campaign over the summer of 1923.[59]

For all his purported optimism, Lynch, was intensely critical of leading IRA commandants and continually advised improvements. On 22 January, he complained to the heads of all IRA departments, that:

> in some cases Divisional and Brigade O/Cs are the only officers who communicate with me ... If you find that O/Cs are communicating with you it means that the officer responsible for the Department is not acting. In such cases arising you will query why the Head of the Dept concerned does not communicate with you. We cannot stand for 'one man Units'.[60]

In a particularly searing communication to all divisional O/Cs two days later, Lynch complained about the lack of information sent to him from divisions on the strength of both the enemy and their own side. Thus, the republican resistance after six months was 'in the ridiculous position of not knowing how we stand in this area'. Such information was important, as in 'these circumstances it is impossible for GHQ to direct the situation effectively, deal with areas which are not making effective use of the resources at our disposal, or strengthen the weak areas. However, we must be in a position to judge if we are in a position to enforce army Orders, Government Decrees and Instructions ...'[61] In addition, Lynch emphasised that such information was necessary for both GHQ and the Republican Government to determine strategy.

One especially trenchant criticism came from Séamus O'Donovan, the IRA's director of chemicals. Writing to Lynch at the end of January, he remarked on the 'almost complete out-of-touchness with affairs' of the IRA leadership, not to mention with the 'general impotence in coping with a situation which daily becomes increasingly grave' in light of the executions thus far. O'Donovan insisted 'the enemy are too well established and … and further weakness on our side … will leave us simply a wasted shadow'.[62] A disgusted Lynch responded, 'Plainly, I do not want to be receiving such communication as yours.' He felt the issue was that his orders were not being carried out, and insisted 'the general situation is quite satisfactory … The army in all areas in now very well re-organised …'[63] Lynch continued to pepper his communications with such words of encouragement and the promise of republican success. For instance, while assuring Joe O'Connor, quartermaster of the First Southern Division, at the end of January that 'it is only a matter of time until we come out on top', Lynch admitted that GHQ 'have realised that enemy has steam-rolled the area' leading to a lack of IRA actions.[64]

IRA inactivity was a frequent concern. In early 1923, Lynch was particularly troubled by the lack of IRA organisation in Kildare, given the National Army forces based at the Curragh. On 22 January, he urged senior officers there to action, stating that in such an area 'the possibilities of operations … must be immense'.[65] In late January, the depletion of forces on the ground forced Lynch to alter slightly the terrain covered by some brigades in Dublin, the east and the midlands. In Lynch's thinking, these reorganised commands were to allow greater co-operation amongst anti-Treaty IRA forces in areas 'where the enemy [is] … only holding big towns and Civic Guard holding the remainder'.[66] He was also concerned enough about the lack of military initiatives in the area of the Southern Command to travel there directly in February 1923. The main inspiration for this on Lynch's part was the capture of one of his key allies and the events that followed.

★★★

More aggressive peace efforts on the republican side were to develop in early 1923, to Lynch's frequent consternation. In one striking development, Commandant Tom Barry became involved in peace proposals. The beginning of Barry's involvement in such efforts in early 1923 are notable given his pedigree as a capable IRA commandant and Lynch's reliance on him for military success as recently as December. However, Barry's efforts in the field of battle had collapsed by January.

Barry was joined in his peace moves by Fr Tom Duggan, a cleric with republican sympathies.[67] Duggan initially proposed a 'dumping of arms' on the part of both sides, and Barry was impressed enough to take the proposal before a council of the First Southern Division. When both men travelled to meet Lynch at GHQ in Dublin, not surprisingly, Lynch rejected their proposals.[68] He was furious with Barry and, in a fit of particularly high emotion, admitted privately to Madge Comer that he felt like having Barry killed for having brought Duggan to meet him – a sure sign the stature of the one-time leader of the West Cork flying column had greatly diminished in Lynch's eyes.[69] Their relationship was to further sour in the weeks ahead, as Barry's efforts to be an intermediary in these independent peace efforts continued. But a worse betrayal in Lynch's eyes was to come from one of his most trusted subordinates.

As commander of the territory encompassing First Southern Division, and as deputy chief of staff, Liam Deasy was one of the most crucial IRA figures on the republican side and deeply respected by Lynch. After his ascension to the position of O/C of the First Southern Division, Lynch communicated with Deasy frequently, and arguably even more since the Civil War began, their close working relationship built on a firm sense of comradeship. On 18 January, Deasy was captured in arms at a supposed IRA safehouse in Clonmel. Several days later, Lynch was in no doubt about the impact of Deasy's capture, and told Kathleen Barry Moloney, '[his] arrest is the worst blow … he is an extraordinary leader and his loss cannot be filled'.[70] At Deasy's later court martial, he was sentenced to death. He requested a stay of execution to see if he could convince Lynch and the other members of the IRA Executive to end the conflict.[71] Deasy was allowed to forward a personal letter to each member of the republican leadership, and this remarkable document laid out at length his reasons for wishing an end to the war. It should be read partly as a severe criticism of Lynch's leadership and the direction of the military resistance.[72]

Deasy implored his allies to end the fighting and open peace negotiations with the Free State, and thus recognise the strength of their opponents' military forces in contrast to the 'entire defensive position of our units in many areas and the general decrease in fighting'. He also invoked the public support of the Free State government, making clear that 'because I believe this fight will eventually end in negotiations do I make this appeal'.[73] Deasy had requested that his correspondence be directed first to Lynch.[74] Lynch replied with a curt, 'I am to inform you officially ... that the proposal contained ... cannot be considered'.[75] Lynch's private reply to Deasy was couched in blunt and condescending terms, rejecting 'your views that we should become British subjects' and that 'you should have realised that our forces would fight to the death rather than accept this'. Lynch did temper his tone towards the end: 'I assure you I will do my utmost to obtain a cessation of hostilities but this must be within very definite lines'.[76] The rest of the IRA leadership, while acknowledging Deasy's integrity, disagreed with his idea of peace negotiations where the pro-Treaty side would have the clear advantage. A closing of ranks followed.[77]

In the aftermath of Deasy's plea, which was published for maximum effect by the Free State authorities, Lynch embarked on a considerable degree of damage control with senior officers, allies and other supporters. He admitted to Joseph McGarrity, the Clan na Gael benefactor in the United States, that it may take some time for the republican forces to recover from the incident.[78] He insisted to Kathleen Barry Moloney that she should not 'fret over the Deasy affair, this blow will fade away within a week, our position is too strong to have this affect it', adding that the 'enemy are on their last days… I wish our people all over could be made to realise this'.[79] Lynch told Frank Barrett, O/C of the First Western Division, that once the 'whole facts are put up to the Senior Officers we should get over this and then our position will be stronger than ever'.[80] Correctly,

Barrett had expressed fears that the incident was 'sure to produce the most disastrous results amongst out Troops'.[81] Lynch remarked in a similar vein to Pa Murray, O/C of Britain:

> Deasy's documents and subsequent efforts have had an effect on morale of our forces mainly in South, but when our position all over the country is explained to officers everything will go ahead as usual. I am satisfied South will stand firm and act with the rest of the country. My view on the position has not changed since my previous communications to you.

Lynch even bizarrely put forward the idea that the temporary 'lowering of our morale of course has had its effects also on enemy'.[82]

Despite his firm, public dismissal of Deasy, Lynch was personally devastated since he held Deasy in such high regard. He also feared that the letter would have a considerable effect on republicans, both in prison and in the field.[83] The Provisional Government thought so too and made another offer of amnesty, which promised immunity to all republican fighters who surrendered their arms by 18 February.

In private discussion, Lynch's response to Deasy's actions appears to have been contradictory. Moss Twomey felt 'Lynch almost thought Deasy's stuff was a forgery'.[84] To one senior IRA officer, Lynch tried to justify the uncharacteristic action of his one-time deputy: 'it is clear his action was entirely the cause of his fear … he was prepared to temporarily set aside the demand of maintaining our full ideals'.[85] He also attempted to understand his former comrade's motives, writing, 'it is clear to me that Liam did not fear death but wished to be alive to try to save nation from its present disastrous troubles'. To Kathleen Barry Moloney, he stated that '[Deasy] did not expect his appeal would be acted on but hoped it would delay negotiations'.[86]

Following Deasy's surrender plea, discipline within the IRA, as well as keeping up morale, were paramount concerns for Lynch. In the immediate aftermath of Deasy's statement, republican prisoners in Limerick, Cork and Clonmel jails had either signed forms of undertaking to no longer take part in the fighting or implored the IRA leadership to end the conflict.[87] Lynch's initial communication was to the O/Cs of all IRA commands, divisions and brigades. Attaching a copy of Deasy's statement, he suggested to them that it had 'taken place at a vital moment when our position was most hopeful'. He reminded the O/Cs that previous peace efforts that granted everything except Irish independence had already been turned down (consistent with the decision made at the IRA Executive meeting the previous October). Lynch attempted to counter Deasy's points and returned to a typical refrain: the 'general position is most satisfactory'. Reminding his O/Cs of the strength of the republican resistance in the south, as well as in Britain and America, Lynch felt 'all our forces must steel themselves to face the final efforts that our ideals may be realised'. Lynch asked them to hold divisional councils to explain the position to officers, and requested that all officers 'do their utmost to counteract enemy propaganda in their areas'.[88]

Several days later, after Deasy's statement became public, Lynch issued a further memorandum to all ranks. He presented to his soldiers a summary of the challenges facing the republican resistance, accompanied by praise for their efforts thus far. Describing 'a supreme crisis ... in the defence of the Republic', Lynch qualified any pessimism by adding, 'the army has withstood all efforts to break it by force in the field ... it is to-day in a much stronger military position than at any period in its history'. He implored his men not to be deluded by 'present wiles' into 'surrendering the strong position you have so dearly won' and reminded them of peace agreements broken by the pro-Treaty forces. Lynch assured them that the IRA and Republican Government would handle any peace negotiations, and that the 'situation can only be destroyed by the ill-considered and precipitate action of individuals' (perhaps an allusion to Deasy's recent letter). He ended the message by reminding those reading of 'the sacrifices of some of Ireland's best and noblest soldiers' and finally, in rhetorical style: 'Are we now to falter when on the threshold of victory and rob the Nation of the fruits of these sacrifices?'[89]

On the journey to the south in February, Todd Andrews recalled seeing a letter from Lynch to Barry instructing him to discontinue further peace talks.[90] Several weeks later, a conference between Fr Duggan and Lynch in the village of Ballingeary, County Cork again failed.[91]

Lynch had made the decision to venture south due to his pressing concerns over developments in the area of Southern Command. After Deasy's capture, he admitted to Kathleen Barry Moloney, 'I would wish to be moving among the officers of South of pushing the fight there.'[92] Tom Barry and Tom Crofts, the latter O/C of the First Southern Division, had visited Lynch at GHQ Dublin early that month to impress upon him that the 'position is very bad in the South.'[93] Although he had told Moss Twomey and P.J. Ruttledge 'that if another man had written it [Deasy's letter] he would laugh at it', Madge Comer felt Lynch was a 'broken man' when venturing south as he had taken 'Deasy's action very badly' and it spurred him into going.[94] In Comer's understanding, Lynch was to set up a new headquarters within the First Southern Division area, and both she and Twomey would join him later.[95] Lynch wrote to de Valera that he hoped the 'longer I can remain in the South the surer we will be of saving the position'.[96]

✻✻✻

It was in early February that Captain Todd Andrews, then assistant director of organisation to IRA GHQ, was summoned to meet Lynch. They met at a safehouse in Leighlinbridge, County Carlow, ahead of Lynch's journey south.[97] Andrews described his chief of staff as 'a handsome, six-foot tall man, oval faced, with a noticeably high forehead from which light brown hair was slightly receding ... Being short-sighted, he wore thick-lensed, gold-rimmed glasses.'[98] After drinking tea together, Lynch explained how he planned to go to Cork to 'pull the South together' and wished to take Andrews as his adjutant.

Despite Andrews having his own view on the collapse of the republican military resistance, his chief of staff 'was, in my mind, a significant figure for whom I felt great respect'. He was nonetheless greatly puzzled as to why Lynch chose him for the role, and what he was expected to contribute. He was further surprised when Lynch then asked him as to 'the state of affairs' across the country: 'I did not think my opinion could be very valuable to the Chief of Staff, certainly not to the point of influencing his decisions.'[99]

Using the opportunity, Andrews told Lynch, from his first-hand experience, 'the military situation [for the IRA] was going very badly'. He explained that, aside from Frank Aiken's Fourth Northern Division, there was no action north of the border. The Dublin Brigade was so reduced in personnel as to be 'militarily ineffective'. While Andrews had a high opinion of the South Wexford IRA officers he had just left, there was nothing to be hoped for from North Wexford, Carlow or Kilkenny. He had little knowledge of the west or of the south, where he and Lynch would be heading.

As was typical with junior subordinates to whom he was not personally close, Lynch immediately projected an air of confidence and optimism. He dismissed Andrews' bleak appraisal of the republican resistance and was 'cheered by my account of conditions in South Wexford, expressing the view that with effort, the rest of the country could be brought to the same level of effectiveness'. Lynch returned to a popular recurring topic of conversation in these last few weeks: Deasy's surrender plea. While Lynch was still disappointed with Deasy personally, he did not foresee his effort to bring about a surrender impacting the strength of the republicans' military effort. Andrews was bemused at the mention of Deasy and admitted to himself that his chief of staff was 'probably right, because those who continued to be active at that stage of the war had been immunised against anything short of catastrophe'.[100] Such an exchange strongly demonstrates the effect Lynch's air of confidence had on those under his command, even at this late stage.

Andrews was concerned when Lynch said he could seize the initiative from a base in the south and expressed his confidence in Con Moloney doing the same in the South Tipperary command. Andrews recalled having seen a copy of a communication of Moloney's in Dublin that in his view 'expressed a most pessimistic view of the situation'. It is likely Lynch himself saw such a communication but, as he often did in these months, projected positivity to his junior officers. As the initial conversation came to an end, Andrews felt he had to point out, 'rather timidly, that we didn't seem to have any coherent plan of action either at local, brigade or divisional level'. In retrospect, he also regretted not making the point that having Con Lucey, the IRA director of medical services, 'acting as secretary-cum-chauffer to the Chief of Staff was not the best evidence of good organisation'.[101] In any case, whatever his doubts, Andrews joined Lynch's staff as adjutant and became an important observer of his chief of staff in the following crucial weeks.

***

In December 1922, an organisation had been formed called the 'Neutral IRA', made up of pre-Truce Volunteers who wished to take no part in the Civil War. One of its leaders was Florence O'Donoghue. As John Borgonovo noted, the 'group tried to settle the strife, but achieved few significant accomplishments'.[102] Brief asides in Lynch's various communications reveal his suspicion and dislike of the group, whatever their aims. In early December, he had speculated the group would disband when they learned ex-British officers were being recruited into the National Army.[103] A few weeks later, he had made mention of a rumour that 'the enemy' was using an ex-IRA association group to reorganise the formerly influential IRB.[104]

Though the Neutral IRA had a republican bias in constitutional matters, its public efforts for a truce were exploited by the Free State authorities to the ire of Lynch.[105] His intense dislike of the organisation was not unique, as Todd Andrews recalled: 'the Neutral IRA was despised equally by both sides despite their generous motivation'.[106] Nonetheless, by late January, Lynch seemed impressed at the thousands allegedly recruited to the group and made the suggestion that 'we should leave nothing undone to have as much control as possible and also arrange they be of assistance to us from time to time'. He seemed to believe there was a chance the group could be swayed by republican propaganda, and 'in the South we are fairly certain of controlling this organisation and use it where possible to our advantage'. Lynch also contemplated a link-up with 'the Labour people'.[107]

The Neutral IRA, led by O'Donoghue, made its most prominent peace proposal in early February. The proposal involved a truce of one month, during which all military activities by both sides were to be suspended. It was supported by a wide variety of public bodies.[108] To O'Donoghue's disgust, Lynch had de Valera publicly reject it.[109] Lynch then replied personally to O'Donoghue, making his contempt for the Neutral IRA clear. In a condescending tone, he indicated that he 'need not point out to you the numerous advantages the enemy would gain by even a temporary truce and the corresponding disadvantages to our forces'. Lynch, as always, insisted that only when the Free State side accepted the independence of Ireland could negotiations begin. He ended on a blunt note, clearly for the benefit of a Free State audience who might doubt the IRA's capabilities: 'it is clear to me that you do not realise the position of our army throughout the whole country or the general resources at our disposal'.[110] Lynch, not long after, forbade his officers from meeting Neutral IRA members so their efforts would not gain further momentum.[111] Likely as a result of the poor response by the military and political leadership to the prospect of this month-long truce, O'Donoghue disbanded the group in March.[112] Of more concern to Lynch were efforts to end the conflict from within his own ranks.

On 26 February, the council of the First Southern Division met, with Lynch present. Hopkinson felt this meeting 'could not have been franker about the Republican military position and prospects'. There was an overriding pessimism among the officers present regarding the prospects of success in their area and elsewhere in the country.[113] However, Lynch made clear his firm belief in the IRA's 'ability to carry [on] the struggle'.[114] Nonetheless, Lynch ultimately deferred to the officers' wishes to put their concerns to a future Executive meeting.[115] Ted Sullivan, a member of the divisional staff later admitted that the entire division was prepared to surrender that day until all present witnessed how 'Liam Lynch was fighting against it and it changed me'.[116] Clearly, for some, Lynch remained a man who could inspire, even in such a difficult period.

Writing to de Valera after the meeting, Lynch felt his arrival in the area 'was only in time to avert a serious difficulty' that arose as a result of

'Deasy's action'. Lynch felt morale within the division should now improve, having settled the debate over ending their part in the republican military effort.[117] Andrews, however, wondered whether Lynch's 'quite astounding and detailed knowledge of the First Southern Division … produced … an illusory belief in a potential which was no longer there, thus distorting his judgement of the true military situation'.[118] Nevertheless, an Executive meeting could no longer be deferred, particularly as Lynch appeared to fear some officers may act independently of GHQ. Of the southern officers, he wondered '[w]hat they mean by acting on their own views'.[119]

In the midst of the debate over peace proposals, de Valera's controversial Document No. 2, his alternative to the Treaty, re-emerged into public debate by way of his endorsement of it following his rejection of the Neutral IRA's proposals. The Free State government issued a pamphlet denouncing the document, which had already been brought to public attention previously at the Treaty debates. This resulted in de Valera publicly responding that peace could be agreed if the proposals outlined in Document No. 2 were adopted.[120] Lynch felt de Valera's public advocacy of Document No. 2 'had a very bad effect on army and should have been avoided' and told him so.[121] Several days later, in a reply to Lynch copied to all Republican Government ministers, de Valera defended his position. Something of de Valera's own frustration with the treatment of the Republican Government is reflected in the reply. He encouraged the IRA Executive to think more about a political means of ending the conflict, or 'leave all political matters to the Government within the wide range and the understanding … on which the Government was formed'. If the Executive were to take the lead on political matters, de Valera wrote, they 'will have to think intelligently along political lines and discuss the political problems as they would discuss military ones'.[122]

Interestingly, after this exchange over Document No. 2, there is no further existing correspondence directly between Lynch and de Valera in the latter's archive. Instead, Moss Twomey replied to de Valera on Lynch's behalf. By early March, de Valera was expressing surprise that Lynch was no longer sending him reports directly.[123] Lynch's lack of engagement with de Valera demonstrated his continued negative attitude to the nascent

Republican Government. In late January, in a lengthy memorandum to the cabinet, Lynch had alleged that 'members of cabinet have not given general assistance in direction of policy to army'. He felt his own 'position of C/S is rather difficult' given the unavailability of the members of the Executive or Army Council during the fighting.[124] While Lynch may not have been enthusiastic to communicate with the president from this point, the two were both at an IRA Executive meeting in late March. De Valera was a marginalised presence at this final Executive meeting headed by Lynch, indicative of their relationship by then.[125] Meda Ryan felt a main reason for Lynch's move to the Southern Command area was 'to prove de Valera wrong' in his belief that republicans should seek peace, as well as refute any implication that the republican forces were already beaten.[126] Alternatively, Lynch's efforts can perhaps be seen as an acknowledgement that action was needed to reverse the military fortunes of the anti-Treaty IRA by direct involvement on his part, thereby avoiding serious consideration of a political solution that was unpalatable to him.

The main issue preventing a peace settlement in the early months of 1923, as Kissane noted, was that 'the longer the conflict progressed, the less realistic peace proposals seemed'. As early as four months into the Civil War 'the common ground among the political elite had entirely disappeared'.[127] In the view of Kissane, for those who sought this common ground, such as Duggan or O'Donoghue, 'the main obstacle to a negotiated peace was … the obduracy and intransigence of the leaders on both sides who preferred a policy of violence and force to that of negotiation and persuasion'.[128] By 1923, this was as true of Lynch and much of the IRA Executive as it was for those in the political and military leadership of the Irish Free State. What was clear now, however, were the considerably greater resources available to the pro-Treaty elite. As Macardle noted, it was during March that Lynch 'at last became convinced that it was necessary to consider whether any way, short of surrender, could be found to bring the Civil War to an end'.[129] Lynch's instinct, his choice, was to devote his energies to introducing new military initiatives, further decreasing the chance of changing his focus to peace negotiations. This can be seen in the much-mocked orders to disrupt amusements and for

IRA Volunteers to issue dog licences to the public in early 1923.[130] Yet, it demonstrated the myriad of increasingly desperate ways in which he sought to create a new military advantage for the IRA through various means in the final weeks of his life.

∗ ∗ ∗

In early February, the government of the Irish Free State had temporarily suspended the executions of republican prisoners in the vain hope it may end the military phase of the conflict. There is no evidence that Lynch or the remainder of the republican leadership attempted to take advantage of this pause in the executions to work towards such an end. The executions soon recommenced (amounting to between seventy-seven and eighty-one in total), as did the increasingly controversial extrajudicial killings of republican prisoners. March 1923 was to herald a particularly bitter month of violence in County Kerry, which conversely had seen relatively little action during the War of Independence. In response to the killing of three National Army soldiers by a booby-trap bomb on the night of 6 March, nine republican prisoners were tied around a landmine, which was then detonated. Only one of the nine survived the subsequent explosion.

Todd Andrews recalled that he and Lynch first heard of these events at Ballyseedy while travelling on the Cork/Kerry border, with both feeling 'nauseated' at the news. Andrews believed that at the heart of Lynch's deep personal upset was the knowledge that members of the Dublin Guard, formerly of the pre-Truce Dublin IRA, were responsible – men whose names they both knew. Andrews felt Lynch 'seemed to live with the ineradicable belief that Irish men, particularly if they had served in the pre-Truce IRA, were born without the stain of the original sin.'[131] Lynch wondered aloud how the 'Free Staters justified to their own conscience' the killing of republican prisoners at Ballyseedy. He received a detailed report of the tragic, violent events from Humphrey Murphy, O/C of the Kerry No. 1 Brigade, a few days later. In terms of a response, Lynch was shocked when he learned Bill Quirke, Vice O/C of the IRA's Tipperary No. 3 Brigade, had issued a proclamation targeting civilian supporters of the Free State should any members of the brigade be executed.[132] Did Lynch perhaps remember Mulcahy's arguments against his similar proposal towards loyalists in mid-1921?

From late 1922, Lynch became determined to aggressively pursue the acquisition of heavy artillery. Central to such schemes were figures such as the Irish-American benefactor Joseph McGarrity of Clan na Gael and J.T. Ryan, who went by 'Jetter' and was based in Germany.[133] In late January, Lynch had indicated to Joseph O'Connor, quartermaster of the First Southern Division, 'If we had a small piece of artillery I feel we could finish this war now very quickly … We here are leaving nothing undone in this matter.'[134] Writing to Lynch in mid-January, McGarrity felt the 'scales could turn in our favour' if the artillery purchases got moving in a month or two, but he also urged caution: 'I feel it dangerous to talk of projects in mind until they reach a point of maturity which promises results.'[135] Just after Deasy's surrender plea, Lynch had indicated to de Valera that the acquisition of artillery could yet turn the tide: 'it would be easy to make terms with the enemy'.[136] De Valera worried 'that a piece of artillery will hamper the mobility of our columns and will be difficult to keep concealed and to retain under the conditions of this war'.[137] Nonetheless, he expressed some hope that the much-desired artillery would affect the balance of the war. In March he advised Lynch that if 'we had two or three of these mountain guns in each Division, with proper concentration of our forces, we would smash up all the enemy posts'.[138]

Lynch's great faith in what the weaponry could achieve for the republican war effort seemed to heighten in March. On the type of weaponry republicans could receive, Lynch noted, 'small guns would do us … if big one with gunners and other experts can be landed, so much the better. We can then make a clean sweep.'[139] On 16 March, from the United States, Seán Moylan, as a representative of the Republican Government there, assured Lynch that he realised the importance of the artillery and had 'done everything but shoot people in order to impress its urgency on the men here'.[140] Correspondence in this period showed Lynch attempting to plan the transport of such materiel. Writing again to O'Connor in early March, Lynch speculated, 'If these supplies cannot come by submarine, a cargo landing is impossible on the South or South-west Coast therefore, you must perfect elsewhere.' Lynch went as far as to consider a pilot landing in the west.[141] The west was an area where, Andrews remembered, 'for some not very apparent reason he [Lynch] had still hopes of our making a comeback'.[142] Lynch's faith in the area of the Western Command, under the leadership of Seán Hyde, was considerable in the weeks before his death.

According to Deasy's memoir, the chief reason for this was Hyde. Deasy felt that Hyde's 'enthusiastic reports to Liam Lynch ... did much to encourage and strengthen Liam in his determination to carry on the fight'.[143] An examination of reports sent by Hyde to Lynch in this period bear this assessment out. Some weeks after Deasy's plea for surrender, Hyde assured Lynch, 'Deasy's action had no effect whatever in this area ... the situation generally in this area is satisfactory. Developments are slow but in the right direction.'[144] Towards the end of February, Hyde again assured Lynch: 'Activities are becoming more widespread every day, many of them are not reported in the press ...'[145] The effect of Hyde's reports seems to be confirmed by Twomey's remark to Moylan on 2 March: 'Things are going very well since last report especially in the West, where our activities have increased immensely ...'[146] Twomey later reflected, 'I think Liam was disappointed in the west for he thought they should have done more' if those over-optimistic reports were to be believed, which Lynch clearly did.[147]

* * *

On 1 March, Tom Lynch wrote to his older brother from New South Wales. The siblings had not communicated since Tom returned to Australia in December. Later study of this surviving letter has resulted in the determination it was never received by its intended recipient. The letter was delivered to the Connell family, based in north-east Cork, who had functioned as a conduit for post sent to Lynch. Having been sent from Australia, it is unlikely to have reached Cork before the end of the month. By this juncture, Lynch was frequently on the move in the First

Southern Division area and, in his last three weeks, was far from the vicinity of Conna where the Connells resided. Perhaps surprisingly, given the considerable surviving abundance of correspondence from Lynch to Tom, this is the sole surviving correspondence from the latter to his older brother, and is instructive as to Tom's place as a close personal and political confidant of Lynch.

In the letter, Tom praised his brother's response to Deasy's surrender plea and admitted he feared Lynch and the other IRA leaders would compromise, 'but it seems ye are wide awake'. Making mention of the republican support organisation in Australia, Tom felt from his perspective that the IRA 'are putting up a great fight. Only remember the motto (no surrender) and all will be well, you have led well so far.' On the prospect of his older brother facing execution, Tom assured him 'you will be able to look into the rifle barrels: Life is short, what matter a few years extra. Brugha and Mellows will help you in the supreme test …' Taken in isolation, this remark may seem shocking, in that it comes across as wistful at the prospect of martyrdom for Lynch. However, given the brothers' closeness and their long-shared enthusiasm for republican politics, it was clearly typical of many discussions they had had over the years. While Tom was not part of the revolutionary elite, he knew his value as a confidant to his beloved older brother, one whom – as Lynch acknowledged – gave him great encouragement and instilled in him a self-belief during uncertain, difficult times in his revolutionary activities. Reminiscent of how Lynch had addressed those under his command in the previous months, Tom now talked positively of the republicans' prospects in the continuing conflict.

In the letter's closing lines, Tom acknowledged to his brother how 'yours is an awful life now, terrible responsibility but be brave, true and humble. Fight on to the last man. The nation's honour is being vindicated. God bless you in Ireland's cause and enable you to continue a rebel unchanged and unchangeable.'[148]

Chapter 10

'I'm glad now I'm going from it all' (Late March–Early April 1923)

PRIOR TO THE IRA EXECUTIVE meeting held on 23–26 March, Moss Twomey composed a lengthy memorandum to Lynch from GHQ in Dublin. In it, he summarised the array of difficulties facing the IRA in various areas, including propaganda and arms supplies. One key point Twomey succinctly made was 'News is not encouraging these days. There has not been a decent operation, whatever the cause is.'[1] With regular armed actions in key fighting areas proving difficult, for Lynch it was important for the IRA somehow to regain this momentum.

Nonetheless, by mid-March, for all his previous purported optimism, even Seán Hyde admitted in a communication that mass arrests were now leading to a devastating impact in his Western Command.[2] Todd Andrews recalled a request by Lynch, possibly inspired by this, for Andrews to take over the Western Command before the latter's departure for the March Executive meeting. To Andrews, such a request was extraordinary as he had never commanded anything above a company and was unfamiliar with the area.[3] His final exchange with Lynch 'shook my confidence in him', and he recalled, 'I remember Liam Lynch saying to me before I first left him: "You ought to turn your mind to the question of uniforms. I don't like the Free State uniform."' To Andrews, it was shocking that their leader should be focused on such a seemingly trivial matter at such a desperate time for the IRA in the conflict. Of interest, Andrews completely omitted this exchange from his own memoir but summarised it in a later interview with Ernie O'Malley.[4]

Lynch was under no illusion as to the importance of holding the Executive meeting and that it was 'of vital importance' to make clear the 'actual Army and general national position'.[5] Before the meeting, he confided in Seán Hyde that he 'would not be coerced into a surrender position' – very much setting out his stall for the intense debate ahead.[6] Lynch's firm view, notwithstanding the losses, was to continue military resistance, 'until their opponents were forced to negotiate'. The other two options, neither of which Lynch advocated, were to abandon the military fighting or to dump arms.[7]

Apparently, before the meeting began there was a debate among some present about whether de Valera, as the head of the Republican Government, should be allowed to participate. It was agreed he could be present, but without voting rights. This was symbolic of the IRA's dominance over the direction of the Civil War on the republican side.[8] It also demonstrated a further marginalisation of the Republican Government since its formation the previous October. At the meeting along with Lynch and de Valera were Frank Aiken (deputy chief of staff), Austin Stack (Republican Government's minister for finance and also Executive member, replacing O'Malley), Seán Dowling (IRA director for organisation), Humphrey Murphy (O/C, Kerry No. 1 Brigade), Seán MacSwiney (quartermaster, Cork No. 1 Brigade), Tom Derrig (adjutant general), Seán Hyde (assistant chief of staff), Tom Crofts (O/C, First Southern Division), Bill Quirke (O/C, Second Southern Division) and Tom Barry (operations officer, Southern Command). Aiken, in his capacity as Lynch's deputy, chaired the meeting.[9]

It was in a grim atmosphere that the much-delayed Executive meeting took place, with severe differences of opinion among the IRA leadership. Further complicating matters were the National Army raiding parties in the area, which resulted in the meeting having to move to different secret locations around the Nire Valley.[10]

Lynch began the meeting with a report on the 'general military situation of the Army', with mention of the meeting of the First Southern Division he had attended. He stated that his reason for holding this Executive meeting under difficult circumstances was due to pressure from senior officers, such as Barry, following Liam Deasy's capture and communication with the republican leadership. Each officer present then proceeded to give a report of the 'military situation' in their areas and an estimate of how long they could hold out. (Of note, for all of Lynch's hopes in the west, reports relating to the Western Divisions, as well as the Third Eastern Division, had not reached him in time for the meeting.)[11] The total strength of the IRA at this juncture was determined as 8,000, with 13,000 in prison. In contrast, it was estimated the Free State government had nearly 40,000 in their ranks.[12]

The minutes of the Executive meeting then refer to a 'long discussion' that followed on several subjects – among them the consequences of Deasy's capture, the response of republican prisoners in Limerick and Cork to Deasy's letters, Tom Barry's peace efforts with Fr Duggan and other peace efforts.[13] Aiken proposed a motion, seconded by MacSwiney, that on the direction of the IRA Executive, the Republican Government 'be empowered to enter upon negotiations' with the government of the Irish Free State. The vote resulted in a tie, with Lynch himself not voting.[14] Barry then put forward a proposal, that 'in the opinion of the Executive further armed resistance and operations against the Free State government will not further the cause of independence of the country'. The result was five votes for, six against – with Lynch the last, deciding vote.[15]

During the lengthy discussions, mention was frequently made – likely with interventions by Lynch – of the ground artillery Moylan was trying to secure, now focused on efforts in Germany. Lynch remarked he 'thought a few pieces at least would be landed before three weeks'. His confident assurance seemed to have an impact on proceedings. According to the meeting minutes, those who voted against Tom Barry's resolution 'stated they did so because they wished to see whether the artillery would come or not', as well as waiting for the detailed reports from the areas that had not yet sent these to Lynch.[16]

Given that it was impossible to reconcile the divergent views of those on the Executive, it was decided to adjourn the meeting for three weeks and to reassemble at Araglen on 10 April, while de Valera was charged with bringing definite peace proposals he had been discussing with intermediaries before the conference.[17] This was perhaps more a sop from Lynch to the head of the Republican Government and his supporters, and there is little indication this assigned task was deemed particularly important by Lynch.

Frank Gallagher, a sympathetic biographer of de Valera, later wrote of an exchange between Lynch and de Valera following the Executive meeting. As they walked down a country road from the site of the farmhouse where it took place, Lynch remarked, 'I wonder what Tom Clarke would think of this decision' – in reference to the executed Fenian and key figure in the IRB leadership who masterminded the Easter Rising. De Valera stopped in his tracks, and replied, 'Tom Clarke is dead … He has not our responsibilities. Nobody will ever know what he would do for this situation did not arise for him. But it has arisen for us and we must face it with our intelligence and conscious of our responsibility.'[18]

This exchange is often referred to in accounts of the Civil War as an example of Lynch's unrealistic thinking at this time, and the contrast between the two men at this crucial juncture.[19] However, the sole source for the quote is a sympathetic biographer of de Valera and, if it is taken as valid to some degree, Lynch's response – if any – to these remarks is disappointingly not recorded for posterity in Gallagher's notes. What is clear is that to the end, de Valera and Lynch's relationship was a troubled one.

It was extraordinary the Executive meeting was soon to reconvene under such difficulties in the midst of the National Army sweep. Yet, Lynch realised it was necessary in order to retain unity among the IRA leadership and convince those with doubts a viable path to regain military momentum was still possible.

* * *

On 30 March – Good Friday – Lynch, Aiken and Hyde stayed at a flying column's billet in Kilcash. It was there that Lynch reiterated to his courier and friend Kathleen Barry Moloney the three courses he felt were left for the military resistance: 'to fight on, to surrender, or a third he would not name, but did not like – which was in fact a dumping of arms'. Above all, to Barry Moloney, as he discussed with others, he maintained the firm and deeply misguided belief that the area under the Western Command could carry on the fight.[20] However limited their military successes, however dim their prospects, for Lynch it was important that some strain of sustained military resistance to the Free State continue. As well as expecting positive news of the the ground artillery, this represented the very limit of his thinking for future strategies in the days leading up to his death.

At Graigavalla, Lynch stayed at the Kirwans' home, so familiar to him since the aftermath of the Fermoy arms raid of September 1919. Jerry Kirwan repaired his boots, worn from his long travels.[21] It was at the Kirwans' that Lynch met Bridie Keyes for the last time. Of the substance of this encounter, Meda Ryan briefly described it as 'a very memorable visit, the Republic's cause was foremost in their conversations'.[22] While the couple must still have held fast to their dreams, both no doubt realised such a happy future was still out of reach.

Up to 9 April, Lynch and others stayed in various safehouses, including a shed referred to as 'Katmandu' on a farm in the townland of Poulacappal. This hiding place was constructed by Jim O'Brien, the local IRA battalion engineer, and was a room measuring 10 x 5 feet and accessed through a cow shed. Still retaining a strong faith, even in these troubled times, Lynch was spotted one day during this stay on his knees saying the Rosary.[23]

On 9 April, a dispatch rider, Owen McCarthy, informed Lynch of the presence of National Army soldiers in the area, with a round-up anticipated in the next day or two. Lynch opted not to head towards Araglen that day and requested McCarthy return with another report in the next day or two.[24] He was never to receive it.

That night, the group billeted in several farmhouses along a small road at the base of the Knockmealdown mountains. This was at Croagh, one mile east of their location the day before. The Tar River, flowing eastward to join the Suir, formed the northern boundary of the billet area that night. Lynch, Aiken and Hyde stayed at the home of Michael Condon. Croagh was at the far eastern end of the area of the Sixth Battalion, Third Tipperary Brigade, and the guards on the farmhouses consisted of Volunteers from that battalion under the command of their vice-commandant, Seán Myles. Myles ensured the billeting area was well protected from the north, east and west. To the south, were the Knockmealdown mountains themselves.[25]

It was at Michael Condon's that Lynch wrote one of his final dispatches to his very disgruntled O/C of Britain, Pa Murray, and said that 'I am confident if we stand united that victory is certain and that in a short time.'[26] For Lynch, this was a typical statement to one of his leading commanders, demonstrating once again his determination to maintain a very optimistic tone to encourage those under his command whatever his private concerns. Since the beginning of his command of this doomed republican military resistance, to the very end, such encouragement was the consistent note in his communications to officers, whatever his private doubts and anguish.

∗∗∗

In the early hours of 10 April, forces of the National Army were still on the hunt for the republican leadership in the area. Colonel Thomas Ryan's troops were getting increasingly close, though neither they nor their intended targets knew it yet. Under Ryan's command were 400 men that made up the four columns of the National Army's Second Southern Division. On his order, the columns began a major sweep through the Ballybacon area just north of the Knockmealdown mountains, which stretch from east to west along the borders of Counties Tipperary and Waterford. The highest peak, Knockmealdown Mountain itself, measures nearly 3,000 feet.

Travelling in his army-assigned Ford car, Ryan was eager to check the progress of each of these four columns. He had reason to be highly confident in these early hours of the morning. At the end of March, he had received 'most reliable voluntary information' that the leadership of the republican military resistance was moving between the Ballybacon and Newcastle parishes for a pivotal meeting to discuss future strategies. Scattered and diminished though the ranks of his opponents, the so-called 'Irregulars', were, it was the view of Ryan's superiors that they seemed to be determined to continue their fight and had to be crushed. Recent intelligence indicated the existence nearby of a secret dugout in a small farmer's house, the entrance being through a sideboard in the parlour, which then led to an office and sleeping quarters. From the time he received this intelligence, Ryan resisted ordering a round-up in the area until he knew the house's exact location.[27]

While he bided his time, on 8 April a special messenger reported to Ryan that the republican leadership was again in Ballybacon, billeted in a series of known houses in Goatenbridge at the foot of the Knockmealdown mountains. Ryan promptly informed General Prout and issued an operation order. He had four columns detailed, with 100 men in each column following specific instructions. For instance, No. 1 column was ordered to sweep the mountainside and the valley, and then to proceed to carry out a flanking movement on the mountain over Newcastle.[28]

One advantage of Ryan's was that he knew this area well. Not only did Ballybacon adjoin the parish of his birth but it was also his old company area, where he once served as vice-commandant of the Sixth Battalion, Third Tipperary Brigade during the War of Independence. Ryan recalled it as being one of the safest areas for retreating flying columns of the IRA brigade during that earlier conflict – he had been centrally involved in the flying column in several key engagements with the enemy.[29]

However, Ryan's confidence was quickly tempered by a rather farcical development. In consultation with his officers on the night of 9 April, Ryan had deemed the most important part of the operation to be that taken on by the No. 2 column, which was to venture to Goatenbridge Cross. This group was to take the road which led to the mountain and proceed by it towards the hillside. The troops were to spread out to cover both gaps on the crests of the hills which commanded the valley and Goatenbridge. Leading this group was Captain Thomas Taylor, who, like Ryan, was an old member of the Tipperary IRA flying columns and knew the area well. Ryan, however, was a little wary of giving Taylor this command, recalling he was 'unreliable and erratic when he took drink'. Nonetheless, he felt Taylor's local knowledge, as commander of the troops in Clogheen, would prove key. Just to be certain, Ryan met Taylor and stressed to him the importance of his troops occupying the gaps on the hills to prevent any escape by the enemy. Taylor assured Ryan that his troops would occupy the area at daybreak.[30]

Ryan drove into Goatenbridge around 6 a.m. to find, to his utter amazement, members of the Clogheen column visibly standing or sitting along both sides of the bridge leading to the local pub. Some were even asleep. Demanding the location of the absent Taylor, Ryan was told the captain had entered the pub on the column's arrival and had not come out. A furious Ryan immediately entered the premises and pulled the inebriated Taylor out of the public house. He took Taylor's belt off and gave him several wallops with it in front of his troops. In his recollection of Taylor's response, Ryan sardonically noted, 'There was no necessity [for Taylor] to seek an explanation.'[31]

Precious time had now potentially been lost. Ryan was privy to the fact that the owner of the public house was the brother-in-law of a battalion commandant of the local anti-Treaty IRA. Not surprisingly, the owner had been more than welcoming to Taylor, delaying him with several glasses of whiskey in what Taylor originally intended to be a quick drink before heading up the mountainside with his men.

Ryan realised the enemy had most certainly been alerted in the interim and, by his own account, he was now in a 'towering rage'. He assigned Lieutenant Laurence Clancy to immediately head a search party for the elusive republicans. Clancy had been second-in-command to Taylor and had just witnessed the mortifying exchange between his two superiors. He quickly gathered his group to head up the nearby mountainside. While Ryan felt Clancy seemed unfamiliar with the surrounding countryside, he was nonetheless impressed by how quickly he took to the task. Likely the young lieutenant was eager to impress Ryan, given what he had just witnessed.[32]

The National Army Census of November 1922 identified Lieutenant Clancy as serving in L Company of the Second Southern Division of the National Army, based at Fethard Military Barracks. Twenty-two years of age at the time of the census, he hailed from the townland of Ballylusky in Tipperary.[33] The 1911 census identified him as the oldest of seven children, born to Martin and Margaret Clancy. Both he and his younger brother Patrick seem to have been born in England before their parents moved back to the home of Martin's father, also Laurence.[34] Lieutenant Clancy also had not one, but two, tragic connections to the previous conflict, which were to prove important in his upcoming brief, though fateful, encounter with a prisoner in his custody several hours later on that April day.

Venturing uphill, Clancy and his party were surprised by a sudden burst of gunfire in their direction. He later recalled 'splinters flying from the rocks along with whizzing bullets', the gunfire coming from raised ground to their right and a few hundred yards in front of them. He quickly ordered his men nearby to take cover, briefly assuming it was some of their own troops mistaking them for the enemy. Hiding behind a large rock, Clancy took out his field glasses and carefully looked in the direction from which the gunfire was coming. Instead of their own men, Clancy was 'surprised to see a group of men daringly standing on rocks above us wearing big black overcoats and hats' firing down on them. Clancy felt sure these were some of the republicans for whom they were searching.

As his men returned fire, Clancy – after firing two shots himself – observed the men jump off the rocks to begin their withdrawal. As the gunfire from Clancy's column continued, he watched as the overcoated men moved up the hill towards the skyline. Through his field glasses, he observed one tall figure among the group fall forward suddenly and remain on the ground, undoubtedly hit.[35]

* * *

Frank Aiken, when he wrote later to Lynch's brother Tom, told of the alarm being raised at 4 a.m. He admitted, 'It was a much bigger round-up than we expected. There must have been at least 6,000 Staters on the warpath that day.'[36] Seán Hyde remembered the subsequent perilous journey: 'several times when each one of us came close to being hit, earth and bushes splashed around us. There was one occasion when a blast of gunfire rained rocks and soil along an area between us and the boys in front.'[37]

Aiken and Quirke led the small party, while Lynch and Hyde brought up the rear. Ahead of these four were Tom Barry and Jack O'Meara. Aiken referred to a running fight between the group of republicans and the National Army column lasting for about twenty minutes.[38] He realised their small group was exposed 'on a mountain as base as a billiard table [sic]'. The republicans were hamstrung by only carrying revolvers, while their numerous pursuers were responding with gunfire from long-distance rifles. After a sudden pause in the firing, lasting a number of seconds, a single shot then rang out and hit Lynch. At the time, Hyde was holding him by the hand helping him through a particularly difficult part of the terrain.[39] On later hearing the account of the day, Madge Comer got the impression that Lynch 'was worn out for he had not been used to crossing country, on account of his close confinement in Dublin. The others tried to push him on …'[40] Speculation has also endured that Lynch was suffering a bad flu that morning, which would certainly have affected his ability to move quickly across the terrain.[41] Given that Lynch was perhaps moving slowly and that he was tall in height, he may have been an easier target for his pursuers.

Hyde recalled how the bullet 'which got [Lynch] whizzed past me'. He indicated to Meda Ryan that the fatal shot came from the road below, from the direction of the party of National Army soldiers.[42] Lynch fell to the ground and exclaimed, either 'My God … I'm hit!' or 'I'm hit lads!'[43] Aiken summarised the group's shock: 'We could hardly believe him when he said he was hit.'

Unable to take full account of their leader's injuries in the moment, Aiken, Quirke and Hyde quickly lifted him up and carried him for a distance. The three began saying the act of contrition, with Lynch repeating it. Despite such assistance, even this effort took much out of Lynch, whom the group quickly realised was suffering from a serious wound.[44] Lynch ordered the group to leave him, feeling he was the near the end.[45] Some weeks later, in the letter to Tom, Aiken recalled how he felt that to 'leave him was the hardest thing any of us ever had to do. I was last leaving having been carrying his feet. I was afraid to even say "good-bye Liam" least it would dishearten him … in the excitement of the fight we knew how terrible was the blow that had fallen on the Nation and Army on being deprived of his leadership.'[46]

Tom Ryan claimed Lynch's wound was accidental, an unnamed soldier having fired one shot when members of Lynch's party fired on them. Ryan stated 'they [the republicans] made the mistake of firing on the troops searching the furthermost houses on the mountainside' – the latter had not initially spotted the republicans.[47]

Clancy watched two of the fallen man's companions return to him and attempt to drag him along the hill with them, while the rest continued hesitatingly. He shouted to this troops, 'We have got one of them shot, fire again and don't let them take him, they are dragging him away; let them have it! They are diehards alright!'

Clancy and his own party were then interrupted by fire from their rear, a temporary case of 'friendly fire' from some in their own flying column who were linking up with the party. When this firing ceased, Clancy ordered all present to follow him. He ran towards where the man was lying, now alone; his companions nowhere to be seen. A soldier twenty yards ahead of Clancy was nearing the wounded man and Clancy called out to him, 'Keep that fellow covered with your rifle as you approach him.' To the rest, he said, 'Keep spread out lads. Don't bunch in together.'

As the first soldier approached the wounded man, Clancy noted the latter had a coat bundled under his head like a pillow. As Clancy approached the pair, the soldier, covering the wounded man with his rifle as instructed, suddenly exclaimed, 'We have Dev! We have Dev, sir!' It was then that Clancy noted the man on the ground wore glasses, but he would have recognised Éamon de Valera by sight and that was certainly not the man they had just found. Looking down on him, a confused Clancy replied, 'No, it's not Dev.'

He asked the tall, bespectacled man with the sallow complexion who he was. Their prisoner answered, 'You didn't get Dev, it's Liam Lynch this time, get me a priest and a doctor, I'm dying.'[48]

Clancy immediately recognised the name, dropping to one knee beside the wounded Lynch. 'Are you the bloody chief-of-staff of the Irregulars?'

Even in his weakened state, Lynch could not tolerate the use of the hated term. Qualifying the statement, he answered more definitely, '*I am General Liam Lynch, Chief-of-Staff of the Irish Republican Army.* Get me a priest and doctor, I'm dying.'

Clancy asked where Lynch's guns were as he began to search him, to which Lynch replied, 'My friends took my guns.' He then let out a moan of pain. As Clancy searched Lynch's pockets, he asked him where he was hit, and Lynch touched the lower part of his stomach. 'Oh there!'

Clancy was temporarily distracted as his entire party of soldiers had now crowded around the wounded Lynch. Scolding his troops for not continuing the search for the rest of Lynch's group, he ordered his men to continue after them. After a follow-up search and a scan of the landscape with his field glasses in the aftermath, Clancy concluded that the other republicans had successfully escaped, having been forced to abandon their leader.

Returning to Lynch, Clancy found him being tended to by some soldiers. A search of Lynch's person revealed some ammunition, money, a pocket watch, two fountain pens (silver and gold) and a number of documents related to operations of the anti-Treaty IRA.[49] One particularly intriguing item was deposited in a cache of documents found near Lynch: a series of handwritten notepad pages, penned by Austin Stack, which appeared to be a draft order for a republican surrender.[50]

The weakened Lynch again insisted he was dying. Clancy and others opened Lynch's clothes to find the wound. Immediately, they noticed a small entrance wound above one of the hip bones and an exit wound above the opposite hip bone. Clancy noted an inch of intestine protruding from the exit wound and a few drops of blood. He grimly concluded the bullet had torn through Lynch's intestines.

Incredibly, almost none of the group possessed any field bandages. One soldier, a veteran of the Great War, admitted to having one but refused to give it to a 'bloody die-hard' and insisted to Clancy he needed it himself. He undressed to reveal he had a scorch of a bullet across one buttock. 'So near and yet so far,' Clancy noted darkly. Dismissing the soldier's injury as a 'little burn', Clancy insisted he hand over the bandage. The soldier gave out 'hells delight' to 'all and sundry' and only finally surrendered the bandage when Clancy threatened him with his revolver. (Clancy later recalled the soldier deserted the army after this exchange.)

Clancy realised the bandage was inadequate and noticed Lynch growing more and more pale. The troops were forced to carry the six-foot Lynch down the mountain in an improvised stretcher made of rifles and a soldier's great coat, forcing the agonised man into a semi-sitting position. Every few yards he had to ask the men to stop and let him down. When they finally reached the bottom of the mountain, Captain Taylor arrived with his own party of troops, which only complicated the situation.[51] Taylor asked Clancy what he was going to do, and when Clancy mentioned seeking medical aid for Lynch, Taylor replied, 'I don't approve at all, and your handling of the whole situation is questionable.' Clancy recalled that 'hot words' followed and the two men pulled guns on each other. After a tense moment, Taylor insisted he was taking back all the troops.

'You won't take my men,' Clancy insisted.

'Who is in charge of this column, you or me?' Taylor replied.

Clancy insisted he was remaining in charge of the men with him. He recalled later his indifference as to the consequences of defying Taylor, who subsequently returned with forty men to nearby Clogheen, with the remainder staying with Clancy – he decided to lead his group to a public house in nearby Newcastle, where he could contact the barracks in Clonmel. Along the way, the group encountered a priest, who tended to Lynch. Not long after, the party came across a farmer with a horse and trailer of hay, which was used to convey Lynch to the public house.

On reaching the premises with the wounded Lynch, Clancy rang Clonmel Barracks, informing the military authorities of developments and asking for an ambulance to come as soon as possible.[52] At some juncture, a local doctor tended to Lynch and complimented Clancy on the dressing of the wound.[53] Clancy, along with the publican (an ex-RIC man), ensured Lynch was comfortable, providing him with blankets, a mattress and a glass of brandy in the front parlour. Following this, Clancy, who was in the adjoining room, was summoned by the soldier guarding Lynch, as the prisoner wished to speak to him.

On returning to the parlour, Lynch said to Clancy, 'Is it getting dark?'

'No,' Clancy replied. 'It's not three o'clock yet. Are you comfortable? You are here only an hour or so yet.'

The answer seemed to inspire a haste in the weakened Lynch. 'I thought it was getting dark, I must be dying and I want to ask you to do a couple of little things for me. ... When I die tell my people I was to be buried with Fitzgerald of Fermoy.' The name registered with Clancy as Michael Fitzgerald, the Cork-based IRA officer who had been the first republican hunger striker to die in late 1920. He asked Lynch if it was the same individual.

'Yes,' Lynch replied. 'The greatest friend I ever had on this Earth.'

The weakened Lynch seemed curious Clancy had realised to whom he was referring. 'Are you one of the old crowd, the IRA, I mean?'

Clancy replied that he was. He made mention to Lynch of his two brothers, who had served in the Tipperary IRA and were killed during the Tan War, and noted that he was an IRA member and had been tried by field court martial in Victoria Barracks in Cork.[54] Clancy's brother Patrick had been unarmed when shot dead by a member of a British Army patrol near the family's home in Ballyuskey, Drangan in November 1920. His brother Martin was shot dead during a British Army raid on a secret IRA battalion meeting in Knockroe in March 1921.[55]

Lynch raised his right hand toward Clancy. 'Shake hands. I'm glad one of the old crowd got me.' Tears began to stream down Lynch's face and Clancy realised he, too, was sobbing as the men shook hands. 'God bless you, I will pray for you,' Lynch continued, 'and you sometimes think of poor Liam Lynch and say a little prayer for me. All this is a pity, it never should have happened. I'm glad now I'm going from it all. Poor Ireland, poor Ireland!'

Lynch then asked Clancy to ensure his gold watch and fountain pen go to his brother, a member of the Christian Brothers, and silver watch to his sister. He then said, 'My silver fountain pen you may keep for yourself as a small token of appreciation for the way you treated me from the time I fell into your hands. God bless you and the boys, who carried me down the hill, I am so sorry for all the trouble I caused you and them.' Clancy repeated all of Lynch's requests back to him to ensure their accuracy, and assured Lynch he would see to them. The ambulance then arrived, which included General Prout and a captain Clancy did not recognise, along with a military medical doctor and orderlies.[56]

At the inquest into Lynch's death the following day, Dr Raymond Dalton, the local military medical officer, described arriving at the public house in Newcastle in an ambulance. He noted two bullet wounds in the body – one entrance wound being somewhat behind and to the right between the lower border of the ribs and the hip. The exit wound also appeared to be on the same level at the left side. Lynch was suffering very severely from shock, and Dalton determined there was a fair amount of external and internal haemorrhaging. In consultation with the attending local doctor, they determined it was best for Lynch to be moved to the military hospital in Clonmel by ambulance.[57]

Lynch and Clancy clasped hands again and parted with tears in their eyes. The last words that Clancy claimed Lynch spoke to him were, 'I will live until about ten o'clock tonight.'[58] Lynch was conveyed to St Joseph's Hospital and arrived there at 6 p.m., where he was placed in the military ward. Dalton noted the patient was 'low all the time'. At the inquest, his death was put at shortly before nine o'clock, not too far from Lynch's own prediction.[59]

In another coincidence, Tom Ryan recalled that on being taken to the ward, Lynch was put in a private room which was vacated by the occupant to make way for him. That occupant was none other than Ryan's first cousin, Tom Doyle, a National Army officer who had been wounded during a skirmish in Waterford. Another cousin of Ryan's was present: the attending nurse, Bridget Halley. Halley nursed Lynch, assisted by Doyle despite his own injury, until Lynch passed later that night, as recalled by Ryan, 'in the arms of both cousins of mine'.[60]

★★★

The inquest into Lynch's death was held on 11 April at Clonmel Workhouse. It was presided over by the deputy coroner, Dr Patrick Stokes, with a jury of twelve being sworn in.[61] Lynch's body was viewed by the jury in the mortuary nearby.[62]

Colonel Jerry Ryan, deputy O/C of the National Army in Waterford, identified the body in the mortuary as that of Liam Lynch. His age was given inaccurately as thirty-three years old. Doctor Raymond Dalton, a lieutenant, then gave evidence about how he went to Newcastle and examined Lynch in the public house. Dalton summarised Lynch's wounds: 'There was a fair amount of external, and a considerable amount of internal haemorrhage, and he was suffering very severely from shock.' Dalton explained that the decision was made, in consultation with the attending doctor, to bring Lynch to the military hospital in Clonmel. He concluded that Lynch's death was due to shock and haemorrhaging following the wounds he had suffered.

Captain Taylor, identified as being of the Sixth Battalion in Clonmel, gave evidence and explained how he was in charge of a party of soldiers going up the mountain. Around 10 a.m., after 'fire was opened on us by a number of Irregulars', his party returned fire. When the firing ceased after a half hour, the soldiers went in the direction of where the IRA members had withdrawn and found Lynch lying face-up. Taylor makes mention of one of his soldiers – almost certainly a reference to Clancy – dressing Lynch's wounds. In Taylor's brief narrative, he referred to how he engaged Lynch in conversation at some point after the latter's capture, who confirmed who he was and asked to be buried with Michael Fitzgerald in Kilcrumper. Taylor added that Lynch had no arms on him when he was found. It is unclear why Clancy was not called as a witness.

After a brief consultation, the jury agreed the cause of death 'was due to a shock and haemorrhage due to bullet wounds caused by a party of the National Army in the execution of doing their duty.' A vote of sympathy was taken for Lynch's relatives.[63] The entire inquest was later reported as being 'brief and formal'.[64]

Like the wave of speculation that continues to endure about Michael Collins' death at Béal na mBláth, there does, albeit on a smaller scale, exist a similar conspiracy theory about the circumstances of Lynch's end. In summary, in the words of Meda Ryan, in some areas 'it is said that there was an organised plot to get rid of Lynch', the belief being that 'he was a stumbling block for those of the cease-fire, dump-arms element'. In essence, an unknown actor, possibly someone in the escaping party accompanying Lynch, is believed to have fired the fatal shot. Central to this speculation is the fact that Lynch was the only one wounded during the incident.[65]

Ned Murphy, at the time a National Army intelligence officer, who carried out his own internal investigation and interviewed numerous National Army soldiers present on the scene, told Ryan that one unnamed soldier in the column spotted the fleeing republicans 'and aimed at one of them, he was aware that he had hit a man, this turned out to be Lynch'. In Murphy's view, it was a war situation and an enemy had been hit by a long-range shot; the idea that the bullet came from any source 'other than a National Army rifle should not arise'.[66] Furthermore, Ryan noted at the inquest 'there seemed to be no doubt that the fatal bullet was a long-range shot fired from a National Army weapon and admitted to by them'.[67]

At no point did the Free State government, National Army or the otherwise censored national press issue statements raise the possibility of Lynch having been removed by those on his own side – despite a precedent for using scurrilous allegations to discredit their enemies throughout the eleven-month conflict. One would also have to consider how the five other men in the fleeing party – Aiken, Hyde, O'Meara, Quirke, Barry – would have managed to keep such a secret between them or have the considerable foresight to know such drastic action would play out to their advantage.

During the course of research for this biography, this author has met relatives of Lynch, historians and republican political activists, and it is clear that speculation and a degree of oral tradition around such a theory into Lynch's death still endures into the present day and will continue to do so well into the future.[68] In conversation, the idea comes across as a well-intended reflex of the endurance of a particular image of Lynch in popular memory: the idea that this brave and iconic republican martyr had to be 'done in' by something far grander than a lucky shot. However, ultimately such enduring speculation does nothing to illuminate the real existing facts of Lynch's death and what his passing meant for Irish republicans going forward in an increasingly desperate Civil War, or his own legacy. On the enduring speculation into the circumstances of Michael Collins' death, the historian Michael Hopkinson wrote, 'it matters more that Collins was killed than how he was killed'[69] – this is also true in the case of Liam Lynch.

✳✳✳

Only two days after Lynch's passing, President de Valera issued a written statement addressed to IRA members. It started, 'Soldiers of the Republic, bulwark of our Nation's Honour and Independence' and referred to Lynch as 'your Chief – the "Lion Heart" whose exalted soul and tenacious will, backed by his royal allies the hills, more than any other baffled the forces of an Empire and brought them to terms'. De Valera encouraged IRA Volunteers to renew their commitment to the republican cause. He acknowledged with past losses, 'your task is a hard and a sad one … it is better to die nobly, as your Chief has died, than live a slave'.[70] A day earlier, on 11 April, de Valera remarked to Countess Markievicz, 'Poor Liam! It is so awful to see these men who loved Ireland so deeply … killed off one by one. Ireland has far too few of such and cannot spare them.'[71] Whatever the difficulties between them in the last few months, de Valera was genuinely upset at Lynch's death and later kept an envelope of Lynch's final dispatches on which he wrote, 'Very precious. General Liam Lynch's last despatches. National treasures.'[72]

Naturally, the loss of Lynch greatly impacted those to whom he had been closest in the intervening months. Lynch's faithful courier and dear friend Kathleen Barry Moloney, admitted to her then-imprisoned future husband, Jim, that 'I'll be a long time forgetting the horror of the time of the Chief's death and afterwards ... I have nightmares about it still.'[73] While many close to Lynch in the closing weeks had doubts as to his decision-making, they recognised that his death ended any prospect of momentum on the part of the IRA. Todd Andrews was of the opinion Lynch had become 'so blind to the realities ... He had developed some mental blockage which prevented him from believing that we could be beaten.'[74] George Power received a 'letter ... full of optimism' from Lynch just hours after his death.[75] Yet Andrews admitted that with 'Lynch's death I knew the end of the Civil War had come. Only his iron will had kept it going in the last few months.'[76] In his letter to Lynch's brother Tom, Aiken admitted, 'in the excitement of the fight we knew how terrible was the blow that had fallen on the Nation and Army on being deprived of his leadership.'[77]

Not surprisingly, after Lynch's death, communications ground to a halt for Seán Moylan. His efforts to secure the much sought-for ground artillery had led him to Germany; as a result, he was left adrift in the country without updates on the military situation back in Ireland.[78] In this instance, it can be appreciated how Lynch at least attempted to keep the flailing, desperate strands of the republican resistance together in this last phase. Pa Murray, the reluctant O/C of Britain, opined in a letter to Moylan in early May, 'they have not sent me one written word since Liam's death ... I do not know how matters stand.'[79] Later that month, Moylan lamented how he awaited 'a definite reply from Ireland together with some news as to conditions ... Lynch certainly believed in keeping in touch with his outposts.'[80] Perhaps indicative of a lack of interest amongst the new leadership on the IRA Executive, in its first meeting after Lynch's death it was noted simply that there 'was no good news from the men who had been endeavouring to purchase cannon' – it is not clear if anyone had recently attempted to contact Moylan.[81] In late April, on hearing of the final suspension of military operations by Aiken, Moylan, given that his efforts continued to be unsuccessful, made no further attempt to arrange an arms deal and returned to Ireland.[82]

✳✳✳

On the news of Lynch's death, Willie Ryan, a family friend, along with Hanna Hyland, a cousin of Lynch's, made the journey to the Lynch homestead in Barnagurraha to covey the news to his mother, Mary. On reading their faces, Mary spoke first: 'He is dead, Willie … Thank God he did not let down his comrades.' In his biography of Lynch, Florence O'Donoghue claimed, 'in the order of the days that followed she carried her grief proudly and kept her tears unshed'.[83] Lynch's brother Seán, then in Limerick Jail, sadly admitted to a comrade, 'I always felt he'd go by the bullet.'[84] Both Seán and James, themselves active in the republican forces and then incarcerated in Limerick Jail, were denied permission to attend the funeral of their younger brother as they refused to sign a form undertaking to recognise the legitimacy of the Free State and promising not to rejoin the republican fighting, which was necessary to ensure their temporary release.[85] According to family tradition, Mary was upset that the youngest Lynch sibling, Tom, could not return from Australia to say farewell to the brother to whom he was so close.[86]

With the prospect of a major republican funeral, de Valera saw an important opportunity, and suggested to Count Plunkett that Lynch's body be brought to Dublin to be buried with the usual pomp and ceremony in Glasnevin Cemetery. The cemetery had been the site of many a grand republican funeral, especially since that of the Fenian Jeremiah O'Donovan Rossa in 1915. With an eye on recently deceased comrades, de Valera felt the 'proper place for his [Lynch's] body is beside that other great lion – Cathal [Brugha].' De Valera asked Plunkett to form a funeral committee and added, 'No time should be lost.'[87]

At the inquest in Clonmel, one juror had asked if Lynch's request to be buried with Fitzgerald in Kilcrumper would be carried out, to which General Prout, attending as a representative of the military, replied that he 'had given an assurance to that already'.[88] On 12 April, de Valera admitted to Plunkett he had not been aware of Lynch's wishes and they 'will naturally be paramount'. De Valera and the Republican Government nonetheless still privately requested that the Lynch family allow Liam's remains to be brought to Dublin for burial, but they refused.[89] The denial of this request was in some way a fitting postscript to the turbulent dealings between de Valera and Lynch in the latter's final months. Given it was impossible for de Valera to attend the funeral, he requested that Plunkett, along with Mary MacSwiney and Margaret O'Callaghan, represent the Republican Government.[90] (Unfortunately, all three were arrested on to the way to Lynch's funeral by Free State authorities.)

On 13 April, Lynch's remains lay in the church attached to Clonmel Workhouse. The funeral was delayed for a day due to the concern that much of his family had yet to arrive. All through the previous night, members of Cumann na mBan stood guard at the bier as crowds passed through the church and viewed Lynch's remains, dressed in the green uniform of an IRA officer and laid out in a massive oak coffin. *The Irish Times* noted the presence of Lynch's mother at the bier, and 'several soldiers of the National Army, who had come to pay a tribute of respect to their late opponent' kneeling in the body of the church. Lynch's brother Martin arrived from Omagh and, 'as he looked down on the grey drawn face in the coffin, he betrayed much emotion'.[91]

Meda Ryan described the scene as Bridie Keyes, Lynch's fiancée, approached his coffin, based on an interview with a friend of Keyes: 'she stood and looked on him. Then she held his hand and stroked his face … She did not cry. Her eyes just glazed. She froze. She never expected Liam would get shot, he was such a determined person, and so strong. Bridie had a belief that he was invincible.'[92]

On the day of the funeral, National Army soldiers were posted along the route and within the cemetery. Many in attendance noticed a military aeroplane flying over the cemetery itself.[93] Alongside his mother, sister and two brothers, the news coverage noted thousands in attendance in and around the graveyard at Kilcrumper, which included friends, former comrades and sympathisers. A 'regular fleet of motor cars passed through Fermoy to Mitchelstown, while many hours before the funeral arrived the graveyard was crowded'. Lynch's coffin was carried to the grave draped in a tricolour bearing the letters 'I.R.A.' along with his cap and belt. The Rosary was recited in Irish, while the republican TD Professor William Stockley gave the oration in Irish, the first of many beside Lynch's graveside.

Press coverage noted hundreds of wreaths at the graveside, including from the sisters of Terence MacSwiney, but it was the message on one that was deemed worthy of report: 'When Emmet's epitaph shall be written, Ireland will write yours, Liam. – Éamon de Valera.'[94]

***

Lynch's death certainly curbed the resilience of the waning republican military resistance in the weeks thereafter, but for the surviving IRA leadership, the war was not yet quite over. The new Executive met on 20 April, with Frank Aiken elected the new chief of staff. As Hopkinson has noted, 'intentionally or not, [Aiken's] appointment improved prospects for the adoption of a more flexible negotiating stand' on the part of republicans. It was at this meeting that Aiken ordered the suspension of hostilities and the beginning of negotiations with the Free State government.[95] The minutes from the meeting also reveal that 'the President was unanimously requested to take charge of any negotiations which might follow ...'[96] Though de Valera was visibly upset at Lynch's death, his most recent biographer has speculated that he must have realised the main impediment to peace with the Free State government had now been removed.[97] At last, he had the more central role he had long desired and a chance to influence the outcome of the conflict. This was remarkably similar to a scenario Lynch speculated on to de Valera two months before. Writing to him on 7 February, Lynch wondered if republicans 'should know that if possible first if there is a way out by which peace can be attained. At least should give the enemy our minimum terms and receive his and have these latter finally reviewed...' Lynch was not however directing de Valera in such efforts at the time, adding it was not a 'good moment' for a such a discussion.[98] It is worth speculating whether Lynch, by late April, may have also reached the same conclusion as Aiken: that such a moment had arrived.

Nonetheless, this new era of leadership for de Valera did not get off to an auspicious start, as the next few weeks were to prove. When all entreaties to the Free State government were rejected by Cosgrave's cabinet, the much-fabled and hoped-for peace agreement never emerged. In consultation with de Valera, Aiken used his authority as chief of staff to issue a 'dump arms' order to all anti-Treaty IRA units on 24 May – thereby ending the military phase of the Civil War. Intriguingly, one line from the order encouraged IRA Volunteers to take part in political activity in the form of participation in Sinn Féin.[99]

There was to be no formal declaration of the end of hostilities on the Free State side, no negotiated settlement between the warring factions. Yet, in essence, Aiken's dump arms marked an ending point of sorts: the Irish Civil War of 1922–23 and the military resistance of republicans to the Free State that Lynch promised to continue to a bitter end was now over. In the midst of this, de Valera immediately devoted his energies towards beginning to plan a new means for republicans to organise politically within the Irish Free State. Within three years, this would take the form of the Fianna Fáil party, whose constitutional form of republicanism would see it win mass support. De Valera led the party to power in 1932, and his government would go on to dismantle the terms of the Anglo-Irish Treaty and create the 1937 Constitution. For over eight decades, the party would dominate the political life of the state. De Valera's constitution envisaged the state, now simply referred to as 'Ireland', as a republic in all but name. Ironically, it was in 1948, when the political heirs of the pro-Treaty tradition, Fine Gael, passed legislation in government that cemented the state's status as a republic with its withdrawal from the British commonwealth. Such political developments were beyond the comprehension of Liam Lynch and his peers in 1923.

Whatever Lynch's own personal disinterest in political activism, whatever his poor relations with de Valera, the memory of Lynch would remain an important component of Fianna Fáil's political tradition, which views its own beginnings as the republican opposition to the Free State during the Civil War. Thus, every September, around the anniversary of the Fermoy arms raid, the local cumann of Fianna Fáil chair a commemoration to Lynch at his graveside in Kilcrumper. This long-standing commemoration, called the General Liam Lynch National Commemoration, had its origins in a non-political commemoration begun by Lynch's comrades, such as Florence O'Donoghue and Moss Twomey, in the early 1950s. In 2011, party leader – and future Taoiseach – Micheál Martin told those gathered that his party 'is proud to have been founded by republicans of the generation which secured independence'. In an intriguing modern-day defence of the anti-Treaty tradition, Martin also reminded those present that Lynch 'rejected the Treaty like many, many others for reasons which were motivated by the highest ideals'.[100]

The IRA as an organisation emerged from the Civil War defeated and demoralised, and over the following four decades, became a pale shadow of the revolutionary force that shaped the events of 1916–23. Never again to operate in open warfare against the Irish Free State, yet still refusing to recognise it, the IRA's most notable efforts were an ill-fated bombing campaign in England from 1939 to 1940 and a border campaign to destabilise Northern Ireland from 1956 to 1962. The organisation split in 1969, at the outset of the conflict popularly known as 'the Troubles', which were sparked by the violent repression by the unionist government of Northern Ireland of the demand for civil rights from the local nationalist population. The IRA faction associated with the 'provisional' republican movement would become best known as the modern-day iteration of the IRA, claiming both descent from, and a continuation of the revolutionary tradition of the IRA begun by Liam Lynch's generation.

While the IRA was a chief participant in a violent conflict with the British security forces and loyalist paramilitaries, it was to be ordinary civilians who would make up the majority of casualties in 'the Troubles'. The republican movement engaged with a peace process begun in the 1980s involving the Irish and British governments. Following a final IRA ceasefire in 1997, the Good Friday Agreement emerged, with representatives of Irish nationalism and unionism committed to peace and power-sharing within a Northern Ireland government. Crucially, a key component of the agreement was the possibility of a border poll, giving the chance for a majority in Northern Ireland to vote to become part of a united Ireland at an underdetermined point in the future. This agreement was signed on 10 April 1998 – remarkably seventy-five years to the day of Liam Lynch's death.

***

A fascinating private family archive shown to this author revealed the considerable level of contemporary correspondence sent to the Lynch family – primarily Lynch's mother, Mary – on his death. Messages of sympathy arrived from republican prisoners in both Gormanston camp and the Curragh. The message from the Curragh was signed by imprisoned members of the East Limerick Brigade, who asked Mary to let them 'share your grief, for if you have lost a loving member of your family we have lost a loving and beloved Chief'.[101] Bodies from various corporations and councils also paid tribute to Lynch. One such message, from the Waterworks Committee of Cork Corporation and addressed to Mary, expressed 'their very sincere sympathy and condolences on the sad demise of one who had done so much for the emancipation our country at large'.[102]

One notable letter in this private archive was from Cáitlín Brugha, widow of former Minister for Defence Cathal Brugha. Cáitlín assured Mary:

> [Your] greatest consolation is as mine when Cathal made the supreme sacrifice … I had always looked upon Liam as a personal friend. I had heard Cathal speak of him so often with such great admiration … do not grudge Liam the great reward of his noble sacrifice and I am sure you are worthy to be the mother of so great a soldier of the Republic.[103]

The items Lynch requested be given to various individuals during his final hours, including the pen he offered to Lieutenant Clancy, seemingly never reached their intended recipients. Clancy wrote cover notes in order to detail where each item was to go, which he gave to General Prout when the latter retrieved the items from his junior officer. Prout informed Clancy they would be given to army intelligence officers before being passed to the Lynch family in a few days. Over a week after Lynch's death, Clancy, now stationed at Coolville House in Clogheen, was confronted by Lynch's brother Martin, who accused him of stealing the items given to him shortly before Lynch's death. A surprised Clancy offered to go in Martin's car to talk to General Prout at Clonmel Barracks, to which Martin angrily replied, 'I have something to do besides driving Free Staters around the country.' Clancy told Martin that he had not received the fountain pen gifted to him by Lynch. Some weeks later, Clancy approached Prout and asked him what had become of Lynch's belongings, to which Prout replied that they had been sent to the Lynch family.[104] A niece of Tom's and Liam's, Bridie O'Callaghan (née Lynch) told a journalist in 1981 that Clancy, after several years, managed to locate the watch for Martin. One surprising detail about the watch, is that it was once the property of Lynch's father, Jeremiah, and was believed to be over 200 years old.[105] Of the fountain pen that Lynch wished to give to Clancy, a letter writer to *The Irish Press* in 1972 suggested it may have come into the possession of Captain Taylor, who showed it to a group ten days after Lynch's death.[106]

Tragedy would again strike the Lynch family in 1933. Liam's older brother James died at the age of forty-two in St Vincent's Hospital in Dublin, while undergoing an operation.[107] James' death registration recorded the cause as lipoma and pulmonary embolism (a blood clot). He was listed as being a bachelor farmer and still resided at the family home in Barnagurraha.[108] A brief obituary in *An Phoblacht* noted that he was active in the Cork No. 2 Brigade and summarised his imprisonment during the Civil War and a later hunger strike. It called him 'a heroic figure of the Pre- and Post-Treaty conflicts in the South of Ireland'.[109]

Of Bridie Keyes, Meda Ryan wrote that she moved from the locality of Mitchelstown at an undetermined point after her fiancé's death. She then worked in the offices of the Irish Hospital Sweepstakes, a lottery established in the 1930 to fund Irish hospitals.[110] Despite this author's best efforts, it has proven difficult to illuminate much more about Keyes' later life beyond what is provided by Ryan, other than that she seemed to be present at some commemorations for her fiancé in the years thereafter. Keyes' death registration reveals a rather remarkable detail about the date of her death: 20 November

1970, seventy-eight years to the day of Liam's registered birthdate. It made mention that she worked as a clerk, and the cause of death is listed as as tox-aemia, atherosclerosis and hypertension. Her sister was present at her death. An additional detail also stands out: Bridie never married.[111]

In 1934, the extension of the Military Pensions Act allowed for those who participated on the republican side of the Civil War (or their dependants) to claim for a military pension. Tom Lynch filled out an initial application on behalf of his mother, and made mention that Frank Aiken, then minister for justice, had personally promised to see it through. In 1933, Mary Lynch received a once-off dependants' gratuity of £110 10s. She died on 3 October 1937, aged seventy-six. No medical reason is given for her death beyond 'senile decay', and Seán Lynch is listed as being present at her death.[112]

Of interest, the two referees required to sign off on this pension payment to Mary were both former comrades of Lynch, who themselves served on opposite sides of the Civil War: Moss Twomey, then the IRA's chief of staff, and Lynch's old friend in the Limerick IRA, Donnacha O'Hannigan.[113] O'Hannigan wrote that Lynch was 'an enthusiastic pioneer in the movement and was all that could be desired from a military point of view ... he gave his whole time to the cause.' His praise for his late comrade is perhaps surprising, given O'Hannigan was central to the leadership of the National Army contingent that, in Lynch's view, broke the truce in Limerick. It has been inferred to this author that O'Hannigan's assistance to the Lynch family was not appreciated by some of his fellow former National Army comrades.[114]

Twomey's participation in the pension application is notable, given that much of the rump of the still existing anti-Treaty IRA he led would have felt that receipt of a pension would amount to an acknowledgement of the existence of the Free State. While Twomey most certainly never applied for a pension himself, this was his chance to help the mother of his late chief of staff whose memory he cherished for decades. It was Twomey who, along with George Power, approached Florence O'Donoghue about the possibility of writing the first biography of Lynch and assisted him with research for the project.[115]

Twomey was also on the committee responsible for constructing the 60-foot-tall round tower memorial to Lynch on the spot where he was mortally wounded in the Knockmealdown mountains.[116] Twomey's appearance at the unveiling of the tower in April 1935 was a media sensation, given that he was on the run from the Free State authorities (and de Valera's government no less) at the time. Until his death in 1978, Twomey remained well-regarded among adherents of latter-day republicanism. He was the chief of staff of the IRA from 1926 to 1936, finally departing the organisation in 1939, yet he remained a hugely respected figure in republican circles.[117]

In 1973, on the fiftieth anniversary of Lynch's death, a frail Twomey appeared on crutches at the Knockmealdown memorial, as the latter-day iteration of Sinn Féin (associated with the 'provisional' republican movement) held a commemoration there. Too weak to mount the platform and address the crowd, a note penned by Twomey was read out. He urged his fellow republican veterans – in reference to the heightening conflict in Northern Ireland, in which a new IRA was involved – to 'stand today, as you stood under Liam Lynch for Liam Lynch's ideals, to defend and uphold the sovereignty and unity of the Republic'.[118]

The tower itself today remains an important place of pilgrimage for commemorations for Lynch, such as the Liam Lynch National Commemoration every July, not aligned to any group or party. Sinn Féin too holds two commemorations to Lynch, at the memorial tower in September and at the memorial at his birthplace in Barnagurraha. Also, within Newcastle village, where Lynch was taken to Nugent's pub, locals hold a memorial Mass and there is another commemoration committee.

That these political traditions still embrace Lynch in annual commemoration in different locations and at different times of the year is entirely unique for a figure of this period.[119] What is not unique is how those attending these events embrace Lynch as true to their own tradition. Whatever the difference in the politics of these parties and groupings, this sort of commemoration of Liam Lynch will undoubtedly endure far beyond the centenary of his death.

EPILOGUE

LIAM LYNCH'S JOURNEY OVER THE last seven years of his life to his place in the annals of republican martyrdom seemed most unlikely to those who knew him as a quiet child. He was often regarded in those earlier years as a shy, bookish man whose diligence and pleasant manner suited his career as an efficient and well-liked shop assistant. His family and closest contemporaries spoke of him as a warm, humorous, friendly personality, if somewhat shy and socially awkward. Swept into the tide of political fervour in the second decade of the twentieth century, the course of his life changed when he joined the Irish Volunteers. Not lacking in enthusiasm and having a fervent belief in his cause, he proved adept at organising and training as the Volunteers morphed into the IRA. He had no experience as a regular soldier, and yet his dedication to his role resulted in enormous respect for him among his comrades in the areas under his command.

In many respects, in those early years, he was exemplary of the sort of volunteer who made up the organisation. Florence O'Donoghue insisted Lynch 'was not a military genius. ... He was a good soldier, mainly because he was a good man.'[1] Yet, O'Donohgue emphasised how Lynch became a 'master' of guerrilla tactics.[2] What drove Lynch to such a level of commitment was an extraordinary self-belief in his own capabilities and the righteousness of his cause, the latter motivated by contemporary events and also his family background. It was almost inevitable that such a natural leader would become head of the Cork No. 2 Brigade when it was formed, a position which led to Lynch becoming one of the most celebrated guerrilla commanders in the country during the Irish War of Independence. The famed actions associated with his tenure are testament to this: the Fermoy arms raid, the kidnapping of General Lucas and the attack on Mallow Barracks. Not surprisingly, this made him an ideal candidate for the position of O/C of the First Southern Division.

Most of those Lynch encountered during his revolutionary activities he kept at a personal remove. This often led to him being described as self-serious, with a 'priestly' demeanour that made him somewhat inscrutable to many who served with him. Yet, he had genuine, strong friendships with comrades such as Moss Twomey and George Power, and perhaps more surprisingly, despite a supposed shyness, with female activists in the movement such as Siobhán Lankford and Kathleen Barry Moloney. Lynch was not lacking in displays of physical courage during the operations he helped plan and execute. While cultivating a strong relationship with the IRA leadership, he repeatedly demonstrated he was capable of independent action in deed and word. Lynch's objects were always that of Irish independence, the overthrow of British rule in Ireland and the endurance of the Irish Republic. Even his relationship with Bridie Keyes, which gave him the prospect of a life beyond the fighting, always came second to the cause.

By the time of the Truce, Lynch had amassed considerable prestige within the military wing of the Irish revolutionary movement. As it split over the Anglo-Irish Treaty, he immediately associated himself with the anti-Treaty section of the IRA. Yet, he was determined that the IRA could function as a mechanism by which the comrades split over the Treaty settlement could unite. This was especially important, in Lynch's view, if the IRA was to face a renewed war with Britain. However, while supporting efforts at army unity, he always stuck to the approach that such unity must be along the lines of maintaining the Republic as already declared. By 1922, Lynch had seen many of his contemporaries die for the cause, which cemented his belief that the pure republican ideal could not be abandoned. Regarding the terms of the Treaty as a bitter betrayal of the Irish independence for which he and others had fought, he nonetheless remained deeply involved in attempts to find a peaceful solution to the looming conflict. The outbreak of civil war between the IRA and the Provisional Government and National Army of the new Irish Free State was a decisive blow to such efforts. The attack on his comrades in the Four Courts was perceived as an attack on the Republic, and Lynch did not hesitate to take command of the anti-Treaty IRA's military resistance to the new Irish state.

His leadership, military strategies and decision-making during the Civil War were controversial at the time and have remained so. His genuine gifts as a local guerrilla commander did not translate into being an effective commander of the entire IRA across the country. He also faced an array of enormous challenges given the anti-Treaty IRA had no experience of fighting a conventional war and, despite the initial higher number of personnel in their ranks, they lacked military resources, weaponry and vehicles – all of which the Free State side had in abundance – which led to the swift loss of republican territory and a return to guerrilla warfare.[3] It is very difficult to see how any other figure in Lynch's place could have overcome these challenges. In looking through his formal correspondence over the crucial first weeks, there is little evidence that Lynch worried about the loss of territory. Retrospectively, it is not really surprising that other senior IRA leaders pointed to this as a key, early failure on his part.

Lynch's most successful military endeavour was the return to the guerrilla tactics and the flying columns of the War of Independence, despite certain disadvantages not faced during the previous conflict: the lack of a foreign enemy in the form of Britain, opposition from much of the local populace and few results from propaganda efforts. While guerrilla tactics ensured military victories for republicans, albeit on a limited, localised scale, they prolonged the Civil War. Lynch's frequent praise for local operations revealed another key personal failing as the military leader of the anti-Treaty forces: he still viewed the conflict through the prism of a local commander and lacked a vision for the national picture. It is not surprising he had little success in introducing new innovations to republican fighting during the Civil War, a fact which is apparent in the difficulty he had in enforcing a truly ruthless reprisals policy in response to executions, and in the convoluted efforts to acquire heavy artillery.

While maintaining a firm military policy, Lynch consistently stuck to a particular line when peace negotiations with the Free State arose, insisting that these had to be on republican terms. His firm goal by the end of 1922 was that of a war of attrition intended to bring the institutions and infrastructure of the new Irish state to the brink of collapse perhaps to reignite negotiations, or even conflict, with the old enemy of Britain. That Lynch admitted to de Valera in December 1922 that he did not foresee total victory for his side, or a wholesale defeat of the Free State, is intriguing, and far removed from the optimistic proclamations and communications about a republican victory. Whenever one considers his private despair over the Civil War, or even his nuanced reaction to Deasy's surrender plea, there was clearly more to Lynch's thinking during the conflict than his popular image may suggest, however flawed. His approach as chief of staff may have seemed increasingly doomed and hopeless as the Civil War continued into early 1923, but Lynch was familiar with the hard, uncertain life of a guerrilla revolutionary and despite only scattered, small victories, he expected the ranks of his IRA to endure towards ultimate victory as they had supposedly done in the previous conflict. Yet, the nature of this war was different, as Lynch privately acknowledged to family members and even, in his dying hours, to Laurence Clancy. That he was rigidly determined that the fighting would continue was consistent with his approach in times of war. As a leader of the IRA, he knew no other way.

While Lynch proved flexible when promoting the move from conventional fighting to guerrilla tactics, he could not muster a similar suppleness in the political arena. O'Donoghue's referred to those close to Lynch observing 'that there was an element of poetic dreaming in his character' in terms of his personal republicanism. Lynch looked beyond conflict with Britain 'to the day when buildings now housing a foreign army would be [used] for the peaceful purposes of religion and learning. That was one way in which he saw a free Ireland using its freedom.' These are rare descriptions of Lynch's republican views beyond that of military engagement with the British.[4] His increasingly unhelpful disdain for the political wing of the Irish revolutionary movement was clear from the time he joined the Volunteers in 1917, and manifested rather bleakly in his serious suggestion in late 1921 that Sinn Féin could function as some sort of civil reserve force for the IRA. As events through late 1922 were to demonstrate, he was consistently naive and lacking in political acumen, while bereft of the self-awareness to diagnose this. His distrust of politicians ensured he was unwilling to confer genuine political authority on those, such as de Valera, who had acquired experience in such matters during the War of Independence. Ultimately, Lynch lacked the political vision to develop a republican political programme or to understand how to approach any peace negotiations with the Free State. None of these flaws were unique to him as an IRA leader, but they were particularly problematic in an individual who insisted on being the final decision-maker on political matters.

Lynch is often blamed for unnecessarily prolonging the Civil War, yet little is stated in the existing secondary literature of his surprising endurance in the role of chief of staff throughout the conflict. Even in the waning days of the republican resistance, as victory perhaps seemed more uncertain to his allies, Lynch firmly maintained the loyalty of those under his command. In spite of their doubts, their respect and admiration for Lynch remained considerable. As Deasy conceded in his memoir, which is consistently critical of Lynch's decision-making, 'we were soldiers and we felt our duty was to continue to obey orders'.[5] However, he tempered this criticism of Lynch with, 'I have always felt that, if he had survived, our life-long friendship would not have been damaged'.[6] Andrews was of the opinion Lynch 'was so blind to the realities ... He had developed some mental blockage which prevented him from believing that we could be beaten'.[7] Yet Andrews admitted that with 'Lynch's death I knew the end of the Civil War had come. Only his iron will had kept it going in the last few months'.[8] When reflecting on the failed truce in Limerick, even a pro-Treaty military figure liked Michael Brennan conceded that Lynch was a natural leader who commanded loyalty.[9] Rogue peace efforts by the likes of Tom Barry all had the ultimate aim of bringing Lynch on side with whatever the proposed terms were. Lynch consistently had the support and help of most of his senior officers, ensuring his final word on crucial decisions and tactics remained paramount throughout the conflict. As can be seen from the minutes of the final IRA Executive meeting he attended, it was Lynch's hoped-for ground artillery that influenced the majority vote for the war to continue.

It is worth wondering, if Lynch had survived to the next Executive meeting, how a debate on the same topic would have gone, given that Seán Moylan's efforts to secure the much-desired weaponry had come to nothing. Having briefly alluded to de Valera in February that he might encourage the opening of peace negotiations if circumstances allowed, and mentioning to Kathleen Barry Moloney that he may have to consider dumping arms, it is clear Lynch was aware he may eventually have to contemplate such decisions. Perhaps he was beginning to recognise the political realities long obvious to many, but we cannot know how much his views may have shifted if he had survived to the next Executive meeting. That he was willing to have such a meeting held under dangerous circumstances demonstrated that he recognised the need to continue reconciling the differing views among Executive members and also that some sort of change to the republican conduct of the war had to emerge from it. What is certain is that up to the time Lynch died, he was completely unwilling to end the military republican resistance to the Irish Free State, despite the entreaties of his closest officers, and it was left to his successor, Frank Aiken, to make the difficult choice of seeking peace terms and ultimately ending the fight. That Lynch was not faced with this choice benefitted his historical reputation among his admirers, as he remains an icon frozen in time, unbowed and unbroken in his devotion to the republican cause.

It is unquestionable that Lynch was brave and devoted to the republican cause, despite his disregard for the mass political activity and the underground institutions that formed his Irish Republic. As a local guerrilla commander during the War of Independence, his fighting record is genuinely exemplary and that is where much of his historical reputation is grounded. When it comes to the period of civil war, while he retained the devotion and belief in the endurance of the Republic, in terms of his military leadership, his record is decidedly more mixed. He was a moderating figure within the anti-Treaty section of the IRA prior to the Civil War, yet the outbreak of the conflict cemented his militancy against the emerging Irish Free State. With the attack on his comrades, and the betrayal of the truce in Limerick city in July, Lynch never again seriously contemplated peace proposals put to him, no matter the changing political realities into early 1923. Ultimately, he was ill-suited to the role of commander of the republican forces during 1922–23. Yet, at the outset of the conflict, that the anti-Treaty IRA faced enormous, numerous challenges and a formidable opponent familiar with their tactics and personnel must be emphasised. As the Civil War progressed, Lynch knew there were increasingly few paths to an IRA victory, yet instead of seeking peace, he attempted to improve republican fortunes, and these efforts almost certainly contributed to the heightened ruthlessness of his orders and his increasingly ineffective ideas for future strategies, to say nothing of the persistent diminishing morale of his forces. None of this has impacted on how Lynch is celebrated in popular memory, with the admirable recollections of his character among those who knew him well remaining a huge influence.

In the very first oration by Lynch's graveside, Professor Stockley remarked: 'Ireland should be allowed to live her own life … It was in that spirit that Liam Lynch lived, and acted and died.'[10] For those across Ireland who continue to revere him, Liam Lynch still represents the purest ideal of Irish republicanism and one of the greatest of that generation, a heroic example to inspire into the future. Alongside his considerable contribution to the achievement of Irish independence, this remains the most enduring legacy of the short life of this important and influential Irish revolutionary.

ENDNOTES

PROLOGUE

1   On his appointment as chief of staff of the anti-Treaty IRA in April 1922, Liam Lynch gained the rank of general. Thus, he is often referred to as General Liam Lynch in popular memory and commemoration.

2   C.S. Andrews, *Dublin Made Me* (Dublin: Lilliput Press, 2001), p. 305.

3   Florence O'Donoghue, *No Other Law: The Story of Liam Lynch and the Irish Republican Army, 1916–1923* (Dublin: Irish Press Ltd, 1953); Meda Ryan, *The Real Chief: Liam Lynch* (Dublin: Mercier Press, 2005).

4   O'Donoghue, *No Other Law*, introduction.

CHAPTER 1

1   *The Irish Press*, 17 April 1978.

2   O'Donoghue, *No Other Law*, p. 1.

3   Saint Fanahan's Holy Well by Visit Ballyhoura: https://visitballyhoura.com/explore/saint-fanahans-well (accessed 6 November 2021).

4   See O'Donoghue, *No Other Law*; Ryan, *The Real Chief*.

5   Birth registration of William Lynch (No. 31), Superintendent Registrar's District in Mitchelstown (Registrar's District Galbally), Ref. No. 01870067. I am grateful for my conversations with historian Bill Power, who first alerted me to this error.

6   1901 census Lynch family listing, www.census.nationalarchives.ie/pages/1901/Limerick/Anglesborough/Baurnagurrahy/1505674/ (accessed 4 November 2020).

7   O'Donoghue, *No Other Law*, p. 2; *Daily News*, 4 July 1904.

8   Liam Lynch to Tom Lynch, 28 October 1922 [typed copy], National Library of Ireland (hereafter NLI), Seán O'Mahony Papers, Manuscript 44,109/2.

9   For more detail on the Lynch siblings, see O'Donoghue, *No Other Law*, pp. 2–3.

10   'The Hardware Trade and the Irish Volunteers (1910–1919)' by Br Pat Mullins, n.d., private collection. Mullins is a nephew of Lynch's and quotes extracts from an account written by Fr Tom Lynch on his brother. I note Florrie O'Donoghue seems to sometimes quote Tom's account in *No Other Law*, but a copy is not found in his papers in the NLI, unlike the piece in the following note.

11 Untitled family history by Tom Lynch, n.d. [*c.* 1920–21], NLI, Florence O'Donoghue Papers, Ms 31,421(4); *The Cork Examiner*, 16 January 1846.

12 'John O'Mahony', *Dictionary of Irish Biography* (hereafter *DIB*), entry by Maureen Murphy and James Quinn, www.dib.ie/biography/omahony-john-a6878 (accessed 3 August 2021).

13 Bill Power, *Another Side of Mitchelstown* (Cork: PsyOps Books, 2008), p. 30.

14 Seán Lynch to Florence O'Donoghue, 16 May 1951, NLI, O'Donoghue Papers, Ms 31,421/4. Strangely, O'Donoghue only mentions John Lynch as a Fenian member despite confirmation of Jeremiah's membership by Seán and Hanna Cleary: see O'Donoghue, *No Other Law*, p. 4; Hanna Cleary interview, University College Dublin Archives (hereafter UCDA); Ernie O'Malley (hereafter EOM) notebooks, P17b/132, 56L. Tom Lynch identified John Lynch as three years older than Jeremiah, see citation 11.

15 Hanna Cleary interview, UCDA, EOM notebooks, P17b/132, 56L.

16 O'Donoghue, *No Other Law*, p. 4.

17 Seán Lynch to Florence O'Donoghue, 16 May 1951, NLI, O'Donoghue Papers, Ms 31,421/4.

18 Hanna Cleary, a daughter of William Condon, identified him as both 'a Fenian and a Nationalist'. Hanna Cleary interview, UCDA, EOM notebooks, P17b/132, 56L.

19 O'Donoghue, *No Other Law*, p. 4.

20 Ibid., pp. 3–4.

21 Patrick Kiely interview with Ernie O'Malley, UCDA, EOM notebooks, P17B/130, 50L.

22 Ibid.

23 Report/Reference on Liam Lynch by Patrick Kiely, 4 December 1909, NLI, O'Donoghue Papers, Ms 31,421/4.

24 Hanna Cleary interview, UCDA, EOM notebooks, P17b/132, 60L.

25 'The Uncivil War: Liam Lynch' radio documentary, RTÉ (2002).

26 Hanna Cleary interview, UCDA, EOM notebooks, P17b/132, 56L, 57L.

27 Terence O'Reilly, *Rebel Heart: George Lennon Flying Column Commander* (Cork: Mercier Press, 2009), p. 121.

28 Hanna Cleary to Florence O'Donoghue, n.d., NLI, O'Donoghue Papers, Ms 31,421/4.

29 Hanna Cleary interview, UCDA, EOM notebooks, P17b/132, 56R, 56L, 57L.

30 O'Donoghue, *No Other Law*, p. 9.

31 'Patrick Sarsfield', *DIB*, entry by Liam Irwin, www.dib.ie/biography/sarsfield-patrick-a7924 (accessed 3 August 2021).

32 O'Donoghue, *No Other Law*, p. 5.

33 1901 census Lynch family listing, www.census.nationalarchives.ie/pages/1901/Limerick/Anglesborough/Baurnagurrahy/1505674/ (accessed 4 November 2020).

34 1911 Lynch family census listing, www.census.nationalarchives.ie/pages/1911/Limerick/Anglesborough/Baurnagurrahy/634382/ (accessed 14 March 2021).

35 Hanna Cleary interview, UCDA, EOM notebooks, P17b/132, 57L.

36 O'Donoghue, *No Other Law*, pp. 2, 5.

37 Hanna Cleary interview, UCDA, EOM notebooks, P17b/132, 57R.

38 O'Donoghue places this in 1910, *No Other Law*, p. 5. This contradicts the mention of Lynch as a resident at the family home in 1911, see endnote 31. Given O'Donoghue

also mentions Lynch visiting 'every Sunday' and this census was taken on Sunday 2 April, it is possible Lynch was only home for a visit.

39   Andrews, *Dublin Made Me*, p. 291.

40   Patrick Kiely interview with Ernie O'Malley, UCDA, EOM notebooks, P17B/130, 50L.

41   Power, *Another Side of Mitchelstown*, p. 9.

42   Joe Walsh, *The Story of Liam Lynch* (Cork: Lee Press, 1974), p. 30.

43   O'Donoghue, *No Other Law*, p. 5.

44   F.S.L. Lyons, *Ireland Since the Famine* (London: Fontana Press, 1985), p. 229.

45   Liam Lynch to Tom Lynch, 9 November 1917, NLI, Liam Lynch Papers, Ms 36,251/3.

46   David Dwane to O'Donoghue, 16 March 1952, NLI, O'Donoghue Papers, Ms 31,423/6/5.

47   O'Donoghue, *No Other Law*, p. 5.

48   Lyons, *Ireland Since the Famine*, p. 262.

49   George Power to Florence O'Donoghue, 22 June 1950, NLI, O'Donoghue Papers, Ms 31,421(11).

50   Patrick Joseph Luddy, Bureau of Military History (hereafter BMH), Witness Statement (hereafter WS) 1151, p. 1.

51   From Mullins, 'The Hardware Trade and the Irish Volunteers'.

52   Patrick Joseph Luddy, BMH WS 1151, pp. 2–3.

53   See O'Donoghue, *No Other Law*, p. 6 and Military Service Pension (hereafter MSP) of Liam Lynch, Irish Military Archives (hereafter IMA), DP5482 (accessed 1 February 2021).

54   O'Donoghue, *No Other Law*, p. 6.

55   John Dorney, *Peace After the Final Battle: The Story of the Irish Revolution 1912–1924* (Dublin: New Island, 2014), p. 92.

56   George Power to O'Donoghue, 22 June 1950, NLI, O'Donoghue Papers, Ms 31,421/11.

57   Hanna Cleary interview, UCDA, EOM notebooks, P17b/132, 57L. Cleary tells O'Malley she does not recall Lynch becoming a member of the National Volunteers, but this can be determined from other sources.

58   Liam Lynch's National Volunteer membership card, NLI, Lynch Papers, Ms 36,251/31.

59   Dermot Meleady, *John Redmond: The National Leader* (Dublin: Irish Academic Press, 2014), p. 321.

60   O'Donoghue, *No Other Law*, p. 7.

61   Martin Lynch to Florence O'Donoghue, 16 February 1951, NLI, O'Donoghue Papers, Ms 31,421/4. The 'Molly Maguires' nickname was a slur often used for supporters of the IPP. It refers to the Irish-American secret society of that name and its alleged connection to the American-based AOH, though this had no formal link with the similarly named Irish organisation.

62   From Mullins, 'The Hardware Trade and the Irish Volunteers'.

63   'Liam Lynch said he hoped we would be able to organise and educate the people to the position of opposing the Treaty propaganda in favour of the Republic, for he remembered that he had once been a National Volunteer and he requested it', quoted from Liam Manahan interview, UCDA, EOM notebooks, P17b/117, 36R.

64   O'Donoghue, *No Other Law*, p. 6. Further details on his employment in Mitchelstown from Martin Lynch to O'Donoghue, 16 February 1951, NLI, O'Donoghue Papers, Ms 31,421/4.

65   Work reference for Liam Lynch by P. O'Neill, January 1913 [photocopy], NLI, O'Mahony Papers, Ms 41,109/1.

66   Work reference for Liam Lynch by M.J. Flavin, 3 February 1914 [photocopy], NLI, O'Mahony Papers, Ms 41,109/1.

67   Work reference for Liam Lynch by P. O'Neill, 29 May 1916 [photocopy], NLI, O'Mahony Papers, Ms 41,109/1.

68   Death Register of Jeremiah Lynch, Entry No. 318, Mitchelstown Registrar's District, Ref No. 04471645.

69   O'Donoghue, *No Other Law*, p. 10.

70   Ibid., p. 6.

71   Bill Power, *Fermoy on the Blackwater* (Cork: Brigown Press, 2009), pp. 261–3, 287–92.

72   Ibid., p. 261.

73   Hanna Cleary interview, UCDA, EOM notebooks, P17b/132, 56L. O'Donoghue also refers to the National Volunteers non-existence in Fermoy by this time, but feels it was not reflective of the situation in the wider county itself, see *No Other Law*, p. 7.

74   Hanna Cleary interview, UCDA, EOM notebooks, P17b/132, 56L.

75   Ibid.

76   O'Donoghue, *No Other Law*, p. 9.

77   'Thomas Kent', *DIB*, entry by Desmond McCabe and Lawrence William White, www.dib.ie/biography/kent-ceannt-thomas-a4511 (accessed 23 July 2021).

78   Meda Ryan, *Thomas Kent (16 Lives)* (Dublin: O'Brien Press, 2016), p. 295.

79   O'Donoghue, *No Other Law*, pp. 8, 9.

80   Hanna Cleary interview, UCDA, EOM notebooks, P17b/132, 57L.

81   Stan D. O'Brien, *John Joe's Story: Commandant John Joe O'Brien* (self-published, 2016), p. 28.

82   Mullins, 'The Hardware Trade and the Irish Volunteers'.

83   Dorney, *Peace After the Final Battle*, p. 148.

84   Cahir Davitt, BMH WS 993, pp. 22–3.

85   O'Donoghue, *No Other Law*, p. 12.

86   Pádraic Agnew, Alan Bogan and Marcus Howard, *The Louth Volunteers 1916* (Louth: The Write Space Publishing, 2016), p. 332.

87   O'Donoghue, *No Other Law*, p. 12.

CHAPTER 2

1   Laurence Condon, BMH WS 859, p. 1.

2   George Power, BMH WS 451, p. 1. Of note, Power places the Fermoy Volunteers being founded in July; most accounts suggest earlier that year, such as Condon in citation 1.

3   Laurence Condon, BMH WS 859, p. 1.

4   John Fanning, BMH WS 990, pp. 1–2.

5   O'Donoghue, *No Other Law*, p. 14.

6   Ibid., p. 9.

7   Untitled typed notes by George Power on Liam Lynch for Florence O'Donoghue, n.d. [*c*. 1952], NLI, O'Donoghue Papers, Ms 31,421(11).

8   Ibid.

9   Siobhán Lankford, *The Hope and the Sadness: Personal Recollections on an Irish Intelligence Network 1916–1923* (Cork: Celum Publishing, 2020), p. 116.

10 MSP34REF478, MSP of George Power, IMA (accessed 2 March 2021).

11 George Power, BMH WS 451, p. 1.

12 'Maurice "Moss" Twomey', *DIB*, entry by Brian Hanley, www.dib.ie/biography/twomey-maurice-moss-a8690 (accessed 3 August 2021).

13 Walsh, *The Story of Liam Lynch*, p. 30.

14 Thomas O'Riordan, *The Price of Freedom: The Life Story of Mick Fitzgerald (Commandant) O/C 1st Battalion Cork No. 2 Brigade* (Cork: Barrys, 1970), pp. 1–2, 3, 5, 8, 11–13, 22, 22a, 25.

15 Ibid., p. 28.

16 *An Phoblacht*, 9 February 1929.

17 Walsh, *The Story of Liam Lynch*, p. 29.

18 Bill Hammond, *Soldier of the Rearguard: The Story of Matt Flood and the Active Service Column* (Cork: Éigse Na Mainistreach Publications, 1977), p. 8.

19 Séumas Robinson, BMH WS 1721, Appendix 5, p. 2.

20 Various instances arise in Siobhán Lankford's, *The Hope and the Sadness*, and correspondence in the Kathleen Barry Moloney Papers.

21 Walsh, *The Story of Liam Lynch*, pp. 30–1.

22 Ibid, p. 29.

23 George Power, BMH WS 451, p. 1.

24 Patrick Ahern, BMH WS 1003, p. 2.

25 Dorney, *Peace After the Final Battle*, p. 162.

26 Patrick Ahern, BMH WS 1003, p. 2.

27 *The Cork Examiner*, 27 June 1917.

28 Pat Casey to Moss Twomey, 15 May 1950, NLI, O'Donoghue Papers, Ms 31,423/4.

29 Dorney, *Peace After the Final Battle*, p. 163.

30 Maryann Valiulis, *Portrait of a Revolutionary: General Richard Mulcahy and the Founding of the Irish Free State* (Dublin: Irish Academic Press, 1992), p. 24.

31 Ibid.

32 O'Donoghue, *No Other Law*, p. 10.

33 Ibid., p. 9.

34 Liam Lynch to Tom Lynch, 10 October 1917, NLI, Lynch Papers, Ms 36,251/1.

35 Liam Lynch to Tom Lynch, 26 October 1917 [typed copy], NLI, O'Mahony Papers, Ms 44,109/2.

36 Valiulis, *Portrait of a Revolutionary*, pp. 24–5.

37 *The Cork Examiner*, 9 October 1917.

38 *The Kilkenny People*, 3 November 1917.

39 Liam Lynch to Tom Lynch, 1 November 1917, NLI, Lynch Papers, Ms 36,251/2.

40 Ibid.

41   Ibid.

42   Liam Lynch to Tom Lynch, 9 November 1917, NLI, Lynch Papers, Ms 36,251/3.

43   Ibid.

44   O'Donoghue, *No Other Law*, p. 19.

45   John Fanning, BMH WS 990, p. 2.

46   Walsh, *The Story of Liam Lynch*, p. 31.

47   Lankford, *The Hope and the Sadness*, p. 138.

48   O'Donoghue, *No Other Law*, p. 38.

49   Ryan, *The Real Chief*, p. 31.

50   Birth registration of Bridie Keyes (No.116), Superintendent Registrar's District in
      Mitchelstown, Ref No. 01946008.

51   Of interest, the 1901 census accurately lists her age as thirteen, whereas the census ten
      years later listed her age as nineteen. 1901 census return for the Keyes family: www.
      census.nationalarchives.ie/pages/1901/Cork/Mitchelstown/Kilshanny/1153217/
      (accessed 16 November 2021); 1911 census return for the Keyes family: www.census.
      nationalarchives.ie/pages/1911/Cork/Mitchelstown/Kilshanny/438939/   (accessed
      16 November 2021).

52   Liam Lynch to Tom Lynch, 9 November 1917, NLI, Lynch Papers, Ms 36,251/3.

53   Ryan, *The Real Chief*, pp. 30–1; O'Donoghue, *No Other Law*, p. 40.

54   Moylan to O'Donoghue, 20 August 1952, NLI, O'Donoghue Papers, Ms 31,421/5.

55   Mullins, 'The Hardware Trade and the Irish Volunteers'.

56   Liam Lynch to Tom Lynch, 12 December 1917, NLI, Lynch Papers, Ms 36,251/4.

57   Ibid.

58   *The Cork Examiner*, 15 December 1917.

59   Mullins, 'The Hardware Trade and the Irish Volunteers'.

60   Ibid.

61   Valiulis, *Portrait of a Revolutionary*, pp. 27–8.

62   O'Donoghue, *No Other Law*, p. 19.

63   George Power, BMH WS 451, p. 1.

64   O'Donoghue, *No Other Law*, p. 29.

65   Ibid., p. 19.

66   'Tomás MacCurtain', *DIB*, entry by Patrick Maume, www.dib.ie/biography/
      maccurtain-tomas-a5147 (accessed 12 July 2021).

67   O'Donoghue confusingly places the creation of the Fermoy Battalion in September
      1917, *No Other Law*, p. 19. Early 1918 is more accurate; for instance see, O'Riordan,
      The Price of Freedom, p. 28, and Patrick Ahern, BMH WS 1003, p. 3.

68   O'Riordan, *The Price of Freedom*, p. 28.

69   Lynch, *No Other Law*, p. 20.

70   George Power, BMH WS 451, p. 2.

71   O'Donoghue, *No Other Law*, p. 22.

72   Ibid., pp. 22–3.

73   Mullins, 'The Hardware Trade and the Irish Volunteers'.

74   O'Riordan, *The Price of Freedom*, p. 32; O'Donoghue provided no date beyond
      'summer' of 1918 for Tobin's arrival in *No Other Law*, p. 30; Siobhán Lankford
      misidentified the year as early 1917, *The Hope and the Sadness*, p. 116. This was

unlikely as Tobin was still in Frongoch for much of that year, see 24SP2764, MSP of
Liam Tobin, IMA (accessed 3 February 2021).

75   'Liam Tobin', *DIB*, entry by Patrick Long, www.dib.ie/biography/tobin-liam-a8572
     (accessed 14 July 2021); 24SP2764, MSP of Liam Tobin, IMA (accessed 3 February
     2021).

76   Lankford, *The Hope and the Sadness*, p. 115.

77   Ibid., p. 116.

78   Lynch's letters to Kathleen Barry Moloney have a warmth and friendly, even teasing,
     tone to them during a period in which she was his courier during the Civil War. See
     UCDA, Barry Moloney Papers, P94/28.

79   Lankford, *The Hope and the Sadness*, pp. 117–18.

80   Ibid., p. 232.

81   Hammond, *Soldier of the Rearguard*, p. 25.

82   Ryan, *The Real Chief*, p. 10.

83   O'Donoghue, *No Other Law*, p. 25.

84   Ibid., p. 23.

85   *An tÓglach*, 14 October 1918.

86   Con Leddy, BMH WS 756, pp. 5–6.

87   John Fanning, BMH WS 990, pp. 3–5.

88   O'Donoghue, *No Other Law*, p. 23.

89   George Power, BMH WS 451, p. 1.

90   Diarmuid Ferriter, *A Nation Not A Rabble: The Irish Revolution 1913–23* (Dublin:
     Profile Books, 2015), p. 183.

91   John Fanning, BMH WS 990, p. 6.

92   Laurence Condon, BMH WS 859, p. 3.

93   Pat McCarthy, *The Redmonds and Waterford: A Political Dynasty 1891–1952*
     (Dublin: Four Courts Press, 2018), p. 97.

94   O'Donoghue, *No Other Law*, p. 17.

95   Ibid., pp. 188–9.

96   Leon Ó Broin, *Revolutionary Underground: The Story of the Irish Republican
     Brotherhood 1858–1924* (Dublin: Gill & Macmillan, 1976), p. 178.

97   Valiulis, *Portrait of a Revolutionary*, p. 45.

98   Con Leddy, BMH WS 756, pp. 4–5.

CHAPTER 3

1   Michael Hopkinson, *The Irish War of Independence* (Dublin: Gill Books, 2004), p.
    25.

2   Valiulis, *Portrait of a Revolutionary*, pp. 38–9.

3   Séumas Robinson, BMH WS 1721, pp. 19, 22.

4   Daniel Breen, BMH WS 1739, p. 21.

5   Daithí Ó Corráin and Eunan O'Halpin, *The Dead of the Irish Revolution* (New Haven
    and London: Yale University Press, 2020), pp. 104–5.

6   Arthur Mitchell, *Revolutionary Government in Ireland: Dáil Éireann 1919–22*
    (Dublin: Gill & Macmillian, 1995), p. 68.

7   Charles Townshend, *The British Campaign in Ireland 1919–1921: The Development of Political and Military Policies* (Oxford: Oxford University Press, 1978) p. 28.
8   Dorney, *Peace After the Final Battle*, p. 181.
9   O'Donoghue, *No Other Law*, p. 35.
10   Ibid., p. 36.
11   Power to O'Donoghue, 11 September 1952, NLI, O'Donoghue Papers, Ms 31,275.
12   'Seán Moylan', *DIB*, entry by Seán Kearns, www.dib.ie/biography/moylan-sean-a6011 (accessed 17 July 2021).
13   O'Donoghue, *No Other Law*, p. 36.
14   Ibid.
15   O'Riordan, *The Price of Freedom*, p. 38.
16   George Power, BMH WS 451, p. 2; O'Donoghue put the brigade number at 3,800 in *No Other Law*, p. 49.
17   O'Donoghue, *No Other Law*, p. 49.
18   Ibid., p. 36.
19   Ibid.
20   Typed account on 'Communications' by George Power, n.d. [*c.* early 1950s], NLI, O'Donoghue Papers, Ms 31,421/11.
21   O'Donoghue, *No Other Law*, pp. 38, 40.
22   Ibid., p. 39.
23   P.J. Paul, BMH WS 877, p. 60.
24   Handwritten account of Liam Lynch's life by unknown individual, n.d., UCDA, Éamon de Valera Papers, P150/1750.
25   O'Donoghue, *No Other Law*, pp. 38, 39.
26   Walsh, *The Story of Liam Lynch*, p. 31.
27   O'Donoghue, *No Other Law*, pp. 39–40.
28   Ibid., p. 41.
29   Hopkinson, *War of Independence*, p. 25.
30   Mitchell, *Revolutionary Government*, p. 69.
31   Ibid., p. 66.
32   Dorney, *Peace After the Final Battle*, pp. 181–2.
33   Ibid., p. 188.
34   George Power, BMH WS 451, p. 3.
35   Pax Whelan interview by Ernie O'Malley, UCDA, EOM notebooks, P17b/103, 63L.
36   O'Donoghue, *No Other Law*, p. 45.
37   Ibid, pp. 45–6.
38   O'Riordan, *The Price of Freedom*, pp. 43–5.
39   O'Donoghue, *No Other Law*, p. 46.
40   Con Leddy, BMH WS 756, p. 6.
41   O'Donoghue, *No Other Law*, p. 42.
42   Risteárd Mulcahy, *My Father, the General: Richard Mulcahy and the Military History of the Revolution* (Dublin: Liberties Press, 2010), pp. 156–7.
43   Mulcahy's view on Lynch in this period is taken from Valiulis, *Portrait of a Revolutionary*, p. 55.
44   For examples of IRA GHQ difficulties with regional IRA officers during the War of

Independence, see Valiulis, *Portrait of a Revolutionary*, pp. 53–69, 72–3 and Tom Barry, *Guerilla Days in Ireland* (Cork: Mercier Press, 2010), pp. 185–6.

45 Séumas Robinson, BMH WS 1721, Appendix 5, p. 5.

46 Ibid., Appendix 6, p. 1.

47 Ibid., Appendix 5, p. 2.

48 Hanna Cleary interview by Ernie O'Malley, UCDA, EOM notebooks, P17b/132, 57R.

49 O'Donoghue, *No Other Law*, pp. 46–7.

50 'A Ramble to a Tomb' by Tom Lynch, n.d., April 1921, NLI, O'Donoghue Papers, Ms 31,421/4.

51 Thomas Barry, BMH WS 430, p. 3.

52 O'Donoghue, *No Other Law*, p. 48.

53 Patrick Ahern, BMH WS 1003, pp. 7–8.

54 George Power, BMH WS 451, p. 3.

55 O'Donoghue, *No Other Law*, p. 49.

56 Laurence Condon, BMH WS 859, p. 5.

57 Patrick Ahern, BMH WS 1003, p. 9.

58 Ibid.

59 O'Donoghue, *No Other Law*, p. 49.

60 John Fanning, BMH WS 990, p. 8.

61 DP5426, MSP of John Hynes, IMA (accessed online 1 February 2021).

62 Cork No. 2 Brigade Activity Report, IMA, MSPC/A/2(1).

63 Laurence Condon, BMH WS 859, pp. 5–6.

64 Leo O'Callaghan, BMH WS 978, p. 3.

65 O'Donoghue, *No Other Law*, p. 50.

66 Laurence Condon, BMH WS 859, p. 6.

67 Paddy Ahern to O'Donoghue, 22 October 1953, NLI, O'Donoghue Papers, Ms 31,423(1).

68 Patrick Ahern, BMH WS 1003, p. 12.

69 O'Donoghue, *No Other Law*, p. 50.

70 William Sheehan, *A Hard Local War: The British Army and the Guerilla War in Cork 1919–1921* (Dublin: The History Press Ireland, 2017), p. 25.

71 Patrick Ahern, BMH WS 1003, p. 12.

72 *Evening Echo*, 8 September 1919.

73 O'Donoghue, *No Other Law*, p. 30; MSP34REF5427, MSP of Matthew Flood, IMA (accessed online 1 February 2021); O'Riordan, *The Price of Freedom*, p. 48.

74 Leo O'Callaghan, BMH WS 978, p. 4.

75 O'Riordan, *The Price of Freedom*, p. 48.

76 O'Donoghue, *No Other Law*, pp. 50–1.

77 Laurance Condon, BMH WS 859, p. 6.

78 For example, see P.J. Power, 'Mick Fitzgerald: Gallant Soldier of Fermoy', in Various, *Rebel Cork's Fighting Story 1916–21* (Cork: Mercier Press, 2009).

79 Transcription of letter from George Power to Ernie O'Malley, dated 20 December 1957, George Power interview by Ernie O'Malley, UCDA, EOM notebooks, P17b/132, 61L.

80 O'Donoghue, *No Other Law*, pp. 52–4.
81 *Evening Echo*, 8 September 1919.
82 O'Riordan, *The Price of Freedom*, p. 49.
83 O'Donoghue, *No Other Law*, pp. 56–7.
84 O'Riordan, *The Price of Freedom*, pp. 49–50.
85 *The Freeman's Journal*, 9 September 1919.
86 Ibid.
87 Ibid.
88 *The Cork Examiner*, 9 September 1919.
89 Sheehan, *A Hard Local War*, p. 23.
90 Ibid., pp. 34–5.
91 *The Cork Examiner*, 9 September 1919.
92 Power, *Fermoy on the Blackwater*, p. 301.
93 *An t-Oglách*, 15 December 1919.
94 Transcription of letter from George Power to Ernie O'Malley, dated 20 December 1957, George Power interview by Ernie O'Malley, UCDA, EOM notebooks, P17b/132, 61L.
95 O'Donoghue, *No Other Law*, p. 54.
96 Ibid.
97 Martin Lynch to Florence O'Donoghue, 16 February 1951, NLI, O'Donoghue Papers, Ms 31,421/4.
98 O'Donoghue, *No Other Law*, p. 54.
99 'Michael Doheny', *DIB*, entry by Desmond McCabe and James Quinn, www.dib.ie/biography/doheny-michael-a2655 (accessed 4 April 2021).
100 Pax Whelan interview by Ernie O'Malley, UCDA, EOM notebooks, P17b/103, 61R.
101 O'Donoghue, *No Other Law*, p. 36.
102 Laurance Condon, BMH WS 859, p. 7.
103 O'Donoghue, *No Other Law*, p. 60.
104 Patrick Luddy, BMH WS 1151, p. 8.
105 Liam Lynch to Tom Lynch, 29 October 1919 [typed copy], NLI, O'Mahony Papers, Ms 44,109/2.
106 Liam Lynch to Tom Lynch, 13 November 1919 [typed copy], NLI, O'Mahony Papers, Ms 44,109/2; O'Donoghue, *No Other Law*, p. 19.
107 Dorney, *Peace After the Final Battle*, p. 189.
108 Mitchell, *Revolutionary Government*, pp. 54, 57.
109 O'Donoghue, *No Other Law*, p. 60.
110 Ibid., pp. 60–1.
111 Seán Lynch to O'Donoghue, 29 November 1952, NLI, O'Donoghue Papers, Ms 31,421(4).

CHAPTER 4

1 Liam Lynch to Tom Lynch, 2 January 1920, NLI, Lynch Papers, Ms 36,251/5.
2 Untitled typed notes by George Power on Liam Lynch for Florence O'Donoghue, n.d. [*c.* 1952], NLI, O'Donoghue Papers, Ms 31,421(11).

3   Hanna Cleary interview by Ernie O'Malley, UCDA, EOM notebooks, P17b/132, 57R.

4   Ibid.

5   Ryan, *The Real Chief*, p. 30.

6   O'Donoghue, *No Other Law*, p. 60.

7   Mullins, 'The Hardware Trade and the Irish Volunteers'.

8   O'Donoghue, *No Other Law*, p. 61.

9   Walsh, *The Story of Liam Lynch*, p. 29.

10 O'Donoghue, *No Other Law*, p. 61.

11 Liam Lynch to Mary Lynch, 1 March 1920 [typed copy], NLI, O'Mahoney Papers, Ms 44,109/2.

12 Liam Lynch to Tom Lynch, 22 February 1920, NLI, Lynch Papers, Ms 36,251/6.

13 O'Donoghue, *No Other Law*, p. 61.

14 Ibid.

15 Liam Lynch to Tom Lynch, 7 March 1920, NLI, Lynch Papers, Ms 36,251/7.

16 Liam Lynch to Tom Lynch, 31 March 1920, NLI, Lynch Papers, Ms 36,251/8.

17 Ibid.

18 Hopkinson, *The War of Independence*, p. 49.

19 Dorney, *Peace After the Final Battle*, p. 190.

20 Brigade activity report for Cork No. 2 Brigade, IMA, MA/MSPC/A/2(1).

21 Dorney, *Peace After the Final Battle*, p. 184.

22 Mitchell, *Revolutionary Government*, pp. 140–1.

23 O'Donoghue, *No Other Law*, pp. 63–4.

24 Lynch to Gearóid O'Sullivan (IRA Adjutant-General), [date unclear] March 1920, IMA, Michael Collins Papers, 3/27/(13-14).

25 Ibid.

26 Lynch to O'Sullivan, 5 April 1920, IMA, Collins Papers, 3/27/(18).

27 Mulcahy to Lynch, 8 April 1920, IMA, Collins Papers, 3/27/(20-21).

28 Lankford, *The Hope and the Sadness*, p. 134.

29 O'Sullivan to Lynch, 12 April 1920, IMA, Collins Papers, 3/27/(22).

30 O'Donoghue, *No Other Law*, pp. 64–5.

31 Lynch to Mulcahy, 15 June 1920, IMA, Collins Papers, 3/27/(47).

32 Lankford, *The Hope and the Sadness*, pp. 135–6.

33 Ibid., p. 136.

34 Ibid.

35 MSP34REF9380, MSP of Bartholomew Walsh, IMA (accessed online 8 March 2021).

36 Lynch to [unidentified member of GHQ], 26 March 1920, IMA, Collins Papers, 3/27/(12).

37 Liam Lynch to Tom Lynch, 28 March 1920 [typed copy], NLI, O'Mahony Papers, Ms 44,109/2.

38 Ibid.

39 Lynch to O'Sullivan, 29 March 1920, IMA, Collins Papers, 3/27/(14).

40 O'Sullivan to Lynch, 10 April 1920, IMA, Collins Papers, 3/27/(23).

41 Hopkinson, *The War of Independence*, pp. 49–51.

42 Liam Lynch to Tom Lynch, 19 April 1920, NLI, Lynch Papers, Ms 36,251/9.

43 Ibid.

44 Liam Lynch to Tom Lynch, 30 May 1920, NLI, Lynch Papers, Ms 36,251/10.

45 O'Donoghue, *No Other Law*, pp. 75–6.

46 Seán Moylan, BMH WS 838, p. 87. Moylan does not indicate which commandant, but O'Donoghue identifies the intelligence as coming from the Fermoy Battalion, see *No Other Law*, p. 76.

47 O'Donoghue, *No Other Law*, p. 75.

48 Laurence Condon, BMH WS 859, pp. 8–9.

49 O'Donoghue, *No Other Law*, p. 76.

50 Ibid.

51 George Power, BMH WS 451, pp. 5–6.

52 Seán Moylan, BMH WS 838, pp. 88–9.

53 George Power, BMH WS 451, p. 6.

54 Seán Moylan, BMH WS 838, p. 89.

55 George Power, BMH WS 451, p. 6.

56 O'Donoghue, *No Other Law*, p. 77.

57 Ibid.

58 Ernie O'Malley, *On Another Man's Wound* (Dublin: Anvil, 2002), p. 219.

59 See O'Donoghue, *No Other Law*, p. 77, or George Power, BMH WS 451, p. 7.

60 O'Malley, *On Another Man's Wound*, pp. 209–10.

61 24SP13358, MSP of Owen Curtin, IMA (accessed online 1 February 2021).

62 O'Donoghue, *No Other Law*, p. 77.

63 Ibid., pp. 77–8. Also see George Power, 'The Capture of General Lucas', in *Rebel Cork's Fighting Story*, p. 87.

64 O'Donoghue, *No Other Law*, p. 78.

65 Seán Moylan, BMH WS 838, p. 90.

66 Ibid. O'Donoghue, in *No Other Law*, p. 78, placed the return of the second car after the shooting of Danford; Moylan implies in his BMH WS that he returned and witnessed it.

67 Power to O'Donoghue, 3 March 1953, NLI, O'Donoghue Papers, Ms 31,421(11).

68 From George Power, 'The Capture of General Lucas', in *Rebel Cork's Fighting Story*, p. 87.

69 Ibid.; O'Donoghue, *No Other Law*, p. 78.

70 Power to O'Donoghue, 3 March 1953, NLI, O'Donoghue Papers, Ms 31,421(11).

71 Seán Moylan, BMH WS 838, p. 90.

72 John O'Connell, BMH WS 1211, p. 4.

73 Michael O'Connell, BMH WS 1428, p. 5.

74 O'Donoghue, *No Other Law*, p. 78.

75 Michael O'Connell, BMH WS 1428, p. 5.

76 From George Power, 'The Capture of General Lucas', in *Rebel Cork's Fighting Story*, p. 87.

77 George Power interview by Ernie O'Malley, 17b/100, 123, 132.

78 John O'Connell, BMH WS 1211, p. 5.

79 Power, *Fermoy on the Blackwater*, pp. 311–12.

80 Liam Lynch to Tom Lynch, 28 June 1920, NLI, Lynch Papers, Ms 36,251/11.

81 Michael O'Connell, BMH WS 1428, p. 6.

82 Hopkinson, *War of Independence*, p. 53.

83 O'Malley, *On Another Man's Wound*, p. 209.

84 Lankford, *The Hope and the Sadness*, p. 137; Power to Seámus Lankford, 9 January 1946, NLI, O'Donoghue Papers, Ms 31,275.

85 Ronan McGreevy, 'Revealed 100 years on: The letters of a British general kidnapped by the IRA', *The Irish Times*, 18 June 2020: www.irishtimes.com/news/ireland/irish-news/revealed-100-years-on-the-letters-of-a-british-general-kidnapped-by-the-ira-1.4281705 (accessed 4 March 2021).

86 Liam Lynch to Tom Lynch, 3 July 1920, NLI, Lynch Papers, Ms 36,251/12.

87 Liam Lynch to Tom Lynch, 4 July 1920, NLI, Lynch Papers, Ms 36,251/13.

88 Lankford, *The Hope and the Sadness*, p. 137. All quotations from Lankford in this section come from Lankford, op cit., pp. 137–9. While Lankford does not date the meeting with Bridie Keyes, I have opted to do so in August 1920, given the reference to 'an autumn Sunday' – placing it before or after Lynch's imprisonment in Cork Jail. She wrote of it in the same chapter in which she discussed Lucas's kidnapping, suggesting it occurred sometime in that same year.

89 Ryan, *The Real Chief*, p. 31.

90 Ibid., pp. 95–6. Ryan refers to Keyes as Lynch's fiancée, p. 191.

91 Patrick McCarthy, BMH WS 1163, p. 9. Surprisingly, O'Donoghue was unable to determine why Lynch was in City Hall that night, see O'Donoghue, *No Other Law*, p. 87.

92 O'Donoghue, *No Other Law*, p. 89.

93 Ibid., p. 90.

94 Patrick McCarthy, BMH WS 1163, pp. 9–10.

95 Ibid., p. 10.

96 O'Donoghue, *No Other Law*, pp. 89–90.

97 Ibid., p. 91.

98 Patrick O'Brien, BMH WS 764, p. 16.

99 Tom Crawford to O'Donoghue, 5 January 1953, NLI, Ms 41,423/5/9/(2).

100 O'Riordan, *The Price of Freedom*, p. 68.

101 Crawford to O'Donoghue, 5 January 1953, NLI, Ms 41,423/5/9/(3).

102 Patrick McCarthy, BMH WS 1163, pp. 10–11.

103 Owen Harold, BMH WS 991, pp. 10–11.

104 Leslie Price, wife of Tom Barry, later donated it to the National Gallery of Ireland before her death in 1984. See photograph section.

105 Hammond, *Soldier of the Rearguard*, pp. 22–3.

106 O'Donoghue, *No Other Law*, pp. 146–7.

107 Lynch to Tom Lynch, n.d., September 1920, NLI, Ms 36,251/16.

108 Hopkinson, *War of Independence*, p. 65.

109 Valiulis, *Portrait of a Revolutionary*, pp. 55–6.

110 O'Donoghue, *No Other Law*, p. 97.

111 Ó Corráin and O'Halpin, *Dead of the Irish Revolution*, p. 161.

112 O'Donoghue, *No Other Law*, pp. 97–8.

113 'Ernie O'Malley', *DIB*, entry by Richard English, www.dib.ie/biography/omalley-ernest-bernard-ernie-a6885 (accessed 18 October 2021).

114 Lynch to O'Sullivan, 29 March 1920, IMA, Collins Papers, 3/27/(14).

115 O'Malley, *On Another Man's Wound*, p. 209.

116 O'Donoghue, *No Other Law*, p. 98.

117 O'Malley, *On Another Man's Wound*, p. 210.

118 William C. Regan, BMH WS 1069, p. 7.

119 Daniel Daly, BMH WS 743, pp. 6–7.

120 Seamus O'Mahony, BMH WS 730, p. 10.

121 Patrick McCarthy, BMH WS 1163, p. 11.

122 Walsh, *The Story of Liam Lynch*, p. 29.

123 O'Malley, *On Another Man's Wound*, pp. 210–11.

124 Richard Willis and John Bolster, BMH WS 808, pp. 20–1.

125 O'Malley, *On Another Man's Wound*, p. 211.

126 Ibid., pp. 211–12.

127 Richard Willis and John Bolster, BMH WS 808, p. 21.

128 Tadg McCarthy, BMH WS 965, p. 6.

129 Leo O'Callaghan, BMH WS 978, pp. 7–8.

130 O'Malley, *On Another Man's Wound*, pp. 212–14.

131 Richard Wallis and John Bolster, BMH WS 808, p. 22.

132 O'Malley, *On Another Man's Wound*, p. 214.

133 Hammond, *Soldier of the Rearguard*, p. 18.

134 William C. Regan, BMH WS 1069, p. 2.

135 Patrick O'Brien, BMH WS 764, p. 23.

136 O'Donoghue, *No Other Law*, p. 100.

137 William C. Regan, BMH WS 1069, p. 3.

138 Ibid.

139 O'Donoghue, *No Other Law*, p. 100.

140 Hammond, *Soldier of the Rearguard*, p. 23.

141 O'Donoghue, *No Other Law*, p. 101.

142 O'Malley, *On Another Man's Wound*, p. 217.

143 Patrick Lynch, 'Successful Raid on Mallow Barracks', in *Rebel Cork's Fighting Story*, p. 124.

144 O'Donoghue, *No Other Law*, p. 100.

145 Details of Flood's story are taken from Hammond, *Soldier of the Rearguard*, pp. 23–5.

146 O'Donoghue, *No Other Law*, p. 102.

147 Seán Moylan, BMH WS 838, p. 117.

148 O'Donoghue, *No Other Law*, p. 103.

149 Hammond, *Soldier of the Rearguard*, p. 25.

150 O'Donoghue, *No Other Law*, p. 103.

151 Hammond, *Soldier of the Rearguard*, p. 26.

152 Seán Moylan, BMH WS 838, p. 120.

153 Ó Corráin and O'Halpin, *Dead of the Irish Revolution*, p. 192.

154 O'Donoghue, *No Other Law*, p. 106.

155   O'Riordan, *Price of Freedom*, pp. 79–80.

156   Patrick Ahern, BMH WS 1003, p. 21.

157   Hammond, *Soldier of the Rearguard*, p. 28.

158   O'Riordan, *The Price of Freedom*, p. 83.

159   Hammond, *Soldier of the Rearguard*, p. 29.

160   Paddy Ahern to O'Donoghue, 22 October 1953, NLI, O'Donoghue Papers, Ms 31,423(1).

161   Walsh, *The Story of Liam Lynch*, p. 29.

162   For a more detailed summary of the development and activities of Cork No. 2 Brigade's flying columns, see O'Donoghue, *No Other Law*, pp. 103–10.

163   O'Donoghue, *No Other Law*, pp. 104–5.

164   Robinson's account of this, with the accompanying quotes, comes from his BMH WS 1721, Appendix 5, pp. 1–6.

CHAPTER 5

1   Dorney, *Peace After the Final Battle*, p. 206.

2   Ibid., p. 212.

3   O'Donoghue, *No Other Law*, pp. 149–50; Séumas Robinson, BMH WS 1721, p. 75.

4   O'Donoghue, *No Other Law*, pp. 152–3.

5   Lynch to Collins, 13 February 1921, IMA, Collins Papers, 5/2/8(19).

6   O'Donoghue, *No Other Law*, pp. 135–7.

7   Collins to Lynch, 2 March 1921, IMA, Collins Papers, 5/2/8/(24).

8   Mulcahy to Lynch, 8 March 1921, UCDA, Richard Mulcahy Papers, P7/A/17(6).

9   O'Donoghue, *No Other Law*, p. 137.

10   Lynch to Mulcahy, 19 March 1921, UCDA, Mulcahy Papers, P7/A/38(24).

11   Lynch to Collins, 4 March 1921, IMA, Collins Papers, 5/2/8/(28).

12   Collins to Lynch, 9 March 1921, IMA, Collins Papers, 5/2/8/(31).

13   Leo O'Callaghan, BMH WS 978, p. 21.

14   Tadg McCarthy, BMH WS 965, p. 12.

15   Seán McCarthy interview by Ernie O'Malley, UCDA, EOM notebooks, 17b/124, 19L.

16   George Power interview by Ernie O'Malley, UCDA, EOM notebooks, 17b/100, 123, 132.

17   Seán McCarthy interview by Ernie O'Malley, UCDA, EOM notebooks, 17b/124, 19L-20R.

18   Tadg McCarthy, BMH WS 965, p. 12.

19   George Power interview by Ernie O'Malley, UCDA, EOM notebooks, 17b/100, 123, 132.

20   Ibid.

21   Ibid.

22   Leo O'Callaghan, BMH WS 978, p. 21.

23   Ibid., p. 18.

24   Ibid., pp. 19–20.

25   Florence O'Donoghue (I/O for 1st Southern Division) to unidentified member of GHQ, n.d. [*c.* early 1921], UCDA, Mulcahy Papers, P7/A/20(309-310).

26 Lankford, *The Hope and the Sadness*, p. 211.

27 Tadg McCarthy, BMH WS 965, p. 14.

28 Lynch to Mulcahy, 19 March 1921, UCDA, Mulcahy Papers, P7/A/38

29 Mulcahy to Lynch, 26 March 1921, UCDA, Mulcahy Papers, P7/A/38.

30 Lankford, *The Hope and the Sadness*, pp. 199–200.

31 Valiulis, *Portrait of a Revolutionary*, p. 71.

32 Mulcahy to Lynch, 8 March 1921, UCDA, Mulcahy Papers, P7/A/17(12-13).

33 Lynch to Mulcahy, 12 March 1921, UCDA, Mulcahy Papers, P7/A/17(316).

34 Ibid.

35 Ibid.

36 O'Donoghue, *No Other Law*, pp. 188–9; see also Seán Ó Murthuile to IRB Supreme Council, 14 March 1921, NLI Ms 31,237(1-2).

37 Ibid., p. 189.

38 'Liam Lynch A Comrade's Personal View' by George Rice, published in the 2019 commemoration booklet by the Liam Lynch National Commemoration Association. My thanks to Tim Horgan for bringing this to my attention.

39 Mulcahy to Lynch, 13 April 1921, UCDA, Mulcahy Papers, P7/A/17(199-200).

40 Ibid. O'Donoghue puts the exact number as '30,620 officers and men' across all nine brigades.

41 O'Malley, *Another Man's Wound*, pp. 329, 339–40.

42 Barry, *Guerilla Days*, pp. 157–9.

43 O'Malley, *Another Man's Wound*, p. 341.

44 Barry, *Guerilla Days*, p. 159.

45 Uinseann MacEoin, *Survivors: The Story of Ireland's Struggle as Told through Some of Her Outstanding Living People Recalling Events from the Days of Davitt, Through James Connolly, Brugha, Collins, Liam Mellows, and Rory O'Connor, to the Present Time* (Dublin: Argenta Publications, 1987), p. 374.

46 P.J. Paul, BMH WS 877, p. 60.

47 Barry, *Guerilla Days*, p. 162.

48 Ibid., p. 163.

49 O'Malley, *Another Man's Wound*, p. 341.

50 O'Donoghue, *No Other Law*, pp. 115–16.

51 Ibid., p. 155.

52 George Power, BMH WS 451, p. 19.

53 Lynch to Mulcahy, 1 May 1921, UCDA, Mulcahy Papers, P7/A/18(16).

54 Mulcahy to Lynch, 5 May 1921, UCDA, Mulcahy Papers, P7/A/18(15).

55 Dónal Ó hÉalaithe (ed.), *Memoirs of an Old Warrior: Jamie Moynihan's Fight for Irish Freedom 1916–1923* (Cork: Mercier Press, 2014), p. 30.

56 Ibid., p. 31.

57 Ibid., p. 29.

58 Ibid., pp. 30–1, 188.

59 Terence Dooley, *Burning the Big House: The Story of the Irish Country House in a Time of War and Revolution* (New Haven and London: Yale University Press, 2022), p. 94.

60 Ibid., p. 96.

61   Ibid., p. 98.

62   William C. Regan, BMH WS 1069, p. 12.

63   O'Malley, *On Another Man's Wound*, p. 346.

64   Order No. 24 (General Orders, New Series), 9 June 1921, UCDA, Mulcahy Papers, P7/A/45.

65   Dorney, *Peace After the Final Battle*, pp. 214–15.

66   Peter Hart, *The IRA and its Enemies: Violence and Community in Cork 1916–1923* (New York: Oxford University Press, 1999), p. 291.

67   Dorney, *Peace After the Final Battle*, pp. 216–17.

68   Lynch to Mulcahy, 4 May 1921, UCDA, Mulcahy Papers, P7/A/20(39).

69   Mulcahy to Lynch, 7 May 1921, UCDA, Mulcahy Papers, P7/A/21(40).

70   Lynch to Mulcahy, 10 May 1921, UCDA, Mulcahy Papers, P7/A/21(41)

71   Lynch to Mulcahy, 5 July 1921, UCDA, Mulcahy Papers, P7/A/21(130).

72   Valiulis, *Portrait of a Revolutionary*, p. 70.

73   Lynch to Mulcahy, 11 July 1921, UCDA, Mulcahy Papers, P7/A/20(117).

74   Mulcahy to Lynch, 12 July 1921, UCDA, Mulcahy Papers, P7/A/21(156).

75   Copy of 'Women Spies' signed by Liam Lynch, 9 November 1920, Willis and Bolster, BMH WS 808, p. 64.

76   Seamus Fitzgerald, BMH WS 1737, p. 33.

77   Liam Manahan interview by Ernie O'Malley, UCDA, EOM notebooks, P17b/117, 35R.

78   Owen O'Shea, *Ballymacandy: The Story of a Kerry Ambush* (Dublin: Merrion Press, 2021), pp. 78–9.

79   Seán 'Bertie' Scully, BMH WS 788, p. 13.

80   Ibid., pp. 14, 29–30.

81   Lynch to Collins, 8 March 1921, IMA, Collins Papers, 5/2/8/(32).

82   Collins to Lynch, 15 March 1921, IMA, Collins Papers, 5/2/8/(33).

83   O'Donoghue, *No Other Law*, pp. 153–4.

84   Piaras Béaslaí, *Michael Collins and the Making of a New Ireland: Volume II* (Dublin: Edmund Burke, 2008), p. 154.

85   Barry, *Guerilla Days*, p. 163.

86   O'Donoghue, *No Other Law*, pp. 174–5.

87   Dorney, *Peace After the Final Battle*, pp. 217–18.

88   Tadg McCarthy, BMH WS 965, p. 18.

89   Michael O'Connell, BMH WS 1428, p. 23.

90   Lynch to Mulcahy, 10 June 1921, UCDA, Mulcahy Papers, P7/A/19(101-102).

91   William C. Regan, BMH WS 1069, p. 13.

92   Ó hÉalaithe (ed.), *Memoirs of an Old Warrior*, p. 218.

93   Pádraig Óg Ó Ruairc, *Truce: Murder, Myth and the Last Days of the Irish War of Independence* (Cork: Mercier Press, 2016), pp. 55–60.

94   Ibid., p. 60.

95   Interview of Moss Twomey by Seán O'Mahony, n.d., Seán O'Mahony interview, NLI Ms 44,126/4.

96   Ó hÉalaithe (ed.), *Memoirs of an Old Warrior*, p. 219.

CHAPTER 6

1 Liam Deasy, *Brother Against Brother* (Cork: Mercier Press, 1998), p. 27.
2 Interview of Moss Twomey by Seán O'Mahony, n.d., Seán O'Mahony interview, NLI Ms 44,126/4.
3 Deasy, *Brother Against Brother*, p. 27.
4 Ibid., pp. 27–8.
5 Valiulis, *Portrait of a Revolutionary*, p. 89.
6 Liam Lynch to Mary Lynch, 22 July 1921, NLI, Lynch Papers, Ms 36,251/17.
7 'Material for "Liam Lynch"' by Michael O'Connell, n.d., NLI, O'Donoghue Papers, Ms 31,421(5).
8 Walsh, *The Story of Liam Lynch*, p. 30.
9 Valiulis, *Portrait of a Revolutionary*, p. 98.
10 Lynch to Mulcahy, 19 July 1921, UCDA, Mulcahy Papers, P7/A/22(220).
11 Mulcahy to Lynch, 22 July 1921, UCDA, Mulcahy Papers, P7/A/22(222-223).
12 Valiulis, *Portrait of a Revolutionary*, p. 99.
13 Liam Lynch to Tom Lynch, 22 August 1921, NLI, Ms 36,251/18.
14 Lynch to Mulcahy, 23 August 1921, UCDA, Mulcahy Papers, P7/A/23(96).
15 Valiulis, *Portrait of a Revolutionary*, pp. 83–4.
16 Lynch to Tom Lynch, 30 August 1921, NLI, Ms 36,251/19.
17 Conor Kostick, *Revolution in Ireland: Popular Militancy 1917 to 1923* (London: Pluto Press, 1996), pp. 162–3.
18 Valiulis, *Portrait of a Revolutionary*, p. 93.
19 Lynch to Mulcahy, 13 October 1921, UCDA, Mulcahy Papers, P7/A/34(165-167).
20 Deasy, *Brother Against Brother*, pp. 29–30.
21 Lynch to Tom Lynch, 26 September 1921, NLI, Ms 36,251/20.
22 Ibid.
23 Ibid.
24 Lynch to O'Sullivan, 21 November 1921, UCDA, Mulcahy Papers, P7/A/30(16).
25 Private Secretary to Éamon de Valera, n.d. [*c.* late 1921), UCDA, Mulcahy Papers, P7/A/30(124).
26 Lynch to O'Sullivan, 24 November 1921, UCDA, Mulcahy Papers, P7/A/30(117-120).
27 Ibid.
28 Ibid.
29 Andrews, *Dublin Made Me*, p. 191.
30 Annie Farrington, BMH WS 749, p. 5.
31 Ibid.
32 Lynch to Tom Lynch, 11 November 1921, NLI, Ms 36,251/21.
33 'List of decisions at meeting of the ministry on Friday 4th November, 1921' [copy], 7 November 1921, UCDA, Mulcahy Papers, P7/A/37(1).
34 Valiulis, *Portrait of a Revolutionary*, pp. 102–6.
35 Various divisional commandants' communications with Brugha, *c.* November 1921, UCDA, Mulcahy Papers, P7/A/37(2-22).
36 Lynch to Brugha, 6 December 1921, UCDA, Richard Mulcahy Additional Papers, P7a/5.
37 Ibid.

38   Ó Broin, *Revolutionary Underground*, pp. 191–2.

39   O'Donoghue, *No Other Law*, p. 188.

40   Ibid., p. 192.

41   Deasy, *Brother Against Brother*, pp. 95–6.

42   O'Donoghue, *No Other Law*, p. 192. O'Donoghue referred to Collins telling them there may be compromise as Deasy in the previous citation but, unlike Deasy, he does not mention Lynch telling Collins not to say anything.

43   Ó'Broin, *Revolutionary Underground*, p. 196.

44   All quotes here from Seán Ó Muirthile's unpublished untitled memoir, UCDA, Richard Mulcahy Additional Papers, P7a/209.

45   John M. Regan, *The Irish Counter-Revolution 1921–1936: Treatyite Politics and Settlement in Independent Ireland* (Dublin: Gill Books, 2001) p. 30.

46   Interview of Moss Twomey by Seán O'Mahony, n.d., Seán O'Mahony interview, NLI Ms 44,126/4.

47   Untitled communication from 1st Southern Division leadership rejecting the Treaty [copy], 10 December 1921, NLI, O'Donoghue Papers, Ms 31,239.

48   Ó'Broin, *Revolutionary Underground*, p. 196.

49   O'Donoghue, *No Other Law*, pp. 190–1.

50   Lynch to O'Donoghue, 11 December 1921, NLI, O'Donoghue Papers, Ms 31,240.

51   Lynch to Tom Lynch, 12 December 1921, NLI, Lynch Papers, Ms 36,251/22.

52   Ibid.

53   O'Donoghue, *No Other Law*, p. 192.

54   Ó'Broin, *Revolutionary Underground*, pp. 198–200.

55   Deasy, *Brother Against Brother*, p. 32.

56   Seán O'Hegarty (Brigade O/C of Cork No. 1 Brigade) to all TDs in Cork No. 1 area, n.d. [*c.* mid-December 1921], UCDA, Mulcahy Papers, P7/A/33(122).

57   Mulcahy to Lynch, 17 December 1921, UCDA, Mulcahy Papers, P7/A/33(121).

58   As quoted in Valiulis, *Portrait of a Revolutionary*, pp. 119–20.

59   Ibid., p. 120.

60   Mulcahy to Lynch, 3 January 1922, UCDA, Mulcahy Papers, P7/A/32(139).

61   Lynch to Mulcahy, 4 January 1922, UCDA, Mulcahy Papers, P7/A/32(109).

62   Valiulis, *Portrait of a Revolutionary*, pp. 120–1.

63   Mulcahy to Lynch, 5 January 1922, UCDA, Mulcahy Papers, P7/A/33(44-45).

64   Lynch to Mulcahy, 6 January 1922, UCDA, Mulcahy Papers, P7/A/32(142).

65   Typed list of questions put to Oscar Traynor by Florence O'Donoghue, n.d. [*c.* 1952], NLI, O'Donoghue Papers, Ms 31,421(13). Aiken identified de Valera as also being present, see citation 68 below.

66   Oscar Traynor interview, UCDA, EOM notebooks, P17b/98, 53R.

67   Typed list of questions put to Oscar Traynor by Florence O'Donoghue, n.d. [*c.*1952], NLI, O'Donoghue Papers, Ms 31,421(13).

68   Oscar Traynor interview, UCDA, EOM notebooks, P17b/98, 53R-54R.

69   'Notes of interview with Frank Aiken at Leinster House' by Florence O'Donoghue, 18 June 1952, NLI, O'Donoghue Papers, Ms 31,421(13).

70   Ibid.

71   O'Donoghue, *No Other Law*, pp. 231–2.

72   Michael Hopkinson, *Green Against Green: The Irish Civil War* (Dublin: Gill & Macmillian, 2004), p. 59.

73   IRA GHQ Staff, Divisional Commandants, etc., to Mulcahy, 11 January 1922, UCDA, Mulcahy Papers, 7/B/191

74   Mulcahy to IRA GHQ Staff, Divisional Commandants, etc., 13 January 1922, UCDA, Mulcahy Papers, P7/B/191.

75   Valiulis, *Portrait of a Revolutionary*, p. 124.

76   Lynch to Mulcahy, 13 January 1922, UCDA, Mulcahy Papers, P7/B/191.

77   All quotes here from Seán Ó Muirthile's unpublished untitled memoir, UCDA, Richard Mulcahy Additional Papers, P7a/209.

78   Lynch to Tom Lynch, 16 January 1922, NLI, Lynch Papers, Ms 36,251/23.

79   Rory O'Connor to Mulcahy, 18 January 1922, UCDA, Mulcahy Papers, P7/B/191.

80   Mulcahy to all divisional commandants and brigade commandants, 21 January 1922, UCDA, Mulcahy Papers, P7/B/191.

81   Hopkinson, *Green Against Green*, pp. 60–1.

82   Ibid., p. 58.

83   Ryan, *The Real Chief*, p. 106.

84   Deasy, *Brother Against Brother*, p. 36.

85   Leo O'Callaghan, BMH WS 978, p. 25.

86   Lankford, *The Hope and the Sadness*, p. 199.

87   *Evening Echo*, 17 February 1922.

88   *The Cork Examiner*, 20 February 1922.

89   This incident is summarised, among similar IRA actions, in Kostick, *Revolution in Ireland*, p. 164.

90   *The Cork Examiner*, 9 February 1922.

91   *Irish Independent*, 9 February 1922.

92   Lynch to Tom Lynch, 6 March 1922, NLI, Lynch Papers, Ms 36,251/24.

93   Ibid.

94   Pádraig Óg Ó Ruairc, *The Battle for Limerick City* (Military History of the Irish Civil War) (Cork: Mercier Press, 2011), pp. 28–42.

95   Ibid., pp. 43–4.

96   Lynch to Tom Lynch, 31 March 1922, NLI, Lynch Papers, Ms 36,251/25.

97   O'Donoghue, *No Other Law*, p. 214.

98   Ibid.

99   Ibid.

100   Cabinet notes for Richard Mulcahy, 15 March 1922, UCDA, Mulcahy Papers, P7/B/192(60-61).

101   Ibid.

102   Valiulis, *Portrait of a Revolutionary*, pp. 135–6.

103   O'Donoghue, *No Other Law*, pp. 232–3.

104   Ibid., p. 233.

105   Pádraig Ó Caoimh, *Richard Mulcahy: From the Politics of War to the Politics of Peace, 1913–1924* (Dublin: Irish Academic Press, 2019), p. 105.

106   Interview of Moss Twomey by Seán O'Mahony, n.d., Seán O'Mahony interview, NLI Ms 44,126/4.

107 Memorandum on offer made by Minister for Defence at a meeting of the 1st Southern Division, n.d. [*c*. 20 March 1922], UCDA, Mulcahy Papers, P7/B/191.

108 Ó Caoimh, *Richard Mulcahy*, p. 105.

109 *The Irish Times*, 23 March 1922.

110 Andrews, *Dublin Made Me*, p. 233.

111 Interview of Moss Twomey by Seán O'Mahony, n.d., NLI, Seán O'Mahony interview, Ms 44,126/4.

112 Andrews, *Dublin Made Me*, p. 233.

113 O'Donoghue, *No Other Law*, pp. 220–1.

114 Report on IRA Convention, 25 March 1922, UCDA, Mulcahy Papers, P7/B/191.

115 Report on IRA Convention, 26 March 1922, UCDA, Mulcahy Papers, P7/B/191.

116 O'Donoghue, *No Other Law*, p. 220.

117 Report on IRA Convention, 26 March 1922, UCDA, Mulcahy Papers, P7/B/191.

118 Joseph O'Connor, BMH WS 544, pp. 2–3.

119 Ibid., p. 3.

120 Oscar Traynor interview, UCDA, EOM notebooks, P17b/98, 53R.

121 Joseph O'Connor, BMH WS 544, p. 3.

122 MacEoin, *Survivors*, p. 291.

123 Lynch to Tom Lynch, 31 March 1922, NLI, Lynch Papers, Ms 36,251/25.

124 O'Donoghue, *No Other Law*, pp. 224 and 230.

CHAPTER 7

1 *Irish Independent*, 15 April 1922.

2 O'Donoghue, *No Other Law*, p. 231.

3 *Éire*, 19 May 1923.

4 Lynch to Tom Lynch, 18 April 1922, NLI, Lynch Papers, Ms 36,251/26.

5 Ibid.

6 Michael Fewer, *The Battle of the Four Courts: The First Three Days of the Irish Civil War* (London: Head of Zeus, 2018), p. 62.

7 MacEoin, *Survivors*, p. 376.

8 O'Donoghue, *No Other Law*, pp. 233–4.

9 Paddy Mullaney to O'Donoghue, 1 October 1952, NLI, O'Donoghue Papers, Ms 31,421(2).

10 O'Donoghue, *No Other Law*, p. 234.

11 Ibid., pp. 235–6.

12 Hopkinson, *Green Against Green*, p. 83.

13 Ibid.

14 John Dorney, *The Civil War in Dublin: The Fight for the Irish Capital 1922–1924* (Dublin: Merrion Press, 2017), p. 57.

15 Robert Lynch, *The Northern IRA and the Early Years of Partition 1920–1922* (Dublin: Irish Academic Press, 2006), p. 138.

16 Kieran Glennon, 'The Boys of the Old Brigade – The IRA Third Northern Division', The Irish Story, www.theirishstory.com/2018/06/05/the-boys-of-the-old-brigade-the-ira-third-northern-divsion/#.Yk3QGMjMK3A (accessed 2 February 2022).

17 Woods to Lynch, 8 May 1922, UCDA, Mulcahy Papers, P7/B/192.

18 Dorney, *Civil War in Dublin*, p. 58.

19 Lynch to Tom Lynch, 1 May 1922, NLI, Lynch Papers, Ms 36,251/27.

20 Text of Truce signed by Eoin O'Duffy and Liam Lynch, 4 May 1922, UCDA, Mulcahy Papers, P7/B/191.

21 O'Donoghue, *No Other Law*, pp. 238–9.

22 Jeremiah (J.J. 'Ginger') O'Connell, *DIB*, entry by Marie Coleman, www.dib.ie/biography/oconnell-jeremiah-joseph-j-j-ginger-a6561 (accessed 5 August 2021).

23 Unpublished memoir of J.J. 'Ginger' O'Connell, NLI, O'Connell Papers, Ms 22,126.

24 Ruth O'Hara, 'Women of the Revolution: Hannah Condon Cleary on her service in Cumann na mBan 1918–1923', https://mulibrarytreasures.wordpress.com/2018/11/23/women-of-the-revolution-hannah-condon-cleary-on-her-service-in-cumman-na-mban-1918-1923/ (accessed 7 March 2021).

25 Transcribed in Hanna Cleary interview, UCDA, EOM notebooks, P17b/132, ends midway through 61L.

26 Lynch to O'Duffy, 4 May 1922, UCDA, Mulcahy Papers, P7/B/192(310).

27 Memorandum on 'Irish Army Pact or Truce (4 May)', n.d., UCDA, Mulcahy Papers, P7/B/192(26-56).

28 Untitled minutes of 14 May meeting by Richard Mulcahy, 14 May 1922, UCDA, Mulcahy Papers, P7/B/193(13).

29 Hopkinson, *Green Against Green*, p. 98.

30 Lynch to Tom Lynch, 31 May 1922, NLI, Lynch Papers, Ms 36,251/28.

31 Quoted in O'Donoghue, *No Other Law*, p. 241.

32 Lynch to Mulcahy, 7 June 1922, UCDA, Mulcahy Papers, P7/B/192(157).

33 Lynch to Mulcahy, 8 June 1922, UCDA, Mulcahy Papers, P7/B/192(156).

34 O'Malley to Mulcahy, 10 June 1922, UCDA, Mulcahy Papers, P7/B/192(159).

35 Mulcahy to O'Malley, 12 June 1922, UCDA, Mulcahy Papers, P7/B/192(154-155).

36 O'Donoghue, *No Other Law*, p. 184.

37 Memorandum on resolution passed at IRA Executive meeting on 14 June 1922, 15 June 1922, UCDA, Mulcahy Papers, P7/B/192(145).

38 T. Ryle Dwyer, *Michael Collins and the Civil War* (Cork: Mercier Press, 2012), pp. 231–2.

39 Bill Kissane, *The Politics of the Irish Civil War* (Oxford: Oxford University Press, 2005), p. 183.

40 O'Donoghue, *No Other Law*, p. 184.

41 Lynch to Tom Lynch, 18 April 1922, NLI, Lynch Papers, Ms 36,251/26.

42 Kissane, *Politics of the Irish Civil War*, p. 183.

43 Quote from O'Donoghue, *No Other Law*, p. 245. Curiously, no record of the 16 June 1922 letter exists, as with previously quoted letters to Tom Lynch, NLI, Lynch Papers, Ms 36251(145).

44 Joseph O'Connor, BMH WS 544, pp. 3–4.

45 Interview of Moss Twomey by Seán O'Mahony, n.d., NLI, O'Mahony Papers, Ms 44,126/4.

46 Dorney, *Civil War in Dublin*, p. 63.

47 Joseph O'Connor, BMH WS 544, pp. 5–6.

48   Deasy, *Brother Against Brother*, p. 39.

49   Interview of Moss Twomey by Seán O'Mahony, n.d., NLI, Seán O'Mahony interview, Ms 44,126/4.

50   Deasy, *Brother Against Brother*, p. 40.

51   Joseph O'Connor, BMH WS 544, p. 6.

52   Joseph McKelvey, *DIB*, entry by Marie Coleman, https://www.dib.ie/biography/mckelvey-joseph-a5719 (accessed 6 March 2022). I am also grateful for insights into the enigmatic McKelvey from historian Kieran Glennon.

53   Ibid., p. 9.

54   Dwyer, *Collins and the Civil War*, pp. 240–1.

55   Hopkinson, *Green Against Green*, p. 112.

56   Dorney, *Civil War in Dublin*, pp. 66–7.

57   Valiulis, *Portrait of a Revolutionary*, p. 154.

58   Hopkinson, *Green Against Green*, p. 118.

59   Interview of Moss Twomey by Seán O'Mahony, n.d., Seán O'Mahony interview, NLI Ms 44,126/4.

60   Deasy, *Brother Against Brother*, p. 45.

61   Ibid., pp. 45–6.

62   Joseph O'Connor, BMH WS 544, p. 9.

63   Ibid.

64   Deasy, *Brother Against Brother*, p. 46.

65   Moss Twomey interview by Ernie O'Malley, UCDA, EOM notebook, P17b/96, 86R.

66   O'Donoghue, *No Other Law*, p. 258.

67   Deasy, *Brother Against Brother*, p. 46.

CHAPTER 8

1   Deasy, *Brother Against Brother*, p. 47.

2   Dorney, *Civil War in Dublin*, p. 69.

3   O'Donoghue, *No Other Law*, p. 258.

4   Deasy, *Brother Against Brother*, p. 46.

5   Ibid, pp. 46–8.

6   O'Donoghue, *No Other Law*, p. 259.

7   Dorothy Macardle, *The Irish Republic* (Dublin: Wolfhound Press, 1999), p. 745. Macardle is alone in the existing literature in suggesting Lynch sent such a message.

8   Moss Twomey interview by Ernie O'Malley, UCDA, EOM notebook, P17b/96, 86R.

9   Ibid.

10   Those who identify Lynch as the author, with differences of opinion as to where and when he wrote it, include C. Desmond Greaves, *Liam Mellows and the Irish Revolution* (Belfast: Lawrence & Wishart Ltd, 2005), pp. 345–6; Macardle, *Irish Republic*, pp. 744–5; and Calton Younger, *Ireland's Civil War* (London: Fontana Press, 1986), p. 336. To further confuse the matter, Rory O'Connor and Joseph McKelvey have been put forward as authors, see Liz Gillis, *The Fall of Dublin* (Military History of Irish Civil War) (Cork: Mercier Press, 2011), pp. 44–5.

11 Moylan to O'Donoghue, 1 September 1952, NLI, O'Donoghue Papers, Ms 31,421/15/9(1).

12 Deasy, *Brother Against Brother*, pp. 48–9.

13 O'Donoghue, *No Other Law*, p. 259.

14 Cahir Davitt, BMH WS 1751, p. 75.

15 Deasy, *Brother Against Brother*, p. 49.

16 Moylan to O'Donoghue, 1 September 1952, NLI, O'Donoghue Papers, Ms 31,421/15/9(1-2).

17 Deasy, *Brother Against Brother*, p. 50. Notably, no mention is made of Lynch and the other offices being invited to the barracks for a meal in O'Donoghue, *No Other Law*, pp. 259–60.

18 Deasy, *Brother Against Brother*, p. 50.

19 Quoted in O'Donoghue, *No Other Law*, p. 259.

20 Deasy, *Brother Against Brother*, p. 50.

21 Robert Brennan, BMH WS 779 (Section III), p. 723.

22 Ryan, *The Real Chief*, p. 141.

23 Statement printed in full in O'Donoghue, *No Other Law*, p. 260.

24 Younger, *Ireland's Civil War*, p. 371.

25 O'Donoghue, *No Other Law*, p. 267.

26 As well as the myriad of examples of papers with contemporary IRA material referred to elsewhere, O'Donoghue does not refer to a 'Munster Republic' in *No Other Law*.

27 See Dorney, *The Civil War in Dublin*, pp. 89–99. See also Gillis, *The Fall of Dublin*.

28 Séumas Robinson, BMH WS 1721, pp. 76-7.

29 Joseph O'Connor, BMH WS 544, p. 15.

30 MSP34REF2091, MSP of Florence O'Donoghue, IMA (accessed online 1 February 2021).

31 Ibid.

32 Robert Brennan, BMH WS 779 (Section III), pp. 723-4.

33 Hopkinson, *Green Against Green*, pp. 146-7.

34 Younger, *Ireland's Civil War*, p. 370.

35 Ibid., p. 372.

36 'Minutes of [IRA] Executive meeting held October 16th/October 17th, 1922', NLI, Ernie O'Malley Papers, Ms 10,973/15/4.

37 Deasy, *Brother Against Brother*, pp. 53-4.

38 Younger, *Ireland's Civil War*, p. 372.

39 Hopkinson, *Green Against Green*, p. 148.

40 O'Donoghue, *No Other Law*, p. 262.

41 'Agreement between Executive Forces and Gen. Hannigan', 3 July 1922, UCDA, Moss Twomey Papers, P69/28(243).

42 'Agreement between Comdt. Gen. Hannigan and & C/S Executive Forces', 4 July 1922, UCDA, Twomey Papers, P69/28(242).

43 Open letter from Lynch and Hannigan, 7 July 1922, UCDA, Twomey Papers, P69/28(241).

44 Ó Ruairc, *The Battle for Limerick City*, p. 73.

45   McManus to Lynch, 5 July 1922, UCDA, Twomey Papers, P69/28(220-221).

46   Ó Ruairc, *The Battle for Limerick City*, pp. 75–6 or O'Donoghue, *No Other Law*, pp. 263–4.

47   Younger, *Ireland's Civil War*, p. 375.

48   Quoted in ibid., p. 374. For Brennan's issues with his senior officers and government over the agreement, see ibid., pp. 374–6.

49   Lynch's quotes, and views of anti-Treaty contemporaries, from Hopkinson, *Green Against Green*, p. 148.

50   Ó Ruairc, *The Battle for Limerick City*, p. 79.

51   Ibid., pp. 68–9.

52   O'Donoghue, *No Other Law*, p. 265.

53   O'Meara to Lynch, 8 July 1922, UCDA, Twomey Papers, P69/28(171).

54   Lynch to O'Meara, 8 July 1922, UCDA, Twomey Papers, P69/28(172).

55   O'Meara to Lynch, n.d., UCDA, Twomey Papers, P69/28(170).

56   Hopkinson, *Green Against Green*, p. 149.

57   Robert Brennan, BMH WS 779 (Section III), p. 719.

58   Séumas Robinson, BMH WS 1721, p. 76.

59   Lynch to O/C Operations Limerick City, 12 July 1922, UCDA, Twomey Papers, P69/28(142).

60   Ó Ruairc, *The Battle for Limerick City*, p. 92.

61   Ibid.

62   Lynch to Acting Director of Intelligence, 15 July 1922, UCDA, Twomey Papers, P69/28(108).

63   Deasy, *Brother Against Brother*, p. 65.

64   As quoted by Hopkinson, *Green Against Green*, p. 149.

65   MacEoin, *Survivors*, p. 230.

66   Ibid., p. 245.

67   Hopkinson, *Green Against Green*, p. 103.

68   Lynch to Deasy, 8 February 1923, UCDA, de Valera Papers, P150/1749.

69   For one example of its use in a obituary, see *Kilkenny People*, 14 April 1923. It is also referred to in Tom Garvin, *1922: The Birth of Irish Democracy* (Dublin: Gill & Macmillan, 1996), p. 43.

70   'Minutes of [IRA] Executive meeting held October 16th/October 17th, 1922', UCDA, O'Malley Papers, Ms 10,973/15/4.

71   O'Donoghue, *No Other Law*, p. 272.

72   Ernie O'Malley, *The Singing Flame* (Cork: Mercier Press, 2012), p. 180.

73   Deasy, *Brother Against Brother*, p. 85.

74   Hopkinson, *Green Against Green*, p. 164.

75   Lynch to Deasy, 6 August 1922, UCDA, Twomey Papers, P69/24(30).

76   Dorney, *Peace After the Final Battle*, p. 269.

77   Robert Brennan, BMH WS 779 (Section III), pp. 723–4.

78   Email conversation between author and historian and photographer Bill Power, 15 March 2021.

79   Lynch to O'Malley, 10 July 1922, UCDA, O'Malley Papers, P17A/60.

80   Lynch to O'Malley, 25 July 1922, UCDA, O'Malley Papers, P17A/60.

81 Ryan, *The Real Chief*, p. 151.
82 John Borgonovo, *The Battle for Cork, July–August 1922* (Military History of the Irish Civil War) (Cork: Mercier Press, 2011), p. 126.
83 David McCullagh, *De Valera: Rise 1882–1932* (Dublin: Gill Books, 2017), pp. 294–5.
84 Ibid, p. 295.
85 Lynch to de Valera, 14 Jan. 1923, UCDA, de Valera Papers, P150/1749.
86 McCullagh, *De Valera: Rise*, p. 296.
87 Risteárd Mulcahy, *Richard Mulcahy (1886–1971): A Family Memoir* (Dublin: Aurelian Press, 1999), p. 165.
88 O'Malley to Lynch, 21 July 1922, UCDA, Twomey Papers, P69/38(44).
89 Lynch to O'Malley, 25 July 1922, UCDA, Twomey Papers, P69/38(35).
90 Greaves, *Liam Mellows*, p. 362.
91 Hopkinson, *Green Against Green*, p. 186.
92 At the first IRA Executive meeting since the outbreak of the Civil War, no discussion among Executive members of Mellows' proposals are apparent, see Minutes of the IRA Executive Meeting, 16–17 Oct. 1922, UCDA, Twomey Papers, P69/179(3-9).
93 Greaves, *Liam Mellows*, p. 359.
94 Emmet O'Connor, *Reds and the Green: Ireland, Russia and the Communist Internationals 1919–43* (Dublin: UCD Press, 2004), p. 68.
95 Ibid., p. 72.
96 Lynch to Todd Andrews, 15 Dec. 1922, UCDA, Twomey Papers, P69/13(93).
97 O'Connor, *Reds and the Green*, p. 73.
98 Lynch to Oscar Traynor, 25 July 1922, UCDA, Twomey Papers, P69/38(21).
99 'Operation Order No. 9: Organisation and Activities of Active Service Units', 19 Aug. 1922, UCDA, Twomey Papers, P69/2(11-12).
100 Hopkinson, *Green Against Green*, pp. 174–5.
101 Interview of Moss Twomey by Seán O'Mahony, n.d., Seán O'Mahony interview, NLI Ms 44,126/4.
102 Lynch to O'Malley, 18 Aug. 1922, UCDA, O'Malley Papers, P17A/61.
103 Lynch to Deasy, re Beal-na-Blath ambush, 28 Aug. 1922, IE/MA/Civil War/Captured Documents/Lot 4.
104 Lynch to O'Malley, 30 Aug. 1922, UCDA, O'Malley Papers, P17A/61.
105 Deasy, *Brother Against Brother*, p. 76.
106 Andrews, *Dublin Made Me*, p. 291. Andrews made a similar observation when interviewed by Meda Ryan, see Ryan, *The Real Chief*, p. 166.
107 A wide sampling of these can be seen in Anne Dolan and William Murphy, *Michael Collins: The Man and the Revolution* (Dublin: Collins Press, 2018), pp. 271–8. Both authors noted the tendency of Lynch to put 'RIP' beside mention of Collins in examples of correspondence.
108 Hopkinson, *Green Against Green*, p. 173.
109 Lynch to Éamon de Valera, 8 Dec. 1922, UCDA, de Valera Papers, P150/1749.
110 O'Donoghue, *No Other Law*, p. 280.
111 Eoin Neeson, *The Civil War 1922–23* (Dublin: Poolbeg Press, 1989), p. 250.
112 Lynch to Liam Deasy, 11 Oct. 1922, UCDA, Twomey Papers, P69/25(161).
113 Lynch to Deasy, 30 Sept. 1922, UCDA, Twomey Papers, P69/25(190).

114   Lynch to Deasy, 30 Sept. 1922, UCDA, Twomey Papers, P69/25(191).

115   Lynch to O'Malley, 17 Sept. 1922, UCDA, Twomey Papers, P69/40(98).

116   Lynch to Deasy, 17 Sept. 1922, UCDA, Twomey Papers, P69/25(217).

117   Lynch to Con Moloney, 7 Nov. 1922, UCDA, Twomey Papers, P69/77(142-143).

118   Lynch to O'Malley, 26 Jul. 1922, UCDA, Twomey Papers, P69/38(24-25).

119   Gerard Noonan, *The IRA in Britain, 1919–1923: 'In the heart of enemy lines'* (Liverpool: Liverpool University Press, 2014), p. 238.

120   Hopkinson, *Green Against Green*, pp. 239–40.

121   Lynch to Pa Murray, 9 April 1923, UCDA, de Valera Papers, P150/1749.

122   Hopkinson, *Green Against Green*, pp. 249–50.

123   Deasy, *Brother Against Brother*, pp. 73–4.

124   'Points for Special Memorandum on Guerilla Tactics' by Deasy, 26 July 1922, UCDA, O'Malley Papers, 17a/15.

125   O'Donoghue, *No Other Law*, p. 269.

126   Lynch to Tom Lynch, 16 Sept. 1922, NLI, Lynch Papers, Ms 36,251/29.

127   Ibid.

128   O'Donoghue, *No Other Law*, p. 270.

129   Younger, *Ireland's Civil War*, p. 444.

130   Lynch to O'Malley, 18 Aug. 1922, UCDA, O'Malley Papers, P17A/61.

131   Moloney to O'Malley, 28 Sept. 1922, UCDA, Twomey Papers, P69/77(70).

132   Lynch to O'Malley, 1 Oct. 1922, UCDA, O'Malley Papers, P17A/64.

133   O'Donoghue, *No Other Law*, p. 275.

134   'Notes of interview with Frank Aiken at Leinster House' by Florence O'Donoghue, 18 June 1952, NLI, O'Donoghue Papers, Ms 31,421(13).

135   Hopkinson, *Green Against Green*, p. 186.

136   Younger, *Ireland's Civil War*, p. 482.

137   Andrews, *Dublin Made Me*, p. 290.

138   Younger, *Ireland's Civil War*, p. 482.

139   Todd Andrews interview by Ernie O'Malley, UCDA, EOM notebooks, P17b/88, 22R.

140   Kissane, *Politics of the Irish Civil War*, p. 90.

141   Resolution at meeting of IRA Executive, 17 Oct. 1922, UCDA, de Valera Papers, P150/1749.

142   Hopkinson, *Green Against Green*, p. 187.

143   Lynch to de Valera, 18 October 1922, UCDA, de Valera Papers, P150/1749.

144   Ibid.

145   Kissane, *Politics of the Irish Civil War*, p. 90.

146   De Valera to Lynch, 23 Oct. 1922, UCDA, de Valera Papers, P150/1749.

147   Lynch to de Valera, 8 Nov. 1922, UCDA, de Valera Papers, P150/1749.

148   De Valera to Lynch, 9 Nov. 1922, UCDA, de Valera Papers, P150/1749.

149   See copy of 'Address from the Soldiers of the Army of the Republic to Their Former Comrades in the Free State Army and the Civic Guard', signed by Liam Lynch and Éamon de Valera, 23 Nov. 1922, UCDA, Twomey Papers, P69/79(123-130).

150   Moloney to Lynch, 21 Nov. 1922, UCDA, Twomey Papers, P69/77(124).

151   Lynch to de Valera, 8 Nov. 1922, UCDA, de Valera Papers, P150/1749.

152   Lynch to de Valera, 16 Nov. 1922, UCDA, de Valera Papers, P150/1749. Lynch

also made his objections to Barton's appointment known to his adjutant general, Moloney, who also sat on the IRA Council. See Lynch to Moloney, 15 Nov. 1922, UCDA, Twomey Papers, P69/77(125). This may imply Lynch directly addressed his concerns about Barton to other individual members of the IRA Army Council.

153   de Valera to Lynch, 17 Nov. 1922, UCDA, de Valera Papers, P150/1749.

154   Draft Proclamation by the IRA, 28 Oct. 1922, UCDA, Twomey Papers, P69/39(136-137).

155   Hopkinson, *Green Against Green*, p. 188.

156   Neeson, *The Civil War*, p. 271; Earl of Longford and Thomas O'Neill, *Éamon de Valera* (Dublin: Gill & Macmillan, 1970), p. 211.

157   Andrews, *Dublin Made Me*, p. 299.

158   Lynch to Joseph McGarrity, 21 Dec. 1922, NLI, Joseph McGarrity Papers, Ms 17,455(1).

159   Lynch to O/C 4th Western Division, 22 Jan. 1923, UCDA, Twomey Papers, P69/42(105).

160   O/C 4th Western Division to Lynch, 9 Jan. 1923, UCDA, Twomey Papers, P69/42(106).

161   Liam Lynch to Tom Lynch, 28 October 1922 [typed copy], NLI, O'Mahony Papers, Ms 44,109/2.

CHAPTER 9

1   Letter from Liam Lynch to Liam Deasy, 7 November 1922, UCDA, Irish Republican Brotherhood Papers, P21/2. All items in the Irish Republican Brotherhood Papers can also be found in their original form in the NLI, O'Donoghue Papers, Ms 31,240.

2   Letter from Deasy to Lynch, 29 December 1922, UCDA, Irish Republican Brotherhood Papers, P21/4.

3   Lynch to Joseph McGarrity, 21 December 1922, NLI, McGarrity Papers, Ms 17,455(1).

4   See John O'Beirne-Ranelagh, 'The IRB from the Treaty to 1924', *Irish Historical Studies*, vol. xx, no. lxxvii (March 1976), p. 6.

5   Ibid., pp. 34–5.

6   Andrews, *Dublin Made Me*, p. 291.

7   Lynch to O'Malley, 3 August 1922, UCDA, Twomey Papers, P69/38(2). Of interest, this tricolour styled with the 'I.R.' lettering still endures in some modern-day republican commemorations, as confirmed in a conversation between the author and Matt Doyle, Secretary of the National Graves Association, 2 February 2022.

8   See Lynch correspondence to this effect, 14 December 1922, UCDA, Twomey Papers, P69/79(97-98).

9   Lynch to Seán McCarthy, 16 September 1922, UCDA, Twomey Papers, P69/79(63).

10   Lynch to Erskine Childers, 8 September 1922, UCDA, Twomey Papers, P69/79(39).

11   Lynch to Childers, 13 September 1922, UCDA, Twomey Papers, P69/79(56).

12   Childers to Lynch, 6 October 1922, UCDA, Twomey Papers, P69/79(88).

13   Moloney to Childers, 13 October 1922, UCDA, Twomey Papers, P69/79(94).

14   'Katherine (Kathleen) Moloney', *DIB*, entry by Lawrence William White, www.dib.ie/biography/moloney-katherine-kathleen-a9950 (accessed 6 August 2022).

15 Lynch to Kathleen Barry Moloney, 22 Dec. 22, UCDA, Barry Moloney Papers, P94/28.

16 Lynch to Kathleen Barry Moloney, 27 Jan. 23, UCDA, Barry Moloney Papers, P94/28.

17 O'Malley, *Singing Flame*, p. 194.

18 Lynch to O'Malley, 30 August 1922, UCDA, O'Malley Papers, P17A/61.

19 O'Malley, *Singing Flame*, pp. 218–19.

20 O'Donoghue, *No Other Law*, p. 277.

21 O'Malley, *Singing Flame*, p. 229.

22 O'Donoghue, *No Other Law*, pp 277–8; Additional material from the article 'The Tower House' by Tim Horgan, published in the 2018 commemoration booklet by the Liam Lynch National Commemoration Association.

23 Ibid., p. 278.

24 Hopkinson, *Green Against Green*, p. 181.

25 'Minutes of [IRA] Executive meeting held October 16th/October 17th, 1922', NLI, O'Malley Papers, Ms 10,973/15/4.

26 O'Malley, *Singing Flame*, p. 218.

27 Séamus Fox interview by Ernie O'Malley, UCDA, EOM notebooks, P17b/106, 44L.

28 Lynch to de Valera, 17 Nov. 1922, UCDA, de Valera Papers, P150/1749.

29 Lynch to Molly Childers, 27 Nov. 1922, UCDA, de Valera Papers, P69/56(46).

30 O'Donoghue, *No Other Law*, p. 279.

31 Lynch to de Valera, 25 Nov. 1922, UCDA, de Valera Papers, P150/1749.

32 De Valera to Lynch, 27 Nov. 1922, UCDA, de Valera Papers, P150/1749.

33 Quoted from O'Donoghue, *No Other Law*, p. 279.

34 'General Order No. 11', 22 Nov. 1922, UCDA, O'Malley Papers, P17A/37.

35 'Operation Order No. 11: Enemy Murder Bill', 30 Nov. 1922, UCDA, O'Malley Papers, P17A/94.

36 Lynch to Johnson, 28 Nov. 1922, UCDA, Twomey Papers, P69/56(41).

37 *Parliamentary Debates: Dáil Éireann: Official Report*, 2/3 (Friday, 8 December 1922).

38 Lynch to O'Connor, 26 Jan. 1923, UCDA, Twomey Papers, P69/25(90).

39 Hopkinson, *Green Against Green*, p. 190.

40 De Valera to Lynch, 15 Jan. 1923, UCDA, de Valera Papers, P150/1749.

41 Lynch to de Valera, 15 Jan. 1923, UCDA, de Valera Papers, P150/1749.

42 Derrig to Honorary Secretaries of Cumann na mBan, 15 Dec. 1922, UCDA, Twomey Papers, P69/56(31).

43 Lynch to de Valera, 14 Dec. 1922, UCDA, de Valera Papers, P150/1749.

44 Regan, *The Irish Counter-Revolution 1921–1936*, p. 115.

45 Hopkinson, *Green Against Green*, p. 190.

46 See ibid., pp. 183–5, for a rundown of peace efforts in this period.

47 Lynch to Twomey, 9 Sept. 1922, UCDA, de Valera Papers, P69/77(150).

48 Moss Twomey interview by Ernie O'Malley, UCDA, EOM notebooks, P17b/96, 89R.

49 Hopkinson, *Green Against Green*, p. 184.

50 De Valera to Lynch, 15 Dec. 1922, UCDA, de Valera Papers, P150/1749.

51 Lynch to de Valera, 18 Dec. 1922, UCDA, de Valera Papers, P150/1749.

52 Lynch to de Valera, 28 Dec. 1922, UCDA, de Valera Papers, P150/1749.

53 Hopkinson, *Green Against Green*, p. 199.
54 Ibid., pp. 198–9.
55 Ibid., p. 280.
56 O'Donoghue, *No Other Law*, p. 289.
57 Hopkinson, *Green Against Green*, p. 228.
58 Macardle, *The Irish Republic*, pp. 837–8.
59 Neeson, *The Civil War 1922–23*, p. 286.
60 Lynch to all IRA Departments, 22 January 1923, UCDA, Twomey Papers, P69/2(95).
61 Lynch to Command O/Cs, 24 January 1923, UCDA, Twomey Papers, P69/2(97).
62 Hopkinson, *Green Against Green*, p. 229.
63 Ibid.
64 Lynch to Joseph O'Connor, 26 January 1923, UCDA, Twomey Papers, P69/25(90).
65 Lynch to Acting O/C of Dublin Brigade, and to O/C 3rd Southern Division, 22 Jan. 1923, UCDA, Twomey Papers, P69/22(175).
66 Lynch to Éamon de Valera, 19 Jan. 1923, UCDA, de Valera Papers, P150/1749.
67 Andrews, *Dublin Made Me*, p. 299.
68 Hopkinson, *Green Against Green*, pp. 232–3.
69 Madge Comer to O'Donoghue, 6 September 1953, NLI, O'Donoghue Papers, Ms 31,423(5).
70 Lynch to Kathleen Barry Moloney, 27 Jan. 1923, UCDA, Barry Moloney Papers, P94/28.
71 Deasy, *Brother Against Brother*, pp. 110–11, 114–15.
72 For full text of this document composed by Deasy in captivity, see ibid., pp. 116–22.
73 Ibid., pp. 119, 121.
74 Ibid., p. 122.
75 O'Donoghue, *No Other Law*, p. 290.
76 Lynch to Deasy, 5 Feb. 1923, UCDA, de Valera Papers, P150/1697.
77 Hopkinson, *Green Against Green*, pp. 230–1.
78 Lynch to Joseph McGarrity, 5 Feb. 1923, NLI, McGarrity Papers, Ms 17,455/5.
79 Lynch to Kathleen Barry Moloney, 9 Feb. 1923, UCDA, Barry Moloney Papers, P94/28.
80 Lynch to Frank Barrett, 9 Feb. 1923, UDCA, de Valera Papers, P150/1697.
81 Barrett to Lynch, 5 February 1923, UCDA, de Valera Papers, P150/1697.
82 Lynch to Murray, 29 February 1921, UCDA, Mulcahy Papers, P7/B/89(33).
83 Hopkinson, *Green Against Green*, p. 232.
84 Moss Twomey interview by Ernie O'Malley, UCDA, EOM interviews, P17b/96, 90R.
85 Lynch to AM L/G, 4 Feb. 1923, UCDA, de Valera Papers, P150/1697.
86 Lynch to Kathleen Barry Moloney, 9 Feb. 1923, UCDA, Barry Moloney Papers, P94/28.
87 Hopkinson, *Green Against Green*, p. 232.
88 Lynch to O/Cs Commands, Divisions and Ind. Brigades, 2 Feb. 1923, NLI, McGarrity Papers, Ms 17,455/4.
89 Lynch to 'All ranks of the army', 9 February 1923, UCDA, de Valera Papers, P150/1749.
90 Andrews, *Dublin Made Me*, p. 299.
91 Ibid., p. 300.

92   Lynch to Kathleen Barry Moloney, 27 Jan. 1923, UCDA, Barry Moloney Papers, P94/28.

93   Lynch to de Valera, 7 Feb. 1923, UCDA, de Valera Papers, P150/1749.

94   Madge Comer (Clifford), interview, UCDA, EOM notebooks, P17b/89, 37R.

95   Madge Comer (Clifford), interview, UCDA, EOM notebooks, P17b/89, 36R.

96   Lynch to de Valera, 6 Feb. 1923, UCDA, de Valera Papers, P150/1749.

97   Andrews, *Dublin Made Me*, p. 286.

98   Ibid., p. 287.

99   Ibid., p. 288.

100   Ibid.

101   Ibid., pp. 288–9.

102   John Borgonovo (ed.), *Florence and Josephine O'Donoghue's War of Independence: A Destiny that Shapes Our Ends* (Dublin: Irish Academic Press, 2006), p. 201; Kissane, *Politics of the Irish Civil War*, pp. 138–9.

103   Lynch to de Valera, 18 Dec. 1922, UCDA, de Valera Papers, P150/1749.

104   Lynch to de Valera, 15 Jan. 1923, UCDA, de Valera Papers, P150/1749.

105   Hopkinson, *Green Against Green*, p. 185; Kissane, *Politics of the Irish Civil War*, p. 141.

106   Andrews, *Dublin Made Me*, p. 275.

107   Lynch to de Valera, 26 Jan. 1923, UCDA, de Valera Papers, P150/1749.

108   Kissane, *Politics of the Irish Civil War*, p. 139.

109   Borgonovo (ed.), *Florence and Josephine O'Donoghue's War of Independence*, p. 202.

110   Lynch to O'Donoghue, 8 Mar. 1923, NLI, O'Donoghue Papers, Ms 31,261(2).

111   Borgonovo (ed.), *Florence and Josephine O'Donoghue's War of Independence*, p. 202.

112   Hopkinson, *Green Against Green*, p. 185.

113   Ibid., pp. 235–6.

114   O'Donoghue, *No Other Law*, p. 296.

115   'Minutes of 1st Southern Division meeting, 26 Feb. 1923', UCDA, O'Malley Papers, P7/B/89.

116   Moss Twomey interview by Ernie O'Malley, UCDA, EOM notebooks, P17b/96, 90R.

117   Lynch to de Valera, 26 Feb. 1923, UCDA, de Valera Papers, P150/1749.

118   Andrews, *Dublin Made Me*, p. 293.

119   Quoted in O'Donoghue, *No Other Law*, p. 297.

120   Longford and O'Neill, *de Valera*, p. 215.

121   Lynch to de Valera, 26 Feb. 1923, UCDA, de Valera Papers, P150/1749.

122   De Valera to Lynch, 7 Mar. 1923, UCDA, de Valera Papers, P150/1749.

123   Younger, *Ireland's Civil War*, p. 500.

124   Lynch to President and Ministers, 30 January 1923, UCDA, de Valera Papers, P150/1749.

125   Ryan, *The Real Chief*, p. 185.

126   Ibid., p. 175.

127   Kissane, *Politics of the Irish Civil War*, p. 99.

128   Ibid.

129   Macardle, *The Irish Republic*, p. 843.

130   'Amusements Order', 13 March 1923, UCDA, de Valera Papers, P150/1710; 'General Order No. 16: Registration of Dogs', 19 Feb. 1923, UCDA, Twomey Papers, P69/2(42-47).

131 Andrews, *Dublin Made Me*, p. 300.

132 Ibid.

133 Hopkinson, *Green Against Green*, pp. 236–7.

134 Lynch to O'Connor, 26 Jan. 1923, UCDA, Twomey Papers, P69/25(91).

135 McGarritty to Lynch, 15 Jan. 1923, NLI, McGarrity Papers, Ms 17,455/3.

136 Lynch to de Valera, 6 Feb. 1923, UCDA, de Valera Papers, P150/1749.

137 De Valera to Lynch, 8 Feb. 1923, UCDA, de Valera Papers, P150/1749.

138 De Valera to Office of Chief of Staff, 2 Mar. 1923, UCDA, de Valera Papers, P150/1749.

139 Lynch to Moylan, 5 Mar. 1923, UCDA, Twomey Papers, P69/9(44).

140 Moylan to Lynch, 16 Mar. 1923, UCDA, Twomey Papers, P69/37(244).

141 Lynch to O'Connor, 12 Mar. 1923, UCDA, Twomey Papers, P69/9(32).

142 Andrews, *Dublin Made Me*, p. 304.

143 Deasy, *Brother Against Brother*, p. 75.

144 Hyde to Lynch, 26 Feb. 1923, UCDA, Twomey Papers, P69/30(214).

145 Hyde to Lynch, 26 Feb. 1923, UCDA, Mulcahy Papers, P7/8/89(29).

146 Twomey to Moylan, 2 Mar. 1923, UCDA, Mulcahy Papers, P7/8/89(69).

147 Moss Twomey interview by Ernie O'Malley, UCDA, EOM notebooks, P17b/96, 89R.

148 Fintan Lane, 'Fight on to the Last Man': A letter to Liam Lynch, March 1923', *Journal of the Cork Historical and Archaeological Society*, vol. 108 (2003), pp. 159–62. The full transcription of this letter is included.

CHAPTER 10

1   Twomey to Lynch, 22 March 1923, UCDA, Mulcahy Papers, P7/B/92(19–20).

2   Hopkinson, *Green Against Green*, p. 244.

3   Ibid.

4   Todd Andrews interview (UCDA, EOM notebooks, P17b/88), 25R.

5   Hopkinson, *Green against Green*, p. 236.

6   Ryan, *The Real Chief*, p. 14.

7   O'Donoghue, *No Other Law*, p. 300.

8   Hopkinson, *Green Against Green*, p. 237.

9   Minutes of IRA Executive meeting, 23–26 March 1923, UCDA, de Valera Papers, P150/1739.

10 O'Donoghue, *No Other Law*, p. 300.

11 Minutes of IRA Executive meeting, 23–26 March 1923, UCDA, de Valera Papers, P150/1739.

12 O'Donoghue, *No Other Law*, p. 300.

13 Minutes of IRA Executive meeting, 23–26 March 1923, UCDA, de Valera Papers, P150/1739.

14 Ibid.

15 O'Donoghue, *No Other Law*, p. 300.

16 Minutes of IRA Executive meeting, 23–26 March 1923, UCDA, de Valera Papers, P150/1739.

17 Ibid.; O'Donoghue, *No Other Law*, p. 301.

18   De Valera's Typescript, n.d., NLI, Frank Gallagher Papers, Ms 18,375(6).

19   Ryan, *The Real Chief*, p. 185.

20   Ibid., p. 301, and O'Donoghue, *No Other Law*, p. 301.

21   O'Donoghue, *No Other Law*, p. 302.

22   Ryan, *The Real Chief*, p. 186. O'Donoghue made no mention of Bridie's visit to the Kirwans in *No Other Law*, p. 302, in keeping with not mentioning her by name in that text.

23   O'Donoghue, *No Other Law*, p. 303.

24   Ibid.

25   Ibid.

26   Lynch to Murray, 9 April 1923, UCDA, de Valera Papers, P150/1749. A similar statement is made in Lynch to all Battalion O/Cs, 4 April 1923, UCDA, O'Malley Papers, P17a/25.

27   Tom Ryan, 'The National Army Engagement that led to the death of Liam Lynch', n.d., UCDA, Mulcahy Papers, P7/D/108a, p. 10.

28   Ibid., p. 11.

29   Ibid., p. 10. See Lieut-Col Thomas Ryan, BMH WS 783 for more on his revolutionary activities prior to the Civil War.

30   Tom Ryan, 'The National Army Engagement that led to the death of Liam Lynch', n.d., UCDA, Mulcahy Papers, P7/D/108a.

31   Ibid.

32   Ibid.

33   The Irish Army Census of November 1922, p. 26: http://census.militaryarchives.ie/pdf/Fethard_2_Southern_Division_Page_26.pdf (accessed 26 May 2020).

34   1911 census, entry for Clancy family, www.census.nationalarchives.ie/reels/nai003380630/ (accessed 26 May 2020).

35   Untitled account of Liam Lynch's capture and death by Lawrence Clancy, n.d., NLI, O'Donoghue Papers, Ms 31,423(4). Several typed copies of this exist in O'Donoghue's archive.

36   Frank Aiken to Tom Lynch, 23 July 1923, NLI, Lynch Papers, Ms 36,251/30.

37   Ryan, *The Real Chief*, p. 194.

38   Clancy refers to it being a brief shoot-out, see NLI, O'Donoghue Papers, Ms 31,423(4), while the evidence at the later inquest, see *The Irish Times*, 12 April 1923 and Frank Aiken's letter in the aftermath, suggests a shoot-out lasting twenty to thirty minutes, see Frank Aiken to Tom Lynch, 23 July 1923, NLI, Lynch Papers, Ms 36,251/30.

39   Frank Aiken to Tom Lynch, 23 July 1923, NLI, Lynch Papers, Ms 36,251/30.

40   Madge Comer (Clifford), interview, UCDA, EOM notebooks, P17b/89, 40R.

41   Author in discussion with historian Michael Desmond, 13 November 2021.

42   Ryan, *The Real Chief*, p. 194.

43   O'Donoghue, *No Other Law*, p. 305.

44   Ibid.; Aiken to Tom Lynch, 23 July 1923, NLI, Lynch Papers, Ms 36,251/30.

45   O'Donoghue, *No Other Law*, p. 305. Ryan identifies Twomey as one of the officers with Lynch's group, see Ryan, *The Real Chief*, p. 188.

46   Frank Aiken to Tom Lynch, 23 July 1923, NLI, Lynch Papers, Ms 36,251/30.

47 Tom Ryan, 'The National Army Engagement that led to the death of Liam Lynch', n.d., UCDA, Mulcahy Papers, P7/D/108a.

48 Untitled account of Liam Lynch's capture and death by Lawrence Clancy, n.d., NLI, O'Donoghue Papers, Ms 31,423(4).

49 Ibid. All quotes from Clancy come from this source, unless otherwise stated.

50 IE/MA/CW/Captured Documents/Lot 78 – Papers found near the body of Liam Lynch. A cursory scan of Austin Stack's papers in the NLI reveal this is his handwriting, and newspaper reports of his capture also reveal this: see various Irish newspapers, April to May 1923. It is likely Stack had given Lynch a handwritten copy in the days previous. There is no evidence suggesting Lynch was to act on this or issue it.

51 Untitled account of Liam Lynch's capture and death by Lawrence Clancy, n.d., NLI, O'Donoghue Papers, Ms 31,423(4). Of interest, Clancy makes no reference to Taylor's confrontation with Ryan earlier that morning from Ryan's account. However, his disrespect for his superior officer is certainly clear in the exchange that follows. It is unclear why he does not mention Taylor's venture to the public house in Goatenbridge, possibly omitting it to prevent embarrassment. It is surprising that Ryan allowed Taylor to remain in command in the area if this account of Clancy's is to be believed.

52 Ibid.

53 *The Irish Times*, 12 April 1923.

54 Ibid.

55 Cody, Séamus, 'The Clancy Family of Ballylusky, Drangan in the War of Independence', *Tipperary Historical Journal* (2020).

56 Untitled account of Liam Lynch's capture and death by Lawrence Clancy, n.d., NLI, O'Donoghue Papers, Ms 31,423(4).

57 *The Irish Times*, 12 April 1923.

58 Untitled account of Liam Lynch's capture and death by Lawrence Clancy, n.d., NLI, O'Donoghue Papers, Ms 31,423(4).

59 *The Irish Times*, 12 April 1923.

60 Tom Ryan, 'The National Army Engagement that led to the death of Liam Lynch', n.d., UCDA, Mulcahy Papers, P7/D/108a.

61 Inquest – Clonmel Coroner's District, 11/4/1923, National Archives, Tipperary Coroner's Inquests 1919–1928, 1C/135/31.

62 *The Irish Times*, 12 April 1923.

63 Inquest – Clonmel Coroner's District, 11/4/1923, National Archives, Tipperary Coroner's Inquests 1919–1928, 1C/135/31.

64 *The Irish Times*, 12 April 1923.

65 Ryan, *The Real Chief*, pp. 16, 193.

66 Ibid., pp. 196–7.

67 Ibid., p. 197.

68 Author in discussion with historian Michael Desmond, 13 November 2021. To be clear, similar to this author, Michael himself does not endorse the view of a conspiracy to have Lynch killed but did confirm to me such speculation still endures in the area.

69 Hopkinson, *Green Against Green*, p. 178.

70 'President's message to the army [on the death of Liam Lynch]' 12 April 1923, UCDA, de Valera Papers, P150/1750.

71 De Valera to Countess Markievicz, 11 April 1923, UCDA, de Valera Papers, P150/1813.

72 McCullagh, *De Valera: Rise*, p. 316.

73 Kathleen Barry Moloney to Jim Moloney, 27 May 1923, UCDA, Barry Moloney Papers, P94/115.

74 Andrews, *Dublin Made Me*, p. 291.

75 George Power interview by Ernie O'Malley, 17b/100, 123, 132.

76 Andrews, *Dublin Made Me*. p. 305.

77 Frank Aiken to Tom Lynch, 23 July 1923, NLI, Lynch Papers, Ms 36,251/30.

78 Aideen Carroll, *Seán Moylan: Rebel Leader* (Cork: Mercier Press, 2010), pp. 203–4.

79 Murray to Moylan, 8 May 1923, NLI, McGarrity Papers, Ms 17,466/1/5.

80 Moylan to unknown, 24 May 1923, NLI, McGarrity Papers, Ms 17,466/1/8.

81 Macardle, *The Irish Republic*, p. 845.

82 Carroll, *Seán Moylan*, p. 204.

83 O'Donoghue, *No Other Law*, p. 306.

84 Ryan, *The Real Chief*, p. 197.

85 From an interview with Seán's daughter, Bridie O'Callaghan, *Limerick Leader*, 3 October 1981.

86 Author conversation with Liz Downes, grandniece of Liam Lynch, 28 July 2021.

87 De Valera to Plunkett, 11 April 1923, UCDA, de Valera Papers, P150/1652.

88 *The Irish Times*, 12 April 1923.

89 Hammond, *Soldier of the Rearguard*, p. 65.

90 De Valera to Plunkett, 12 April 1923, UCDA, de Valera Papers, P150/1652.

91 *The Irish Times*, 13 April 1923.

92 Ryan, *The Real Chief*, p. 191.

93 *Éire*, 12 May 1923.

94 *The Irish Times*, 16 April 1923.

95 Hopkinson, *Green Against Green*, p. 256.

96 Minutes of Government and Army Council meeting on night of 26th–27th April 1923, UCDA, O'Malley Papers, P17a/12.

97 McCullagh, *De Valera: Rise*, p. 316.

98 Lynch to de Valera, 7 Feb. 1923, UCDA, de Valera Papers, P150/1749.

99 Hopkinson, *Green Against Green*, pp 256–7.

100 'Speech by Fianna Fáil leader Micheál Martin TD, Liam Lynch Commemoration, Fermoy: www.fiannafail.ie/speech-by-fianna-fail-leader-micheal-martin-td-liam-lynch-commemoration-fermoy/ (accessed 26 July 2020).

101 Telegram from prisoners in Gormanstown Camp to Mary Lynch, *c*. April 1923, private collection; Daniel Ryan to Mary Lynch, 16 April 1923, private collection.

102 Various correspondence from representatives of councils and corporations to Mary Lynch, *c*. April 1923, private collection; Secretary of Waterworks Committee of Cork Corporation to Mary Lynch, 12 April 1923, private collection.

103 Cáitlín Brugha to Mary Lynch, 23 April 1923, private collection.

104 Untitled account of Liam Lynch's capture and death by Lawrence Clancy, n.d., NLI, O'Donoghue Papers, Ms 31,423(4).

105 *Limerick Leader*, 3 October 1981.

106 *The Irish Press*, 2 March 1972. James Ryan wrote of being shown the pen by Taylor:

'Taylor … claimed he had received [it] from Liam Lynch just before he died … I wonder how Capt. Taylor came to be in possession of this pen … the pen Lieut Clancy should have received?'

107　*An Phoblacht*, 11 March 1923.

108　Death Register of James Lynch (entry no. 254), 4 March 1933, Death Register of the North Dublin Union, Ref No. 04315955.

109　*An Phoblacht*, 11 March 1923.

110　Ryan, *The Real Chief*, pp. 191–2.

111　Death Register of Bridget Keyes (entry no. 163), 20 November 1970, Death Register of Mitchelstown, Ref. No. 422009.

112　Death Register of Mary Lynch (entry no. 372), 3 October 1937, Death Register of Killmallock, Ref. No. 04280130.

113　DP5482, MSP of Liam Lynch, IMA (accessed online 1 February 2021).

114　Author conversation with historian Thomas Toomey, October 2020.

115　For an array of examples of Twomey's input and assistance to O'Donoghue with the writing of *No Other Law*, see numerous letters in NLI, O'Donoghue Papers, Ms 31,421(12).

116　For material related to the committee that organised for the building of the memorial round tower, and Twomey's place on the committee, see NLI, O'Mahony Papers, Ms 44,109.

117　'Maurice "Moss" Twomey', *DIB*, entry by Brian Hanley, www.dib.ie/biography/twomey-maurice-moss-a8690 (accessed 3 August 2021).

118　*The Irish Times*, 10 September 1979.

119　As well as the aforementioned Fianna Fáil-chaired commemoration at Kilcrumper in September, Sinn Féin holds commemorations at the memorial in Anglesboro and in the Knockmealdown mountains in November and June respectively. (The former, however, appeared also to be held around the anniversary of Lynch's death in 2022.) The non-aligned Liam Lynch National Commemoration holds a commemoration to Lynch at the memorial tower in the Knockmealdown mountains the last weekend of every June. Every April, around the anniversary of Lynch's death, the Liam Lynch Commemorative Mass Committee, headed by Mattie McGrath TD, holds a commemorative Mass for Lynch in Newcastle village.

EPILOGUE

1　O'Donoghue, *No Other Law*, p. 307.

2　Ibid, p. 267.

3　Hopkinson, *Green Against Green*, p. 127.

4　O'Donoghue, *No Other Law*, p. 40.

5　Deasy, *Brother Against Brother*, pp. 111–12.

6　Ibid, p. 85.

7　Andrews, *Dublin Made Me*, p. 291.

8　Ibid, p. 305.

9　Younger, *Ireland's Civil War*, p. 375.

10　*The Cork Examiner*, 16 April, 1923.

BIBLIOGRAPHY

PRIMARY SOURCES

Census and Genealogical Records
Census of Ireland 1901
Census of Ireland 1911
Birth Registration records for Mitchelstown
Death Registration records for Mitchelstown

Dáil Éireann
Parliamentary Debates

IRISH MILITARY ARCHIVES

Bureau of Military History Witness Statements
Civil War Captured Documents Collection
Irish Army Census of 1922
Michael Collins Papers
Military Pension Service Collection

NATIONAL ARCHIVES

Clonmel Coroner Inquests 1923

NATIONAL LIBRARY OF IRELAND

Count Plunkett Papers
Frank Gallagher Papers
Liam Lynch Papers
J.J. O'Connell Papers

Florence O'Donoghue Papers
Seán O'Mahony Papers

UNIVERSITY COLLEGE DUBLIN ARCHIVES

Kathleen Barry Moloney Papers
Éamon de Valera Papers
Richard Mulcahy Papers
Richard Mulcahy Additional Papers
Ernie O'Malley Notebooks
Ernie O'Malley Papers
Maurice 'Moss' Twomey Papers

NEWSPAPERS AND PERIODICALS

An Phoblacht (1925–35)
An tÓglach
Daily News
Éire
Evening Echo
Irish Independent
Limerick Leader
The Cork Examiner
The Freeman's Journal
The Kilkenny People
The Irish Press
The Irish Times

SECONDARY SOURCES

Articles

Cody, Séamus, 'The Clancy Family of Ballylusky, Drangan in the War of Independence', *Tipperary Historical Journal* (2020)

Horgan, Tim, 'The Tower House', Liam Lynch National Commemoration Association Booklet (2018)

Lane, Fintan, 'Fight on to the Last Man': A letter to Liam Lynch, March 1923', *Journal of the Cork Historical and Archaeological Society*, Vol. 108 (2003)

Mullins, Br Pat, 'The Hardware Trade and the Irish Volunteers (1910–1919)', private collection, n.d.

O'Beirne-Ranelagh, John, 'The IRB from the Treaty to 1924', *Irish Historical Studies*, vol. xx no. lxxvii (March 1976)

Rice, George, 'Liam Lynch A Comrade's Personal View', Liam Lynch National Commemoration Association Booklet (2019)

Books

Agnew, Pádraic, Bogan, Alan and Howard, Marcus, *The Louth Volunteers 1916* (Louth: The Write Space Publishing, 2016)

Andrews, C.S., *Dublin Made Me* (Dublin: Lilliput Press, 2001)

Barry, Tom, *Guerilla Days in Ireland* (Cork: Mercier Press, 2010)

Béaslaí, Piaras, *Michael Collins and the Making of a New Ireland: Volume II* (Dublin: Edmund Burke, 2008)

Borgonovo, John (ed.), *Florence and Josephine O'Donoghue's War of Independence: A Destiny that Shapes Our Ends* (Dublin: Irish Academic Press, 2006)

— *The Battle for Cork, July–August 1922* (Military History of the Irish Civil War) (Cork: Mercier Press, 2011)

Carroll, Aideen, *Seán Moylan: Rebel Leader* (Cork: Mercier Press, 2010)

Deasy, Liam, *Brother Against Brother* (Cork: Mercier Press, 1998)

Dolan, Anne and Murphy, William, *Michael Collins: The Man and the Revolution* (Dublin: Collins Press, 2018)

Dooley, Terence, *Burning the Big House: The Story of the Irish Country House in a Time of War and Revolution* (New Haven and London: Yale University Press, 2022)

Dorney, John, *Peace After the Final Battle: The Story of the Irish Revolution 1912–1924* (Dublin: New Island, 2014)

— *The Civil War in Dublin: The Fight for the Irish Capital 1922–1924* (Dublin: Merrion Press, 2017)

Dwyer, T. Ryle, *Michael Collins and the Civil War* (Cork: Mercier Press, 2012)

Ferriter, Diarmuid, *A Nation Not A Rabble: The Irish Revolution 1913–23* (Dublin: Profile Books, 2015)

Fewer, Michael, *The Battle of the Four Courts: The First Three Days of the Irish Civil War* (Great Britain: Head of Zeus, 2018)

Gillis, Liz, *The Fall of Dublin* (Military History of Irish Civil War) (Cork: Mercier Press, 2011)

Greaves, C. Desmond, *Liam Mellows and the Irish Revolution* (Belfast: Lawrence & Wishart Ltd, 2005)

Hart, Peter, *The IRA and its Enemies: Violence and Community in Cork 1916–1923* (New York: Oxford University Press, 1999)

Hopkinson, Michael, *Green Against Green: The Irish Civil War* (Dublin: Gill & Macmillan, 2004)

— *The Irish War of Independence* (Dublin: Gill Books, 2004)

Kissane, Bill, *The Politics of the Irish Civil War* (Oxford: Oxford University Press, 2005)

Kostick, Conor, *Revolution in Ireland: Popular Militancy 1917 to 1923* (London: Pluto Press, 1996)

Lankford, Siobhán, *The Hope and the Sadness: Personal Recollections on an Irish Intelligence Network 1916–1923* (Cork: Celum Publishing, 2020)

Longford, Earl of and O'Neill, Thomas, *Éamon de Valera* (Dublin: Gill & Macmillan, 1970)

Lynch, Robert, *The Northern IRA and the Early Years of Partition 1920–1922*, (Dublin: Irish Academic Press, 2006)

Lyons, F.S.L., *Ireland Since the Famine* (London: Fontana Press, 1985)

Macardle, Dorothy, *The Irish Republic* (Dublin: Wolfhound Press, 1999)

MacEoin, Uinseann, *Survivors: The Story of Ireland's Struggle as Told through Some of Her Outstanding Living People Recalling Events from the Days of Davitt, Through James Connolly, Brugha, Collins, Liam Mellows, and Rory O'Connor, to the Present Time* (Dublin: Argenta Publications, 1987)

McCarthy, Pat, *The Redmonds and Waterford: A Political Dynasty 1891–1952* (Dublin: Four Courts Press, 2018)

McCullagh, David, *De Valera: Rise 1882–1932* (Dublin: Gill Books, 2017)

Meleady, Dermot, *John Redmond: The National Leader* (Dublin: Irish Academic Press, 2014)

Mitchell, Arthur, *Revolutionary Government in Ireland: Dáil Éireann 1919–22* (Dublin: Gill & Macmillian Ltd, 1995)

Mulcahy, Risteárd, *Richard Mulcahy (1886–1971): A Family Memoir* (Dublin: Aurelian Press, 1999)

— *My Father, the General: Richard Mulcahy and the Military History of the Revolution* (Dublin: Liberties Press, 2010)

Neeson, Eoin, *The Civil War 1922–23* (Dublin: Poolbeg Press, 1989)

Noonan, Gerard, *The IRA in Britain, 1919–1923: 'In the heart of enemy lines'* (Liverpool: Liverpool University Press, 2014)

O'Brien, Stan D., *John Joe's Story: Commandant John Joe O'Brien* (self-published, 2016)

Ó Broin, Leon, *Revolutionary Underground: The Story of the Irish Republican Brotherhood 1858–1924* (Dublin: Gill & Macmillan, 1976)

Ó Caoimh, Pádraig, *Richard Mulcahy: From the Politics of War to the Politics of Peace, 1913–1924* (Dublin: Irish Academic Press, 2019)

O'Connor, Emmet, *Reds and the Green: Ireland, Russia and the Communist Internationals 1919–43* (Dublin: UCD Press, 2004)

Ó Corráin, Daithí and O'Halpin, Eunan, *The Dead of the Irish Revolution* (New Haven and London: Yale University Press, 2020)

O'Donoghue, Florence, *No Other Law: The Story of Liam Lynch and the Irish Republican Army, 1916–1923* (Dublin: Irish Press Ltd, 1953)

Ó hÉalaithe, Dónal (ed.), *Memoirs of an Old Warrior: Jamie Moynihan's Fight for Irish Freedom 1916–1923* (Cork, 2014)

O'Malley, Ernie, *On Another Man's Wound* (Dublin: Anvil, 2002)

— *The Singing Flame* (Cork: Mercier Press, 2012)

O'Reilly, Terence, *Rebel Heart: George Lennon Flying Column Commander* (Cork: Mercier Press, 2009)

Ó Ruairc, Padraig Óg, *The Battle for Limerick City* (Military History of the Irish Civil War) (Cork: Mercier Press, 2011)

— *Truce: Murder, Myth and the Last Days of the Irish War of Independence* (Cork: Mercier Press, 2016)

O'Shea, Owen, *Ballymacandy: The Story of a Kerry Ambush* (Dublin: Merrion Press, 2021)

Power, Bill, *Another Side of Mitchelstown* (Cork: PsyOps Books, 2008)

— *Fermoy on the Blackwater* (Cork: Brigown Press, 2009)

Regan, John M., *The Irish Counter-Revolution 1921–1936: Treatyite Politics and Settlement in Independent Ireland* (Dublin: Gill Books, 2001)

Ryan, Meda, *The Real Chief: Liam Lynch* (Dublin: Mercier Press, 2005)

— *Thomas Kent (16 Lives)* (Dublin: O'Brien Press, 2016)

Sheehan, William, *A Hard Local War: The British Army and the Guerilla War in Cork 1919–1921* (Dublin: The History Press Ireland, 2017)

Townshend, Charles, *The British Campaign in Ireland 1919–1921: The Development of Political and Military Policies* (Oxford: Oxford University Press, 1978)

Valiulis, Maryann, *Portrait of a Revolutionary: General Richard Mulcahy and the Founding of the Irish Free State* (Dublin: Irish Academic Press, 1992)

Various, *Rebel Cork's Fighting Story 1916–21* (Cork: Mercier Press, 2009)

Younger, Calton, *Ireland's Civil War* (London: Fontana Press, 1986)

Booklets

Hammond, Bill, *Soldier of the Rearguard: The Story of Matt Flood and the Active Service Column* (Cork: Éigse Na Mainistreach Publications, 1977)

O'Riordan, Thomas, *The Price of Freedom: The Life Story of Mick Fitzgerald (Commandant) O/C 1st Battalion Cork No. 2 Brigade* (Cork: Barrys, 1970)

Various, Liam Lynch National Commemoration Association Booklet 2018 (independently published, 2018)

Various, Liam Lynch National Commemoration Association Booklet 2019 (independently published, 2019)

Walsh, Joe, *The Story of Liam Lynch* (Cork: Lee Press, 1974)

Websites

Dictionary of Irish Biography: www.dib.ie

MU Library Treasures: mulibrarytreasures.wordpress.com

The Irish Story: www.theirishstory.com

Visit Ballyhoura: visitballyhoura.com/

Other

'The Uncivil War: Liam Lynch' radio documentary, RTÉ (2002)

ACKNOWLEDGEMENTS

IT WAS NOT EASY WRITING this book during a global pandemic, yet having such a monumental task as completing a biography of General Liam Lynch was an important lifeline for me in those strange first few months. I sincerely wish to thank Conor Graham and the entire team at Merrion/Irish Academic Press for taking a chance on me. My thanks to my editors Patrick O'Donoghue and Wendy Logue and their encouragement and advice through this process. My thanks also to Kevin O'Sullivan for his superb maps.

This book initially began life as a thesis looking at Liam Lynch during the Civil War while I was an MA student in the DCU School of History and Geography from 2017 to 2019. My time there helped shape me both as a historian and writer. I thank Dr William Murphy, my thesis supervisor, and also Dr Daithí Ó Corráin, the head of the MA programme, along with my fellow MA students Bartle Faulkner and Joe Rodgers. I must pay tribute to the staff of various archival institutions, most especially to the staff of UCD Archives, for all their assistance in securing material both during and between lockdowns. Thanks, too, to the staff of the National Library of Ireland, National Archives of Ireland, National Gallery of Ireland, Cork Public Museum, Irish Military Archives and National Museum of Ireland.

I am grateful to have met and talked to several relatives of Liam Lynch. They have shown me photographs, unique family mementos, and regaled me with anecdotes and important information on Lynch and his family. My thanks, in this respect to Helen White, Liz Downes, Christy O'Callaghan, Helena O'Callaghan, Nuala O'Riordan, Dolores Lyne, Bernadette O'Líatháin and the Mullins family. Also, thanks to another relative who wishes to remain anonymous, yet who gave me access to an important private archive.

Thanks also to filmmaker John Foley, and his wife Angela, for hosting me in their Dungarvan home during a memorable weekend as John began shooting his documentary on Lynch's final days. I have enjoyed sharing progress on our mutual Lynch projects. I am grateful to both John and to historian Michael Desmond for taking me around the Nire Valley and helping me understand Lynch's movements in those last few weeks. Thanks also to Mattie McGrath TD and his daughter, Councillor Máirin McGrath, who took me to Newcastle village and on a memorable trek around the Knockmealdown mountains. The McGraths are involved in the Liam Lynch Memorial Mass Committee. My thanks, too, to others who commemorate Lynch and who spoke to me, such as Councillor Deirdre O'Brien, chairperson of the General Liam Lynch Commemoration Committee; Eddie O'Sullivan, chairperson of the General Liam Lynch Sinn Féin Commemoration Committee; and Seán Nugent, chairperson of the Liam Lynch National Commemoration Association.

I would also like to thank those historians and history enthusiasts who have been immensely helpful with suggestions, advice and even the provision of photographs and other material on various aspects of Lynch and this period. There are far too many to name here, but particular mention must be made of John Dorney, Matt Doyle, Bill Power, Tim Horgan, Neil Donovan, Pauline Murphy and Éamon Lankford. I pay particular tribute to two individuals, whose friendship and advice through this process has been of enormous help: Laura Doyle, who helped in too many ways to fully document here, but who gave me a memorable tour around her home town of Fermoy – the streets where Liam Lynch and his peers walked so long ago – and Aaron Ó Maonaigh, who is, in essence, my 'Ernie O'Malley whisperer' and who helped me illuminate the often inscrutable, but so pivotal, interviews Ernie did with IRA veterans in the 1950s.

I had brief seasonal employment in Kilmainham Gaol in 2011 that changed my life more than I could ever have imagined. Two people I met there were Mícheál Ó Doibhlín and Liz Gillis. Their enduring friendship and support over these last few years while navigating the worlds of Irish history has been so important to me. Sadly, Mícheál passed during the final stages of my writing this book; his friendship and conversation are dearly missed.

I should make mention, and give my thanks also, to Ruairí O'Donnell and Patrick Mannix. An additional group of history enthusiasts to thank include

Lorcan Collins, Liam Crowley, Frank Fagan, Frank Whearity, Seán Hogan, Ronan McGreevy, Sineád Brennan and Anne-Marie McInerney.

I'd like to pay particular tribute to my late friend, the great historian of Fenianism, Dr Shane Kenna, whose memory I have carried with me every day in the years since his untimely passing at the age of thirty-three. I am forever grateful to Shane's mother, Olive, for helping keep Shane's memory alive.

I often forget I am a full-time working civil servant, and I do little to hide my interests and history endeavours when I should be focused on other tasks, to the frequent bemusement of those I work with. In this respect, I must thank all my colleagues in the Facilities Management Unit in the Department of Housing, Local Government and Heritage. Thanks especially to Tony Butler, Gareth London, Danny O'Sullivan, Joe Colfer, Radiana Rabissoni, Imelda Dignam and Anne Marie Doyle. Special mention must also be made of Paddy Cunningham, David Dixon and Jerry Kelleher in my old stomping grounds of the Department of the Taoiseach, and to my more recent colleagues in the Office of Public Works.

I must also pay tribute to some dear friends who have been such a great support through this process. While there are far too many names to list here, I must at least make mention of Róisín Jones, Maria Power, Donal Hanks, Jason Coburn, Stephen King-O'Farrell and, of course, Laura Cullen. I am deeply grateful for your friendship, conversation and the continued great times shared with you all – more of an enormous help during writing this than you'd ever believe. Special mention to Cathy Geist who came into my life towards the end of this book.

And finally, most importantly, to my family. To Ross and Michael, thanks for tolerating my quirks and random humour; you are both very dear to me and have grown into more mature and capable men than I ever was at your respective ages. I'm very lucky to have you both as brothers, and you inspire me through your own creative endeavours.

To my two favourite people, Mum and Dad, known to everyone else as Betty and Gerry senior. Your love, support and belief in me always keeps me going and inspires me to pick myself up when times are personally tough. That was never more needed than in these last few years. I love you both so much.

INDEX